BEYOND PERESTROIKA

VIBS

Volume 210

a volume in
Hartman Institute Axiology Studies
HIAS
C. Stephen Byrum and Rem B. Edwards, Editor

BEYOND PERESTROIKA

Axiology and the New Russian Entrepreneurs

Gary G. Gallopin

Rodopi

Amsterdam - New York, NY 2009

Cover photo: ©Morguefile.com

Cover Design: Studio Pollmann

The paper on which this book is printed meets the requirements of "ISO 9706:1994, Information and documentation - Paper for documents - Requirements for permanence".

ISBN: 978-90-420-2735-0
E-Book ISBN: 978-90-420-2736-7

Printed in the Netherlands

To Irene

CONTENTS

Contents

EDITORIAL FOREWORD

What might it be like for an American anthropologist to live for a time with members of Russia's emerging capitalistic entrepreneurs? What trying and exciting ordeals and adventures would he undergo? What obstacles might he encounter, especially if he wanted to get a powerful personality profile, the Hartman Value Profile (HVP), translated into Russian and then persuade a number of Russians to take it so that their patterns of value and valuation could be measured and better understood? As an anthropologist, what would he notice about Russia's then newly independent capitalistic entrepreneurs and about post-Communist Russian society and infrastructure? What dramatic cultural and historical changes would he witness during that time span, and how might his subjects themselves cope with and adapt to the changing times?

Suppose that this anthropologist has a completely novel anthropological focus—centered on what and how early unrecognized Russian entrepreneurs valued, and on measuring and comprehending their values by using a scientific axiological or valuational approach. Would an axiological approach to studying another culture and its members open up a new, promising, and illuminating door for other anthropologists, whether or not they want to take it? Would a concentration on values shed new light upon the culture and its members?

Dr. Gary Gene Gallopin, the author of this book and the world's first axiological anthropologist, addresses such questions and raises many more. How would an anthropologist himself grow and change during the course of his investigations and reflections? Would he affect the values of his subjects? Would he be affected by their values in the course of better comprehending them? Would his understanding and application of formal scientific axiology provide him with powerful safeguards against anthropic bias and error? Would it lead him to discover and to grasp more clearly many subtle and complex things about the members of another culture that other researchers might not see at all, or only dimly at best?

In this book, Dr. Gallopin provides us with fascinating answers to these questions, and to many more. If you like the adventure of science and its application, you will like this book.

Rem B. Edwards
February, 2009

PREFACE

The work for this book began in 1991, several years into my graduate studies, when, thanks to an over-zealous professor (my assigned academic advisor at the time), I was unceremoniously dropped from my planned summer fieldwork among the Maya in Belize. I was deemed to be too unruly in my approach to research, going outside the fashion of the time—moral relativity—into the "never-never land" of "moral absolutism."

I was also accused of violating another one of the unofficial taboos of the time: Did I not know that the use of Western-oriented psychological theories and instruments in ethnology and ethnography was "reductionism?" They had been tried but deemed to be too ethnocentric in conception and form. The best you could do was to create a survey questionnaire based on *ad hoc* facts gathered at the field site about the target culture. The acceptable approach precluded any logical structure derived from systematic formula carefully constructed independently of any cultural considerations.

Extra-agent theories were the norm. The super-organic, a quasi-mystical entity, supposedly ruled men. Cognitive science was acceptable only if it pertained to a carefully circumscribed area of the brain known for its "cultural function" whose outward manifestations included various forms of sorting and classifying the imperfect and often *ad hoc* soup of concepts locked in the mind of "average" man (woman). Apparently, culture (society) rules human beings through this area, a notion with which I most heartily disagree.

Memes and morphemes aside, any social manipulation involving hypnosis must ultimately start with a human agent. I was interested in a more subtle and complex form of social manipulation called *spontaneous order* (emergent complexity), which studies the combined effects of self-interested individuals' simultaneous rule-following activities, and I was interested in the related approach called *methodological individualism* which arises from the Austrian school of economics and says that societies after all consist of individual human organisms, each with a unique brain of its own.

Most of the professors I worked with up until then had "never heard of it," but this approach held great promise in that it purported to explain larger phenomena (something that the super-organic idea claims to do) by studying the nature of the agents involved in that phenomena and by understanding how the combined effect of those agents was the ultimate cause of the larger phenomena. In other words, in order to understand human activity holistically, one must understand individual human nature and also understand how human action is an extension of human nature.

In addition, according to my assigned advisor, my research proposal was considered to be methodologically too "urban" in nature for a target culture such as contemporary rural Maya. To take a pencil-and-paper test they had to be literate, which was not always the case. Even a pictorial version could be confusing to them. I dismissed this "cannot do" spirit, and, as I discovered down the line, many such problems can be overcome with shrewd uses of interpreters who can act as middlemen for such testing.

Also, my view of reality was too fixed on the "objective." Did I not understand that culture did not just filter reality, it also made reality? I was too much of an objectivist to go for that last notion, especially when one departmental theorist (responsible for reviewing my research proposal) claimed that culture created far more than "social reality." I could not operate in an atmosphere where my potential lead committee member thought that mathematics was "culture bound," and the reviewer thought that reality was "all in your mind"—the ultimate form of reductionism! I felt the whole enterprise to be sinking from subjectivism long before it submerged.

But being left without a project was actually a "good thing," as a fairly disinterested archaeologist who was leaving the department told me at the time, provided I looked at my situation as an opportunity. After I scraped through the last qualifying examination in a state of shock, and after I changed advisors with some considerable difficulty, I was left with what many artists kill for in any arena where they normally have little say—creative control. I only had to find a different place to do my summer fieldwork.

The whole enterprise was transferred to Russia in short order, and a new phase of my research life began. That change was accomplished with an accomplice who became the outside reader on my committee and a personal mentor. Long before my academic crisis, my new mentor had asked me if I wanted to join him in his cross-national and cross-cultural research project concerning the objectivity and usefulness of a psychological instrument purporting to be not only non-relativistic but, in fact, well on the way to apodictic. I had considered his idea, dropped the idea, and taken it up again. Now, I made a full commitment.

I entered Russian territory with little institutional support. I had savings from my stipend from a research fellowship and a small grant, but that was it. The rest of the money would have to come from immediate family. I had tacit support from a professor who had yet to prove her value to me as an advisor but would eventually do so nicely. I had logistical support from the cross-cultural researcher but no funding. Having made the switch at the last minute, I lacked the language skills usually attained before fieldwork for my new site. To put it in a more colorful vernacular, I fell into the Soviet Union "ass backwards."

Despite the rocky start, I found that the Soviet Union was the perfect place to experiment with a new untested social science tool. An authority-vacuum occurred between a period of rigid control of foreigners by Soviet authorities, vestiges of which were evident in 1991, and the newer integrated Russian Federation regulations as I later saw in 2000. Part of that vacuum existed during 1992 and 1993, when I did the bulk of my research, and a Wild West atmosphere permeated Russia. I suffered no Russian authority claiming that I was importing some new religion into the country nor was I suspected of spying by an over-zealous KGB. Still, I took a long time to become completely comfortable with my research, and one of my helpers experienced problems with authorities in the Ukraine, where some data she collected on our behalf was confiscated.

Any resistance, suspicion, or interference mainly came from a context that viewed any scientific work not officially sanctioned by the state to be questionable. We kept our contact with Soviet and Russian officials to a requisite minimum. With rare exception did any scientists we met in the field seriously challenge the legitimacy of the basic premise we were operating under, namely that objective standards may be found across nations and cultures.

Relativity was a strong concept in cultural anthropology at the time, and still is. Cultural relativism ruled the approach to ethics of various cultures which were said to have internal logic of their own. Regardless of whether the society engaged in brutal repressive warfare, conducted human sacrifice, and practiced other horrors, or it was peaceful and had prescribed ways of settling disputes, the observer-commentator had to remain neutral.

But ethical situations always occur that cross cultural boundaries. These may include, for example, the contact between anthropologist and isolated tribe, missionary and long lost "children of God," Spanish conquistadors and semi-divine Inca ruler, European pioneer and Native American, colonialist merchant and slave pool, American and Japanese businessmen, Mexican migrant workers crossing the border into the United States, Chief Joseph speaking to Congress, and so on. A commercial disagreement between businessmen from different countries may precipitate a real show of moral relativism or lack of such. Books and courses are devoted to teaching American businessmen more than just the language of the nation to which they will travel. A framework is necessary to guide such transactions, and a laissez-faire policy towards ethics may not always be suitable.

Latin American theft is a good example of this quandary. I was once in Ecuador and beat back an attempt to steal my wallet. I was admonished afterwards for carrying my expensive camera in the open thus attracting thieves. Besides my lack of common sense in a third world country, a question arose concerning whether or not this particular attempted theft was immoral. Some felt I was a hero for successfully defending myself and foiling the robbery, implying the thief was no hero. Others felt that North Americans in general historically exploited South America, and their wealth really belonged to the hoodwinked South Americans, so it was okay to steal from North American tourists. The thief was just attempting to "get his money back." Fortunately my Ecuadorian guide was not of such an opinion.

The point is that hardly any cross-cultural situations are Pollyanna-like. Hard choices usually face the protagonists, and a policy of always giving in to the demands of the host culture may not always be the right thing to do. Thus, in this age of increasing globalization, cultural relativism becomes, whatever other ethical standards might apply, impractical. We are all ethno-centrists to some extent, and we need a way around that reality to deal with the other.

This is why I was so intrigued by my new mentor's proposed research and why I latched onto it as an interested observer-commentator, and occasional participator. He was there to test the validity of the moral science. I was there to assist that and to record the process, keeping in mind that cultural differences were inevitably going to affect the process. They did and how they did became subject matter for my doctoral dissertation.

The book here adds another layer to what I did in my doctorate. It applies the theory of the new value science to the recorded process of unfolding research to add an axiologically illuminating structure to what seemed at the time to be a morally chaotic series of events.

In that vein, this book represents an experimental breakthrough in social science, namely the application of a "hard science" to moral problems encountered in the field. It is an opportunity to "step back" and assess the field experience, something that is becoming increasingly important in the theoretical aspects of anthropology. Formal axiology is applicable to all ethnographic material. This book is a small sample of what is possible.

Finally, this book also provides an interesting and non-routine look at the Soviets and ex-Soviets as they confronted the end of a dream and the beginning of renewed hope for their country. Forget Russia? I think not.

Ethnographic work "fixes" a culture in time and place. The early post-Soviet Russia and late Soviet Russia is immortalized here not by the headline grabbing events but by the ordinary Russians who, willingly or not, took part in the swirl of events that defined the end of an era both for the Soviet Union and the United States. I met a few of them and their story is an integral part of this book.

I would like to acknowledge the following persons and groups for their assistance with this book: Dr. Rem Edwards, for his patient and professional editorial assistance; Dr. Leon Pomeroy, for his continuing encouragement in my career development and for his invaluable assistance with the original research upon which this book is based; The Hartman Institute, for their support of my Russian research and their providing me with a forum to speak about my work; Dr. Ann McElroy and the entire dissertation committee at the University of Buffalo, for guiding me through the doctoral research that provides the spade work and raw data upon which my subsequent analysis is built; the late Dr. Robert S. Hartman, for giving all the moral sciences a chance to become just that, sciences instead of forums for competing ideologies. Finally, I'd like to thank my wife to whom this volume is dedicated. Without her patient support for a writer working *pro bono*, the book would not have been possible to complete.

One

INTRODUCTION

1. Overview

This book is derived from and extends an earlier ethnographic study of Russian entrepreneurs in Soviet and post-Soviet Russia, which was published as my doctoral dissertation (Gallopin, 1999). That work focused on how Russian entrepreneurs used social networks to survive economically and emotionally during the difficult transition from a closed society in a communist controlled state to a more open society within a fledgling constitutional democracy. Here the emphasis is on Russian values.

A period of state sponsored change in the Soviet Union known as *perestroika* eventually gave way to a political upheaval in the early 1990s that swept away the former communist state. Former members of a well-educated nominal upper middle class, above the common laborer but below the ruling class, were forced to adapt to a change in circumstances. This included the confrontation with the fact of their poverty relative to their counterparts in the West. The result included a radical turn to entrepreneurial activity with varying degrees of success.

The new Russian entrepreneurs made effective use of connections, a *de facto* system of mutual favors, which flourished during the heyday of the Soviet Union. This system sustained an otherwise cumbersome economy by subverting and circumventing various forms of red tape embedded in the state sponsored command economy. When the Soviet Union fell apart, this system of favors was employed to cope with a variety of new problems.

The field work for the doctorate was done in the Soviet Union/Russian Federation, starting in July of 1991 through the end of November 1993. My focus site was the city of Leningrad/St. Petersburg, with side trips to other cities and towns in the former Soviet Union. This book is a value oriented examination of a three week span of time taken from my field work. The other portions of the field work are incorporated into supporting material. In 2000, I made an additional trip to the former Soviet Union to collect some more data for the book.

In the dissertation (Gallopin, 1999), for data gathering and analysis, I employed methods both traditional and novel in the field of cultural anthropology. These included participant-observation, social network analysis, ethnographic elicitation interviews, and the use of a new psychometric technique based on a novel theoretical orientation called *formal axiology*—the scientific study of values based on a logical system invented by philosopher Robert S. Hartman.

This book focuses on social network analysis and value analysis of the collected data. The material gained from participant-observation and ethnographic elicitation is used to create a context, supply data for analysis, and supplement analysis. The psychometric and value-metric technique derived from formal axiology is used for stress analysis of several Russian respondents. Formal axiology is further mined to create a value analysis of collected ethnographic material, and social network theory is combined with scholarly research about Russians' use of social connections to analyze the same material. The resulting synthesis provides fascinating insights into what drove the new Russian entrepreneurs by uncovering their hidden motives and emerging values. Rising from the ashes of a fallen empire, the new entrepreneurs come to life as a diverse and complex group.

2. The Development of an Idea

Cultural anthropology is a field with a wide span of subject matter. The unifying concept of this field is culture. Cultural anthropologists continue to debate just exactly what culture is. This book adopts a partial definition of culture as "the cultivation of values" in order to focus attention on the related topics of value, valuation, and evaluation as they pertain to a cultural milieu. The book also studies people coping with stress. Stress plays a key role in human life and drives human activity for better or for worse. When you look at a nation's culture you see that nation's struggle with the stress of living expressed in the daily patterns of its citizens. Specifically, this book is the study of how Russians coped with stressful conditions in an urban context within a larger national context of political turmoil and how that affected their values.

The former Soviet Union in the early 1990s underwent a series of changes that affected the lives of its citizens on many levels. If one constant existed during this period, it was the tension existing in the country. As Russians watched the latest incarnation of their empire once again transforming itself, they faced an uncertain future, a sense of loss, and a possibility of future losses. Coupled with this was the recent exhilaration associated with a period of openness that marked the waning years of the Soviet Union. Social stress, which can result from both positive and negative situations, was in the air. Cultural values were changing. For a social scientist interested in the study of stress, culture, and values, the former Soviet Union presented itself as an unprecedented natural laboratory.

In 1991 I attached my graduate work in cultural anthropology to the ongoing work of an established research scientist, Dr. Leon Pomeroy, a psychologist interested in the exploration of values across nations. I was interested in the ethnographic study of stress, and this scientist introduced me to the Soviet Union during its most tumultuous period. I chose to employ the (purportedly) culturally neutral methodology being developed by Pomeroy, who had adopted an emerging theory of value as a basis for his new orientation in psychology that he called "value-centric cognitive psychology" (Pomeroy, 1998, personal communication) and that could be used to measure stress in individuals.

Robert S. Hartman's theory of values, formal axiology (Hartman, 1967), was being expanded into a potentially scientific discipline through Pomeroy's empirical work. During the early 1990s, I collaborated with Pomeroy to push this research frontier into Russia. Pomeroy was conducting empirical tests on the Hartman Value Profile (HVP)—a "value-metric instrument" that had been developed by Hartman and Mexican psychologists (Hartman and Cardenas, 1970; Hartman, 1973a). Pomeroy had studied nations such as Mexico, the United States, and Japan. He got me into the former Soviet Union and helped me establish the necessary ties to conduct ethnographic field research.

A bridge into Russia was constructed by Pomeroy through his chance 1990 meeting with a Russian industrial psychologist who apparently shared a research interest with Pomeroy and was willing to collaborate with him. In the summer of 1991, I asked Pomeroy to help me find a research site to fulfill a summer research requirement associated with my fellowship at the Anthropology Department at the University of Buffalo, State University of New York. He set up arrangements for me to travel to Leningrad to meet his Russian counterpart and begin a research oriented association as part of his ongoing cross-national data collection project.

My research grew out of my association with Pomeroy's cross-national research, and in effect turned a Soviet-American scientific exchange into an ethnographic pilot study that was used to launch two subsequent returns to the same general field site in 1992 and 1993. The trip in 1993 lasted seven months and constituted the bulk of my ethnographic data gathering.

The Pomeroy research was used to gain the assistance of Russian contacts. Otherwise it would have been very difficult to get into Russia, especially in 1991 when it was still the heart of the former Soviet Union. Pomeroy's compact research design easily translated into research activity for our Russian contacts. Later, once some lasting relationships were established, I was able to pursue the more generalized goals associated with ethnography. My field trips, the first starting in July 1991 and the last, ending by December, 1993, spanned about two and half years and included nine months of time spent in the former Soviet Union. In 2000, I returned to Russia one more time to get an idea of what had become of the country and the people I had met there.

During the course of my fieldwork, I was able to use the traditional field method of participant-observation and other methods drawn from social and linguistic anthropology to assess Russian values and associated social phenomena. My initial trip to the Soviet Union in 1991 helped me select those areas of interest that would be especially helpful in my study of stress and values. One promising area, pointed out to me by my principal contact in 1991, was the use of social networks by Russians and other Soviet citizens to cope with the unique difficulties with which Soviet Russia's command economy saddled its citizens. Social network theory, an already established methodology across the social sciences, helped me map the critical relationships that sustained those Russians with whom I came into contact.

In addition, I had an interest in gathering supplemental data to complement the work I was doing with formal axiology. Self-reports were useful in identifying subjective opinions about internal states and environmental factors. I found Madeleine Mathiot's self-disclosure technique for ethnographic elicitation (Mathiot, 1982) to be most helpful in producing rich texts from tape recorded interviews. Not only could they be used to complement the data collected through the use of the HVP, but they stood in their own right as illuminating windows into what Russians considered priorities in life. Also the search for interview respondents revealed aspects of Russian relationships and helped me map the social networks of my contacts.

My research had a cumulative and intertwined character to it. By following leads and exploring certain ties, I was continually able to uncover new sources of data. Certain of my 1991 side contacts became my 1992 principal contacts, and certain of my 1992 side contacts became important in 1993. Research conducted on the HVP led to interview respondents, and following the chains that led me to more HVP-related contacts or interview respondents allowed me to map social networks. The ease with which one research activity flowed into another reflected on the generally open nature of those Russians I encountered. Groups of Russians struggled for my attention. This competition, while sometimes counterproductive, by and large increased my research opportunities.

Living with Russian families in Leningrad/St. Petersburg also helped me explore social network activity. I found Russians for the most part to be gregarious and socially active. I did not need to push much to meet their relatives and friends. Casual conversations with the Russians I stayed and/or worked with helped me form an impression of their likes and dislikes. Since Russians tended to keep summer gardens outside of the city, this gave me a chance to get into the countryside. Also, since Russian families often helped me with bureaucratic matters that involved trips outside of the city, this sometimes led to travel with family members.

Political events also gave impetus to my research. The August 1991 coup attempt, led by ultra-conservative members of Mikhail Gorbachev's regime, that led to the eventual dissolution of the Soviet Union galvanized my intent to return. A dreary and seemingly hopeless country had suddenly come alive and seemed much more interesting to explore. Also, the new political openness during the early years of the Russian Federation facilitated my re-entry to Russia. Rapid political events and a changing society made it easier to do longitudinal research.

The October 1993 parliamentary rebellion gave me fresh topics to use in my probes of Russian values. The various reactions to this dramatic political event, which dominated Russian media in the fall of that year, showed that Russians held widely diverging opinions, not monolithic political correctness. The run up to the early December 1993 parliamentary elections, which were the result of the political upheavals during September and October, further reinforced this observation.

3. Themes

In my study of Russia I found some recurring themes that I place into four broad categories.

(1) The Russians I met were preoccupied with issues of survival, which would come up often in my conversations with them. The book explores various strategies of survival.

(2) Historically, slavery was a crucial issue in Russia. Many Russians had been serfs—peasant slaves owned by aristocratic landowners (Europeans, some Russian, some not, from a higher class)—for hundreds of years until the emancipation of 1861. Russia was largely a rural country until the Bolshevik Revolution of 1917. After that, Russia became a highly urban country. A set of Soviet laws that required different legal documents, including internal passports, for residency and travel partially re-enslaved most Russians. Much of Russia's recent political history involves a struggle with deeply imbedded institutions that have tended to perpetuate various forms of full or partial slavery. Russians I met expressed ambivalence over whether or not slavery was a cultural institution, a kind of national character trait, or an accident of history.

(3) Related to both is the theme of a national work ethic, or a lack of one. Foreign observers, amateurs, and experts alike were quick to conclude that many Russians are lazy, or, at the very least, imbued with a distaste for work. This quick conclusion facilitated misinterpretations of a failing Soviet economy that contradicted overt Soviet technological achievements. It produced the image that a certain class of Russian scientists could create miracles, such as Sputnik, while in general the Russian people were too sluggish to keep up with the West in terms of consumer goods. One of the things that impressed me during my first trip to Russia was the sense of desperation among my Russian acquaintances to get work, any work. This theme would be repeated in subsequent trips with greater degree of sophistication. Many of the Russian men I encountered were interested in me as a potential business contact.

(4) Russians have a different sense of life than Americans. Once they get you inside their home, they can be extremely engaging. They have a sense of warmth and camaraderie that breaks through in locations they consider to be safe, and they are willing to draw total strangers into their family circles, sometimes entangling them in family matters. So called "kitchen talks" were a commonplace way of venting frustration over official and public life during Soviet times.

Americans are more particular about opening up their souls and tend to treat strangers with polite caution. They also are more circumspect in business dealings sometimes to the point of being long on talk and short on action. Russians by contrast can be reckless in their willingness to plunge into schemes they may not be prepared to handle.

The interplay between the necessity of surviving and a certain devil-may-care attitude to life gave the Russians I met an unusual spiritual dimension. They prided themselves on being resourceful and also full of vigor. Russians had endured so much historically they felt themselves to be immune to shock. Life could not surprise them with any new horror. This contributed to outsiders' impressions that Russians were unusually dormant. By the early 1990s, they had lost all hope and were ready for anything. At the same time, they were capable of embracing positive turns with deep enthusiasm, such as their defeat of the August 1991 coup attempt by so-called "hard-liners," or their participation in the newly freed markets of 1992.

4. Organization of Book

This book is organized into five parts. The first part provides a historical, geographical, and ethnographic background discussion that sets time, place, and cultural atmosphere. The second part is a detailed description of my first three weeks in the Soviet Union. The third part describes in detail the technical aspects of methodology. It focuses on the axiological theory behind the HVP, and introduces social network analysis. The fourth part demonstrates the HVP's use in the field. The fifth part provides an axiological analysis (enhanced by supplemental techniques) of my first three weeks in the Soviet Union.

The first part includes latter portions of this chapter and Chapter Two, "Context." It discusses the genesis of the research, how I came to study Russia. It also provides an historical essay about Russia and the Soviet Union, a description of St. Petersburg and other cities and towns I visited, and some more detail about my research.

The second part is divided into four chapters: Chapter Three, "A Glimpse of a Dying Empire"; Chapter Four, "Social Networks in Action"; Chapter Five, "Negotiating Life"; and Chapter Six, "Values and Their Cost." The three weeks described in close detail are in the form of a personal narrative. (The first trip in 1991 lasted four weeks, but including all four weeks in the narration would have been too cumbersome.)

The narrative chapters are key to the book. In order to have subject matter upon which to base the discussions in the analytical portion of the book, I wanted to create a text. Statistically oriented data provided by the HVP and analytically dissected interviews did not in themselves provide enough raw material. Secondary sources, such as other published accounts of Russia, also did not provide enough material and would make the project a purely academic exercise. Therefore, I decided to use the raw material provided by my field notes, photographs, sketches, and some taped conversations in two ways: first, as anecdotal data used to support and illustrate contentions. This is traditional in an ethnographic work. More importantly, I wanted to create a story from which conclusions could be drawn. Writing the whole story was neither feasible nor desirable. However, a sample drawn from my story could be used not only to orient the reader as is done in ethnography, but could also be used to provide an integrated and exhaustive description of Russia as seen by the author during a certain period of time. Only by placing the reader in Russia does the subsequent analysis make sense.

Participant-observation and its associated detailed record keeping characterize ethnography. Together they are cultural anthropology's most distinguishing contribution to the social sciences. Ethnographic monographs produced from these techniques have been the subject of much controversy in cultural anthropology. Rosaldo for instance noted the sterility of classic ethnography when it came to the flexibility of its descriptions (Rosaldo, 1989, pp. 40–41). Societies as depicted in such ethnographies were surprisingly stiff, more like clockwork mechanisms than flesh and blood communities (Agar, 1996, pp. 4–7; Pratt, 1986; Rosaldo, 1989, pp. 41–43).

The use of narrative in ethnographic texts has been re-examined (Pratt, 1986; Rosaldo, 1989, pp. 128–130) because the descriptive and formal approaches cannot convey the "messages" that a well-written narrative can. The descriptive and formal approaches cover, respectively, the classificatory and formal aspects of ethnography. We cultural anthropologists want to classify native activity, including mental activity. Thus, our descriptions must be focused on cumulative patterns. We also want to uncover hidden rules and formal structures, so we apply our analyses in that direction hoping to construct the appropriate abstract system that will capture the culture of the focus community in terms of essences. However powerful or constructive the classificatory or formal approaches are, paying only lip service to the personal does us no good. When we do, the result is a dry disconnected ethnography that inevitably leads to charges of intellectual colonialism (Rosaldo, 1989, pp. 31–32). The anthropologist arrives, observes, participates, records, and writes an ethnography that satisfies his peers but bewilders the natives, if they ever have a chance to read it.

This disconnect, I contend, is the result of a lack of balance in the writing of ethnography. Every anthropologist has a story to tell, and so often most of that story is left out of the ethnography. The narration of that story constitutes the personal portion of the writing because it is the only chance the reader has to identify with the experience of the ethnographer that, by its very nature, is intimate and, if done properly, includes the personal stories of the various contacts that the ethnographer has made in the field.

I am making a case for a more rigorous inclusion of the subjective (idiosyncratic) elements of a culture in the substance of an ethnography. I believe that the best tool for that inclusion is the use of narrative. The best grounding for that tool, the best source of material for it, comes from the active participation of the ethnographer in the culture he or she intends to represent to the reader. Not only must the ethnographer participate, he or she must discuss the participation. A good example of non-participation is the survey technique, or the remote collection of standardized data where the eventual writer of the results uses only secondary sources to flesh out the details or give them meaning. Anthropologists are well aware of this flaw; and the participant observation technique is used to circumvent this problem, though, curiously, much trouble is taken to avoid reporting very much about the participation. After establishing that he or she was there, the ethnographer suddenly drops out of the picture, the writing becomes "objective," and the authority of the writing then rests on its "non-subjective" nature. This is self and reader deception. The observer never leaves the scene and is always a part of the data, whether discussed or not.

This act of deception is doubly troublesome. Not only is the effect of the observer upon the observed never questioned, but an entire dimension of value is short changed in the process. In order to correct this problem, you must drop the charade and talk about the observer's participation with and effect upon the people being studied at length. Doing so is scientifically honest and makes good sense.

In order to follow through on my ideas, the ethnography in this book contains an extensive narrative. I use the results of participant-observation there to help establish a sense of the mood of the country and how some of its citizens coped with difficult circumstances.

My idea was simply to take my readers into the field with me and keep them there for several weeks. The time frame chosen was the first field trip I took to Russia when it was still part of the former Soviet Union. I write extensively about this trip because it was my rawest and least conditioned experience in Russia. I was a neophyte, learning to be an anthropologist by being thrown into the water. What came out of this exercise was a psychological landscape involving Russians and other Soviet citizens I met on that first trip.

The third part of the book includes the methodology chapter (Chapter Seven). I spend a considerable amount of time discussing the theory behind the HVP in this chapter because it is new to anthropology and somewhat unique in its claim to be culturally neutral. Since Hartman was, and Pomeroy is, after a science of values (*behavioral axiology* is Pomeroy's derivative of formal axiology), this instrument must be as culturally neutral as the law of gravity. As a cultural anthropologist studying in the tradition of relativism, I found the claim to be intriguing.

The HVP-PIV (HVP—Pomeroy Interpretation Validation) was both a way into Russia, an excuse for being there in the first place, and a productive way to measure the levels of individual and social stress that provided a social-psychological context for my work. My work with the HVP-PIV provided a significant part of my participation in the society. The invitations to live with Soviet scientists and later to live with other families from other occupational classes were derived from my work with this test. The ability to keep myself immersed in the society (as opposed to living separate from it as businessmen might do in a hotel or journalists might do in a journalistic enclave) was crucial for doing good work there.

The fourth part of the book (Chapter Eight) involves a detailed analysis of the value structures of three Russians who responded to the HVP. It demonstrates how the HVP's compact design and brevity enabled me to conduct research and gather useful data without too much trouble, once the initial rough spots were overcome. In general, HVP results provided two kinds of information. First, they helped me refine the HVP's translation into Russian, which underwent several phases, by providing feedback about the test's design, where it was consistent with the English version and where it was not. Second, Russian HVP results (when reliable) provided feedback about the respondents' mental states at different times and complemented the respondents' self-reports and my observations about their lives.

The fifth part of the book includes Chapter Nine, an analytical account of material concerning my visits to Russia. Two analytic approaches are used, a value analysis derived from formal axiology and social network analysis.

Cultural anthropology is largely an interpretive science. Interpretations are based on the intellectual background of the interpreter and influenced by a consensus of those currently providing interpretations within the same general area of focus. You may say that the cultural *milieu* of the scientist shapes the interpretation given to the culture under study. The projection of one's own culture onto that of another is bound to lead to problems that go beyond academics. (History is replete with examples of the imposition of one cultural *milieu* onto another, often leading to long term overt or covert conflicts, for example, colonialism.) The problem of cultural projection (often called "ethnocentrism") has been recognized by cultural anthropology. Various attempts to overcome this Gordian knot have yielded mixed results. Formal axiology potentially provides the "sharp scissors" needed to cut the knot.

In this study, formal axiology is applied to interaction between ethnographer and native Russian entrepreneurs, and to the cultural context of the entrepreneurs. The goal is to "objectify" interpretation and thus bring it beyond the slippery realm of subjective analysis that results from cultural projection.

5. The Research Question

My first trip to Russia provided me with all the tools I needed for my subsequent research and writing. As already discussed, I was able to make intellectual progress by forging a connection between values and stress. I was also able to establish the necessary contacts to continue doing work there. These contacts provided every aspect of the possible assistance I would need from dealing with red-tape, finding suitable and affordable places of residence to introducing me to the range of people I would need to meet, while at the same time keeping me safe and fed. My first trip also yielded a focus question. Through an extended contact with my principal informant I was able to uncover the phenomenon of *blat* that permeated all aspects of Russian life.

"*Blat*" is an informal word that means "influence" or "connections." A concept used in America that comes close to *blat* is "networking."

Once I understood how important *blat* was to Russians, I became aware that practically everybody I got to know was, in one way or another, an entrepreneur of sorts. Russian entrepreneurial activity was very informal, contractual law having been a very nebulous thing in the Soviet Union. Over time, specialization would return to Russia. Those who had a knack for business would formalize their activity. Those who did not remained dilettantes or dropped out altogether. My study focused on those Russians whose activities stood out and were also observable.

In a sense "Russian entrepreneurs" covered anyone I met. In another sense, only a handful of those I met were masters at this game. Since I was studying values and stress and since a certain kind of activity presented itself to me, the question I decided to pursue is "How are Russian entrepreneurs coping economically and emotionally in everyday Russia?"

To clarify this further, I needed to categorize activity rather than individuals. Although the nature of the data collection I did involved individuals, I was interested in these individuals primarily as they performed as entrepreneurs. Other issues in their lives, such as the political situation or their personal problems, played supporting roles and formed the raw material from which I could extract their values. The HVP and formal axiology are used here to systematize Russian entrepreneurs' coping activity in terms of their cognitive value structures and social behavior, while keeping in mind that their struggles were those of anyone caught in a difficult situation.

6. Russian Entrepreneurs

I did not originally go to Russia to study the new entrepreneurs. Originally intended to be a much more narrowly defined case study, I found that events in Russia itself began to shape the direction of my research. The revelation that Russian scientists and academicians operate under a different set of assumptions than their American counterparts led me to delve into an area of Russian culture that has become not only a big public headache for that new federated republic, but also a secret source of its vitality.

News headlines screaming about corruption and gangsters in post-Soviet Russia served the previous function of Communist Party controlled government propaganda. The Party covered up the Soviet Union's second economy, underground markets, while its members participated in it (Vaksberg, 1991; Zemtsov, 1985). The newspapers (inside and outside of Russia) covered up entrepreneurial activity, which was now out in the open, by wrongly characterizing it as being illegitimate and corrosive.

The problem did not lie with the entrepreneurs. It lay with a legal structure in disarray because it could not discriminate between legitimate businessmen and crooks. The problem went beyond the law to the culture itself, one in which the idea of a civil society was still new and untested, where the people expected "the authorities" to take care of everything, even when they knew that such authorities were as dangerous as or, in fact, the same thing as the *mafiya*.

The main thrust of the book is to uncover the truths about Russia that pertain to living and prospering, or not, in a state that was undergoing tumultuous change. This change can be called a culture shift as opposed to a culture change. Culture change includes processes that occur over long periods of time as well as those that occur quickly. Culture shift is a particular kind of change, one that occurs quickly with markers that include overt political, social, and economic revolutions.

Boris Yeltsin's revolution, which broke the back of the Soviet Union and ushered in the current age of the Russian Federation, defines the political context of my book. In July of 1991, during my first trip to the Soviet Union, Yeltsin represented the active opposition to Gorbachev and "reformed" communism in Russia. In August, the confrontation between Gorbachev's hand-picked executive cabinet and Yeltsin's democratic forces turned the tables on Gorbachev. Initially seen as the martyr of the failed coup, the isolated victim of the treacherous Committee for the State of Emergency (Dunlop, 1993, p. 191; Satter, 1996, p. 9), Gorbachev quickly became the fool of his savior, Yeltsin, who used the changed political circumstances (characterized by a suddenly weakened Communist Party) to turn the tables on his old nemesis. Yeltsin's actions were pay-back for his public humiliation at the hands of Gorbachev in 1987 (Morrison, 1991, pp. 60–73; Yeltsin, 1990, pp. 177–210). The Yeltsin agenda to dismantle the Soviet Union proceeded unabated, and Gorbachev could only grin and bear it.

In August and September of 1992, during my second trip to the (former) Soviet Union, the Yeltsin agenda was starting to run into its first snags. Prices, which had already jumped at the beginning of 1992—when Yeltsin unleashed most market forces, but, in an attempt to retain employment in large scale industries, not all—would soon jump again as a second wave of inflation would besiege Russia. The problem was that Yeltsin's team was either reluctant to, or found it impossible to, control the credit policies that allowed gigantic antiquated industries to stay in place while the rest of the country had to fend for itself. These industries were slowly dying from a lack of purpose and years of neglect, but they were being propped up in an attempt to avoid the potential social consequences of mass unemployment. Unfortunately, the social consequences of runaway inflation threatened to topple the new government and usher in an era of reaction and backlash (Aslund, 1995, pp. 191–193).

From May to November of 1993, I was in St. Petersburg, while Russia was awash in frantic activity. I watched as residents struggled to make ends meet in unpredictable economic conditions and in frustrating slow downs of the reform movement, while the recalcitrant Russian parliament engaged the Yeltsin agenda in a pitched battle and fought to preserve the system of rank and privilege that the "civil service" had long enjoyed in Soviet times. I witnessed the final confrontation between Yeltsin and the leaders of anti-Yeltsin forces on Russian television, and I later traveled to Moscow to survey the ruins of the bloody event that touched the lives of everyone I knew in St. Petersburg.

The aftermath of the Yeltsin victory in October of 1993 led Russians to the polls in December for the first of a series of post-Soviet elections that would reshape the political landscape and provide the beleaguered Communist forces with other opportunities to take back control of the former empire. The final hurrah of the Communists came in 1996 as Gennady Zyuganov, their hand picked presidential candidate, came dangerously close to ousting the still indefatigable Yeltsin in a hotly contested election.

The Russia of 1999–2000 weathered a series of turbulent times and continued to show its eternal promise. Still, Russia was faced with many problems. Inflation was tamed for the time being, but it occasionally resurfaced, generating new crises. The civil and military services were shattered, and wage arrears threatened yet another form of social catastrophe, as the new government struggled to find equitable ways to collect taxes and pay its employees. Meanwhile, charges of corruption threatened public confidence in the ability of the Yeltsin forces to save the day yet again.

Yeltsin resigned at the turn of the new millennium, with an apology to Russians that he wished he could have done more for his country. However, he did not do so before hand picking his successor, Vladimir Putin, who easily won the election of 2000. Putin has proved to be a popular president for Russia, winning re-election in 2004.

In my opinion, Yeltsin did a lot more for Russia than he gave himself credit. His leadership, brilliant at times, and rocky in others, can be best measured by what did *not* happen. The Soviet state broke up cleanly in a largely peaceful process. A costly and potentially catastrophic civil war did not break out as it did in Yugoslavia. Russians as an ethnic group were not threatened. No disastrous famines occurred as they did in Russia's civil war of the early twentieth century. Finally, a reversion to a totalitarian state did not occur, and, despite occasional questionable assertions of the contrary, still has not occurred.

Putin did inherit many of the nagging problems that plagued Russia during the 1990s. Financial problems and government corruption continue to plague the country. Russia's former status as a superpower is still gone. However, Putin has managed to keep Russia active in foreign affairs. He has managed to retain friendly relations with the United States, joining it in the world wide war against Muslim extremists. Putin is also attempting to reassert the legal authority over big business the Russian government lost during the 1990s, reigning in a powerful oligarchy, and, at the same time, not imposing a centralized economy as in the old days.

Russia's current perceived problems were well under way when I was in the field from 1991 to 1993. Webs of personal relationships that had been employed to advantage in the Soviet Union were being transformed from being clandestine parts of secretive cumbersome dynasties to providing open dynamic structures for transparent enterprises. Setting out to study a narrow problem involving the ethnographic evaluation of an emerging, cutting edge, social science surveying technology, I soon found that the frustrating task of doing straightforward data collection in the Soviet Union was telling me something. I began to pay attention to the various accidents and enigmatic situations that were so confounding. Close to blaming myself for being an incompetent neophyte, I began to discover that Western scientists and businessmen of greater experience than I were having equal difficulty in their attempts to work in post-Soviet Eastern Europe. This discovery led me to re-evaluate Russian circumstances. Initial probing and theory-making led to new revelations and new questions. By reading and studying the literature on Russia and by reviewing my experiences there—some apparently successful and others apparently not successful—I came to the conclusion that the nature of Russia and Russians, after seventy years of communism, posed unique challenges to straight ahead research designs. Real subversion and a willingness to play a game called subversion (the original purpose of the underground networks) were necessary to get things done. In my case, the aim was to collect sufficient data to make an empirical base for theory construction. The indirect ways I went about doing it, as they reflected on the conditions that made direct methods problematical, themselves became a part of the empirical data.

After several frustrating attempts to classify the kinds of people I met in Russia and many discussions with members of my doctoral committee, I came to the realization that the mostly hardworking and mostly honest people I encountered have been considered by Russian and Western presses to constitute part of what they call the Russian "Mafia," but I call the new Russian entrepreneurs. The boundaries between what we in the West refer to as the Mafia and what we refer to as entrepreneurial activity are very much blurred in post-Soviet Russia. Some Russian observers have commented that entrepreneurs in Russia are considered to be "Mafiosi," simply because they do not operate in the traditional channels set up by the Soviet system (Bennett, 1997, personal communication). This is an eloquent statement of the ability of culture to endure beyond the nation-state. The cultural ideal patterns established during the time of the Soviet Union remain while *de facto* practices continue to mutate. A new ideal pattern will eventually emerge from the current chaos and culture change will be complete in terms of a new set of expectations for what it means to be Russian.

Two

CONTEXT: HISTORY, GEOGRAPHY, AND THE EVOLUTION OF THE FIELDWORK

1. Overview

In early July of 1991, I had a chance to travel to Leningrad in the Soviet Union, a country that held deep mystery and fear for me. Four weeks later, after a bewildering, exhausting, and, at times, poignant trip, I left, glad to have been there and glad to be getting out. I did not want to return. Little did I know that, in a couple of weeks, the Soviet Union would be changed forever, and, by the end of 1991, it would cease to exist altogether.

Only the Russian Federation, the heart of the former Soviet Union, remained. Leningrad changed its name to the original, St. Petersburg. Like a woman changing her hairstyle, wearing new clothes, Russia was luring me back. I returned in 1992, and then again for several months in 1993. The experience reshaped my attitudes to Russia and to my home country.

I grew up in the United States, a country that long considered the Soviet Union to be an enemy and that viewed Russians stereotypically, as being "lazy workers" because their economy was sluggish, "drunks" because of reported problems with alcoholism, and "devious" because Soviet spying was a threat during the Cold War. In addition to being immersed in a culture generally hostile to the Soviet Union, I had become repelled by communism not only as a political system but also as a philosophical ideal after reading works of Ayn Rand and other authors opposed at various philosophical levels to socialism in its different forms.

I did not know then that a growing curiosity about things Russian was subverting my overt hostility to the Soviet Union. The haunting Russian landscapes from films like "Dr. Zhivago" and "Dark Eyes," the photographs of the magnificent palaces near Leningrad in tourist brochures, and the vulnerable, all too human Russians behind gruff Soviet exteriors as depicted in various novels, television shows, and movies all conspired to create a compelling sense of enigma and allure about Russia and Russians for me.

At the time, my knowledge of Russia was a patchwork of snippets of information. Early in grade school, I read the boy's adventure story, *Michael Strogoff* (by Jules Verne), set in the steppes of Russia that gave me the impression that Russia was a vast Asiatic land. Later in grade school, after trying to fathom the intricate geography and unmanageable names of the Soviet Union, I felt that any attempt to understand this place was beyond me.

In high school, a friend who had traveled to the Soviet Union told me the thing that had most struck her was seeing people silent in the subways as if in a dream. No one said a word, either in the trains or on the platforms, and they moved as a herd, like cattle. This overt passivity was considered by many to be part of the "Russian character." This kind of public behavior was a reaction to oppressive conditions and could not be considered independently of them, being only "Russian" in the sense that Russians had to endure such conditions.

One of the topics that would come up over and over in the 1970s was the possible future of the Soviet Union, of communism and capitalism. The consensus was that Russia and America would eventually converge. Capitalism would give way to more socialism in America, and Communist Russia would become more democratic and give way to more capitalism. No one spoke of the possible end of communism in the Soviet Union. In the mid-1980s, political commentators saw changes beginning but did not expect the Soviet Union to go away any time soon.

As it turned out, the Soviet Union only lasted a few more years. The warning signs existed. We had long heard about Andrei Sakharov, a prominent scientist responsible for the Soviet development of nuclear weapons who turned away from the Communist leadership and became an internationally recognized dissident. However, dissidents, though organized, numerous, and internationally recognized, still seemed to have no chance. In 1987, Mikhail Sergeyevich Gorbachev, General Secretary of the Communist Party of the Soviet Union, expelled a Communist Party functionary little known in the West by the name of Boris Yeltsin from his position as First Secretary of the Moscow City Party Committee (Aron, 2000, pp. 202–203). This event led Yeltsin (who had intended to resign anyway) out of the Communist fold into uncharted political waters and eventually to a triumph of political will and ingenuity.

Two years later, the visible end of Soviet domination in Eastern Europe began. I was in graduate school at the University of Cincinnati, studying cultural anthropology with a focus on Mayan civilization. Russia was still as distant as ever to me, but I, along with most Americans, was heartened by these events. Gorbachev, soon to be the Soviet Union's first and only President, became prominent. His *perestroika* (restructuring) and *glasnost* (openness) suddenly became household words. Sakharov died and was given credit for influencing the changes underway in the Soviet Union. Yeltsin also began to be noticed as a rising force in Soviet politics, but major Western political figures were slow to embrace him as a genuine Russian reformer.

In early 1990, I received an invitation from the Department of Anthropology at the University of Buffalo to continue my studies in anthropology with two years of funding. Given a fresh opportunity to design research, I contacted a colleague whom I had met in New York City, where I had been working as a computer programmer during the 1980s and contemplating graduate school. Dr. Leon Pomeroy was a clinical psychologist who had acted as my marriage counselor and had grown interested in me as a scientist. Upon my return to college to study in the social sciences, he had invited me to collaborate with him on his values oriented research. We had agreed in principle to cooperate but no opportunity had presented itself. Now one existed. I told Pomeroy that I would try to incorporate his research into mine. I was intrigued by the potential applications of his valuation studies. During this time, Pomeroy introduced me to the HVP and formal axiology.

I was scheduled to do fieldwork during the summer of 1991 among Mayans in Belize. I planned to use the HVP-PIV in my research. However, resistance to the HVP-PIV (by the Belize project director) and other academic politics forced me to abandon this plan. Anxious to get a new field site for that summer, my pursuit of leads included calling Pomeroy in New York City. I had given up on the idea of going abroad that summer. He proposed to send me to Russia. Pomeroy had met Dmitri, a Russian psychologist, at a conference in Japan the previous summer who left a standing invitation with Pomeroy to visit him in Leningrad, or, short of that, to send another American scientist to visit him. Pomeroy wanted a Russian version of his test. I got the assignment to travel to Russia as Pomeroy's proxy.

I barely cracked a book on Russia before I had to get on the *Aeroflot* jet that would take me to the Soviet Union. I had to learn the language in a hurry. Fortunately, I got help from a young library sciences student who taught Russian and had family roots in Belorus (White Russia). This student, Laura, told me about the time she went with a group to the Soviet Union. She found that Russians liked cigarettes, the children liked chewing gum, and everyone liked retractable pens and postcards. She had met and talked with Russian students and done other things typical of a student holiday in a foreign land.

Then Laura scared me: The group leader, a middle-aged female teacher, died on the trip. This woman had been suffering from a nagging condition, her illness became worse during the trip, and the medical attention she received in Soviet hospitals was poor. Complications from her illness and poor care killed her. Instead of immediately returning to the United States when she started feeling worse, the group leader persisted in staying in her role. This cost her her life. Laura's story plus my thin knowledge of the place left me with trepidation about my upcoming journey.

Meeting the Russian psychologist over the phone (with Pomeroy's help) did not do much to ease my anxiety. Dmitri's broken English, heavy accent, and strange intensity tended to leave both Pomeroy and me with a sense of uncertainty. The poor telephone connection did not help (telephone service to Russia has dramatically improved since 1991). Nevertheless, we worked out a rough agreement for a four week stay at Dmitri's home, and I managed to get the necessary documents for travel to the USSR with his help.

My one month field trip in 1991 laid the foundation for further research in Russia. The trip shaped the rest of my research and profoundly influenced my thinking about that country. I devote a good deal of space in this book to a blow by blow account of a major portion of that trip. My initiation into Russian culture provided some indelible impressions. Themes in my account of the trip include Russians' sense of their own destiny, their tenuous position at the end of the twentieth century as a country and as a people, their chances to survive the end of the Soviet Union, and their hopes for a better future.

In order to provide context, sections of this chapter are devoted to acquainting the reader with Russian history and the city known both as Leningrad and St. Petersburg, where I did most of my research. In addition, I provide small introductions to other cities and major towns I visited. Along the way, I introduce several of my Russian and Soviet friends, using first names as pseudonyms to preserve their identities. Some I met in 1991, others later. These are broad sketches and small anecdotes designed to get the reader's feet wet before I turn to the lengthy narrative description that covers Chapters Three, Four, Five, and Six.

2. Sketch of Russian History

Russia (as we know it today) has lasted approximately 850 years, the same age as its founding city, Moscow, which originated as a religious and secular seat of princely power located deep in a wooded region on the northern Eurasian plain. Its remoteness from the steppes and fertile lower regions of (present day) Russia, which were dominated by Asian nomadic warriors, spared it from the fate of Russia's first flowering (known as *Rus*) centered in Kiev. The original Kievan medieval kingdom (the heart of modern day Ukraine) began to decline in the twelfth century and was destroyed by Mongols in the thirteenth century (Riasanovsky, 1969, pp. 43–44). Moscow competed with other principalities for land, prestige, and power to form Muscovy in the late Middle Ages. After the nomadic hordes receded, the once small principality grew into a regional power, defeating many of its former enemies.

Beginning in 1462, the Muscovite state expanded in all directions to reach the continental boundaries of the Arctic Ocean to the north and the Pacific to the east (Barraclough, 1982, pp. 84–85). This land expansion characterized Russia over the next five centuries. In the twentieth century, Russia's expansion began to be checked (Laqueur, 1994, pp. 67–68; Ulam, 1992, p. 5). Russia's tendency to expand helped characterize it as an empire. Without a sizable market economy, it needed fresh conquests to maintain its viability as an empire. During the Soviet period, former territories of the Russian Empire were conquered by the new Communist regime (Pipes, 1974). The Soviet expansion continued into the Baltics and part of Finland, and extended Russian political hegemony into Eastern Europe, Latin America, Asia, and Africa. When the Soviet Union was finally contained by the Cold War with the United States, it was forced to deal with the very real problems of an empire that could no longer sustain itself through expansion (Ulam, 1992, pp. xi–xii).

During its long history, Russia transformed itself three times. First, under the brutal but innovative direction of autocrat Peter the Great (1689–1725), Russians adopted European customs and built a navy that gave them a much needed military presence on the seas and rivers and allowed them to defeat their rivals, the Turks and the Swedes, thus opening up new avenues of commerce, trade, and ideas. Russia's capital shifted west to St. Petersburg at this time. Peter in essence took Russians out of the feudalism of the Dark Ages and began the kingdom's transition into an empire, rivaling those of its European neighbors to the west. Second (1917), under the bloody revolutionary leadership of Lenin, Trotsky, and Stalin, Russia became the Soviet Union, a "people's dictatorship" that subverted various aristocratic classes formerly on top, while at the same time retaining the empire's land base, its anti-democratic nature, and its expansionist tendencies. Moscow became the capital of the revised empire. Third (1991), under the bravado of authoritarian President Yeltsin, Russians broke free from the rotting yoke of the autocratic Soviet Union to form the Russian Federation. Russia has retained the largest part of the former empire with its sweep and ethnic diversity but, at the same time, allowed legitimate democratic forms to emerge.

Every society undergoes numerous changes during the course of its lifetime, Russia being no exception. The changes Russia underwent during its long history were dramatic and unpredictable, largely resting on the shoulders of a series of leaders. Often, before such dramatic upheavals, all would seem quiet. These periods have been referred to as "stagnations" or "stabilizations" by some historians (Malia, 1994, pp. 355, 474–475; Pipes, 1990, p. xxii; Tucker, 1987, pp. 126–127; Ulam, 1992, p. xi; Yanov 1981, pp. 65, 324). For instance, before Peter the Great's reforms shook Russia to its foundations, Russia (in the form of ancient Muscovy) was largely an inward looking country, its administration dominated by elaborate religious ritual, seemingly unconcerned with the rest of Europe (Platonov, 1972, p. 181; Sumner, 1972, p. 188). Devastated by World War I, Russia was a nation adrift before the Bolsheviks accomplished their takeover of the empire during the chaos after Tsar Nicholas II abdicated (Pipes, 1990, p. 195). With its administration unwilling to keep up politically with the internal changes caused by the industrial revolution sweeping Europe, Russia had become cumbersome, militarily impotent, and wrought by internal strife (Pipes, 1990, pp. 233–234).

In the period before Yeltsin's revolution, Russia could be characterized by the same sense of drift and lethargy. Its financial system, long bolstered by the sale of precious reserves of oil (Malia, 1994, p. 377) and other natural resources, was drifting towards a collapse during the early 1980s. Geared primarily to support a military, Leonid Brezhnev's state-run economy was unable to meet the growing consumer demands of its own citizens. When world oil prices dropped, the Soviet Union lost much of its primary source of income (Granville, 1995, p. 12). Brezhnev's golden age came to an end, and so did he, dying after a long period of senility.

The next few years saw the Soviet Union change its leadership three times in a confused effort to infuse the waning superpower with new life and fresh ideas. The end of this tumultuous period brought about the rise of a new generation of Russian leadership destined to change global politics. The most prominent personalities of this new generation, Gorbachev and Yeltsin, struggled for ultimate control of Russia's fate.

A. Mikhail Gorbachev

The attempts by Gorbachev (1985–1991), the last of the Soviet Union's leaders, to shake up Russia enough to get it back on track failed, largely because they were based on the fundamental belief in the Marxist model of history. Gorbachev, as a true believer (Morrison, 1991, 35), could never bring himself to reject utterly a command economy in favor of unrestrained markets. His ultimate purpose was to preserve the Party and the Union (Aslund, 1995, pp. 27–28). Thus, he only took half measures, toying with various economic reforms, some of which had real promise, only to put the brakes on and align himself with the "hard liners" who wished to reject reforms. Gorbachev wanted to have the best of both worlds: Communist Party rule of a nation with an economic engine based on communism's ideological antithesis, capitalism. He also wanted the new Soviet Union to have a more open press. Gorbachev's project was doomed by its own internal contradictions, which were much more evident and final than those which Communists attributed to capitalism. The Communist Party had maintained its rule with a stranglehold on both commerce and information. By weakening its grip on both of these things simultaneously, it wrote its own death sentence.

Gorbachev's actions had consequences that he did not anticipate. The results of his various reform programs and his backtracking and side-stepping, were reminiscent of the (April 1986) Chernobyl disaster (Smith, 1992, p. 64). The nuclear accident had begun with an experiment that got out of hand, overheating a reactor that exploded. In a similar fashion, Gorbachev's experiment with the Soviet Union's financial structure (following a Keynesian approach of deficit spending) and his simultaneous introduction of limited economic and political reforms overheated the Soviet economy and accelerated the formation of organized and open opposition movements. Since prices of state goods were fixed by state fiat, the underlying hyper-inflation first showed up in the form of drastic shortages of state goods and rapid price inflation of privately traded goods (Aslund, 1995, p. 49). By 1991, the Soviet Union's economy had been reduced to a system of coupon rationing. State resources formerly capable of maintaining a minimum level of social security dried up. Gorbachev, who retained the Communist Party chairmanship and had given himself the additional title of President of the USSR, suddenly found himself being criticized openly by the media he had helped to free. Since, as of then, no political safety valves (such as the checks and balances in the U.S. system) existed, the subsequent political explosion in Russia was inevitable and loud.

B. Boris Yeltsin

While Gorbachev fiddled with reforms, Yeltsin took *perestroika* (economic restructuring) seriously (McDonnell, 1994, 26). While he may have lacked the delicate diplomacy of Gorbachev, he had more gumption, and was willing to take risks that Gorbachev was not. Starting off as just another ambitious Communist *apparatchik*, Yeltsin's willingness to tackle problems honestly and to "tell it like it is" quickly made him a "bad boy" as far as the Party was concerned, and he suffered severe—one would think career ending—political set backs. Yeltsin restored his career through successful use of the newly available (thanks to Gorbachev), proto-democratic forum, the USSR Congress of People's Deputies. In 1989, his populist appeal to ordinary Russians bore fruit, and he was elected by an overwhelming majority to the legislative body (Dunlop, 1993, 38-46). His political career took off after that, following a path to success that went through the Russian Soviet Republic (RSFSR). He was elected Chairman of the Russian parliament in 1990 (the post that his future rival, Ruslan Khasbulatov, inherited) and became Russian President in June of 1991 (Dunlop, 1993, pp. 52–53).[is Khasbulatov mentioned again?]

The Russian Soviet Republic unlike the other Union republics had long been under direct control of the Kremlin and lacked its own internal administration. Yeltsin saw to it that the republic's newly revised institutions would have more political muscle. The Soviet Union now had two bases of power, that of Gorbachev's Kremlin and that of Yeltsin's parliament housed in the *Byeli Dom* (White House) (Dunlop, 1993, p. 32; Waitzkin, 1993, pp. 268–269). The standard joke among Russians during the summer of 1991 was that Russia had "two voices." The first, President Gorbachev's, you could find on television Channel One (*Ostankina*). The second, President Yeltsin's, you could find on television Channel Three (*Rossiya*). In effect, Russia was being given a choice—go with Yeltsin, or stick with Gorbachev. Just as, at the time, no other (national) channels were on TV, Russians had no other choice. They were lucky to have any choice.

Yeltsin was in office no more than a couple of months in 1991 before the attempted coup against Gorbachev by hard liners in August of that year forced the issue. Yeltsin, his life and political career on the line, used his office to rally the country against the coup plotters. His legitimacy as a democratically elected leader in the eyes of Russians (Barner-Barry and Hody, 1995, pp. 13–14; Billington, 1992, p. 56) gave him a resilient strength that the coup plotters, steeped in Soviet ways, did not understand—for the first time, they were encountering a *popular* leader. The aftermath of the coup left Gorbachev visibly weakened. Yeltsin wasted no time pointing out that Gorbachev had brought those responsible into positions of power from which they could launch a coup. Gorbachev also had to suffer the humiliation of having Yeltsin, his political nemesis, rescue him from the hands of his own people. Gorbachev could no longer afford to ignore him. Yeltsin, with his sights set on democratic power, used the opportunity to push through many new reforms, beginning the long sought dismantling of the Soviet Union.

Russia had been first an empire and then a socialist union. It was going to become a "tranquil" nation, and it was already becoming "normal" (Yeltsin, 1994, pp. 7–8, 293). The new nation would encompass the territory of what had formerly been the Russian Soviet Republic within the old Soviet Union, but it would assume the international role that the now defunct Soviet Union had had, such as a seat in the United Nations, the nuclear suitcase, and so on. Yeltsin, using his legitimate post as the former Soviet republic's President, soon took over as Russia's new leader, while Gorbachev watched his former empire fall apart and the Communist Party fall from power. Once done, Gorbachev was out of a job.

Despite slips and setbacks, in the end, under Yeltsin's steady hand, capitalism saved Russia and brought it back from the brink of national disaster. During the final hectic days of the Soviet Union and the dawn of Russia's new beginning, many of its citizens feared not only for their country but for their very existence as a people. Like a drunk the morning after a binge with a bad hangover, Russia pulled itself out of its stupor and stumbled out of bed. Hoping to reform themselves, Russia's people decided that it was time to take charge of their own lives, to "be good" and to find "the best within them." You might say that Russia underwent a moral rebirth through its citizens.

Of course, not all Russians thought this way; the nation, even with the resounding defeat of the Communist Party, was divided as to the correct path to follow. During the late 1980s, *perestroika* and *glasnost* (openness), centerpieces of Gorbachev's shakeup, had given many Russians a voice in their own future. Many took up the cause of economic reform, either ideologically or directly for their own profit, and were involved in the formation or promotion of cooperatives (primitive corporations) and the concomitant spirit of free market trade. Others looked to dissident voices such as Sakharov's for blueprints of a new political order that would allow the Union to devolve into a confederation of autonomous republics with more democratic structures and freer markets than their predecessors. Sakharov's call for the repeal of Article Six of Brezhnev's constitution that entitled the Communist Party to a political monopoly bore fruit after his death. (Many would call this Sakharov's greatest political achievement).

In early 1990, Gorbachev succumbed to the political pressure and rescinded Article Six (Dunlop, 1993, p. 97). As proto-democratic structures emerged, new politicians appeared, eager to gain power in a way largely unfamiliar to Russia—by popular appeal. Yeltsin, a failure at conventional Communist politics, rose to power this way. Later, ultra-nationalists like Vladimir Zhirinovsky and General Alexander Lebed would gain positions of power in a similar manner.

At the same time, many voices were calling for a stronger state, one directed by an autocrat in the tradition of Stalin. The trend towards decentralization started by Sakharov was seen as being too dangerous for the Soviet Union and the Party. Nina Andreeva made a name for herself as the spokeswoman for anti-*perestroika* sentiment when she published a neo-Stalinist manifesto during 1988 in a leading Soviet newspaper attacking Gorbachev and the so called "left-liberals" (Dunlop, 1993, pp. 13–14). She was taking advantage of Russians' long standing predilection for the strong boss (Yeltsin, 1994, p. 6). While many welcomed the coming breakup of the Union, others feared it, hoping to restore Russia's former international presence. As the communist utopia unraveled, Slavophiles (those enamored of the Slavic races) began to reawaken nationalist sentiments. The focus shifted away from the alternate models of socialism and capitalism to that of "Russians first." Many looked to the military to restore national prestige and honor.

This conflux of differing intellectual currents vied for prominence in a country that was teetering on the brink of a civil war. The country was literally being pulled apart by forces headed in at least two different directions simultaneously. The hard liners were arrayed against the newer emerging class of democratic reformers. The year 1992 began with a series of crises that lasted into December of 1993 when Russians went to the polls for the first time in a form familiar to Western nations. Two years after throwing off Soviet rule, they were electing a new legislature and were voting in a forum for a new constitution.

3. My Research

Against this backdrop, I decided to return to the former Soviet Union to do ethnographic work after my initial four week pilot study. I was not only concerned for the people I had already met in 1991, but I already felt that I was, in a small way, a part of their struggle, and was sharing their hopes. As a cultural anthropologist, the opportunity to see a large scale transition in process was intriguing. The sweeping economic, political, and social changes were bound to have cultural implications. A last chance to see Soviet structures before they melted away completely and the ever present risk of a collapse gave my mission a sense of urgency and adventure. Whatever the outcome, I did not want to squander a chance to see it for myself and to record the transition from the citizen's point of view, as opposed to the predominantly top down view given by the Western media.

I was fortunate to see Russia close up during that period. Being there as opposed to relying on news sources from afar gave me a unique opportunity to make my own observations. Living with several Russian families and interacting with circles of friends, colleagues, and business partners, I was able to gauge various reactions to national events.

The most prominent feature of the rapidly unfolding events was the flexible reaction of the Russians I got to know. Stripping away the tarnish put on the Russian work ethic by Western journalists and Sovietologists, I found that the Russians I met were, by and large, not adverse to hard work; nor did they lack in creativity and ingenuity. As one informant would say, "We are the only people who work for nothing." As a whole, they could be characterized as a very pragmatic and materialistic people, hardly the romantic idealists or lazy workers they were alternately described as being. They were also slowly learning to work from their own initiative after years of being told what to do and what to believe.

I ended up traveling to Russia three times over a period of three years, and made a fourth trip several years later. My relationship to that country unfolded in unanticipated ways. In the course of my travels to Russia, I changed my career focus and my views on Russia, America, anthropology, history, and values. The experience left a deep impression in my life.

During this time I got to know Russians in a variety of ways. One way was through the institutional contacts I made. These included the University of Leningrad, where I was a student, a teacher, and a visiting scientist. I had status as a student and received some of the benefits, but I was not studying formally. I was invited to participate in and observe English classes and later to teach conversational English. Two departments, one devoted to continuing education, the other devoted to teaching foreign languages, helped with my research. In this book, I refer to the first as the Retraining Department and the second as "Polylog" (many voices). My principal contact at both of these departments was an administrator named Andrey whom I met by chance in Latvia during my 1991 trip. Also associated with my research was an educational facility, the Upgrade Center, located north of the university in the Vyborg section of Leningrad. In 1992, Dr. Leon Pomeroy and I gave a seminar on formal axiology with Polylog's sponsorship at the Upgrade Center. In 1993, I presented a paper with Andrey about our HVP Russian research.

I also met many natives by living with Russian families. Table 1 shows which families I stayed with, identified with pseudonyms. It includes Dmitri's (the Russian psychologist) and Andrey's families. It also introduces some names with which the reader will become familiar. The families are listed in order of duration of stay. The last column shows when I lived with each family. Unless otherwise noted, all stays took place in Leningrad/St. Petersburg.

The third way I met new people, stayed in touch with people who I had already met, or got to know those I already knew better was through travel. Table 1 mentions several places outside of Leningrad (St. Petersburg). The next section discusses places I traveled to while I was in Russia and the former Soviet Union, including Moscow and Riga. Two places mentioned above do not appear in the next section and are only discussed later. These include the village of Privyetneskoye, located northwest of Leningrad, where I spent time in 1992 and 1993. I was introduced to this place by Andrey, when he took me, my wife, and (later) Pomeroy there. Jurmala, a resort town near Riga in Latvia, was introduced to me by (assistants of) Anatol, who was a Latvian contact of Dmitri's in 1991.

TABLE 1 - LIVING WITH RUSSIAN FAMILIES

Family	Total Time Spent Living with Family	Years and Months during which I Lived with Family at Least Part of the Time
Seryozha, Lena, Stepan	19 weeks	1993: May – August, October – November 2000: July – August
Andrey, Amelia * (Leningrad, Moscow)	8–9 weeks	1991: August, 1992: August – September 1993: May, August, September – October
Dmitri * (Leningrad, Riga)	3–4 weeks	1991: July
Fedya	3 weeks	1993: October
Nadia (Privyetneskoye)	1 week	1993: August, September
Nicholas, Ekaterina * (Leningrad, Moscow)	5 days	1993: October, November
Anatol * (Riga, Jurmala)	3 days	1991: July

* Arrangements included staying in places of associated family members or close friends. Amelia, the mother-in-law of Andrey, provided a place in Moscow for an overnight stay in August, 1993. Ekaterina, the mother of one of Nicholas's favorite girlfriends, provided a place to stay in Moscow for a few days during November, 1993. Anatol provided me one overnight guest service in Riga, Latvia plus accommodations in Jurmala, Latvia. (Dmitri and his wife Alisa provided my hotel room in Riga).

4. Leningrad/St. Petersburg, other Cities, and Major Towns.

Over the course of four separate trips to the former Soviet Union I visited several major cities and towns in European Russia and the Baltic region. Six of them stand out, including St. Petersburg (1991–1993, 2000), the central focus of my research, Riga, Moscow, Pushkin, Gatchina, and Vyborg.

During the summer of 1991, when I first arrived in St. Petersburg, it was still called Leningrad in honor of Vladimir Lenin, the most influential and well-known founder of the Soviet Union. Later, in 1992, the city changed its name back to the original St. Petersburg. The capital of Latvia, Riga, was a welcome addition to my itinerary in 1991. It served as a point of comparison to St. Petersburg. I visited Riga only in 1991. I saw Moscow, Gatchina, and Vyborg in 1993. (I made a return trip to Gatchina in 2000). Moscow, being of crucial importance to Russia as well as the Soviet Union, was an important place to visit. I spent two trips and a total of six days there during 1993. Pushkin, which I visited in 1991 and 1993, is an outer suburb of St. Petersburg, yet it has a personality of its own. For such a relatively small place, it played a curiously large part in my field trips.

I spent different lengths of time at each place. Visiting Vyborg, formerly part of Finland, consisted of a one day trip to the east of St. Petersburg, while Pushkin involved a series of three trips with different people for different reasons. I spent several trips visiting two other towns south of St. Petersburg, Petrodvorets and Pavlosk. Both are extensions of St. Petersburg, each containing residences of former Russian tsars that were magnets for tourists. Pushkin also has a tourist attraction, the restored Catherine Palace originally built by Empress Elizabeth. I also visited the resort Zelenogorsk on the northern shore of the Gulf of Finland on my way to and from a small *kholhoz* (collective farm) village (*Privyetnoskoye*) that played a role in my research. Zelenogorsk was little more than a train station and bus depot for me.

Gatchina is located about 45 minutes south of St. Petersburg by rail. It has the feel of provincial Russia, away from the political concerns of a wider world, more family oriented, and more of an economic backwater. Getting to and from Gatchina by myself in 1993 gave me an education in Russian rail travel. The experience of getting myself there and back, deciphering complex railroad timetables (in Cyrillic), purchasing tickets, and dealing with conductors gave me more confidence.

A. St. Petersburg: The City that Peter Built

St. Petersburg was built on a swamp by an implacable emperor, Peter the Great, who commanded it into being, using drafted labor and imported stones to realize his creation. It served as the capital of the Russian Empire from the early eighteenth century until 1917, was the site of the Bolshevik Revolution and other cases of Communist intrigue, endured one of the worst sieges in the history of modern warfare, and became, over the years, the center of Russian high culture.

St. Petersburg's dwellers are aware of its history and often tell tales of woe and heroism. They have an interest in their city that is reflected by their loyalty to it despite its difficult climate and environment.

Lying further north than Stockholm, St. Petersburg is the most northerly major city in the world. Given its extreme northern location, it has some of the longest days of any major city—the so called White Nights of June and early July. It also has the shortest days with the sun rising after ten in the morning and setting between three and four in the afternoon in winter (Lempert, 1996, p. 143; Selby, 1996, p. 14). From September to November, the days grow shorter quite quickly with snow arriving in mid-October. At night, the white orbs of the street lamps on Nevsky Prospect glitter in air that has suddenly gone from being heavy and tired to light and crisp. During the grayer afternoons in November, the damp air penetrates the bones with its icy bite. In the morning hours of late autumn, the sky is still dark, and the cold almost intolerable. Middle-aged ladies display their treasured fur coats and hats on their way to work, walking rapidly to keep warm. Patrons huddle in any heated entryway they can find as they wait for shops to open. The Neva River turns white during this time. In the past, tram rails were laid on the frozen surface to increase the flow of traffic across the river.

Spring does not begin until late in April with the weather rapidly warming during May, obliterating the last of the ice floating on the Neva. The days grow long quickly, marking the advent of events celebrating the approaching White Nights, summer outdoor concerts, and other annual festivals associated with this time of year. The anniversary of the city's founding falls in June. (St. Petersburg celebrated its 290th anniversary in 1993. Local television provided extensive coverage of classical and rock concerts, fireworks, and appearances by dignitaries associated with this event.)

With the first warm days of the middle of May, pensioners make preparations to head to their country *dachas*, sometimes no more than a single room in a converted tool shed. The spring planting season is something very real to city dwellers as well as collective farm workers who live year round in the same places city folk only occupy for a single season. The growing season is short, and city dwellers are amateurs compared to the villagers who have ways to extend the growing season. They use hothouses for growing cucumbers and tomatoes, a technique that requires more investment of time and energy, which are not generally available to the urban gardeners.

During the summer, city dwellers escape to the countryside every weekend and every holiday. Politicians concerned with the popular vote now must take into account this annual custom when scheduling elections. Besides being seasonal gardeners, some city dwellers remember what their parents taught them and go into the forest to collect wild mushrooms and berries. It is a form of relaxation and a hobby that can add variety and nutrition to their diets and medicine to their medicine cabinets. Other city dwellers with more capital and clout have secured the right to parcels of land upon which they have official permission to build permanent dwellings. Small communities consisting of clusters of such housing are popping up here and there next to collective farm villages. Roads, streets, electrical grids, and water systems are being set up to accommodate these new villages. Russia is just beginning, with these small scale projects, to resemble suburban America.

The summer brings water shortages as well. The city authorities take advantage of the warm weather to get at underground pipes for much needed repairs. The pipes are inaccessible during the winter when the frozen earth is too hard to penetrate. The air becomes heavy with moisture and pollution from the many industrial plants surrounding the city. The rustic countryside provides a welcome relief from the harshness of city life.

The long summer days draw tourists from inside and outside Russia and are ideal for gazing at the magnificent collection of architecture and sculpture that makes St. Petersburg's center a living museum. The city offers breathtaking panoramas when seen from the river that divides it in two. Tourists crowd the large tour boats gaping at the sights from the Neva River. Smaller craft owned by entrepreneurs take tourists through the city's many channels and occasionally out onto the Neva. Stately mansions, government buildings, domed cathedrals, and parks grace its banks. The cityscapes include architecture reflecting a style that is largely European painted in an assortment of colors that are not. The colors, pastels mostly, come to life during the long twilight hours after the strongest light has faded and give St. Petersburg an ethereal atmosphere.

The Neva flows to the Gulf of Finland from Lake Ladoga to the east. The Neva divides the city into a northern side—Vasilevsky Island, Petrogradskaya, the Vyborg district, and Kirov Islands—and southern side, which itself is divided by several canals. Both sides of the city stretch along the northern and southern shores of the Gulf of Finland, which narrows as it reaches the city. The western edges of the Vasilevsky Island district and the Kirov Islands border the gulf. To the south, factories and harbor cranes dominate the coast line. The river divides into various branches that flow into the easternmost estuaries of the gulf. Speedy *rokyeti* (hydrofoils) ply the waters of the Neva and its branches, passing small fishing boats and docked naval gunboats, impressive craft in gun metal blue. The *rokyeti* take visitors west and south to Petrodvorets, the former imperial residence of the eighteenth century; Kronstadt, the formerly off-limits military base of historic significance; and Lomonosov, a palatial estate honoring the Russian scientist by the same name. Sometime after midnight, various drawbridges connecting the city's main islands to either bank are raised, allowing the larger commercial, naval, and tourist ships past. Nighttime motorists on the islands must account for the fact that these bridges cut automobile traffic off from the mainland for two hours.

Various summer retreats lie along the northern and southern shores of the gulf outside of the city limits, including holiday *dachas* and sanitariums, highlighted, to the north, by the resort city of Zelenogorsk and, to the south, by Petrodvorets, which is preserved as a museum. Both places attract many vacationing Russians and foreign tourists. Taking the train north lets you see Russian vacationers bathing amidst the reeds and wildflowers that line the marshy shores of lakes in the forests of the Karelian isthmus.

Warm winds blow off the Atlantic, keeping the city temperate year round (Humphreys and Richardson, 1994, p. xi; Kann, 1990, p. 9). For a city so far to the north, St. Petersburg's winters, though bitingly chilly, are endurable and its summers pleasant. Compared to frozen Moscow, with its dangerously low temperatures and fierce wind chills, St. Petersburg is balmy during the winter despite the fact that Moscow lies well south of it. Lying far to the interior, Moscow also has hotter summers than its rival and the outdoor public swimming pools to prove it. Its northern cousin has none, the temperatures rarely rising over 80 F°. St. Petersburg includes its share of sun worshippers who greedily catch the scarce sun rays on the shores of its northern banks during the short spell of long warm summer days. Men sometimes pose like bronzed Greek gods, either with shirts off or in bathing suits, while standing along the exterior walls of the Peter and Paul Fortress.

The weather is troublesome to some *Pyeterburzhtsi* (as Russians refer to the inhabitants of St. Petersburg). Changes in atmospheric pressure, especially during the summer months that bring frequent thunderstorms, make many of them susceptible to sudden headaches and other ailments. "You'll weather the weather in Leningrad, whether you like it or not," was a silly saying employed by my Anglicized Russian friend, Ann, when she wanted to lament over her ailments related to fluctuations in atmospheric pressure. She was entitled to it, suffering from migraine headaches during the summer that kept her at home on days she wanted to work. One of my principal Russian hosts in 1993, Lena, also suffered from headaches and could predict upcoming precipitation based on their occurrence. Sometimes I kidded Lena that she should give the daily *prognosis* (televised weather forecast). The rapid atmospheric pressure fluctuations affected me as well: I started to suffer hearing loss and ear aches, the kind you might get when descending in a passenger jet. I also suffered from sore throats that may or may not have been associated with the pressure changes. A Russian doctor I consulted could not tell me what was causing them. The long twilight of the summer interfered with normal sleeping patterns, and the dreary short winter days contributed to seasonal affective disorder—the kind that acutely affected Andrey's son, Oleg. David Lempert noted these climatic conditions in his ethnography of Leningrad (Lempert, 1996, p. 143).

Despite all of the inconveniences associated with living in a city so far north, most Peterburgians I encountered loved the city and would not trade living there for any other place including, in most cases, Moscow. Having a place to live in the city was very much appreciated, and often families went out of their way to make sure at least one family member retained residence there. This was true of my first interview respondent, Lana, who had been "carried" by her parents to Leningrad from Siberia and left there to live with her grandmother so as to "continue the line." It was also true of my English student Liza and Natalie, her aunt. Liza was the fourth generation of a family living in Leningrad. While her parents remained at a military base where her father worked in Nicolaev in south Russia, Liza was sent to live with Natalie in Leningrad. Natalie had been assigned to Omsk in Siberia to progress in her profession (language teacher) but always wanted to come back to Leningrad and finally did, enrolling in a graduate program at Leningrad (St. Petersburg) University.

In 1993, I was living on Vasilevsky Island, renting a room with meals included in a flat that belonged to Lena's family, where her brother Seryozha lived. I often had to go to the University department where Andrey worked. It was located about four blocks to the west of my flat. If I decided to walk the entire distance, I would inevitably head to the southern side of *Sredny Prospekt* (Central Avenue) and follow it one block west to the next street. Heading south part of the way down that street, a narrow entrance led to an interior yard off to the right. I would then go west again through an intricate series of passages, some simply holes punched in brick walls, crossing interior yards and side streets, one block after another, until I reached the back entrance to the university building where Andrey's department was located. This way I avoided the bulk of the pedestrian traffic as well as trams, trolleys, buses, autos, and all the noise associated with them. I also got a chance to glimpse the underside of the city, the broken walls, trash piles, incomplete construction projects, graffiti, as well as the playgrounds of children and the haunts of vagrants, although these haunts were generally rare. Most vagrants occupied street corners. Many courtyards were overlooked by dozens of windows from which mothers could keep an eye on their children and a lookout for suspicious activity. Andrey introduced me to this shortcut, and I used it often, treating it as a child might a well worn path in the woods. It was a secret of the city dwellers not found in published city guides.

The underlying key to this system of short cuts was political: Since property had been generally held communally in the former Soviet Union, a distinctive lack of gates, fences, and other barriers was associated with segregated private plots of earth. This feature underscored the difference between St. Petersburg and a typical American city. Apartments themselves were locked up tight, but the grounds and yards around buildings were not. This was a kind of dividing line between what was considered to be private property (allotments) and communal holdings.

During 1992 and 1993, St. Petersburg resembled a ghetto. As in a ghetto, things in short supply were shared. Open courtyards were just the tip of the iceberg. A lack of hot water for a shower in one apartment led to a social occasion in another that had hot water. The same thing occurred over a badly functioning oven. Resource sharing acted as social glue. Public transportation, cheap, abundant, and generally reliable, dominated. Private cars were rare and difficult to care for due to a lack of stores selling spare parts or service centers. Petrol stations had long time-consuming lines, and private entrepreneurs took advantage of this by buying gas at the pump, putting it into gasoline canisters, and distributing it at a markup to those waiting near the end of these lines. In 1993, new, neon-lit gas stations appeared, helping to ease the general shortage, but they were expensive, making lines at these places much shorter or nonexistent. The road system inside the city was designed for trams and trolley buses. Going anywhere in a car entailed a bumpy ride and was hard on the car's suspension.

Automobiles, like everything else, were shared. Lena's brother Seryozha acted as my host during the early part of my stay at his flat in 1993. He had owned a car once. During the better days of the early 1980s, his parents had purchased it for him. Unfortunately, it was promptly stolen, and the police never recovered it. Auto insurance was not generally available in the Soviet Union. Seryozha's loss was complete, but his new work in the "apartment business" brought him access to cars: He drove three different models while I was there. Seryozha had no qualms about offering me rides, or any of his friends or relatives. One of his "company" cars, a jeep, was used to transport his father, Stepan, and Stepan's things to the family *dacha* in Suida, a country village about two hours away. Seryozha never accepted payment for the rides he gave, not considering it to be honorable. To take advantage of his boss' cars in this manner would probably have been in bad taste. A sense of chivalry was involved here: Russians generally were suffering from a cash shortage. To ask for cash payment was like asking for the shirt off of someone's back. Seryozha did not want to corrupt his code of ethics by taking advantage of a foreigner even though other Russians saw nothing wrong in asking for money from foreigners.

In 1991, I spent most of my time with Dmitri and his wife. Dmitri's friend, Vasili, had an old jalopy. It looked like a Chevy from the 1960s. His red runabout was his pride and joy. He worked practically every weekend on it at his garage. Garages were available for car owners and were located in commercial and industrial areas of the city. He, like Seryozha, gave me free rides in his car including one to the airport at the end of my trip in 1991. (In fact, the only time I was asked to pay someone other than a stranger was when Andrey's friend, Pyotr, picked me up at the airport in 1993). Since Dmitri had no car of his own, Vasili's car was a prime element in their friendship, making Dmitri willing to share me with them.

As will be described in greater detail later, Dmitri was possessive of me, trying to limit those who could engage an "audience" with me. Liza and Natalie were also this way. One evening while they were walking me to the tram stop near their home after I had visited them, some strangers approached us, noting we were speaking in English. They had surmised that I was an American and were eager to speak English with me. I was willing to oblige them, but Natalie would have none of it, effectively telling them to "find their own American." Thus I discovered that sharing in Russia had its limits. For instance, while Andrey shared my knowledge of the HVP with several of his workers or colleagues, he was reluctant to share it with potential rivals.

Sharing also included information. One typical sight in the city, in its courtyards and parks were the *babushki*, retired female pensioners, many of them widows, sitting for hours on benches discussing the latest news about their neighbors and the city. Word got around. For instance, a few days before the official announcement about the July 1993 changeover of currency (removing the old "Lenin" bills), one of Andrey's student workers, Yuri, told me about it. In fact, I discovered that most people I knew were already aware of the impending change and were busy spending their old bills. After the change, the same *babushki* could be seen handling small denominations in the old currency. Many of the local shops accepted and used the outlawed currency as change. The new official currency did not include such small denominations. Government fiat could not control everything on the streets.

B. Nicholas' Leningrad

I met Nicholas in 1993 through Glasha, a colleague of Andrey. In 1992 at Pomeroy's seminar, Andrey introduced Glasha to me and Pomeroy. She was an "aspirant"—in effect a master's level graduate student—who was using Andrey as an outside advisor for her graduate work. In 1993, Glasha volunteered to assist me with my research in return for help with hers. Nicholas was the second interview respondent whom Glasha arranged for me.

Before Glasha introduced us, she advised me that her friend, Nicholas, came from a wealthy family. For someone whose father was the Soviet equivalent of a millionaire, Nicholas and his divorced mother lived in a very modest flat. You had to look carefully to see the signs of wealth. For instance, the television set was an imported Japanese model as opposed to the inferior and dangerous Soviet variety (occasionally one of them caught fire). In the tiny kitchen, the refrigerator had high quality sausage and imported Georgian wines. The flat itself was small and, besides the expensive TV set, modestly furnished. It did have a rather large and sunny balcony with a nice view of the delicate top branches of trees.

The flat was located in a so called "green" district of St. Petersburg. These sections of the city were characterized by their abundance of wooded areas and parks. One of these parks was located a short walk away from Nicholas's building. Nicholas and I spent a chilly autumn day there. It had a small pond with ducks, benches to sit on, and an abundance of birches and oaks. The ground was littered by yellow leaves, and Nicholas recited Alexander Pushkin's poem about the yellow leaves of autumn for me. It was not the most beautiful park I had seen, but given the barren nature of other districts I had seen, it was not bad.

Nicholas took me to visit his grandmother one day in October while I was staying at his flat. His mother had permitted me to stay there for a few days while I decided on my next place of residence. Grandmother lived in a different section of the city, past a stretch of woods that we walked through, and in a quiet enclave built in the 1930s. It was Stalin-era housing, noted for its strong construction and much more desirable than the shoddy Khruschev-era housing. The apartments were large, set in stout buildings with thick walls. The ceilings were higher than normal. I went inside a couple of these kinds of flats while I was visiting Gatchina.

Nicholas had a way of just showing up at places without phoning ahead. Sometimes he would go to the district where somebody lived and then ring them to see if he could visit. It was the habit of a man used to having time on his hands and used to being treated like a visiting dignitary among his extensive circle. When we showed up at his grandmother's house unannounced, she began to scold him for not giving advance notice and made serious inquiries as to who I was and why I was staying with him. After the courteous treatment I had received from Nicholas' mother, I was a little taken aback by his grandmother's suspicious nature and hostile behavior.

The *babushka* (grandmother) was from an older generation, and it was not unusual for them to be suspicious of foreigners. David Pryce-Jones and Hedrick Smith noted a strong paranoia by many Soviet era Russians towards foreigners (Pryce-Jones, 1995, pp. 15–16; Smith, 1981, pp. 12–13). For instance, Dmitri's parents never wanted to meet me. Nicholas's grandmother may have had something to hide as well. Her son, Nicholas's father, was highly placed and very rich. She did not want a stranger to be aware of signs of wealth in her flat. I only got a glimpse of the entry way and noted nothing remarkable except that the few pieces of furniture I saw were well made. Besides this, the place seemed old and austere, like her.

We had no choice but to leave her place with a tentative invitation to perhaps visit sometime in the future. I was embarrassed for Nicholas, and I could tell that his grandmother's behavior made him uncomfortable. Many of my Russian hosts did not want me to meet their parents, perhaps to avoid scenes like this.

Nicholas and I wandered through his district heading north along the ridge of a hill. The sky was clear that day and the weather warm enough to make the walk pleasant. We passed one of the lakes in the green zone. It was below us to our left partially hidden by trees. Then we came over the crest of a low hill, and I saw a site that was breathtaking. We were passing out of the green zone into one of the newly developed areas on the northern edge of the city (near North Boulevard). It was a large spread of modern skyscrapers, all brand new housing, in white, light blue, aqua, and rose. The contrast from stodgy five-floor heavy green and rust colored housing set amidst the soft greens and yellows of birch trees to these garish and very large houses devoid of surrounding vegetation gave a dramatic effect, as if we had come across a vast new civilization. I had been in this area before, visiting Yuri and his friends or Liza and her family, but I had always come *via* metro, which left me in the center of the zone, and I had always been there on a rainy dreary day or at night. I had not seen a panoramic view of this cityscape from a height under brilliant sunlight.

Soviet architecture, much maligned for its monotony, instant weathering, and overwhelming nature—for instance it took a guide to find a specific apartment in one of these complexes—had a positive quality, its futuristic style. Certain buildings looked to have been conjured up in a science fiction writer's dreams. Still, here they were, very concrete and real. Communists had promised a future utopia and delivered on part of that promise: Their constructions seemed to be from the future. The Soviets invested heavily in new housing stock throughout the country (Kudryavtsev, 1986, p. 49). Unfortunately, the constructions did not live up to the promise of the future. Once you got close to these places, the tell tale signs of squalor would appear, broken or boarded up windows, streaks of soot on the buildings, cracks on the walls, the shoddy entrances, and the ubiquitous clothes lines, reminding one of tenements in New York City and serving notice that clothes dryers were not widely available. The people living there were pretty much the same as in the center. Some had nice clothes; most did not. An alarming amount of vagrants, drunks, hooligans, and street urchins hung around, mingling with the passing crowds. The busiest place in this district was the metro station and its outdoor *kiosk* market, and the most popular direction in the busy underground vaults of the station was due south to the city center.

C. Moscow: Summer and Winter

Moscow is the heart of Russia, and the Kremlin is the heart of Moscow. If the area around it can be any measure of a society, then I had a chance to see it on two occasions and to measure Russia's pulse. The occasions took place in the summer and early winter of 1993. In October of that year, a rebellion occurred in Moscow, leaving a scar on the city and shaking Yeltsin's tenuous rule. During the summer before the crisis, the Kremlin had a leisurely feel about it. Tourists walked amidst the long cobblestone esplanade in front of Lenin's tomb. Many took photos. At the time, Lenin's guards still stood there in dark green uniforms. A sign was posted nearby announcing the times of the guard change but I did not notice any timetable for tours of the mausoleum itself. Lenin had not yet been moved out, but access to his tomb had been curtailed. The late afternoon and early evening brought a certain quietude to the place. I found it difficult to imagine that the broad avenue in front of the esplanade and flanking the Kremlin had been the site of many Soviet soldiers, tanks, and trucks pounding the pavement, of political speeches by Communist Party leaders, and of organized demonstrations in favor of and later against communism. The place had the feel of a park that day, and a pleasant one at that. A short walk away, you could enter a busy commercial district and do some shopping, or you could go to GUM (pronounced "goom"), a large indoor arcade. Since the air was so nice outside, and the weather was so pleasantly warm, I felt those things could wait for a while.

Winter arrived in the middle of November that year. When it did the Kremlin was transformed. The harsh winds drove people along the same esplanade and into the surrounding buildings. While comrade Lenin was not receiving visitors (in fact the guards were gone as well), GUM was open, and so was a small but beautiful Russian Orthodox church.

I visited both places. GUM, smart, pricy, and impressive, seemed to be an oversized version of *Passazh* (a popular indoor shopping mall in St. Petersburg). Some of the shops resembled American stores quite closely. The human traffic reminded me of malls back home.

A short and briskly exhilarating jaunt away was the church, done in white and rose on the outside, and gold and red on the inside, and lit by what seemed to be a thousand candles. It was open for business, and I found it hard to tell the little church apart from a store, except that it did not sell much besides candles. Also like a museum, with tourists and some worshippers walking around it counterclockwise as you might do at an arranged exhibit, the church, nevertheless, did contain people who were praying and offering candles. I took my turn doing so. Though heated, the church was chilly, and the candles flickered each time the doors let more tourists in along with the frigid air.

Escaping the cold that day was no easy task. Even when I had been inside the heated shopping arcade, the fading winter light peeking in here and there, and the papers blowing around outside on the square brought a shiver to my back.

The atmosphere around the Kremlin had changed since the summer. The day before visiting the church, Nicholas and I had jogged by another side of the Kremlin on our way to view the remnants of the 4 October shelling of the *Byeli Dom* (White House). The former Russian parliament building was undergoing extensive renovation, so it hardly resembled the burnt out shell shown on television a few weeks prior. The air was still and the sun was out, but keeping warm was hard, so we half walked and half ran. I commented to Nicholas that "old Boris" was probably up there somewhere in one of the yellow government buildings that peeked over the looming red walls. What was he up to? He was still in charge, thank God. Dmitri's insistent talk of a civil war back in July of 1991 had almost come to pass for the second time in three years. I imagined Boris was plotting a new course, working himself overtime as usual, but at the same time quite pleased with himself, tucked behind those massive walls. He seemed kind of small for the place in a way, lost amidst the complex of structures. He had seemed more imposing when occupying the same *Byeli Dom* to defy the tanks of August, 1991. Since then, he had damaged his former haunt and had shrunk a bit in the process. Yeltsin was no romantic fool, and knew he had lots of work to do still. So the Kremlin no longer resembled a park on a lover's summer day. It had been infused with new meaning. The atmosphere was cold and purposeful. A hard resolve had replaced the softness of Moscow's heart.

Nicholas and I were visiting Moscow during this time. I had to get my visa renewed there, and Lena helped me recruit Nicholas to accompany me on the trip. Nicholas was in a position to help me. Nicholas's position in society made him an "eligible bachelor." Ekaterina, the mother of one of Nicholas's potential fiancées, let us stay a few days at her flat. I compensated him and her by covering the expenses involved. He in turn had a chance to visit his friends in Moscow.

The streets of Moscow in November 1993 showed signs of tension. Plainclothes policemen not far from a McDonald's questioned two men, dark men, probably from the Caucusus. The move to expel those without residence permits was part of a sweep occurring after Yeltsin ousted the rebellious parliament. The state of partial military rule was a part of a two pronged attack. The first goal was to oust those visitors who had joined the mob atmosphere of the October crisis simply to have an adventure. The second was to deal with the ever growing power of the *mafiya* (semi-legal traders), who, many felt, had their roots in the Caucasus. This was part of an overall effort by Moscow to control the growing problem the country was having with Muslims and other minorities.

We were to leave the city that day, and Nicholas and I had a considerable amount of time to wait for the train in the Leningrad Station, a cluster of ticket and waiting areas in several buildings adjoining the outdoor terminal platform. In bitterly cold weather and with no place to go, we walked about the city for hours after purchasing our tickets that morning. At the station, Nicholas and I wandered in circles, killing time. Speaking to some of the people there would have been interesting, but no one seemed in the mood for speaking with a stranger. Besides, the atmosphere was not at all friendly. That morning I watched a man rudely turn down an offer by another to smoke together, creating an odd scene. The man being turned down seemed socially awkward, and, in one bizarre moment, offered the other man some paper rubles to smoke together in a strange twist of the Russian public habit of men joining together to purchase and share a bottle of vodka.

In the evening, the rough feeling of the place intensified. Scalpers were still pestering those waiting to purchase tickets. Policemen roamed the vast but crowded vaults that made up the station, checking for loiterers. At the entrance to the largest hall, security men checked to make sure you had tickets. Those without were not allowed in this waiting area.

At one point, Nicholas and I watched two uniformed policemen questioning a drunken man sitting on the floor of one of the other halls. I had seen the scenario before back in St. Petersburg. The red-faced man would be flanked by two police, questioned, lifted to his feet, and hauled away. This scene, however, was uglier than usual. Suddenly, one of the policemen landed a swift kick on the chest of the drunken man. His eyes looked startled, like he was awakening from a dream. I was riveted for a moment by the flash of violence. I looked around. Most of the crowd around this scene was watching the event, but many were not. Some who were looking on seemed bored or indifferent. A few made comments to neighbors. One woman was looking on grimly, her eyes angry. Drunks were a public nuisance, no doubt, but this maybe was crossing the line. I asked Nicholas why the policemen were being so rough with the man. "It's to make him pay attention," he replied. The police do not like to be ignored. No doubt, Nicholas had seen this scenario before.

We spent time walking amidst the vast throngs waiting for trains to many points in Russia. I sensed the vastness of the country by the variety of people there. Many races and ethnic groups mixed in a swirl of color and facial variety. They stood near or sat on large bundles, old suitcases, or paper cartons. They spilled over into halls, alley ways, stairways, small shops, video arcades, and onto the open square outside lit by the flames of an open fire in an empty oil drum. Vendors hawked shish kabob, hot-dogs, meat pies, and other, less identifiable, items. I watched some men eating hot-dogs at a stand-up counter with steam rising about them. Though frigid outside, these men were relaxed, obviously enjoying themselves. Just thinking about them eating outside made me feel colder.

I purchased the *New York Times*, printed in Russian with Cyrillic lettering, and tried to read it in the main hall for a while. I watched a man playing a gambling card game on a video machine. We went upstairs to the arcade, which was very crowded. Boys were playing video games, including combat and simulated racing. Older men hung around the edges of this gang of youths. We went outdoors, but I could take the cold for no more than a few minutes at a time. We had our dinner with us, some chicken cooked by Ekaterina wrapped in foil, but eating outside was only for the hardiest souls.

Back inside the ground floor of the station's largest structure, I saw signs for a restaurant on the second level. We went upstairs, hoping to take advantage of the Russian laxity about bringing your own food into eating establishments. No restaurant was there—just a hall with some open vending windows with a couple of service clerks selling coffee and warm cola. The waiting travelers had turned the hall into an improvised restaurant, eating food they had brought with them, like us. The few tables and chairs were strewn about, completely dominated by a lucky few groups. Many patrons sat on the edge of the balcony overlooking the staircase. Some sat on the steps.

St. Petersburg's train stations had been equally crowded, but the crowds there had been different. We were in the interior of Russia away from the Baltic states. The pale gaunt faces, brush haircuts, and lean bodies so common in St. Petersburg (and Riga) were joined by a mix of ruddy faces, barrel chests, round cheeks, Oriental eyes, dark skins, curly black hair, and square jaws. Tension existed in this crowd that I had not observed in similar places in St. Petersburg.

The last time I had observed something like it was when I traveled to Leningrad by plane for the first time. The passengers waiting to disembark had been tense when it was time to leave the plane and re-enter the Soviet Union. Here those throngs waiting for their trains perhaps were not looking forward to returning to their homes so far away from this Mecca of commerce and goods.

The day before, we visited the *Byeli Dom*—the old parliament building bombarded by Yeltsin's tanks. It stood at the end of Novy Arbat, a long windy walk on one of the busiest and most modern looking shopping avenues in Moscow. The government wasted little time in repairing the towering structure. Gone were the long blackened areas near the top third of the building where fires had been started by incendiary shells. Yeltsin had the facade scrubbed clean almost immediately. Still, the building did not look white, if it ever had, but rather a dull faded yellow, like an old soiled shirt. A little man was selling black and white photos of the building taken just after the end of its storming. I purchased one. Nicholas and I walked across the bridge where Yeltsin's tanks had lined up to fire upon the old parliament building. As I took photos, I thought a little about the irony of what I was seeing. In an unusual twist of events, Yeltsin had done what the coup plotters of August, 1991 lacked the will to do, open fire on the Russian White House, which Yeltsin had occupied in resistance of that coup. If more ruthless men had done this in 1991, Yeltsin would not have been around in 1993.

I looked away from the White House to take in the sweep of the place. The older fantastic skyscrapers, built by Stalin, looked like something from a Gothic tale with their dark pinnacles. Nearby, factory smoke stacks blew out white puffs of steam that were reflected by the surface of the Moscow River, which snaked its way around the city. The scene had power, but a bleak kind of power. While the sky still held most of its blue, the fading sunlight suffused the otherwise gray buildings with a stark white light, giving them an eerie orange glow. A Stalin tower rose over the river, its back to the sun, cast in a dark shadow. For some reason, the phrase "nuclear winter" entered my mind. We were not far from the Old Arbat Street with its charming atmosphere and narrow alleys, but here the city felt wide, threatening, and cruel.

Moscow, unlike St. Petersburg, had many tall buildings near its center. Western commercialism had invaded with a vengeance, making portions of the city look like Times Square in New York. While St. Petersburg's center was dominated by horizontal lines, Moscow's center was interested in verticality. On our way to view *Ostankina*, the central television station for all of Russia—the complex of structures, set partly inside a park, had been the scene of a gunfight in October—Nicholas and I passed a monument to Soviet space exploration. Anchored by a concrete block, a glass and steel structure swept in a concave arc towards the sky. Taking a step back, I saw the structure as it was meant to be: The sweep of the structure ended in a shiny metal rocket pointed to the clouds.

Off in the distance and, from our current vantage point, dwarfed by the rocket was another tower. Nicholas pointed to it, telling me that it was our destination. As we approached the *Ostankina* television tower, we soon recognized its enormity. Set in a park across from the massive, squat, aqua-gray headquarters of Russia's premier television station, the transmitter that sent Channel One across the plains of Russia to hundreds of cities, towns, and remote villages did not resemble the steel skeletons back home. It rose well over one hundred meters into the sky, a single solid tower, rising up above the trees to pierce the sky. With several rings around its circumference, varying its thickness as it gradually tapered to a thin spire, it looked like part of a science fiction movie set.

This had been the scene of bloody fighting five weeks prior. No signs of it were present now. Small groups of office workers trickled out of the aqua-gray building across the street as quitting time for the day staff approached. Dozens of cars were parked outside. Traffic streamed by the front of the building on the road dividing it from the park. The atmosphere was tranquil and business-like. A period of calm existed, but a guarantee that the calm would remain did not.

D. Riga: The Summer before Independence

When I spent time in Riga during 1991, I noted its increased pace of life as well as the seriousness and intent with which the Latvians conducted themselves. While, at the time, no one in Leningrad seemed to be in much of a hurry, many people in Riga walked briskly with a sense of urgency. In 1993, this same sense of urgency would come to St. Petersburg.

Riga, though small, comforting, and cheerful compared to Leningrad, was not a passive city. Besides being efficient and modern with many smartly dressed pedestrians, it was also a center of modest but determined resistance to Soviet rule. Leningraders grumbled about a lack of simple items like decent tea, coffee, cheese, fruits, or sugar, while Rigans had things hard to find in Leningrad. Their city seemed to be filled with flowers, ice cream, and busy shops while Leningrad, in 1991, seemed to be filled with dusty plazas, military trucks, and broken pavement. By 1993, the *mafiya* brought fruit and flowers to St. Petersburg, and city planners finished paving its main thoroughfares with a fresh layer of asphalt.

The streets in Riga ranged from regular, broad, flat avenues bordered by trees, to narrow cobblestone alleys, chaotically arranged, as one neared the Daugava River. Rigans lived away from the Daugava and left the old city near the river for tourists. In Leningrad, the Neva was flanked by planned streets, majestic buildings, and manicured parks. Chaos was reserved for interior streets and squalid courtyards. Leningraders also lived away from the river and let the tourists enjoy the fine planning.

Riga was both an insult and an attraction to Soviets. It was a holiday haven for weary Soviet *apparatchiki* (Communist Party and government bureaucrats). Those same bureaucrats were desperately trying to head off independence for Latvia, where Riga was located. Latvia and the other Baltic states wanted to go their own way in 1991. Rebellion was in the air of the charming streets of Riga. Anti-Soviet graffiti covered street barriers and complemented newspaper headlines speaking of the tension between Moscow and the Baltic states. Vacationing officials could not get away from the consequences of their own policies in more ways than one. The pollution that plagued Leningrad and all of Soviet industry had reached the shores of the Gulf of Riga making swimming there hazardous.

When I asked my Latvian guide, Eva, about the Soviet Union, she dismissed it with a shrug. Riga was in the Soviet Union, but to her the Soviet Union was a foreign country. "They ruin everything" she stated flatly, and later she made sure to remind me that the street she lived on, named after Lenin, would soon have a new name.

E. Gatchina: Off the Tourist Beaten Track

I visited Gatchina (Lena's home town) during 1993, and briefly in 2000. It is located almost directly south of St. Petersburg, and can be reached by a trip of about forty-five minutes by rail. It is located some distance from the Gulf of Finland on broad, flat, sparsely wooded land. Gatchina's tall structures rise suddenly from the surrounding barren plain. At night, its brightly lit buildings can be seen at a distance from an approaching train.

In 1993, a small watch tower, complete with sentry, hung over a street somewhere in Gatchina's center. A military base was there at the time devoted to military construction. Not far from the base was the young woman's college where Lena taught. It had been a woman's college, but it had recently been changed to include boys. (In the Soviet Union, colleges taught ages fifteen to nineteen). Inside, it resembled an American high school with a couple of exceptions. One was the sentry posted near the door, a friendly woman, who nevertheless required visitors to state their business. The other was the portrait of Karl Marx gracing the classroom where Lena gave piano lessons. Not primarily used as a music room, as indicated by the maps on the walls and the portrait that signified its function for studying history, only a corner of the classroom was reserved for a piano.

On the opposite side of the military base was the flat where Lena (recently divorced) lived alone with her son, Misha. He was an active boy of fourteen, who seemed to want to spend more time out than in. The building where they lived had been designed in the "Stalin" style. The walls were thick, the ceilings were high, the light dim, and the air warm. Upstairs lived Roza, Lena's mentor and friend. She lived with her husband, who liked to play chess. We started a game one evening but had to abandon it as my train was scheduled to arrive at any moment. Stepan, who was visiting Lena, walked with me back to the train. He knew the shortest route. While we hurried along, he proudly mentioned that the street his daughter lived on was named after a famous Russian cosmonaut.

Gatchina was stubborn and solid. The thick white walls of the Gatchina's Palace (built for Paul the First) seemed to anchor the city. The palace and surrounding park, which could have made Gatchina a popular tourist attraction was barely used for this purpose. A tiny portion of it had been renovated and was as beautiful as Pushkin, Petrodvorets, and Pavlosk. Gatchina was changing a little around the edges just like the palace. More *kiosks* (enclosed stands selling a variety of items) and shops had opened up. Still, few tourists ventured here. It was a backwater and seemed to like it that way.

Gatchina could be likened to an average American suburban town (population about 76,000 in 1980 according to the *Rand McNally World Atlas*, [1987]). A large factory located near one of its two train stations was the city's main employer. Gatchina was primarily devoted to raising children and the family life that went along with that. The changes going on in big cities like St. Petersburg and Moscow would come to it, though there seemed to be no hurry at the time.

I revisited Gatchina in July, 2000. Little seemed to have changed though signs existed in the country in general that an economic recovery would soon begin. During the 1990s Russia had lurched from one financial crisis to another though its political situation remained relatively steady. Late in his final term, Yeltsin finally selected his replacement, Vladimir Putin, to carry on his democratic revolution. The general air in Gatchina as in the rest of the country was that of somber realization that continuing the revolution would require a steady grinding effort. Seryozha brought this home to me when on one of our walks together he pointed to classic symbols of the Soviet Union embossed on a wall as forgotten as those times, the hammer and the cycle. "This is what Gatchina is about," he told me. My first impulse was to protest. Surely the new Russia did not need this reminder of its failed past. Upon reflection, I realized that he did not mean communism but rather the symbols that communism had expropriated, that hard labor both in the cities and in the countryside, the necessity to grow the food the country needed and to build new places, would provide the backbone to a successful reinvention of the nation.

F. Pushkin: An Odd Attraction

Named after the famous Russian poet of the nineteenth century, who spent a portion of his life studying there, Pushkin is a tourist attraction known for its splendid palatial park. Originally named *Tsarskoye Selo* (Tsar's Village), Pushkin changed its name back to the original in 1998 (Phillips, et al., 1998, p. 153). While I was there, I knew it as Pushkin.

Svetlana, who lived in Pushkin with her family, showed me a different side of the town, a little bit removed from the eyes of tourists. I met her in St. Petersburg during my 1992 visit. In the spring of 1993, she acted as my guide for a few days.

Somewhere beyond the complex of gardens that housed the carefully restored, eighteenth century, blue and white Catherine Palace, the main attraction at Pushkin, stood the extant ruins of what appeared to be an ancient fort that had sunk partly into the ground. Its medieval feel and ornate designs would have made the fort an interesting exhibit in its own right, but it remained as is, showing no signs of esthetic or scientific attention.

Pushkin seemed slightly neglected. The research building where Svetlana's friend, Ludmilla, studied biology, remained unfinished, with unpainted portions and incomplete landscaping. Going to a restaurant was "tricky business" according to Svetlana. Apparently, the *mafiya* controlled all restaurants in the town. For some reason, careful planning was required to go to a restaurant there. (I got a similar reaction in 1991, when I offered to take Dmitri to a restaurant in Leningrad. Another informant later explained that going out to a restaurant was considerably more expensive to a Russian relative to what an American might pay in terms of percent of one's income).

The authorities were not completely in charge at Pushkin. After visiting Svetlana one afternoon, I boarded my train heading back to St. Petersburg. The train was about to pull out when I heard a commotion outside on the platform. I saw a *militsiya* man rush past my window apparently chasing somebody. Then I heard the sounds of footsteps and a crash that sounded like somebody had fallen in the entry vestibule of the car in which I was sitting. The train pulled out. As it did, I could see the *militsiya* man still standing on the platform. He had missed his quarry. Sounds of laughter came from the vestibule, and the sliding door opened. Four men, one of them completely inebriated, stumbled into the car. Another one of them was carrying some kind of duffel bag with unidentifiable contents. They found a place to sit (benches facing each other) and they became just more passengers. These unshaven men, their dirty clothes, their unkempt appearance, and their swagger all gave them a look of desperadoes. I found it hard to sit there without feeling uncomfortable. Nobody else seemed to give them a second thought. That was the way that Russians seemed to react to unusual events—as if there was nothing at all amiss. Eventually, I got up and moved to another car.

What struck me about the whole incident was that once they had escaped the lone policeman chasing them, no further action was taken. The train was not prevented from leaving the station. Policemen did not board the train at a subsequent station, or if they did they did not do anything to the men. (I was not on the same car at that point). When we disembarked at St. Petersburg, the men got off the train with everybody else. I did not know exactly what they had done, but just minutes before they had been "running from the law." Now they just were ordinary citizens. The whole experience gave me the sense that no one was really in charge of Russia at the time (May 1993).

Looking back on this incident now, a few things come to mind. First, the policeman was probably chasing these men not because they had stolen something but because of their public behavior. One of them was plainly drunk. Public drunkenness is a punishable offence in Russia. Second, these men probably had not committed a serious enough crime to be worth pursuing beyond the station at Pushkin. If they had, a simple phone call to the next station would have sufficed. Third, the precise problem with public safety was the lack of a policeman or some other kind of security man on the train itself. This may have been due to governmental budget difficulties.

G. Vyborg: Stalin's Prize

In the fall of 1993, Nicholas insisted that my wife and I visit Vyborg with him. Vyborg, set on the Gulf of Finland about two hours away from St. Petersburg to the northwest near the Finnish border, was a nice city to visit. Dating back to medieval times, it was older than St. Petersburg. Although some modern looking structures had been put up near the train station, the main part of Vyborg had steep, narrow streets and iron wrought signs that carried medieval trade guild markings. The center of the old town was dominated by a castle which we visited. It had a tower from which you could see the whole town. The castle had controlled access to a river that ran through the small city and out to the gulf. A museum inside showed its history. This had been Finland once, before Stalin had stolen back some territory through a short but costly war against his outnumbered but tenacious foes.

We visited a large indoor market and one outside as well. The one outside seemed to be dominated by vendors selling cheap, colorful, plastic children's toys. I had seen something like this before in a very different part of the world, a small town outside of Quito, the capital of Ecuador.

The indoor market at Vyborg seemed more like one you might find in St. Petersburg with a slight difference. In St. Petersburg, a *reenok* (farmers' market) would only sell edibles—vegetables, fruits, and meats, and perhaps some flowers. This market, inside a damp, dimly-lit hall, sold those items, but it also had a large section devoted to selling clothes and intricately woven linens (bedspreads, tablecloths).

Vyborg is a place where you can lose track of time. Sitting in a wooded area near the shore of the gulf, Nicholas started to tell us the story of his upbringing. When we got lost in the details, we forgot to monitor the time. We had meandered about the town all afternoon mostly in a direction away from the train station and had lost our sense of how far it was to the station. So, by the time we were heading back, we knew we had miscalculated. A final dash to the train left us only tens of seconds behind schedule, but we had to watch it slowly receding into the distance without us.

We learned three things from this. First, Russians, despite their other problems, run very accurate train schedules. If you need to catch a train, you must leave yourself plenty of time. You cannot be a minute late.

Second, if you are spotted being depressed in public, you may be asked to share vodka with a stranger. This happened to me. My wife and I had planned to see a ballet that evening in St. Petersburg, and missing the train had left us without a way to get back in time to see it. My initial reaction was that of disgust and chagrin. Then I became gloomy. A wiry man, no older than me, approached me making gestures and using words that indicated that he wanted to drink with me. When I protested, he grabbed my arm as if to force me to accompany him to the nearest source of vodka. Nicholas intervened at that point and got the man to leave me alone.

Third, ways around systemic problems in Russia exist if you have the cash. With an hour to go before the next train was scheduled to leave, we decided to try our luck elsewhere. The bus station was nearby, but it ran so few buses that waiting for the next train still seemed to be our best option until a man hanging around the bus station picked up on what was going on and offered to find us a ride. Soon, a second man appeared in a modern minivan with enough room for the three of us plus another passenger. We negotiated with the driver to get us to Zelenogorsk, about an hour away by train. We figured, if he drove fast enough, we could catch up to the train we had missed at Zelenogorsk. So for twenty bucks he gave us a lift there. The ride was uneventful even though tourist guides spoke about the "swarms" of bandits that harassed travelers on the very highway we took. Had highway robbers been about, little would have stopped them. The road from Vyborg to Zelenogorsk was empty almost the entire way. The only company we had were the miles of thin, straight birch trees, looking like toothpicks with leaves, lined up along each side of the road.

We eventually got to Zelenogorsk and caught a train there back to the city. My wife and I ended up missing the first part of the ballet. However, the adventure we shared getting back to town made up for it.

Three

A GLIMPSE OF A DYING EMPIRE: U. S. S. R., JULY 1991

1. Overview

This chapter begins a reconstructed narrative drawn from my first trip to Russia. This narrative is inspired by David Maybury-Lewis's detailed travelogue (Maybury-Lewis, 1965) of his first expedition into a remote corner of Brazil where he went to study the Shavante. In his monograph, Maybury-Lewis gives the reader a sense of the adventure of ethnography and portrays a more intimate sense of what it means to do fieldwork. It is a contrast to more stodgy and analytical ethnographic studies. It is not a complete ethnography in itself, but it provides an ethnographic account of his formal study of the Shavante (Maybury-Lewis, 1967). My narrative will orient the reader in Soviet society with all its grandeur, faults, and wonders. It illuminates the analysis that follows. The narrative was reconstructed using field notes, letters, photos, and audio-tapes.

This chapter covers the first part of my 1991 trip. It includes the flight to the Soviet Union, meeting Dmitri, his family, and his friends, and a camping trip to Karelia with Dmitri, his wife, Alisa, and his son, Ilyia.

Several themes run through this chapter. The first is the sense of being in a city that has a deep history. Leningrad is like a living museum, and my hosts are eager to show me its best parts.

Second, an ubiquitous public mood of general apathy, perhaps resignation, combined with signs of military activity runs through the story. The train ride to Karelia best illustrates this.

Third, the sense of struggling with more difficult material conditions is ever present. For instance, Dmitri is well-off relative to other Russians and appears to have high status. Yet he has no car, and relies on his friend for car transport. The shower at his apartment is not always working. His living quarters are cramped. Relative to someone in the United States with equal status, Dmitri is poor.

Fourth, Russians struggle with each other over scarce resources. I as an American visitor am a scarce commodity. During my stay I am the center of much attention, haggling, and bargaining. The trip to Karelia begins this process, which continues later as covered in subsequent chapters.

Fifth, Russians could be quite aggressive when it came to business negotiations, as my experience with Alisa shows. My experience with Russians' evolving ideas about enterprise and business would unfold in various directions during all of my trips.

Finally, I should note my own condition during the trip. I frequently felt ill and almost always ill at ease. A large part of my energy was spent struggling to keep control over situations that baffled me. Consequently, I tended to be overly-reticent and bashful, not always, but a good deal of the time. Other times, I would become full of adrenaline and tended to over-react. A lot of time passed before I was able to feel at home in Russia. During this trip, I did not feel comfortable very often. Familiar points of reference, provided by my Irish friend, Eileen, and, in the next chapter, Latvian interpreter, Eva, became invaluable.

2. Arrival (6–7 July 1991)

Saturday, 6 July 1991, the day I was to leave, was gray and misty. My wife and I took a long time to get to JFK airport from New Jersey, where we had stayed with friends over the Fourth of July weekend. Locating the well-hidden Aeroflot ticket counter had not been easy. While we waited on a line for the announcement to board, I noticed that most people carried the reddish-brown passports of the USSR. Some of the Soviet passengers lugged portable stereos, toys, and other items still in their original boxes. Nice souvenirs, I thought. I looked through the terminal's window at the Aeroflot jet waiting to take me. I saw that it was a large, four-engine jet. It seemed like an older model—not the Boeings with which I was familiar. I wondered if it was safe. I began to wonder how I would get along in such an exotic place as Leningrad, alone without support.

Boarding began, and I said goodbye to my wife. When my passport was checked at the ticket collection point, I had technically entered the Soviet Union. In several hours, I would be immersed in a different culture. Stepping into the Aeroflot jet was a change in itself. The feeling was different from other flights I had taken.

Flying Aeroflot to Leningrad was a unique experience. Since it was an international flight, the Soviets were putting forth extra effort to provide good service. Notorious for their poor domestic flight service, Aeroflot's international service was of mediocre quality compared to flying most other airlines. Still, despite some flight associated annoyances, I found the service to be adequate.

When I boarded, the first thing noticeable was the smell. Russians tended not to use deodorant like Americans and other fastidious nationalities used because of a shortage of deodorants in the Soviet consumer market. This changed after 1992 as the availability of imported goods increased.

A stale, acrid stink began to creep into the cabin. The smell disappeared later when the air conditioning was turned on. Overhanging this smell was an old familiar smell, from the times I had flown to Mexico—disinfectant. The second thing noticeable was the music, a funky, synthetic rock-and-roll with unfamiliar melodies. The plane had no stereo headphones, no movie screens. Groups of chatting Russians began to form toward the back. The plane was large, a dull silver color, and Soviet made, (IL86—a large capacity airliner). On the wing was the stenciled Cyrillic "*CCCP*" (SSSR—Russian acronym for

USSR). Flight instructions were given in Russian and in English with a carefully intoned nasal tone. The voice of the smartly uniformed stewardess was melodic, exotic, and slightly intimidating. I noticed a doorway leading to a lower level when I boarded. Occasionally, the flight attendants dwindled in number during the flight, probably resting in a lounge below.

When the plane took off, it felt heavier than an American jet. I snapped a photo of the wing to record my flight. I felt lonely, afraid, as the weight of what I was doing sank in. The plane left around 6 p.m. and landed in Leningrad late the following morning. The plane had two intermediate stops, one in Canada at Ganders airport in Nova Scotia and another in Ireland at Shannon airport. I was alone for the first two legs of the journey, sitting near the window next to two empty seats. Having no confidence in the little Russian I knew, and hearing an endless sea of Russian speakers on the plane, I stayed to myself and settled in to read my Russian translation book. I jotted notes and flipped through a flight magazine (half in English, half in Russian) that extolled the virtues of Leningrad.

The flight was tedious. The food, though plain, included a generous quantity of meats, fish, cheese, potato salad, bread, butter, sweets, fruit, a little wine, cola, and unlimited tea. A large, barely edible roll was served along with an apple after the meal. I felt the roll had a function that I could not fathom. Russians like to have bread with every meal. Several passengers, not satisfied with airplane food, brought their snacks and meals wrapped in foil and paper.

We reached Ganders for a short layover, the pilot landing the plane like an elephant balancing on tiptoes. Everyone disembarked onto a tarmac and into a dull, sterile waiting area. At a concession stand, a steward distributed coupons for free cans of Pepsi that were not refrigerated. Some shops and food stands occupied the travelers. Others just sat or stood around in little groups. More tedium, I thought, as I sipped my tepid drink. Then I was treated to a bit of Russian life. Someone returned with a large bottle of vodka from one of the shops and joined a group of six to eight people. Soon, a drinking party began.

I decided to pay attention. The young men were wearing silk or rayon black shirts with pleated stylish pants worn long over fancy looking shoes. Those Russians who could afford to travel and had permission to generally came from the upper echelons of society. Others wore printed shirts over plain pants. Of the group, four were drinking: three men and one young lady, perhaps a wife or girlfriend of one of the men.

One of the young men returned with the large (1.5 liter) bottle, flourishing it, apparently to impress his friends. Having later seen the more common pint-sized bottles of vodka in Russia, I can see how this large bottle impressed them. The boy showed the bottle to the assembled group clustered around one of the waiting area's sofas and table arrangements. Some of them looked at each other and were interested but apparently skeptical over the idea. The boy further produced plastic cups that had been obtained at the same place that the free Pepsi had been distributed. The four—the boy who had purchased the bottle, his young male friend, and an older but still youngish couple—eventually shared all three plastic cups. The woman had blonde hair. She called her companion "*mooszhik*" (a simple man or a husband) when he joined in the drinking. The boy carefully poured three equal portions of vodka into each glass. Then he opened one of the cans of Pepsi and carefully divided it three ways into each cup. The ratio of vodka to Pepsi in these drinks was about one to one. I guessed about two jiggers of vodka were in each of these strong drinks. The boy's friend drank first along with the couple. He quietly downed most of it. The woman carefully sipped her drink. I could not see how the *mooszhik* drank. The boy serving turned out to be heaviest drinker. After waiting for his friend to finish, he poured himself a similar drink, opening a fresh can of Pepsi in the process. Then he downed all of it at once. The soda, by being room temperature, made the drink easier to down.

As the vodka ceremony continued, I noticed that the two boys were drinking more heavily than the couple, who were nursing their drinks. A similar amount of vodka had been poured out after the first round. At one point, the boy stood up and toppled a big metallic standing ashtray making a tremendous crash and ringing sound. The top came off, scattering cigarette butts and ashes all over the floor. The boy showed no reaction and with indifference strolled over to another cluster of passengers to say something. I began to get tense wondering why this boy suddenly appeared to be irresponsible. I was self-conscious and wondered if they had noticed me watching them. The boy returned to right the ashtray carefully and put its top back on.

After awhile, the little group finished drinking, having knocked off about a pint of vodka. Soon the passengers filed back on the plane. I felt uneasy and compulsively checked my carry-on luggage. We were flying across the Atlantic, deep into the night. Non-stop conversations after the lights were dimmed kept me awake. I fell into a stupor only to be roused for another layover.

Shannon airport was a little gayer than Ganders. Spotlights on the edge of the terminal illuminated orange flowers outside and, a little beyond, brightly colored small cars in a car park. This terminal had better shops, and CNN International was broadcast on a giant screen. The washroom was large and clean with many stalls and sinks.

The layover was longer and the wait interminable. The news reports on CNN were repeated. I toured a small display of unremarkable iron sculptures three times and tried to locate Shannon on a map of Ireland to kill time. We did not board the plane again until 4 a.m.

I had just settled in for the last leg, maybe to sleep before we reached Leningrad, when a casually dressed, young Irish girl named Eileen appeared by my seat and asked to sit in one of the empty ones. I welcomed the English speaking company. She seemed bright, had a flirtatious manner, and spoke with a distinct accent. Eileen said she had boarded at Shannon, noticed that I might be an American, and decided she would feel more comfortable with someone who spoke English in a flight full of Russian speakers.

Eileen was being sponsored as a volunteer to help in Russian hospitals by an international organization that had connections to the Smolny Institute in Leningrad. Like me, she had arrangements to stay with a Russian family. I noticed that part of her carry-on luggage included a large plastic bag full of large green apples (Granny Smiths). Russians hardly get any fruit, she explained to me, something of which I was not aware. The value of well-chosen gifts became apparent later in my trip.

I immediately liked this companion who would give me a familiar point of reference during my stay. We chatted over breakfast while a rising orange sun sent its light through the window on my left. We exchanged our Leningrad phone numbers before we parted and promised to meet in a week to share our experiences.

Arriving in Leningrad was a traveler's nightmare. The first warning sign came when the plane stopped. I noticed the odor of perspiration when the air conditioning was turned off while we were let out the back of the plane. The mood on the plane became somber and purposeful. The passengers, most of them Russians returning to the Soviet Union, lost their gaiety. Coming home to a Soviet obviously did not invoke the same kind of feeling you would expect from an American. Some of the passengers may have been worried that the goodies they had purchased abroad might be confiscated by the authorities.

The tarmac was vast, a wasteland of dusty, broken concrete, spotted with grasses. A little red flag, perched on top a small building, flapped in the distance. We assembled outside the plane, the roar of the engines in our ears. I could spot figures in the distance while we waited.

An airport bus appeared, its yellow metal sides shaking. We were shuttled by a series of these rattling buses to the terminal, a plain concrete building with a sign on top saying "Welcome to Leningrad" in English. Another sign said the same thing in Russian. Men in dull green uniforms loitered nearby. We filed through an entrance to the terminal. Stepping out of the hot, bright sunlight into a dark series of rooms, my eyes took some time to adjust. More uniformed men stood inside, some in green, others in blue. We were quiet and passive.

Customs inspection of documents was smooth and efficient. Passing by a wood and glass booth, my visa and passport were stamped a couple of times by one of the green uniformed men, and I was nodded through. The document checkpoint led to a larger room. A shop (closed) of some kind was to the right. To the left was a small room where most of the arrivals were standing. In front was the baggage inspection point, where men in light blue uniforms (KGB) were waiting. I gathered that the bags would arrive in the room to the left.

I went inside to look around. The room was filling up quickly, and I was overwhelmed by the smell. I asked Eileen if she wanted help with her bags. I pointed to my nose. She smiled. Then the conveyor started to move, and, at the same moment, the silence and the passivity of the crowd were shattered. Packed into a tiny stuffy room, men, women, and children banged into each other, cursed and shouted, grabbing at the luggage coming on a tiny, wobbling conveyer—huge cardboard boxes, canvas sacks, oversized bundles, labeled packages, and boxes obviously bought in American stores. Among this loot from America, I noticed a lot of boxes of electronic equipment—stereos, boom boxes, televisions. My subsequent experiences suggested that these items might be distributed as gifts, kept for prestige, or exchanged on the black market because of their general scarcity.

Eileen and I joined the fray, helping each other retrieve baggage. Eileen, overwhelmed by the chaos, bailed out before she got all her bags. I brought our bags out one by one to her in the central area so she could watch them. I became aggressive, bullying my way through the crowd at points to grab a bag.

Glad finally to get out of the chaos, I rejoined Eileen. Beyond was an opening stuffed with people waiting to meet the arrivals. Struggling to remember what he looked like in the photograph that Leon Pomeroy had shown me, I scanned the crowd for Dmitri and hoped to get through baggage inspection intact. Then I spotted him—a wiry, bearded, dark, and intense looking man. He smiled and gave me the thumbs-up sign. He seemed less intimidating than he did in his photo.

While we waited to clear customs, Eileen pulled two small bottles of fruit juice from her luggage and gave me one along with an apple. People stared at us while we drank and munched on the fruit. Fresh fruit was scarce in Russia at the time. Things I took for granted back home were highly valued here, arousing curiosity and envy.

Eileen was worried that she would not find her hosts. She only had an address and phone number. Was someone coming to meet her? She did not know. I thought of asking Dmitri to help, but, as she cleared customs just ahead of me, a young Russian emerged from the crowd at the door, obviously looking for her. I cleared customs shortly after she did; the blue uniformed inspector (KGB) did not open my baggage.

3. Prince Dmitri (7–14 July)

I had just taken my last bag off the inspection table when Dmitri came, shook my hand, and grabbed all my bags. I had three heavy bags. I offered to take one. He refused. I carried only a small light nylon bag with more important stuff in it. We trudged out into the sunlight. Birch trees swayed in the distance. A tree lined road led away to another road. Dmitri said that we had to walk a ways. "Where are we going?" I inquired. "To bus," Dmitri muttered in his broken English. We stopped a few hundred feet away from the terminal on a patch of grass near a road. I did not see anything indicating that this was a bus stop and felt disoriented.

Sure enough, a bus pulled up to the stop. Dmitri leaped on, groaning with the weight of the bags. I stumbled on after him. He asked me to hold the bags while he fished some small scraps of paper out of his pockets and punched holes in them with a puncher attached to the bus window. The bus rattled off, kicking up dust as it went. I clutched the metal rail. People stared at us. I felt self-conscious. They probably guessed I was a foreigner. Later I found that Russians stared a lot. It was not considered to be rude. (In 2000, this public habit was gone; Russians seemed more lively and less stupefied.)

As we rumbled along with the engine roaring, people were crammed together, sweating, and blocking my view out the window. I turned my attention to Dmitri. I noticed his beard was thicker and darker than mine. His hair was long and almost jet-black, the skin on his gaunt face pale and pockmarked. He was wearing a dark necktie and pale yellow shirt under a windbreaker with dark slacks. Studying the other Russian men on the bus, casually dressed for a Sunday afternoon, I wondered why Dmitri had put on a tie. Perhaps he felt the occasion called for one, but I felt uneasy.

Dmitri warned me that we would be getting off soon, edging toward the door. I did not know if the people noticed that he spoke English with me, or even cared. The doors burst open, and we plunged onto the street with my bags. As we gathered ourselves on the street, I heard someone call my name. It was Eileen. She and the young man who had met her at the airport had ended up where we were by coincidence. I waved to her. The coincidence, for a brief moment, made Leningrad seem not so imposing and gave me hope that our plans to meet in a week would be realized. Leningrad would turn out to be a little more complicated than I thought, and the brief interval was replaced by a harsh reality.

While Dmitri hunted for a taxi, I had a minute or two to look around. My first impression of Leningrad was that I was a visitor from another planet. Any pictures I had seen beforehand failed to convey the sensation of being there. We were standing in strong sunlight on a wide street (Moscow Boulevard), where a plaza extended the width of the already wide road. Beyond, facing me, stood a massive light gray, official-looking building, the House of Soviets, misted with a yellow haze, adorned with red flags and sculptures. Beyond it was another similar building and, closer to me, a gigantic gray-green statue of Lenin, an imposing giant, was frozen in action, one arm outstretched. The sound of trucks, buses, trams, and boxy compact cars bounced off the vast concrete surface of the plaza, creating an incredible din. The heavy machinery made the sidewalk shiver. The buildings seemed weighty and menacing. I was unfamiliar with this architecture, which had no European sense of human scale, and was dominated by straight lines and huge blocks of stone. I sensed might and an energetic presence. I wondered how they had achieved it—this was not a land of capitalism.

I had little time to contemplate it. Dmitri hurried me into a taxi, and, with giant groans, heaved two of my bags into the trunk. I wondered why he was hurrying. His groaning started to sound theatrical. He had collected me, and we should have been relaxing by then. Dmitri smiled a lot but said little during the trip. Jammed into the back seat of a tiny car with Dmitri and one of my larger bags, I took a moment to stare out the window, trying to soak in the place as it whizzed by. The thing that most struck me was the poor condition of the roads, sidewalks, grassy areas, and apartment blocks we were passing. We had swept off the main thoroughfare with its shop windows and crowds, over a bridge, and into a park-like, quieter section of town. Dmitri lived in a section northeast of the Neva River. Our route had avoided the center. As we whizzed down a main avenue, lean, suntanned, off-duty soldiers with hardened faces, wearing dark green pants and dull yellow open-collar shirts, stopped to stare at me unabashedly.

We were traveling along a bumpy road, passing narrow streets, grasses and bushes running riot over broken sidewalks, and the junk and garbage of empty lots. Trees leaned out onto the road. The vegetation, which seemed to threaten to win nature's battle against civilization, grew quickly, vigorously. I saw no flowers, just green competing with yellow dust. If things were ever trimmed, a long time passed between trimmings. Compared to the vast concrete plaza I had seen before, this was a jungle. The inhabitants seemed lax to deal with it. The vista gave me a sense of abandonment or indifference. Because nobody really owned the land, nobody took care of it, I thought. To me, the conditions were a sign that not enough capital and labor were available to deal with this kind of public problem.

Labor and money are required to maintain public landscaping, and the attitude that it is worth the trouble. After all, lots of labor and capital went into the vast structure that greeted me when I stepped off the bus. Russians, it turns out, seem to like the wildness of vegetation overgrowing parts of their cities. Leningrad (St. Petersburg) is surrounded, not by suburbs as cities are in America, but by forest. At the southern edge of town the contrast is most dramatic: tall apartment complexes face large stands of pine trees. The concrete, asphalt, and steel of a city are out of place, not the trees and weeds. Though they enjoy well-kept parks, Russians like to see unkempt patches of wildness here and there because it relieves the tedium of civilization. City dwellers, no matter how rich, powerful, or poor, always head for the untamed countryside on summer weekends.

A. Dmitri's Flat

We finally arrived at two narrow blocks of white concrete split by a side street. I looked up at the apartment building to which Dmitri was leading me. It was a "Khruschev house"—prefabricated, noted for its low cost and lack of appeal, (Smith, 1992, p. 259)—consisting of a series of boxes stacked neatly together, five boxes high and about twenty across. Each box had a window, every third box across, a balcony. Three boxes across made up one flat, flanked by airshafts. The window to the right or left of the balcony was for the kitchen; the window on the other side was for the bedroom. The balcony was attached to the centered living room. The complex of boxes was sectioned into paired columns of flats, side-by-side, and each section was served by its own staircase.

I was led through a narrow, broken, wooden door, partially hidden by overgrown bushes. It looked like the door to a backyard shack, not the entrance to an apartment building. It was patched and covered with graffiti. The stairway inside was dingy. The building had no elevators, and we climbed five flights to reach his flat. By now, Dmitri was letting me help him with the bags. Though more graffiti was on the walls, and a lot of dust was in the air, the smell was not bad. I had been in New York City apartment houses that smelled worse. I noticed that some of the doors had some kind of vinyl padding probably for sound insulation.

We struggled to the top floor, which accessed three flats. Dmitri knocked on a door to our left, shouting at the same time. I stood there, panting. Dmitri's wife greeted us at the door. Alisa was shy, giggled, and spoke no English. I noticed she was tall, about the same height as Dmitri, and, though not especially attractive, she may have been sometime in the past. She wore a plain dress. Her high pitched articulations contrasted with his low gruff voice as Dmitri introduced me. I went into the apartment and noticed how small it was, just three rooms, including a little kitchen, and a low ceiling.

They immediately asked me to take off my shoes while they gave me some *tapochkee*, a pair of oversized slippers to wear indoors. This is a Russian tradition passed through the generations to this day, and is meant to keep dirt off the floors of city and town dwellings.

I was shown to the back room where I would be staying. I did not see any bed in this narrow room, just a couch crammed next to a tiny icebox and an antique looking chair. A sliding plastic partition separated the room from an open closet near the living room that contained an old crib and hanging clothes. My cramped quarters had one nice redeeming touch. An Oriental rug covered the wall above the couch. The window was covered with a wispy, thin, white curtain that let light into the room and was framed by an orange colored drape that had been drawn back. A single potted plant hung in front of the window. I wondered if I would have to sleep on the couch. It looked too narrow. I deposited my bags and returned to the central part of the flat.

I was nervous and exhausted, and the only thing I wanted to do was sleep. I was also getting uncomfortable because they expected me to eat a heavy meal with liquor. I appreciated their enthusiasm, but they would have been wiser to give me tea, let me sleep, and ply me with food and drink later. I had run into a Russian custom of immediately treating an arriving guest lavishly. To do any differently would have, in their minds, left them open to criticism. This Russian was sometimes abused practice (according to Lena, my friend from Gatchina). For example, a long lost relative from Siberia might show up unexpectedly, putting pressure on the host family to produce a feast.

A large table was being set up in the living area. Dmitri instructed me to wash up in the bathroom. It was of American style—the toilet was in the same room as the sink and bathtub. It was dimly lit by a single naked light bulb and had no window. It did not look clean. The tile walls and yellow paint had lost any luster. The sink and tub were stained.

The water that came out of the faucets was tinged with a noticeable brownish color. It was not rust; it left no residue. This off-colored water would appear again and again in different parts of Leningrad and the Soviet Union. It may have been due to asbestos or a heavy metal like lead. I had been told many times before my trip that the tap water in Leningrad was undrinkable. Seeing it made me think the warnings had been unnecessary.

Their bathroom had a large tub but no shower. The toilet seemed different somehow. Two types of toilets are used in Russia. This one was the Russian style, which used less water than an American toilet and usually required more than one flush. I later encountered flats with more expensive imported Finnish toilets, which resembled the American ones in the way the water was used.

The conditions in Dmitri's flat did not help the little appetite I had for a meal. I had been fed many times on the plane. Besides, I was running on nervous energy. I started a talking jag with Dmitri (mimicking his broken English the best I could and trying a Russian word here and there) when I sat at the table, which by now was covered with food. I knew I had to eat some to be polite. The food turned out to be good, and my appetite came back. The liquor, cognac, champagne, and vodka being poured into tiny glasses fascinated me. They also served Pepsi that was warm, just like at Ganders airport. Slightly woozy from jet lag, I hesitated over drinking.

Here I am, I thought, in Russia, being treated like a visiting dignitary, sitting in front of a lavish feast being served up by my host's shy bride. I would have to spend the next month of my life here with these strangers in their cracker box apartment, to get to know them, to get my task done, and to get out. Nervously considering the moment, I felt that I had plunged into something beyond me.

I sample the champagne, while Dmitri explains to me that he can only drink a little. While we speak, Dmitri translates the conversation for his wife. He has stopped drinking for five years, or so he says. He claims that he did not touch a drop while he was in Japan. Dmitri's stories of his trip to Japan, where he met Pomeroy, become an obsessive recurring theme throughout my stay. I wonder if he is not telling me this to also reassure his wife, and if drinking has been a problem for him at some time in his past.

The food is served in courses. The first one includes appetizers—an egg, fish, and garlic salad on top of little round pieces of toasted bread, a diced potato, celery, ham, and leek salad with some kind of dressing mixed in, lightly pickled fresh cucumbers, and thinly sliced *kolbasa* (salami type sausage).

I try the cognac. It is too harsh and warming for a summery day. The apartment is warm enough. Alisa, who appears to understand my displeasure, tastes it and says "*normalna*" (average). I try to explain that I do not drink much hard liquor—only beer and wine. I concentrate on the champagne and try a little Pepsi. Soon the combination of the exotic little delicacies and drink makes me feel nauseous.

I realize that I have been feeling sickly since setting foot in his apartment. I got over some kind of intestinal flu shortly before my trip. Now, I am faced with more gastrointestinal discomfort. It is a strange sort of discomfort. I am constantly teetering on the edge of becoming ill, but never do.

David Lempert, who spent time studying Leningrad in 1989, reported distress associated with nutrition and environmental conditions (Lempert, 1996, pp. 144–145, 205). Soviet preoccupation with heavy industry left shortfalls in pollution control and consumer goods. A Russian friend once showed me a map of Leningrad that sectioned off parts of the city according to prevalent types of pollution.

The second course, richer still, consisted of potatoes in sour cream, garnished with sprigs of dill, and beef brisket. The meat had gristle and fat, but not so much as to make it unpalatable. I noticed the quantity of food I was served was enormous. I could not possibly finish it.

Dmitri and I talked enthusiastically about the HVP project. Alisa got worried because we talked more than we ate. I apologized for not eating enough as I sensed Alisa's disappointment. I told Dmitri that I ate a lot on the flight and how tired I was after my long trip. They finally understood that I needed to sleep, and Alisa went to prepare my room. She pulled the couch away from the wall and, flipping down its back, converted it into a small bed. She brought in some bedding. Before sleeping, I smelled ancient mildew.

B. Dmitri's Friends

At eight o'clock in the evening of the same day, I was roused from a shallow sleep by Dmitri, telling me to get ready because his friends were coming soon. I looked out the window at the sky to try to get a sense of what the time was, as my watch was on New York time, and I did not know the exact adjustment yet. The sky was still blue, not so bright as before. Sometime in the middle of a summer afternoon, several hours before sunset, I thought. Then I remembered that we were to do something after eight. I was surprised that evening had already come.

Dmitri gave me tea in their tiny kitchen and told me to get a jacket and a camera, if I had one. My head was still foggy. A little while later, I heard a car running in the street below, then a couple of honks. Dmitri's friends, Vasili and his wife, Sonia, had arrived.

Soon, I found myself in a red jalopy. I waited in the front seat next to Vasili, while Dmitri, Alisa, and Sonia finished getting themselves out of the apartment house and into the car. Vasili spoke no English but began communicating with signs. He motioned that I was to wear my seat belt, but it did not have to be buckled since it was only for show so the police would not stop us. He was busy looking at a map. At one point he tried to show me where we were going. I pretended to be interested, but the map was meaningless to me. It did not matter. My task was to carry the map so he could refer to it. Apparently, Vasili did not drive downtown often. As it turned out, Leningrad was criss-crossed by all means of public transportation. He only used his car on "special occasions."

We rumbled off toward the center, the engine roaring, gears grinding, a camera in my jacket pocket, a map on my lap. Vasili drove fast until we got near downtown. Soon we parked near a big Russian Orthodox church. It was a series of structures, colored pale blue and trimmed in white. Tall and narrow columns, supporting light gold "onion" domes topped with crosses, set off the central structure from the flanking buildings. I took photos. Dmitri took a picture of me standing with the others in front of this church. I later found out that we were standing in front of the Smolny Convent, near the Smolny Institute, which was sponsoring Eileen. I was unaware of this at the time. Had I known where I was, the place would have had more meaning for me. Lenin and the Bolsheviks used the Smolny Institute as headquarters before the Bolshevik Revolution in 1917.

The tour continued. Our group went further downtown. We parked near a fantastically complex, multi-colored, and ornately decorated Orthodox church called the Cathedral on the Blood. The church had been built on the spot where Tsar Alexander II had been assassinated (Selby, 1996, p. 190). I noticed that part of it was being renovated. I tried to take some pictures of the scaffolding as well as the cathedral, while my Russian friends directed me to angles avoiding the scaffolding. They wanted me to record the best parts of their city.

Tired of taking photos, I started wandering about a bit. At this point Vasili approached me and attempted to "speak" with me. Somehow this gesture warmed me a little. Vasili, shorter than Dmitri, was a swarthy fellow, thin, wiry, and strong looking. His tanned face was permanently flushed with the color of a man who drinks. He had sandy hair and a wry expression. He had been a navy captain at one point and worked in a factory now. I began to like him, and we started communicating somehow. Dmitri came over and started explaining to me that Vasili was interested in "Dale Carnegie."

I wondered how Dale Carnegie, a Westerner interested in business communication, made his way into Soviet culture. Later, I discovered that, in Mikhail Gorbachev's Russia, many new ideas were being introduced by visitors from Western countries. This influx of new ideas would have great influence on Russia over the next decade.

We strolled along a mostly deserted stretch of the city. Dmitri walked ahead with Sonia and Alisa. I stayed behind with Vasili, who was quiet by now. I had a few moments to contemplate my surroundings as we entered a great square in front of the Winter Palace, formerly the residence of Romanov tsars. A few pedestrians were wandering about there. Sunset was finally beginning around ten at night. I felt calm and took in my surroundings.

We reached a tower (Alexander Tower) maybe a hundred feet tall planted in the middle of the square (Palace Square). A yellow hued building with an enormous arched opening was to our left—I was told that the statues on top of this building depict the Russian generals who defeated Napoleon. The green hued Winter Palace was to our right, an impressive, ornate complex, several stories high. Dmitri took me over to a structure, the Little Hermitage, near the Winter Palace. The columns in front of it were sculptures of giant naked men of monumental strength (Atlases) "holding up" the building. The quality of the work was outstanding. The polished dark brown stone had the texture of skin. Its sensuality attracted you to the smooth, rounded surfaces. I wanted to reach out and touch the feet of one of the statues. Two youths were watching me, so I self-consciously avoided touching it. I was sure that my foreignness was apparent.

We walked along a narrow canal spanned by little arched bridges. The sun reflected off the surface of the water. The alleyway was dark. I anticipated the sight of a sunset right ahead. We emerged from the alley onto a river-front view. I was not mistaken about the sunset and took my first memorable photograph of Leningrad. Across shimmering ripples of the Neva River lay the straight horizontal lines of the Peter and Paul Fortress, accented by a single spire, and dramatized by the last rays of the sun. The light behind it made it mostly a dark silhouette set against a backdrop formed by brilliant silver-yellow and streaks of orange and violet. Jagged black clouds overhead added a menacing touch. The vista reminded me that I was in Peter the Great's city, for, more than anything else, this city was the creation of this one man who was cruel and brilliant.

We spent the rest of the time in Vasili's car going from site to site. I was struck by the apparent emptiness of Leningrad. This was a big city. Millions supposedly live here. Where was everyone? Then we turned a corner, and I saw hundreds of people who seemed to float in the yellow and white lights of shops, theaters, hotels, and street lamps.

Nevsky Prospect, the central avenue of Leningrad, attracts city residents and tourists like a magnet. In early summer, the low light of dusk lingers, giving the city's widest boulevard an eerie, softly illuminated quality. These are the White Nights, when the sun takes forever to set and the apparently endless afterglow is interrupted by only a couple of hours of darkness before giving way to dawn.

At some point, we stopped to see a bronze statue of Peter on a rearing horse, facing the Neva. In the dim light, it was mostly a shadow perched on an irregularly shaped, pale granite rock. Dmitri explained how the statue had been carefully balanced on the horse's rear legs and a tail barely touching the twisted form of a bronze snake being crushed under the horse's hooves. A short walk away was a massive cathedral of an entirely different design than the Orthodox cathedrals I had seen before. This massive structure, St. Isaac's Cathedral with its domed top, loomed over us, engulfed in its own darkness.

Running through Leningrad in the little red jalopy, Vasili informed me that the city has four hundred bridges, a fact hard to swallow without the knowledge that, besides the River Neva and its branches, the city is criss-crossed by numerous canals and ditches. My flight's magazine had mentioned that Leningrad was experiencing a Renaissance of sorts. I could tell that the city was getting a facelift, because of the ubiquitous scaffolding on the cathedrals all over Leningrad.

At some point, we stopped so Alisa and Sonia could buy Pepsis. They offered me some of the tepid cola. By then, Sonia was making efforts to be friendly and communicate with me. She was a short energetic woman, speaking with a voice full of life, expressively gesturing with her hands.

Back in Dmitri's flat again, we shared a midnight meal. The sky had finally turned dark. Unlike Dmitri, Vasili was not reluctant to drink and insisted I join him. We were treated to the leftover portions of the earlier feast. I joined in, the drink woke up my inquisitiveness, and we began to talk. They asked me my opinions of Boris Yeltsin and Gorbachev. I told them that Gorbachev was much admired in the United States for his openness to the West, that Yeltsin was also seen as a courageous reformer, but he was also rumored to drink and act in ways that Americans did not understand. They said that it was "*normalna*" (a typical observation). I asked them to give their opinions of Gorbachev, Yeltsin, or about any political topic. They were hesitant to do so. Finally, Vasili suggested that it was better to wait until we knew each other better.

I liked Dmitri's friends. Vasili was making an effort to communicate, and Sonia's enthusiasm added cheer to our party. Dmitri and Alisa took the table from the living room and converted the couch there to a bed after the party was over and their guests had left. I had made it through one day without getting sick. I was exhausted twice over and managed to sleep until 5:30 in the morning.

C. Alisa's Payment

When I woke up, the daylight was already strong. I could see tall skinny birch trees outside with their profuse green leaves and white bark. They blocked the view of the apartment building across the street. A little vent on top was open, but it let in little air. I opened the window wide and breathed in the fresh morning air. The humidity was not bad. The day would be sunny. The air helped my headache. I fiddled with a tape recorder, wondering if it was worth recording city sounds.

The morning of 8 July was a Monday, but nobody appeared to be going to work. At 6 a.m., I heard a factory whistle but no response to it. The morning seemed to drift on and on, with only an occasional human voice or the sound of a distant car. Then I remembered that this month is a national holiday. Students and workers were on vacation. The motor of the little refrigerator in my room stopped, and I could hear birds but little else. I recalled that Laura told me that when she visited Leningrad it was "dead." A little later, I heard a radio go on in the living room. The radio played for a while and went off again. Dmitri and Alisa were not up yet. Eventually, I heard voices in the street below and more cars rolling down the main avenue. Then Dmitri came to my room to tell me to wash up for breakfast.

Breakfast was unremarkable, except for the quality of the tea. It was a strong black tea that Dmitri drank quite often. I noticed his teeth were stained from it and hesitated to drink it, but he assured me the staining was not permanent. I discovered that getting any kind of juice or even milk for breakfast was not possible. A little jam served on tiny glass saucers helped make the tea palatable and was the only source of Vitamin C and sugar for breakfast. Granulated sugar was not available. I was told that sugar was scarce and being rationed by the government. They showed me the ration coupons for it. They had bread but no toaster. I wondered how Alisa managed to toast bread the day before. Coming from a land where juice, milk, dry cereal, and toast were readily available, I saw that the going would be tough awhile. I forgot about it as Dmitri and I were soon lost in a theoretical discussion. It was a redeeming quality of the situation. My talks with Dmitri continued throughout my trip. Our enjoyment of the exchange of ideas made the hardships bearable.

We worked out our plans for the day, which included visiting the city center. Dmitri took me downtown on a bus to the Finland Train Station, its last stop. A beautiful clear day, warm and sunny, enveloped our leisurely walk along the blue Neva on a long, tree-lined promenade. The shady inner path we followed was dotted with benches where weary pedestrians could rest. Across the river was a panoramic view of Russo-European architecture built during first two hundred years of Leningrad's (St. Petersburg's) history. I could see some of the landmarks we visited the night before.

During the day, we criss-crossed the city, mostly on foot, occasionally using trolley buses or the less frequent gasoline powered buses. Leningrad also had a *metro* (subway) system, and a network of trams, neither of which Dmitri favored. We visited the Peter and Paul Fortress, the Central Post Office, and the Hotel Leningrad.

I enjoyed the fortress. The little church in the center had a tall golden spire that rose high above the fort. It was the same spire I photographed the day before, and now I was standing below it. Inside were sarcophagi of famous Russian rulers. The interior of the church was richly decorated. Half of it was under renovation.

Dmitri treated me to ice cream and coffee in a little cafe on the grounds of the fort. He was pleasantly surprised by the refreshments, and, while we sat and chatted, he told me that the place was a real treasure. Apparently, table sitting, ice cream, and even coffee were not often found in cafes. Dmitri said that it was a "private" cafe (a cooperative). Under Gorbachev, the Soviet Union was experimenting with small scale private ventures that provided some relief to average consumers that were all too familiar with the lack of simple pleasures such as these.

After we finished our coffee, we left the fort. Outside, men and women were sunbathing on a golden sand beach near the water. Some of the sunbathers were fully dressed; others wore bathing suits. Many of the men posed like statues against the outer wall of the fort. Since the sun never shines directly down at any time in Leningrad due to its extreme northern latitude, the most effective way to get a tan is standing. Also, the beach there is too cold to lie on comfortably, even in the summer. (Russians are very sensitive to differences in temperature. For instance, some believe that lying on cold ground can permanently injure your health.)

On our way from the Peter and Paul Fortress, we crossed the Neva on a long bridge (*Kirov Mohst*). Dmitri pointed to a double-headed eagle decoration that repeated all along the iron railing of the bridge. I noticed that a pointed stem separated the heads. He told me that, in the past, crowns were on the stems before the Bolsheviks cut them off. They had all the crowns from such designs removed everywhere in Russia. I thought of the enormity of the task and the implacable determination to eradicate any symbol of the imperial aristocracy.

I offered to pay for the coffee and ice cream, but Dmitri refused. He was insisting on paying for everything. Because, during the negotiations by long-distance telephone, Dmitri had apparently turned down my offer to directly pay them for room and board, I found his insistence on paying for everything else troubling.

I remembered that Eileen had brought a large bag of beautiful green apples for her hosts. I brought cartons of cigarettes, inexpensive, retractable ball-point pens, and boxes of gum, which were suggestions of Laura, and more suitable for a tourist to bring for children and strangers. For example, later, when I was more independent. I found these items to be useful. A few times, at Palace Square outside of the Winter Palace I did give away some pens and gum. Near the metros, I occasionally was asked for a cigarette.

Dmitri smoked, and so did Vasili. Alisa and Sonia did not. Dmitri thought my cigarettes were fine but refused my offer of a couple of packs. Every time I offered him one of my Camels, he offered me one of his cigarettes. He preferred a mild Bulgarian brand of cigarette, which he got with coupons when he could. I thought I should buy some gifts for him and Alisa, but I did not know what they might like. I did not want to change all my dollars into rubles and had no idea as of yet how to convert traveler's checks. I was still groping around looking for familiar guideposts.

As the day wore on, I felt a rising apprehension that something was amiss. I felt nervous around Dmitri because his manner was that of constant urgency. I had felt this way since the first day when he hustled me out of the airport. Dmitri's urgency contrasted with the slow pace of Leningrad. I also had trouble understanding Dmitri's English, which did not improve with practice. The little Russian I knew did not help much. I was under a constant strain to make myself understood.

To make matters worse, our continuous exchange of ideas left little time to discuss the practical aspects of my trip. Once I realized that Dmitri was not a wealthy man, I wanted to show him that I was willing to compensate him for what he was doing for me, but did not as yet have a clue as to how to do it. Cash (American dollars) would have been the simplest solution if I had not taken most of my money in the form of travelers checks. Finding a place to cash them for dollars, a routine transaction back home, turned out to be much harder than I expected. The only bank we stopped in did not accept them, and the hotels were only willing to turn them into rubles. Commercial banking was virtually nonexistent in the Soviet Union.

We went to the Central Post Office so I could send a promised letter to my wife. Dmitri asked me to include a preliminary translation of Pomeroy's test along with a short note in my letter. Knowing that normal post took forever to get to the United States, I inquired about an expedited service. After discussions with several clerks, Dmitri found the right location for the express service. I asked Dmitri to tell me the cost in rubles, telling him that when I got my money exchanged I would pay him. He agreed but asked me to wait until we got home.

Our last stop was the Hotel Leningrad, a large hotel, modern-looking with lots of marble floors, and occupied mainly by Europeans. On the mezzanine level was a foreign currency exchange where I converted some dollars to rubles so I could pay the postage bill. The going rate was about twenty-seven rubles to the dollar. Dmitri was curious about the exchange process and asked me questions.

Though I was anxious, the day had gone well. We got things done. I took more photos and saw plenty of the city. As we headed home on a bus, I relaxed awhile.

Back at the flat, Dmitri and I discussed the HVP. Alisa, who had stayed pretty much in the background, told Dmitri that she wanted to speak with me. Immersed in my discussion with Dmitri, I was distracted, wondering what she could possibly want. This was the first time that Alisa initiated a conversation with me.

Suddenly, I am talking to Alisa with Dmitri as the interpreter, and she wants to know where I plan to stay. By this time, I am completely disoriented. "Where am I planning to live during my visit?" Alisa begins (Dmitri's translation). I plan to stay with them, or is that not understood? Well, she has children to take care of. I wonder where they are. Working to take care of them and me is going to be taxing for her. Was I planning to pay?

I explain that I do not know anything about this, and that no formal arrangements had been made before I left my country. Pomeroy negotiated with Dmitri on the phone, and the understanding at the time was that they were not making any formal request for rent. I understood that to mean that it was up to me to purchase gifts for them and provide informal compensation. Still, while giving me no acknowledgment or denial of this, Alisa persists in asking me when I am going to pay her and how much.

Prior to making the trip, I had asked Pomeroy to ask Dmitri how much I should pay them. The reply was curious. They did not want to be paid in cash; they asked instead that I bring them a stereo. I did not want to bring such a bulky item, and Pomeroy relayed this back to Dmitri. The matter had then been left unsettled, but I was left with the impression that they did not want to be paid directly for their services, and that Dmitri was wealthy or being funded.

I intended to buy them presents after arriving in Russia and had not counted on the lack of normal banking services, which made cashing my traveler's checks more than inconvenient. The process of negotiating *via* long distance phone calls plus cultural differences laid the groundwork for further misunderstandings.

Rattled, I tell Dmitri that I do not understand for what his wife is asking. He wants to know why I do not understand when just a few moments ago I did. After pausing, I ask Alisa to name a price, hoping that she does not have a clue. She names a sum, 500 U. S. dollars, that is almost precisely what I have brought with me only less a few dollars. I get the feeling that it is not a lucky guess and am at a loss as to what to do.

Alisa, as I put together later, was a skilled negotiator. She had acquired the talent and social confidence for this over time, stemming from her early days living in the port of Odessa, where street trading was rampant. She was a member of the Communist Party. She officially worked for Intourist, a Soviet monopoly for tourism, although she seemed to be on some kind of leave of absence from them at the time and was much more involved with helping Dmitri in various ways. At the time, I did not know any of this.

One of my first impulses was to get out of there. I was not enjoying the negotiations. I felt like I was being ambushed. As I looked out the window at the darkening sky, I knew that running would not solve anything. The mood of my trip had turned from nervous excitement to gloomy realization. I was completely unfamiliar with this place and spoke hardly any Russian. I could not imagine trying to get new accommodations. Although a bluff in that direction may have been effective, I had absolutely no confidence in such a move. From pre-trip reading, I knew that the normal tourist hotels were so expensive that all my money would be gone in a few days. Whatever price these people wanted was better than that. Besides, how was I going to work with Dmitri and stay in a place where I could be so close to a Russian family? A main point of my trip was to get an ethnographic experience. I could not do that in a hotel. I also had to work closely with Dmitri to make sure he translated the HVP into Russian correctly.

However, the thought of turning over almost all of my money, in effect putting myself completely at their mercy, at such an early stage in my trip was chilling. I continued to stall. First, I said that, until I got my visa processed for residency, I could not do any business with them. My travel agent instructed me to have my visa stamped during the first few days of my stay. Remembering that most of my money was in traveler's checks, I decided to show them. "This is what I can pay you with," I explained. Alisa looked at the traveler's checks curiously. She had not seen these before. Sensing that they were a little bit at a loss, I continued to press, "As soon as I can go get these exchanged, we can negotiate." Alisa was not going to give up so easily. She continued to insist that we settle on a price.

I tried to keep as calm as possible so I could think. They had gotten me in the sense that they knew what I could pay, so the time worn trick of pretending to have less money was not going to work. Even though they had never seen these funny checks before, they knew how much currency I had. Just how they knew was an interesting question that I turned over in my mind. Finally, I tried a gambit: "I cannot pay you what you want; I won't have any money left over for gifts." They hesitated. So I proposed a sum that, while still high, was considerably less than what they wanted. We bickered some more over this until, leaving the exact amount unsettled, we agreed upon a ball park figure or range (200–300 U. S. dollars). They succeeded in extracting a concession from me in the form of a promise, but I still had my money. Then Alisa, who apparently had been briefed about all my transactions that day by Dmitri, angrily insisted I pay the postage bill immediately. Relieved, I counted out the rubles.

Later, mulling over the incident, I reconstructed the day and discovered what happened. Shortly before we arrived at the hotel where I changed some of my small bills into rubles, Dmitri asked me to wait while he used the phone, explaining that he wanted to let his wife know when we would be returning. When he came back, Dmitri began asking me a lot of questions. Innocently, I explained what the process of exchange entailed. Dmitri then wanted to look at the documents involved for "scientific" reasons. I let him look at them. My judgment was not good.

The documents included the amount of money I was carrying. Alisa had enough knowledge or savvy to deduce this and instructed Dmitri on precisely what to look for when that phone call was made. Their spying made me mad. I resolved to find out what Eileen was paying when I met her, as I hoped to do at the end of that week.

One thing that stuck in my mind was how little I knew Dmitri's wife. Behind that "fawning" exterior lay a tiger. I also started to see how Dmitri was taking full advantage of his knowledge of English, placing himself in the center of everything as interpreter, while staying away from any responsibility. After all, I was negotiating with his wife, not him. But he was the beneficiary of the negotiations as well as she. The sum I had agreed to pay (up to 300 U. S. dollars) was still high given Soviet economic conditions at that time as I would discover (Bennett, 1991, personal communication). I put the incident behind me, and the subject of payment was not raised for the time being.

The next day, the first order of business was my visa. For some reason, even though I was to stay in Leningrad, my "destination" was given as Riga, Latvia, one of the Baltic countries to the southwest of Leningrad. There I had been invited by an Anatol S. to a meeting of the Latvian Managers Club. This, according to Dmitri, was done to expedite the visa. So I was under the impression that I would not necessarily be traveling to Riga. This turned out not to be the case. Dmitri was holding back information, and they discussed their plans to travel to Riga only after sorting out the visa situation.

According to Soviet law, my address had to be verified when I arrived in the Soviet Union. Since my visa named Riga as my destination, this complication would have to be resolved. Alisa and I walked to a police station, where she said they would take care of my visa. As we went into the dank gloomy atmosphere of the narrow dark corridors, I saw many old and worn out people, mostly women, waiting on a line that ended at a closed office door. Expecting a long delay, I was surprised when Alisa, ignoring the line, went right to the front of it, opened the closed office door, and took me inside. (Alisa belonged to the Communist Party—see Chapter Five.)

Several blue uniformed men were inside. Alisa spoke to one of them and asked me to have a seat. I surrendered my passport and visa to her, and she disappeared into an inner office. Several anxious minutes later, she emerged. I got my passport back, and she said that they would have to keep my visa for a while to have it stamped. That was it; no trip to Latvia was entailed. I was partly relieved but also worried about having to be without my visa.

After Alisa and I returned from the police station, Dmitri and I worked in his living room for a long time, concentrating almost entirely on the project. I noticed that he liked to work with frequent interruptions for tea or a cigarette break. I did not mind. I enjoyed the conversations we had during these breaks. The work itself was tedious and consisted of close examination of virtually every word involved in Pomeroy's test. Still, we were making progress. I got Dmitri's permission to tape record our sessions.

During our breaks, we often stood outside on his tiny balcony to have a smoke. His wife did not want smoking in the apartment. The balcony was high up, where some birds had their nests. They were of the species, *lastochka*, a kind of swallow or swift. They were super fast flyers. At times, I thought one of them would crash into me only to have it veer sharply away at the last second. These birds helped control the insect population around Dmitri's flat.

Five stories up, breathing in the fresh cool air of an early evening, Dmitri and I often discussed some of his theories about history and culture, and he inquired into my life. At night, we continued our conversations in the kitchen, sitting on little stools with some tea and *sushkee* (hard, ring-shaped biscuits) on the small table in front of us. Occasionally, I learned something about him, like the time he took one of his professors deep into the Caucasus Mountains, or the time he participated in a "hunger" experiment. The experience left a lasting mark on Dmitri, judging from pictures of him with lots of color and fat on his face before the experiment and his gaunt, almost haggard, appearance after he recovered.

D. Vasili's Flat

I had not showered or bathed since leaving New Jersey. On the evening of my third day there, I told Dmitri that I must bathe (since he had no shower). He explained that the hot water had been turned off in his flat while the pipes in the street were being repaired. I remembered seeing some street repairs going on toward the far end of our block. During my stay, the water supply system seemed to be always under repair. You never knew when water, hot or cold, was going to be available. Sometimes an entire section of the city lost its water. I inquired when we might have hot water. Dmitri said that he had no way of knowing. He called Vasili.

Later that evening, we had a "shower party" at Vasili's home. Sonia prepared a sumptuous feast for us. I welcomed the relief from Alisa's tiresome cooking. Though still early in my trip, I already had a sense that the meals would not improve. The meal Alisa prepared for my arrival had been a one-time event. After this, she cooked the most boring meat available, and I quickly got sick of potatoes and the fried squash that inevitably accompanied our meals. I longed for salads and fresh fruit.

Once, they tried to persuade me to eat some gray-colored hot dogs that looked too disgusting to eat. Some kind of *kasha* (hot grain cereal) was always available for breakfast. One variety, which tasted similar to my favorite dessert, rice pudding, made me feel better. They also served me dairy dishes that were too rich for my palate. Occasionally, sprats or some other kind of tinned fish were served for breakfast. Cheese could be had for a snack. Dark thick bread and black tea accompanied every meal. We rarely had eggs.

I had already spent a lot of time in Dmitri's tiny kitchen with the refrigerator that hardly worked, the bare sink, and the gas burning stove. I never cooked. Alisa and Dmitri always took care of it. I sat there, balancing myself on a tiny stool while trying to avoid shifting it into a hole in the floor that they never bothered to fix. A picture of a tiger hung on the wall, probably torn from an old calendar. By contrast, Sonia's kitchen had a complete calendar with a picture of a Russian cathedral.

This night, I ate roasted chicken and lots of vegetables, which, I was told, came from Vasili's garden. Private gardens were kept near the outskirts of the city in special designated areas or in the surrounding villages. Before dinner, I took a five-minute shower in Vasili's cramped bathroom and put on fresh clothes. I could not use all the hot water, as Dmitri and Alisa were planning showers too. As we shuffled around in *tapochkee* waiting for dinner, I started to feel at home. The place reminded me of my grandmother's apartment in Queens, New York—full of knickknacks, and a chicken roasting in the oven.

The slight difference was that Vasili's place had a style of bathroom more typically found in Leningrad. The toilet (water closet) was segregated from the rest of the bathroom. It was in an adjoining but separate room, with its own door to the hallway.

I temporarily solved my gift problem. Before leaving my country, I had packed postcards of Buffalo, New York and Niagara Falls to show Russians where I lived. I brought a couple of these for Sonia and Vasili. When I got there, I found that an additional member of their family was waiting to meet me. It was Vasili's mother, Valentina, who lived with them. So I gave the postcards to Sonia and Valentina, and I gave Vasili a pack of Camels. They seemed pleased, especially by the postcards.

As I sat in the kitchen, Alisa was busy telling Sonia about our upcoming camping trip. I was let in on this anticipated adventure during the afternoon before the party. I was feeling hesitant about going.

In one of our early conversations, Dmitri and Alisa told me about an adventure they had in the Karelian forest. They were camping, got lost, and found themselves walking on an unfamiliar road. Apparently they had wandered into a "closed" zone and were promptly arrested and taken to a local police station. The police held them for several hours, and confiscated Dmitri's camera and film. They wanted to know what Dmitri and Alisa were doing there. After convincing the authorities that they were not "spies" or "saboteurs," Dmitri and Alisa were able to leave. They were given a warning, and the film and camera were returned. When Dmitri had the film developed it was blank.

I was scared by this story. Dmitri assured me that this was years ago, and where we were going had no closed zones. Many parts of the Soviet Union were closed to regular citizens for military or political purposes. I was also worried about the climatic conditions and being in a remote place. They told me it was just a normal camping trip. Did I not go camping in the United States? I finally relented but had the feeling that they did not trust leaving me alone in their flat while they were camping. As my hosts, they were responsible for any trouble I got into, so they wanted to keep an eye on me.

After dinner, I was treated to some serious Russian drinking. Russians like to get the measure of a man by the way he handles drink. The new member of my expanding network, Valentina, joined the party. She was a husky woman, a real bear. She had the same reddish complexion as her son. This was my first encounter with a Russian *babushka*. I was seated on a divan next to her for the festivities that were held in their living room, which was larger and more richly decorated than Dmitri's. They had a piano. Valentina asked me if I wanted to play it. I apologized that I did not know how.

We sat around a large coffee table containing an assortment of snacks and bottles of liquor. I was fascinated by one of the snacks—pickled watermelon. The concept was strange to me, but my Russian friends insisted that I sample some. I liked it. The *babushka* explained to me that she had developed a recipe for this treat and insisted on showing it to me. It was written in Russian, and I could not understand it, but she seemed pleased that I was looking at it.

I drank more than I intended. Tipsy, my reticence disappeared. The party became more animated as everyone relaxed. I lost track of time.

Vasili has just shown me an atlas of which he is proud. It has maps of all parts of the world. I like looking at it, trying to decipher the different names of places in Cyrillic on the maps. We look at the United States and the Soviet Union for a long time. Dmitri boasts about how large the Soviet Union is. I point out places in the United States to them. With Dmitri interpreting, Valentina explains to me that she once worked as a military engineer in a place that is near the Norwegian border, a northern location. Her job was connected with radar defenses. Was it cold there? Yes, she tells me, but maybe not so cold as I might think. It starts to dawn on me that this amiable woman, now retired, had worked for a superpower that could destroy our country. Here I am sitting inches from "the enemy."

The vodka and sweet fruit liquors start getting to me. Vasili asks if I want to smoke, and we go in to the kitchen while the women stay behind. Dmitri translates for us. Vasili shows me a book by Dale Carnegie, translated into Russian. Dmitri stops interpreting and begins a conversation with Vasili. I interrupt occasionally to ask Dmitri to translate. The conversation has something to do with their interest in going into business together as partners. What exactly they are planning to do is not evident. This is followed by talk about Vasili's car in a garage somewhere. The edge of Leningrad has numerous groups of small tin shacks clustered together. They are storage and repair places where city dwellers can lock up their cars when they are not using them. Repair work is done, usually by the owner, at these places.

The women are missing us and call us back to the living room. After the break, I resume drinking along with the rest of them. Sonia keeps bringing out more and more bottles for me to sample, while Vasili shows me a picture of his son, Oleg, who is away studying at a military school. The black and white photo shows a boy with a look on his face that could stop a tank. I comment that he looks like an intelligent boy. They are pleased and ask me if I could do something for him. I do not have the faintest idea what that could be, so I say nothing.

The conversation turns to another subject—the danger of a possible civil war in the Soviet Union. Dmitri has been going on at length about this ever since the day after my arrival. The only time he kept his opinions to himself was when Vasili and Sonia were at his flat the night before.

I sample some flavored vodkas and more fruit liquors. I especially like a plum liquor and tell them so. I almost sing its praises. Vasili says something to the effect that it is nothing special.

By now I am drunk and talkative. While Dmitri translates, I launch into a monologue. First, I exclaim that their flat is just like ones you could find in the United States. Then I change the subject back to the topic of civil war. "You know we have a very serious situation now in the world," I say, paraphrasing one of Dmitri's favorite English expressions. He would say things like "this is [a] very dangerous situation," or "this is [a] very unusual situation."

I go on to talk at some length about what I understand to be a precarious situation in the Soviet Union. I say that the need for a "peaceful resolution" to conflicts all over the world is more pressing than ever. I say something to the effect that the need for a war between our countries does not exist. I say that some people are trying to prevent the Soviet Union's progress. They agree with this. I say that no matter what happens, resorting to guns and rockets is out of the question. Dmitri indicates that Vasili does not agree with this, but understands my position. I say that we owe it to the future, to the children, pointing to the photo of Vasili's son. I go on and on like this. At one point Vasili comments on Dmitri's excellent translation.

When the party broke up, I was tired. Everyone seemed pleased by the evening. I left wondering what had prompted me to make such a speech. I had a history of being reserved at parties regardless of how much I drank.

Vasili walked with us all the way home to see we got home safely. On our way out, he showed me the entrance to his apartment house. The thick glass windows of the lobby had bullet holes in them. I was glad that I was not going to walk home alone.

Vasili lived in an apartment house more similar to those with which I was familiar. It had a large single entrance, elevators, and was much taller than Dmitri's place. The grass outside had been cut. The soft carpet of green made for nice walking.

As we neared Dmitri's flat, walking ahead of them on the gravel path that provided a short cut between the two homes, I felt at peace. Then I noticed some strangers walking behind us, and I felt a little apprehensive, but nothing happened. We reached Dmitri's flat safely. Glad to be home, I went to sleep immediately.

E. Camping in Karelia

The next day (10 July) we went camping. This was the beginning of the second phase of my trip. I had already met many of the principal adult players in the drama. I would soon meet Dmitri's older son as well. As far as Dmitri's circle in Leningrad was concerned, I had already met just about everyone I was going to meet. Dmitri knew more people but these were the holidays. His regular academic work would resume again after I left. I never met his parents or Alisa's. For some reason, I was kept away from them. Those we met camping were not regulars in Dmitri's life. Later in Latvia, I would meet members of Dmitri's network outside Leningrad.

My hangover was not as bad as I thought it would be, and I was soon able to organize my thoughts. I knew we had to leave that day and spent the morning deciding what to take and what to leave behind. Alisa went out in the morning and returned with my visa, complete with the proper stamp. I was glad to have it with me and found a place to keep it.

While I was musing, I could hear Dmitri and Alisa bustling about, putting together what seemed to be an inordinately large amount of stuff. I came out to look. I saw Alisa wearing pants—this was the first time I had seen her do so. Dmitri had jeans on and a navy blue zip-up sweatshirt. I noticed they both seemed to be strongly built. They were packing two large backpacks. A huge canvas sack containing who knew what was in the middle of the living room. Dmitri explained that they were bringing their kayak. It was of a type that could be disassembled. I asked if they needed any help packing, but they refused it.

Just before we left, Dmitri and I had a smoke on his balcony. At one point, our conversation became rather animated, and our voices were raised. Dmitri finished his cigarette first and went back in to help Alisa. I lingered a moment, and, as I was turning to go back in, I caught sight of an unfamiliar face disappearing into a window near our balcony. It was the partially visible face of an old woman, only one eye showing. The image stayed in my mind. She had been surreptitiously peering at us.

When I turned toward her she disappeared. She must have heard us speaking and been curious about it, since we were not speaking in Russian. The look on her face was that of an innocent bystander accidentally overhearing a criminal conspiracy. I had a flash of paranoia and wondered if the authorities would be summoned. I had caught a remnant of Stalin's days—an extreme suspicion of foreigners held by older generations who were encouraged to spy on their neighbors.

We walked to a train station near the flat, where we would be taking a train up north into Karelia. I was given a disassembled tent to carry, a heavy bundle. Dmitri had a little dolly that he used to wheel some of the baggage. Soon a train rumbled into the station. Dmitri, Alisa, and I boarded.

The train was right out of World War II movies I had seen, dark green, with a metallic crest bearing the hammer and cycle in front. It was mostly empty, and we took our time getting a seat. A small metal rack was above our seat where extra luggage could be put. We put the bundled kayak up there. I held on to my shoulder bag. That and a waist pack held my things. I also had a little zippered wallet tied around my chest, kept under my shirt.

The train was old and dusty inside. Most of the bench seats were polished wood. Some had padding; others had only a plank on which to sit. The seats were arranged in pairs facing each other. Three passengers could squeeze into one of these bench seats. The windows were dirty. Some were broken, some open, and others missing a pane of glass. The day was hot, and not much air came in until we were moving. The cars had a manually operated metal sliding door at each end leading to a vestibule where passengers got on and off the train through automatic doors.

The trip was divided into four legs. The first leg lasted until Alisa's son joined us at a stop on the outskirts of town. The second leg lasted from then until we changed trains. The third leg took us to our destination town. The fourth and final leg consisted of getting to our campsite from the train.

Odd little things stick in my memory about the trip—like Dmitri's bad breath. At the beginning of the train ride, Dmitri was sandwiched between Alisa and me. Alisa was near the isle, and I was near a window on my right. We sat backwards to the direction of travel. The bench opposite us was occupied with some of our bags. The hard wooden benches were uncomfortable. The really annoying thing was Dmitri's trying to speak with me. I had never been so close to him. His breath reeked and was making me nauseous. I tried to ignore him and stare out the window. Finally, I got up and, without explanation, went to an empty seat nearby to sit down and breathe. Dmitri started getting annoyed, but I remained reticent.

While I was sitting alone, I had a chance to absorb some of the atmosphere of the train. The old women were striking. Their faces were so worn, wrinkled, and haggard that I thought they were beggars, but their clothes showed that this was not the case. Though not so smartly dressed as women in Leningrad, they wore clean, printed, cotton dresses with heavy plain boots made of rubber. They had shawls tied around their heads and clutched cotton bags, bundles, or leather purses. They appeared sullen and their glances were full of suspicion. They also seemed resigned to their fate, somehow defeated.

I wondered what ravages they had endured that had brought them to this state. I looked at other younger looking people. Though the ravages of time were not on their faces, the same look of resignation was. Then a horrible thought struck me—as if all the years of our government's Cold War propaganda was flashing before my eyes. This old beaten up train with these old beaten people—were these the fierce, technologically advanced warriors that threatened the American way of life? These people needed to be rescued, not defeated.

I went back to my seat after a short while. Dmitri, puzzled and probably angered by my mysterious behavior, kept to himself and gave up trying to talk with me. We managed a few words between us. Alisa was also not saying much. I tried to get comfortable by stretching my left arm across the back of the bench, freeing up a little elbow room between Dmitri and me. A few minutes later lost in thought, I felt Alisa's head resting on my hand and turned to look. She was dozing. Dmitri had turned his head away from me and also gone to sleep. I felt awkward, considered moving my hand, but then thought, why wake them? Glad to have Dmitri's breath out of my face, I watched buildings, factories, rusty shacks, and empty patches of wild grass go by. Empty train stations flashed by. We had reached the outskirts of the city. I glanced over at Dmitri and Alisa at one point. An old lady was staring at us. We probably looked like a romantic triangle to her. I did not care. In the Soviet Union, strangers often passed judgment on other strangers.

At some point, Alisa woke up, and I freed my hand nonchalantly. Dmitri woke up, and Alisa left her seat. The train rolled to a stop. People crowded onto it. Alisa returned with a boy, maybe twelve years old. This was "Ilya," Dmitri and Alisa's older son. One of the bags on the seat opposite us was moved up to the overhead rack to give him room. Ilya had been staying with Alisa's parents in a town or village slightly north of Leningrad. He was a quiet boy with dark hair like Dmitri's, but more shy like Alisa. They told me Ilya was studying English in school, but besides saying hello in Russian and English, I did not speak much to him. Alisa fussed over her son for a while, and then he faded into the background. I kept to myself and looked out the window while his parents chatted.

The city gave way to countryside. We entered a pine and birch tree forest. Then we came to a lake near some *dachas* (country homes) and cabins. I could see people in bathing suits wading in the lake amidst reeds along the shore. Dmitri commented that it was a nice place.

At one point, Alisa got my attention and said something in Russian while pointing to her left. I strained to look and saw some large structures. Dmitri explained that Alisa was joking that I might see some "military secrets." The structures made up a chemical and nuclear research center. A few minutes later, a freight train passed us, carrying car after car of gravel, then another one carrying timber. Finally, a train came by carrying the bottom half of military tanks.

I again recognized that energetic presence I had felt when first setting eyes on Leningrad. The rest of this journey would reveal tantalizing but fleeting images that, in part, contradicted my impression that Russia was a worn out country. My impressions competed with each other. The military, industrial, and architectural features spoke of energy and might, but the encroachment of nature and the gloominess of the people spoke of disillusion and decay. The Soviet system of rule was weighing down the people it was supposed to protect and for whom it was meant to provide.

Our journey north continued. The train stopped every so often. More people came on at each stop than left. We had to abandon the two remaining seats to strangers. Dmitri was carrying a bag on his lap by now. Then Dmitri told me we had to get off soon. I helped him get the sacks off the rack. We assembled in the vestibule with our stuff, along with others ready to get off the train. We had to be quick. People would be anxiously waiting to board it.

The train rolled to a stop, and we got off in good order. We waited on the platform while Dmitri decided what to do next. He said we had two options, to take another train or to catch a long distance bus.

We had to wait awhile. Alisa broke out some grape juice that Ilya has brought along, a contribution by her parents. She was carrying several large jars of this juice called "*compote*." They gave me a cup from which to drink, and I had my share of the sticky, sweet juice.

I noticed some soldiers drilling near the station. They seemed inexperienced and sluggish. Dressed in green fatigues, their faces struck me as being unusual. At first, I thought they may be Chinese, but this made no sense. After a while, I determined that, while being definitely Oriental in appearance, they were not Chinese. They had flat, oval faces and Oriental eyes. Their complexion was yellow like Asians but not pale. Their general appearance reminded me of depictions of ancient Meso-Americans. The only thing I could conclude was that they were from Asiatic Russia (Siberia). Only their leader was Occidental in appearance, probably a Russian. They continued to train while we waited.

A stranger in a navy blue sweat suit—I had seen men dressed like this, standing on the flat tops of empty rail cars that passed by—came right up to me and, without saying a word, started looking at my waist pack. Then he went away. I wondered what he wanted. My pack had the name of an U. S. state park on it. I noticed that I was wearing it so the label was upside down. I was glad of this. The further we were from Leningrad the more afraid I became of being "unmasked." The continual military presence made me uneasy.

Alisa wandered off to a market near the station. I followed her, curious to have a look at the market. Among the items were what looked like tiny apricots. Alisa wanted to buy some for me. I begged her not to. I asked Dmitri to explain that I was afraid of food from these markets, which may carry bacteria harmful to me.

Dmitri decided to catch the next bus, and we moved our bags a few yards to the nearby bus stop. A military officer was waiting there. He wore a tan uniform with red trimming and an officer's cap with metallic insignia. He was young. I saw men dressed like this in Leningrad. There they blended in with the crowds. Here, standing alone, this one man seemed more threatening.

A long distance bus pulled up a few yards away. It had large windows with curtains drawn over them. Dmitri was anxious for us to get on the bus. A crowd rushed for the doors as many other people had the same idea. Dmitri was ready to jump on. Seeing the crush and realizing that we probably would not find a place to sit, I yelled at Dmitri to give up. I did not want to get on. I did not feel like standing for a long haul, packed into an overcrowded bus. He yielded to my wish. We went back to the platform.

We were rewarded, because a train came by shortly thereafter, and it was half-empty. This leg of the journey was uneventful. The train was going through more forest than town. As we neared our stop, we crossed a bridge over a river. When we got off, Dmitri told me that it was where we were going. A fence blocked any direct path to the river, and we had to go another way to reach it.

We walked through a village. Dmitri told me that it was a Finnish village. The people living there looked different, more Nordic. Their houses were small. Little vegetable and flower gardens were kept in the yards. I was thinking of taking a photo when an army jeep came by. This deep into rural Russia, I did not want to be mistaken for a spy. So I decided to wait until the jeep disappeared. I was in fear of their fear of foreign espionage. Later one of my Russian friends pointed out that, by then, Russian authorities were much less worried about foreigners than they had been ten years before. I was not in as much danger as I thought, but I preferred to err on the side of caution.

We stopped at a little store. Dmitri wanted me to have a look inside. It looked like a tiny "five and dime," some bar soap on one shelf, clothes on another, toys, and trinkets behind the single glass counter, and some sewing materials. I did not want to buy anything. This was the first sign of further attempts by Dmitri to get me involved in the Russian market. As time progressed, his attempts became more elaborate.

We trudged down a long path that led to the river we had seen before. As we passed a large apartment building, I was told it was a holiday resort. It looked shabby and run down. A big sign stood outside with aquatic symbols, but I could not tell what it said. Already late in the day, maybe 5 or 6 p.m., Dmitri was in a hurry. I wanted to take a photo. Dmitri asked me to wait until a little later. We finally reached our first destination—a little sandy beach on the river, next to a concrete pier. The river looked as wide as a small lake here. A couple of small sailboats, painted blue and red, sails drawn, were tied to a floating dock. Their shape had a Nordic quality. One had a crude masthead in front, basically a carved plank.

Dmitri told me to take a break while he and Alisa unpacked the kayak and assembled it. Ilya stood by and watched. Sometimes Dmitri asked him to fetch something. I wrote awhile in my notebook and took some photos of the river and the boats. I also noticed a small painted shack nearby and photographed that. It had a raised wooden platform in front, reachable by a sharply inclined set of steps. A powerful-looking electric search light was at one corner of the platform. Two donut shaped life preservers were attached to the stilts, which supported the front of the platform.

I watched the kayak assembly process unfold. First, aluminum tubing was assembled into a skeleton. Then canvas was stretched over the tubing and anchored at several places. A green colored outer nylon or plastic sheath went over that. The oars were made from the same light metal as the skeleton of the boat and consisted of tubes attached together. Fully formed, the boat was a long canoe with sides that wrapped over the edges to keep water from splashing into the boat, giving it the look of a kayak. Gear could be stored under the overhanging canvas to keep it dry.

While Dmitri and Alisa struggled to put the boat together, I sat on a bench near them on the concrete pier and searched my pockets for a pack of cigarettes and matches. I wanted to smoke while waiting.

After a time, two young men approached Dmitri. The first, Boris, was dressed in the khaki pants and horizontally striped shirt that navy cadets wore. He was well tanned. The other had casual civilian clothes on and seemed more of a "city-slicker." Boris offered Dmitri assistance. The second boy, noticing my cigarettes, approached me and asked me for one. I was having trouble lighting mine in the strong wind, and he helped me. I gave him a cigarette and one for his friend. Then I asked him to pose for a photo. I took pictures of him and his navy buddy. They were young and confident looking.

With the help of Boris, Dmitri got his boat together. It accommodated two persons with a little room to spare, so it would not hold all of us at once. Dmitri asked me to accompany him and Ilya while Alisa walked ahead with the remaining gear. I told him I had little experience with such boats. He handed me one of the kayak style paddles and said he needed my help. Some more boys appeared. A couple of them helped Alisa with the bags left on shore. A large blue truck pulled up, and the bags were hoisted onto it. Alisa rode with them to our camping spot.

The wind, which was only a breeze when we first got there, has been steadily getting stronger as the sun begins to sink in the sky. Dmitri is in a hurry, because he knows the weather may turn even worse, and he does not want to be on the lake without sufficient light.

I take off my socks and shoes and roll up my pants. We store all our stuff in plastic, nylon, and canvas bags, try to keep everything as dry as possible, and push the boat into the water. Ilya comes along to give the boat more balance. Dmitri shows me how to get into the boat without tipping it. Then he gives me brief instructions on how to paddle, and we set off.

Our canoe trip does not last long. As we head out into the choppy water, I feel the push of Dmitri paddling behind me. I strain hard to paddle. The wind and water blow in our faces. My glasses get wet immediately, and I find it hard to see. The water is choppy; occasionally, waves splash into the boat. Making headway is difficult. If the boat tips over, we have no flotation devices to help us. After a while, we reach the near side of a point of land jutting out from the shore.

We land. Ilya jumps out to meet his mother. Some more young men are there. Some want American cigarettes and ask Dmitri if I am a tourist. After I distribute more cigarettes, I discover that the zipper of my nylon jacket is stuck open. I need to close it to stay warm and dry. While I am desperately tugging at it, Dmitri and Alisa offer to help. They take turns tugging at it. Finally regaining my composure, I realize this should not be a big deal. I tell Dmitri to let me do it, and I free it myself. This is a call for a mini-celebration on their part. "*Molodyets, molodyets!*" (Good job, good job!) they shout. I wonder what the fuss is about and decide I am becoming too dependent on them. They think I am quite helpless.

Ilya goes off with Alisa, taking some stuff from the boat. His mother has found a place to set up camp. Dmitri wants to continue around the point with the canoe. So we set off again. This time, without Ilya in the boat, we do not have the necessary stability to make progress against the wind and waves. We have to head back to shore. Unfortunately, it is a bad spot to land; a lot of sharp rocks and pieces of rusted metal scraps are submerged in the shallow water near the shore. We climb out of the boat. Dmitri begins to push it along the shore. Suddenly Dmitri gets excited and starts shouting "leak, leak!" Our stuff is in danger of getting wet. I help him get as much of it as possible off the boat. Alisa shows up, and together we salvage the situation. I carry some bags to the campsite while they manage the damaged boat.

By now, twilight was approaching. We had only a little time to set up camp. I was worried that my notes and camera, which were in one of the bags on the canoe, had been soaked. Alisa assembled our things in a little clearing in the woods, a short walk from a sandy beach. Several campsites with old-fashioned tents and a few wooden cabins were strewn about the pine forest, which was fairly deep and went up a shallow slope to a ridge. Away from the river was little underbrush, mostly a carpet of pine needles. Though many campers occupied the campsite, it was quiet. I helped build a fire, gathering twigs along with Ilya.

Dmitri and Alisa were putting up a tent, which was made from nylon and of a fairly modern design. I offered to help, but they refused. I examined my baggage: my notebook and camera survived the trip. I wrote in my notebook in the fading light and watched dark colored gulls glide over the lake.

When the tent was ready, Dmitri showed me where to sleep. They brought four sleeping bags, one for each of us. The bags were arranged so Ilya and I slept in the back of the tent, while Dmitri and Alisa slept in the front. Dmitri and I went in search of the park ranger. Dmitri needed advice about getting the canoe fixed. Though the ranger's cabin, complete with a picture of Lenin tacked to the door, was nearby, he was nowhere to be found. Some boys were sawing a tree stump nearby. We returned.

I sat near the fire trying to get my pants to dry. I still felt cold. I hoped the sleeping bag they provided for me was warm. We sat around the campfire for some time. Dmitri and Alisa were discussing what to do about the canoe. They had ambitious plans to move up river every day. Since the canoe was unusable, we had to wait until we could get it repaired. While they chatted, I heard the drone of a large propeller plane high in the sky. I spotted it, and it looked like a military transport of some kind. Dmitri commented that a military airfield was located somewhere in the general area.

Darkness was descending. As in Leningrad, the light took some time to fade. Since we were further north, the perpetual dusk lasted all night. The fire was strong and warming. Alisa provided us with more grape drink as well as tea. We chewed on some *bulka* (thick white bread) for a snack. I decided to try an experiment I put a piece of the bread on a twig and held it over the fire. I singed it enough to make it similar to toast. They seem fascinated by this and tried it themselves. They liked it. I was a "hero" again.

Well past midnight, Ilya went to sleep. The night was as dark as it was going to get, but a dim light remained, giving the scene an eerie quality. I had heard the drone of another plane come and go. The camp was quiet. The wind had settled down. My pants were dry. I finally felt calm after all those nervous and physically exhausting moments on the lake with Dmitri. The idyllic reverie lasted only a few minutes.

If you have ever been near a military jet when it is flying low over the ground, you know that its appearance is most unexpected. It gives no advance warning, no approaching drone. It just shows up. The stillness of the campsite was shattered by the incredibly loud shrieking roar of a Soviet jet fighter flying no more than a few hundred feet overhead. I looked up just in time to see its dark form passing us from the direction of the ridge. It vanished somewhere over the lake, leaving a rumbling sound like the sound of distant thunder. I was shaken but also exhilarated, impressed by the jet's awesome projected power.

F. Russian Outback

Sometimes when you are in a foreign land you forget where you are; your disorientation is complete. On 11 July, I had such a moment when I awakened. I also saw another side of Russia on that day, one less pressured and more open.

In the morning, groggy from sleep, still half-dreaming about the canoe trip, I hear an unfamiliar sound. It is music, a totally alien, melancholy sort of music. Everyone else is asleep, huddled in sleeping bags. I lie there and listen for a long time to the music. It makes me feel sad and lonely. I am held in its grip, and it gives me nothing to fix on, no way of organizing my thoughts.

I crawl out of the tent to hear the music better. I am hearing a Russian folk song. The melody conveys the troubles of Mother Russia to me. I can discern that the song is emanating from a loudspeaker somewhere in the campsite.

I sit outside the tent on a plank that with a couple of boxes Dmitri made into a bench the night before. Last night's campfire is still smoldering. I try feeding it a few twigs to get it going again. A diffuse sunlight shines through the trees. The morning air is chilly, but it is pleasant. I notice that a group of teenage boys and girls has a campsite not too far away. They are talking and laughing among themselves in a relaxed mood. This is the first time I see Russians smiling and joyful in public. Some people come by to visit them, carrying large glass jars with what appears to be stewed fruit *compote* inside.

I wish I can make contact with them but do not have the confidence to do so. After a while, they notice me watching them. A few smiling glances are exchanged. Then a few of them say something to me in Russian. I try to say that I am an American and do not understand. They start giggling after our brief friendly contact.

My reverie was broken when Dmitri came out of the tent. He immediately got busy preparing for breakfast. He told me to gather some more twigs, while he worked on getting a portable Primus stove going. Dmitri took the gathered twigs and expertly built up the fire. He also eventually got the stubborn stove going.

Alisa came out and joined us. She gave me some soap and a towel and told me to wash up at the river. I went there, and Ilya soon followed me. When we returned, Alisa was preparing *kasha* in a white enamel pot and boiling water for coffee in a tin pan on the stove. While I waited, a couple of teenage girls and a boy from the nearby camp brought us a jar of *compote*. I explained to Dmitri that I had "spoken" with them before. The gesture was warmly appreciated; it put us in a good mood. We ate breakfast out of an assortment of metal and plastic dishes. I asked them to assign me a drinking cup, so I do not catch any "foreign germs." This probably struck them as being eccentric, and Alisa joked that maybe she should divide the boiling water in a similar fashion.

After breakfast, Dmitri went in search of help to repair the canoe. Alisa took the dirty dishes to the river to wash them. A light drizzle began. Ilya and I waited in the tent. I showed him some simple games to pass the time, tic-tac-toe, connect-the-dots. He began to speak more with me after this, and occasionally he used English.

A little while later, Dmitri and Alisa returned. Dmitri found a short stocky young man with blonde curly hair to help him with the kayak. The man was in charge of a small group of boys and girls. Something was odd about them. They did not seem to have the vigor of the other youths in the camp; a pallor hung about them. Still, they seemed cheerful enough. Dmitri told him that I was an American in an "unusual situation."

Dmitri told me that the young man wanted to meet me. Though I never asked him, I suspect Dmitri traded the chance to meet an American for help with his kayak. His name was Mikhail, and he was from Belorus (White Russia). He made a point of telling me that White Russian people were never under the yoke of the Tatars or Mongols.

Mikhail was the camp leader of a group of boys and girls from Gomel, a city in Belorus that was affected by the 1986 Chernobyl nuclear accident. I photographed him and the children. Then, borrowing my camera, he took a picture of me with the children. They all had blonde hair like him. He told me he was proud to have a chance to help an American. He also showed me his hunting knife. He related that he was not a supporter of President Gorbachev. This open anti-government statement would have been a punishable offense in the Soviet Union before *glasnost*.

Another factor influenced Mikhail's openness besides the changed political atmosphere. The setting had something to do with it as well. The Karelian forest, far removed from the big cities, conveyed a sense of freedom. The open friendliness of the youths earlier that day would not have occurred so easily in Leningrad.

The canoe repairs were completed in the late morning. Mikhail mended the torn area. Dmitri used resin to fill the cracks and make it watertight. The rain stopped, enabling us to be outside for the rest of the day. In the afternoon, I had a chance to bathe in the river. Dmitri decided that any further camp moves were out of the question. Until the kayak was absolutely seaworthy, he did not want to take a chance. He tested the kayak briefly and was not fully confident that the repair would hold. He planned to seek further assistance before using the kayak again. So we had to stay put that day.

As the sun came out, bathers went to the river, and I got a lesson in Russian modesty. Alisa announced that she would be going swimming and Ilya would be also. She had a skirt on over her bathing suit. She gave me a towel to use if I decided to join them. Ilya was wearing a bathing suit with a tee-shirt. Dmitri was busy with the kayak and other camping needs, so he did not come with us. Alisa and Ilya went to the river first. I stayed behind. They came back a while later. Alisa had her skirt on again, even though she had already been in the water. She told me that the water was warm. I put on my swimming shorts with only a towel over my shoulders, as I would normally do. When I came out of the tent, I startled Alisa. I guessed I was "under dressed" for swimming and ran back into the tent to put on a tee-shirt as well.

I let Alisa and Ilya go on ahead without me. Then I decided to use the opportunity to have a bath. So I looked for some soap but could not find any. A sandy beach allowed swimmers to wade out into a wide part of the river. A shallow slope prolonged the time required to get to water deep enough to swim. I did not see Alisa or Ilya. The shore was uncrowded at the time. A few people were out bathing. Several boats dotted the water, canoes like ours, some powerboats, and a few sailboats. The situation was pleasant and soothing. The water was surprisingly warm, and I swam a little. Ilya joined me at some point. I asked him where Alisa was. He pointed up stream. I could see her in the distance. I did not like the idea of leaving our camp unattended, even though I had the sense that we would not be robbed. I also wanted to ask Alisa about getting some soap. I asked him about soap, and he returned with some and left again. I bathed and then made my way over to Alisa. I wanted to see if she would join me for a swim. I waded toward her and waved to her. She sent Ilya back to me as "emissary." I thanked him for the soap and Ilya headed back to rejoin her. They went back to the camp. I wondered about her shyness. I found the situation amusing and slightly puzzling.

Refreshed, I headed back to the camp and dried off in front of the fire. Dmitri had returned, Alisa was getting midday dinner ready, and Ilya was off collecting firewood. A clothes line had been rigged using a piece of stout fishing line tied around two trees. I hung my wet tee-shirt to dry and changed in the tent.

During lunch, an interesting incident occurred. It was a mini-tragedy for Ilya. Dmitri had given him a tiny fishing apparatus made out of plastic with which to try his luck. He used it earlier in the day and had gotten the line tangled. While we ate *booterbrod* (open faced sandwiches), Ilya was fiddling with his toy. He accidentally dropped it in the fire and let out a cry. Before Dmitri could poke it out with a stick, the fishing contraption was ruined. Dmitri tried to console Ilya, but he would have none of it, ran off a distance. and started to cry in a dramatic way. I was embarrassed for him. I had had my own bad luck with the fire earlier when I was trying to repair my glasses, which had become bent the day before. I ended up partially frying the plastic coating on one of the stems. Only a few minutes later, Ilya returned and was cheerful again. The accident never seemed to bother him or his parents again.

Dmitri decided to try to get some more work done on our project. The first order of business was to set up an "office" where we could work. Dmitri located several logs and another plank and came back to camp to get me to assist him. Dmitri and I chopped and sawed the logs into suitable lengths. He was good at this. I did what I could to help. Alisa watched us. We also split some logs into firewood. Together, all three of us carried the wood and arranged a square of benches around the campfire with an opening so it would be easier to get at the benches. The arrangement served us well, and we worked all afternoon on the project. Later, when we were tired, the conversation turned to earlier subjects from our ongoing discussions about different shared interests. The sun provided us with light, and the campfire kept the early evening chill away.

I was fully relaxed by then; so relaxed that occasionally I immediately and directly grasped what Alisa said to me in Russian. The right side of my brain was operating well. Plunging into a foreign culture is akin to plunging into cold water. Just as the shock of the water wakes up blood circulation, the shock of a new culture wakes up right brain activity.

Early in the day, I ran out of the cigarettes I had brought for the camping trip. I had not anticipated giving half of them away. Dmitri was letting me smoke some of his Russian cigarettes, but they were beginning to turn my stomach. A lack of proper toilet facilities was an added inconvenience. A trench-dug toilet was up the hill near a group of cabins, but Alisa warned me away from using it because she felt it was not sanitary. So, that day, the bushes became my toilet. Despite the inconveniences, my overall mood was positive. This helped Dmitri and me make quick progress in the Russian translation of the test.

While we worked, Dmitri announced that we would be having supper later as guests of Pavel. We met him when we were collecting wood, and he let us use his water dispenser to wash our hands. It was a small metal pail, attached to a tree, with a hole in the bottom. A freely moving steel rod with knobs at both ends acted as a plug. Pushing up on the bottom of the rod released water from the pail.

Pavel ran a kayaking school at the camp and built his own hand-made kayaks. His students occupied the cabins up the hill. He lived in a parked trailer, on top of which he stored the boats when they were not in the water. Since this man's business was kayaks, Dmitri decided to approach him to get a second opinion about the condition of our boat. Pavel promised to examine it the following morning.

Later that evening, three of us were guests of Pavel. Ilya stayed back at the camp. Supper consisted of roasted chunks of beef on skewers, a cold fish salad made from fish caught in the lake mixed with lots of onions and spices, and curds topped with sour cream. Dmitri thought the curd dish was wonderful. Though fresh, the dish was so rich I could hardly digest it. The meat, though tough, tasted good. I never realized beef could have so much flavor.

On this and subsequent trips, I was treated to a variety of Russian foods produced on private gardens and in rural areas. The different foods were much fresher and more flavorful than I was used to eating. After coming home from my trips to Russia, I found most American food bland by comparison. Much of American food is processed and packaged; much of Russian food is pickled or eaten fresh.

Russian food consumes more of an average Russian budget than American food consumes of an average American budget. To save money,

Russians would purchase some food at state shops, but the quality of this food, if available, was generally poor. Keeping a private garden and having access to fresh farm produce was a necessity. Before I paid them, Alisa went out of her way to buy more food at the state stores than she usually did. On subsequent trips to Russia, when I mastered the art of successful negotiations for room and board, I was more well fed by my Russian hosts than in my first trip. They also had access to better food by then, because the Russian consumer market improved after the end of the Soviet regime.

Dmitri introduced me to Pavel, but they spent most of the time talking among themselves until it was quite dark. Electric lights and a fire illuminated the long table and benches on which we sat. At some point, Pavel showed us his trailer. After a while, I started getting bored. I felt like a child since I hardly understood what they were talking about, and Dmitri was too busy conversing to translate for me.

At one point, I began to examine a large hunting knife Pavel had left on the table. Laughing in a nervous manner, Dmitri took it away from me. This annoyed me, but I decided that I should let it go. Besides, I felt tired. I excused myself and went back to the tent. He wanted to accompany me back to the tent with a flashlight, afraid I could not find it in the darkness. Enough light was left so I could see. I told him I would be okay. Already midnight when I returned, they ended up returning well after two in the morning.

I went to sleep immediately, only to wake up a little later. I realized they were still not back. I had to make an emergency trip to the bushes. Fortunately, I found the toilet paper we had brought. Early the next morning, I decided to chance a trip to the outhouse up the hill. It was not a pleasant experience. The main problem was that the crude outdoor latrine had not been dug deep enough. Despite this, I felt better and slept for awhile.

G. Pavel's Story

On Friday, our third day camping and last full day there, we finished the Russian translation of the HVP, and I got to know Pavel. In the late morning, after returning from the river with his pupils, Pavel fixed Dmitri's boat for the last time. While the glue was drying, he took Dmitri, Alisa, and me on a motor boat ride up the river (to the east). Everyone got life jackets and a heavy parka to wear. The weather was cloudy and windy so the river would be cold. My parka smelled bad but was warm enough. Pavel offered me cigarettes along the way. The craft, no more than a rowboat with a motor attached, went pretty fast, and the strong breeze chilled me.

We passed many small cottages along the edge of the river. Pavel told us that Baltic peoples, Swedes, and Russians all lived here with no problems. Perhaps he had expected ethnic tensions among them. He related the history of the land, who had controlled it. He said that it was possible to reach my country from this river. (I checked later, and he was right.)

I was glad that we were going to see the place we would have camped if our boat had not sprung a leak. We landed at a sandy beach where the river divided just about the time the sun broke through the clouds. They asked me if I wanted to go swimming, but I felt it would be too cold. I could see why Dmitri had wanted to camp here. No one was around. We would have had the place to ourselves.

I had a chance to observe Pavel. He was short, shorter than Dmitri, and thin. His face was purposeful, with sharp, aquiline features. This, and his strong neck, gave him an air of authority. He moved his head as a bird does, eyeing me from the side with his brown eyes, but never looking directly at me. His short cropped hair and clean shaven face gave him a military look. He was athletic and every bit as strong as Dmitri, but leaner. His whole manner projected a sharp intelligence and tension, which contrasted with the easygoing manner of Mikhail, the White Russian I met earlier. Alisa and Dmitri referred to him as a "true Russian." They related to me that Pavel claimed to be a champion kayak builder. I felt on edge, uncomfortable around him. He spoke with intensity. His "speech pressure" manifested stress from within him and gave his voice a commanding ring.

He told us that recently one of his pupils had gotten sick with cancer, went to the United States to be treated, and never returned. Later he talked about his family: His wife was in Kiev with their small son, and his older son was in Vietnam. In the past, the Nazi occupation and the subsequent Soviet liberation affected his mother and father. He also had a surrogate family: He was a "supervisor" of some young boys back in Leningrad, and he let some family's *babushka* stay in one room of his place there.

After our boat ride was over, Dmitri and I finished our work on the Russian profile. Dmitri was satisfied. I was pleased but knew that our task was not complete. Pomeroy had requested a sample of Russian responses to the profile. He also asked me to try to find a linguist to verify the translation. I had a challenge still ahead of me.

While we were working, I noticed that the young campers had departed. Some thin and angular people, dark haired, swarthy looking folk, now occupied their spot. They were busy felling a tall pine tree. I was amazed at this brazen behavior in a public park. I told Dmitri and Alisa that these people would have been arrested for doing that in an American public park. It was their turn to be amazed. Dmitri explained that these people came from Central Asia where trees were rare and wood expensive. They probably planned to bring the wood back with them to sell. I explained that this park seemed to be wild, lacking in any rules, and I alluded to the poor sanitary conditions. They seemed interested. I explained that in my country we had national parks controlled and maintained by the state, with the funds provided by tax dollars. Alisa thought that it was a noble concept.

When our work was done, Dmitri took me with him to try out the canoe. It worked fine, and we paddled for a long time up and down the lake. The water was calm. The sun had come out making it pleasant. Occasionally we had to avoid swarms of mosquitoes. Other canoes and boats were on the lake. Wary of the motor boats and afraid a reckless boater might swamp us, I was relieved that they never came close. We went all the way to where the lake narrowed and was fed by the shallow rapid river. There, I could see men in single-occupant sports kayaks practicing maneuvers in the rough water.

During this trip, Dmitri related a cautionary tale to me. Sometime back, a researcher, someone like me, had come to the Soviet Union to study the culture. Unbeknownst to the Soviet authorities, this investigator had a hidden agenda: He was there to study homosexual behavior in the Soviet Union. Eventually the Soviet authorities found out about it. After this, the investigator was asked to leave the country and was put on a list of those not welcome back. Dmitri was not just passing time. He wanted to warn me in case I had any hidden agendas of my own.

After our canoe trip, Dmitri told me that Pavel was interested in speaking with me. I learned more about him from Dmitri. His kayak school was more than just a routine summer camp. He had been training potential Olympic kayakers for some time.

Pavel arrived for supper. He had plenty of time on his hands. The kayaking class had ended. He had given his students their final exam in the morning. One of the girls had refused to take it and was upset. You could hardly blame her, for it consisted of a plunge off a bridge into the river. Single person kayaks are extremely maneuverable, buoyant, and capable of acrobatic feats.

As we sat around the fire, Pavel began to tell more stories. He told us about an incident that occurred when he was a young boy during the Great Patriotic War (World War II). A German had gotten caught behind enemy lines in Russian territory. He sought refuge in the home of his parents. They had kept him for only a short time when a Russian officer came looking for the man. The Russian was a cruel man and, upon arresting the German, began to beat him. Pavel's parents intervened, driving the officer away. Pavel remembered biting the officer on the leg. Pavel did not relate what consequences his parents suffered after this incident. He was still preoccupied with the ethics of the situation. Were they right to protect the German from the Russian officer? After all, the Germans were the enemy responsible for the devastation of Russia.

I expressed the opinion that he and his parents did not act immorally. It was a natural reaction. They were protecting a man's life, regardless of the larger picture. He shook his head and said that it was not so simple. The conversation turned to the general conditions of the Soviet Union at the time. He seemed bitter that many Russians left the Soviet Union. I said that, given the horrendous conditions, they had every right to leave if they could. He countered by saying that they abandoned their country in its time of greatest need.

This is a crucial question when it comes to Russians and the Soviet Union. How did most Russians react to their leaders' calls for sacrifice? What is a country's value? Is it more valuable than an individual human being? Is it an abstraction that is not worth the cost in human toll?

At one point, Dmitri and Pavel discussed something at length. I asked Dmitri to translate. Dmitri told me that Pavel was discussing a personal problem with him. I waited patiently. It struck me how quickly they had become friends. Thinking back on it, Dmitri, as a trained psychologist, had a knack of getting people to open up. He got to work on me later.

Deep into the night, Pavel turned the conversation to its ultimate purpose. He began by relating a story about an American businessman who had come for a visit some years earlier. His visit occurred during the first year after the Soviet authorities had opened the zone in which we were. Before that, the area was closed to foreigners. The American had sought out Pavel. He was interested in buying a large quantity of kayaks that Pavel would build, and he planned to sell them in America. Pavel rejected the man's proposal, feeling that, even though he would have made more money than he ever had before, he was being set up for "exploitation."

An unpleasant incident also contributed to Pavel's general mistrust of visiting tourists. A group of English tourists came for a visit. One of the women in the party lost a nightshirt. A Russian woman had it in her possession. The English accused her of stealing it, and the shirt was returned. Pavel felt the tourists behaved poorly. This puzzled me. Why was it the English people's fault? Maybe something got lost in the translation, so I asked Pavel for clarification, all to no avail. I concluded that it was not a matter of who took what, but that the incident was unsettling, or that the confrontational nature of the English bothered him. By having nice things were they "tempting" the poorer Russians?

Pavel was also worried about Russian officials opening up the area to Finnish tourists such as the kayakers Dmitri and I had seen on our canoe trip that afternoon. This land had been part of Finland until Stalin launched a bloody campaign to push back the border. Pavel reflected that he might be old fashioned.

Pavel told me I was the second American he met. He was interested in doing business, not for profit, but for the enjoyment. He wanted to open his kayak school to foreigners. Could I find interested parties back in the States to do business? I said that I would see what I could do. There, so far away from any pressing responsibilities, I got caught up in Pavel's enthusiasm and flattering hospitality, even if I had no experience in tourism or kayaking. Pavel went into quite a bit of detail about his plans: how long the schooling would last, how it would include a tour of Leningrad, and so on. He would let me be the middleman, making whatever profit I wished. His manner concerning the matter was that it was an ugly necessity. I felt naively ecstatic. Before, I had been treated like a child. Suddenly, I was all grown up, a budding "businessman." We closed the deal with a slug of tea, since no vodka at hand.

Daylight was returning when we finished our business. I was exhausted. Pavel seemed to change his mind at one point and asked me if I might be too busy with my studies back home to do this. I said that I was willing to give it a try, and we left it at that. By this point, I just wanted to get to sleep.

H. Going Home

Saturday was a bright sunny day. The time had come to head back. Pavel left that morning, packing up all his kayaks on a truck. We came to say goodbye. I took a photo or two. He gave me his Leningrad address and told me to write when I was ready. Pavel was not heading home immediately. He and part of his entourage were traveling to another part of Russia. Pavel presented me with some Russian chocolate before he left.

Dmitri took me out on the canoe for a short trip so I could take a photo of the camping site on the shore. Later, I went with Ilya. Without Dmitri's strong paddling, heading back against the current was difficult. Then Dmitri took Alisa in the canoe. Earlier, he had complained to me that Alisa was not a good rower, but he seemed enthusiastic when they went. They made an odd pair. He wore Nordic style swimming trunks, a tee-shirt, and sneakers. She wore a colorful, flower-printed dress. The scene had an old fashioned flavor about it. The young lady was dressed up in her Sunday best, while her admirer took her out on a rowboat in the pond.

We slowly disassembled the camp during the morning. Alisa began packing stuff when Dmitri and I were saying goodbye to Pavel. Dmitri helped her when I took Ilya with me on the canoe. Later, when I was packing, Ilya went for a final swim.

Dmitri decided that he and Alisa would take the canoe back with most of our stuff. Meanwhile Ilya led me to the landing spot along a path. He had become more relaxed around me and often translated simple things for me. He acted as my guide. Along the way, we passed families with small children playing on the shore. I noticed that all the little girls had their hair tied with ribbons. It distinguished their gender because they wore bathing suits with no tops. It was also a display of status—that they were being taken good care of.

We waited with our bags by the landing spot for Dmitri and Alisa. Since this day was Saturday, weekenders had begun arriving in number. Plenty of boaters were on the lake. In the middle was an unusual looking boat, something out of "Sinbad the Sailor." This ancient looking sailboat was a tourist attraction.

The canoe came at last. Dmitri and Alisa spread out a tarpaulin and began the final packing. Dmitri, sensing that I was bored standing there unneeded for the time being, suggested that I go see the Finnish kayakers on the rapids. He sent Ilya, who knew the way to the place, with me. As we followed a trail along the river, I noticed that, besides some rusted pieces of metal scrap in the water, no garbage of any kind littered the bank.

On this my last day at this remote and idyllic spot, I sat on a granite boulder and absorbed the atmosphere. The boaters nearby were busy plying their craft, and some fishermen were a half-kilometer upstream, standing close to a bridge that spanned the river. Many of the fishermen wore the uniforms of authority, including police, but apparently they were off duty. At the time, I wondered if they wore uniforms because they did not have other clothes to wear.

Reflecting on it, I cannot imagine they were that poor. They may have been wearing their uniforms because they wanted to flaunt that, in this place, they could forget about their formal roles. If some of them were supposed to be on the job, nobody cared to find out.

"Policemen fishing?" I thought, and I found it hard to imagine, but that is what was happening. The scene had an amusing and oddly soothing quality to it. The sound of rushing water over the rocks muffled any sound of voices, and almost nobody was talking. I had not felt so at peace in a long time.

I watched the kayakers awhile. Some came quite close to my spot, skillfully maneuvering their craft between rocks, catching little eddies in the current to turn their boats around. They had a characteristic look that was not Russian—red hair, and beards. Most Russians are clean shaven and do not have red hair. Dmitri, with his heavy beard, seemed a throwback to an earlier Russia.

I mused about the place and thought about a danger beyond Pavel's imagination. He had been concerned with Finnish tourists. I thought of America and its fast food places and resort monopolies. I thought that here was a place that did not have and did not need McDonald's, Burger King, and Resorts International. I thought that, if there was any social compensation for years of bloody dictatorship, this was it, a place uncrowded and not commercialized, far off the beaten path, and away from the prying eyes of ambitious businessmen. A reciprocal compensation for the semi-poverty of this half-tamed place was peace of mind and a kind of untamed freedom that is difficult to find anymore in America.

In America, even remote places are under some kind of management or off limits. Freedom in The United States is a matter of a set of laws protecting individuals, and how those laws are interpreted in different situations. Though it was not officially permitted because the Soviet Union nominally owned everything, freedom did exist here. It came from a tacit understanding that you would not be bothered in this place, partly because commercial development was prohibited, and partly because the state at that time was not interested in oppressing everybody within its domain. In the cities, towns, and villages, authority presided. In the countryside, authority could look the other way, and its representatives took the time to relax.

I reflected on the hard work required of me to get to this place, the hurdles overcome. I felt lucky to be sitting on this piece of granite in Karelia. Lost in thought, I suddenly became aware that I was experiencing a mild euphoria. The shimmering water distorted the rocks, and they appeared to be moving in a wave like motion. I climbed out of my deeply relaxed meditative state shortly before Ilya came back to fetch me. I marked the rock I was on with a piece of gum to leave a little bit of my presence in this place to which I had little chance of returning.

I took a photo, and we walked back, passing the policemen fishing near the pier on their day of rest. Dmitri and Alisa were almost finished packing; canvas sacks were lined up near them. The canoe had been disassembled, and they were discussing how to pack it. Alisa had switched back to pants, and Dmitri had on his jeans. I noticed other women wearing pants and realized how this little detail could dramatically alter the image you had of them. The addition of pants to their wardrobe gave the Russian women an up-to-date look I had not considered before.

The kayak's canvas sack was carefully wrapped around the disassembled aluminum structure and the folded skin of the boat. Then it was placed on the dolly as we reached the walkway leading past the apartment complex at the beginning of the park. We made it to the railway station and prepared to rejoin civilization. As we waited, I started to feel tense. Away for what seemed like eternity, soon I would be going back to their flat, back to the problems concerned with paying them, and back to work on finishing the project. As we waited for the train, Dmitri commented to me how different this trip had been. Never had he met so many people. He had not expected the help he received with the canoe. I figured I had something to do with this attention, because for a Russian to have an American tourist in tow here was so novel.

I had had a chance to observe Dmitri and Alisa interact with other people. I was struck by how characteristic Alisa's manner of speaking (high pitched and plaintive) was of Russian women. At times, I mistook other Russian women for her because they spoke with a similar tone of voice.

Dmitri was quite a go-getter, using my presence to his full advantage, thereby steadily climbing the social ladder. Rungs in the ladder were Boris and his friend, who got some Camels for their trouble, the helpful Mikhail, who had a chance to meet an American and take photos, and Pavel, a fixture at the camp, who had a chance to attempt a "joint-venture" with an American. Dmitri managed skillfully to cultivate an enduring relationship with a more important person. Despite this, Dmitri had some flaws that would fully manifest themselves later. Hints existed at the time. I was already upset by the manner in which he and Alisa handled negotiations over money. I offered to pay them up front, but had instead been drawn into a lengthy game of nerves. Even though Dmitri had begun to earn his keep by his continuous translations, and Alisa had been keeping house for me, albeit with poor fare, I still felt apprehensive about how events would unfold, and I felt an overall lack of control of the situation. I was tired of being treated like a child.

On the way back, Ilya was deposited back with Alisa's parents. At the camp, I had been "adopted," being called "Gariski," a diminutive form of my name. I did not think I would be "Gariski" when we got back. Dmitri filled me in on some details on the upcoming trip to Latvia. He first broke the news to me at camp, where I speculated about possibly getting some samples for Pomeroy in Latvia after I found out that many Russians would be there.

Four

SOCIAL NETWORKS IN ACTION: RIGA, LATVIA

1. Overview

This chapter continues the narrative started in the previous chapter. As an anthropologist, in order to do my job, I had to branch out and expand my network of contacts. At first, I was under Dmitri's strict control. He and his wife had mapped out a series of activities that I was to engage in while in the Soviet Union. Other than Eileen, whom I met by chance on my plane trip to Russia, I initially had no other contacts besides Dmitri and those to whom he introduced me. Opportunities presented themselves as time went on, and I was able to take advantage of them. I found that, by being assertive, I was able to expand my social network and get some flexibility in what I wanted to study there. Sometimes assertiveness led to an entirely new contact, such as Andrey. In another case, it led to a creative exploitation of a relationship that Dmitri originated, namely my relationship with Anatol.

As my social base expanded, my relationships and activity became more complex. Soon, I found myself in the middle of intrigues, as my different Russian and Soviet acquaintances struggled with each other and me to influence the direction of my research. Putting it another way, I encountered the different social networks of the natives.

My long range goal was to accumulate time in Russia adequate for ethnographic research. My 1991 trip lasted only a few weeks and was a pilot study. It determined whether I would return to Russia to do follow up work.

Differences between the Soviet satellite state of Latvia and the major Russian metropolis of Leningrad appear in this part of my journey. Latvians were undergoing a low-key revolution at the time. Signs of the tension between the Soviet overlords and the citizens of Riga appear here and there in this portion of the narrative. Also present is the Latvian sense of life, which is Western-oriented and fast paced in contrast to the heavy and depressed spirit I saw in Leningrad at that time. My Latvian friends, toughened by years of Soviet occupation, were still full of optimism for their future. Signs of the crumbling Soviet infrastructure appear in Riga and Leningrad as do signs of the ever present Soviet military. While interaction between civilization and nature is a prevalent theme in the previous chapter, here the focus is on the struggle between competing groups within civilization. Nature takes a secondary role as a backdrop and has a different meaning. Latvia was a playground, like Karelia, to many Russians, albeit a more sophisticated one. This chapter describes how I encountered more of this side of Soviet life.

The narrative resumes the day after Dmitri, Alisa, and I returned to Dmitri's flat from our camping trip in the Karelian forest. On the way back,

Dmitri discussed his plans to travel to Riga, Latvia, where he was going to hold a business training seminar. We had one free day (a Sunday) before leaving Leningrad again. I planned to meet my Irish friend, Eileen, and asked Dmitri to help me find the place of rendezvous, a Polish Catholic Church. Not knowing much about Leningrad at the time of our plane trip, Eileen and I had inadvertently picked a place that was out of the way.

2. Looking for Eileen (14–15 July)

Sunday, 14 July, was overcast. Dmitri took me to the Catholic church where I had arranged to meet Eileen. We left early to see some of Leningrad before heading to the church. Dmitri wanted to show me St. Isaac's Cathedral. Originally a place of worship, it had been converted into a museum by the Communists. After two bus rides, we reached the cathedral.

Upon entering the building, we saw an interior made from rose colored marble and several groups of tourists near some central pillars. I wanted to join one, but Dmitri insisted on showing me around himself. I had grown weary of Dmitri, irritated by his heavily accented, butchered English. I appreciated his enthusiasm, but that just made it more difficult to keep him quiet.

Dmitri was trying to explain one of the exhibits to me. I was having a difficult time understanding him when I heard a much more lucid explanation of the same thing coming from right behind me. An attractive young Russian female guide was explaining the exhibit to a group of tourists. Several seconds passed before I realized that she was not using English but Spanish, a language I had studied. Unlike my earlier struggles with it, I suddenly understood it for a while. The guide spoke a schooled Spanish, free of the oddities of style and accent that can obscure the language to a non-native speaker. I joined the back of the group for a minute or two until I could no longer understand her, the moment of heightened perception having passed.

Dmitri took me to the observation deck at the top of the cathedral. To get up there cost us a few rubles. The observation deck had a splendid view of Leningrad. I took pictures in all directions. In the foreground was an assortment of tourist sights; the blue-green Winter Palace and Palace Square with its central column; the gold spire of the Admiralty, a former dockyard, now a park; Senate Square, where I had seen the statue of Peter the Great the previous Sunday; the former Mariinsky Palace, now "city hall" (Executive Committee of the Leningrad Soviet of People's Deputies); and the Astoria Hotel. Beyond them across the Neva were domed cathedrals, the Peter and Paul Fortress, and the palatial buildings housing Leningrad State University. Far in the distance, tall radio towers, construction cranes, and high rise apartment complexes could be seen. A sea of rooftops, green copper roofs, red tiled roofs, tin roofs, and dark pitch roofs, dominated the cityscape. A melange of colors delighted the senses from the red bricked Astoria, to the bright yellow of the former senate, to the totalitarian gray of city hall. Prince Dmitri was showing me his realm.

We strolled down broad Nevsky Avenue toward the red-rose colored Anichkov Palace, where we would head off the main thoroughfare. I found the famous four horses of sculptor Peter Klodt at the nearby bridge spanning the Fontanka Canal. The quartet depicted the taming of a wild horse by a young man, a symbol of the struggle of civilization to tame the forces of nature. The nineteenth-century sculptures spoke of a time when Russians were confident in their mastery of nature, a stark contrast to the decaying city conditions I witnessed in the late twentieth century.

On the way, we found an open-air market where I bought a chess set that cost the ruble equivalent of a few dollars. I was wary of the police hanging around and asked Dmitri if I could pay with American dollars, as I had a small amount. He was not sure. The vendor was honest and said she would take rubles or dollars; she preferred dollars but taking them was not strictly legal. I decided to play it safe and pay with my remaining rubles. Afterwards, Dmitri mentioned that the policemen hanging around were more for protection against bandits than anything else. This was one of the "gray markets" where trade in rubles was allowed. Trade in *valuta* (foreign currency) was not, but it nevertheless occurred.

Then we went to find the church in a part of town with which I was not familiar. We located it on a side street in the Polish section of the city. Before finding it, while walking on one of the streets off Nevsky, I saw a military jeep, parked outside a building. The men on it jumped out and ran into the building in what appeared to be an exercise or drill. We did not stick around.

The church was not large. No activity was taking place, and the doors were closed. Eileen was not there. After waiting a few minutes, we tried knocking on the door to get someone's attention. A man came out and explained that the service would be later. I wanted to wait in case Eileen arrived. After a while, I became tired, and to kill time we went in search of a street vendor Dmitri had spotted on the way.

Unlike America, where soda pop can be purchased almost anywhere, in Leningrad, it was hard to find. None of the state grocery stores or supermarkets sold soda, and you could not find gas station convenience stores. I later encountered a few kiosks and open-air markets where Pepsi was occasionally available. You could also go to a tourist hotel and pay inflated prices for one. Vending machines as we know them were not to be found. The Soviets had a funny attempt at them. Machines that dispensed some brownish fizzy liquid (*kvas* - a mildly alcoholic, sweet, beer-like drink) into a large plastic glass could be found here and there. Dmitri did not trust them. They had the obvious drawback of being unsanitary. The machines had only one glass with a faucet to let you rinse the glass in tap water, which was insufficient to kill bacteria. Even if the glass could be sanitized, just the idea of sharing it with thousands of others was enough to disgust me. Yet these machines were used. Dmitri found a vendor selling the same kind of drink out of individual glasses set up on a table, like a child's lemonade stand.

We headed back to the Polish Roman Catholic Church. Some people had started to gather in front of it, but no sign of Eileen existed. We still had some time left to kill. Dmitri wanted me to see a different church. I gave up on the idea of hanging around; Eileen would be at the service, or she would not. So we went to see Dmitri's church (Transfiguration Cathedral).

The cathedral was a few blocks away, painted blue with the traditional onion domes. Unlike the Catholic Church, this place was full of people. A service was in progress; the sound of music and chanting combined with the twinkle of dozens of lit candles here and there in the semi-darkness of the interior. Even though the church service was in session, the place had the atmosphere of a hushed market, with independent activities at different locations. Dmitri purchased a couple of small candles at a crowded little counter located in front of the church near the door. At the back to one side, a priest chanted from a book, with a small congregation standing before him. Music came from somewhere hidden, a choir perhaps. To the other side, candleholders sat on tables near pillars that supported a series of interconnected arches. The arches divided the church into a series of domed areas. Gilded icons of saints hung on the pillars. Little clusters of people stood near the icons, praying to the saint of their choice. I followed Dmitri to one icon and watched him light the candles. He was praying for a safe and successful trip to Latvia.

By comparison, the Catholic church was small and plain. We got back in time for the service to begin. Inside was little decoration, with only the crucified image of Christ above the altar. Dmitri and I sat at a pew near the back. My chess set rattled in my bag, and this drew disapproving looks as we edged into the pew. Most of the worshippers were old women. I looked around and did not see Eileen.

The mass was entirely in Polish. Dmitri and I did not understand any of it. I knew the ritual and followed it, except for communion. The whole affair was gloomy for me. I had stopped practicing Catholicism, and only went to masses when visiting my family. My goal had been to meet Eileen. Dmitri found the service interesting. After it ended, he commented that Roman Catholicism seemed like a depressing, pessimistic religion to him, and he found Russian Orthodoxy to be bright and gay in comparison.

I was not entirely surprised that Eileen had not come. By now, I sensed the immensity and complexity of the city and knew a whole range of factors could have prevented her from coming. I knew that I had lost a chance to compare notes with her to determine what I should be paying Dmitri and Alisa before the trip to Latvia. I had decided that, instead of trying to find a place to change traveler's checks in Leningrad, I would wait until I got to Latvia. Then Alisa would expect payment.

The next day, I tried to contact Eileen before we left. I had a thin lead. Eileen, not having much information about the family she would be staying with, gave me two numbers to call at the Smolny Institute. Using that and her name, I asked Dmitri to help me in an attempt to locate her.

Our experience was a lesson in Soviet protocol. Dmitri did the best he could, meeting resistance at every turn. He repeated Eileen's name several times into the phone as if the connection was bad. He explained that she was a foreign volunteer worker at a hospital connected with the institute. At first, the other party said that no person by that name had anything to do with the institute, but Dmitri was persistent. After several calls, a few heated conversations, and following a trail of phone numbers, Dmitri managed to get the name of the family with whom she was staying, but no more. The only clue to Eileen's whereabouts was someone mentioning that she was in the suburbs to the south of Leningrad, visiting Petrodvorets (a restored eighteenth century imperial residence). Lacking a phone number or address we were stuck since Leningrad had no residential telephone directory. (Phone books appeared in 1992, but they had to be purchased in book stores, when available.)

Alisa finally got impatient with us and asked Dmitri to help her. Dmitri was supposed to be preparing for the trip, and she did not want him wasting any more time on my account. Dmitri had to give a seminar at the conference in Riga. He spent the rest of the day preparing for it. I kept busy copying the entire translation of Leon Pomeroy's test into my notebook.

At one point, while I was sitting on the couch in the living room jotting down notes, I noticed Dmitri and Alisa discussing a tape they were planning to use at the seminar. Dmitri had let me listen to this tape earlier on a portable Sony cassette player. The tape was from a course called "Lifespring" that had been given in Leningrad by a group of visiting Americans who produced human potential seminars. Dmitri's and Vasili's families had attended. This is where Vasili had first encountered Dale Carnegie books.

Dmitri was proud of his Sony tape player, which had been presented to Dmitri by Japanese hosts in Kyoto, Japan, where he had attended a psychology conference and met Pomeroy. It had an AM/FM radio as well. Dmitri liked to play it often. One of his favorite songs was entitled "You're in the Army Now," a Russian rock-and-roll remake of the original American marching tune. Dmitri would sing along with the revised English lyrics and hop around the living room: "You're in the Army now! You're not a student now…."

He did not want to risk having his "boom box" stolen or damaged during the trip. I had brought a spare tape recorder. I offered to let him borrow it. I tried to explain that it was mainly a tape recorder not a tape player, but maybe it would suffice. When they played the tape on it, the audio had poor quality, and the musical portions sounded awful. Amused by this piece of inferior American technology, they turned me down and brought the Sony. At moments like these, I became frustrated because I could not demonstrate to them the true nature of the electronic gadgets available in my country. My poor old tape recorder was not representative. I kept my primary recorder, a micro-cassette recorder, mostly out of sight and did not lend it to them.

3. An Excursion to Latvia (15–20 July)

In the early evening, we finished packing and headed for the Baltic Railroad Station, which was located in the southwestern part of Leningrad. To get there, we took a bus to Finland Train Station, located on the north side of the city, and then used the underground metro (subway). Finland Station was a bewildering, crowded place. Inside the main concourse was a connection to the subway. Steeply pitched escalators led deep into the earth. The escalators were faster than I was used to, and I had to concentrate getting on and off. Lamps on posts between the escalators lighted the way.

At the bottom of the escalators were glass booths, each with a female attendant watching the stream of people go by. I was unsure of their purpose; they were not there to collect fares—tokens were purchased before getting on the escalators, and deposited at turnstiles. These women seemed to have nothing to do. I learned later that they did have a purpose. I wished our subways had similar attendants: They were there to watch for hooligans. They also scolded anyone running down the steps of the escalator. They made sure that children held onto the rail of the escalator and that they were traveling accompanied by an adult. They could provide directions. If an escalator stopped they could call for assistance.

People milled around the subterranean platform. Metro trains came often and were packed. They were free of graffiti—the whole place was kept clean. Our ride did not last long, just a few stops. Getting to the up bound escalators involved bucking people streaming into the station. Along with dozens of other travelers, we spilled out from the metro directly onto the main open air platform of the Baltic Railroad Station.

The old and dingy station was a terminal serving points south and southwest of Leningrad. Several locomotives, some military green, others gray, with long trains of similarly colored cars behind them, abutted the concrete platform that marked the northern end of the line. Brass crests bearing the hammer and cycle insignia of the Soviet Union marked the front of each locomotive.

Alisa and I waited by a gray colored train with a faded orange stripe while Dmitri went to an office to ask some questions about our tickets. He had purchased them before I came to Leningrad. Eleven o'clock was approaching. White Nights were over, so the remaining light was fading quite rapidly. Groups like us dotted the station, standing near or sitting on luggage.

When Dmitri came back, he told me that he and I would be traveling together, and Alisa would be in a separate coach. Dmitri and I had second class tickets. These tickets gave us two spots in a four person compartment called a *coupey*. Alisa would be traveling in a third class car, apparently a communal arrangement. These were the only tickets Dmitri had been able to muster. Alisa and Dmitri bid each other a good night.

Dmitri explained to me that I would be traveling "as a Russian" and that this was a "very dangerous situation." He wanted me to be alert and cautious because, technically, foreigners were supposed to ride in special Intourist coaches, which were much more expensive. Intourist was the monopoly controlling tourism in the Soviet Union. I was not to speak in English—not speak at all if possible—until we found our compartment on the train. A young brown-uniformed conductor, probably in his teens, examined our tickets before we got on the front end of our coach. I kept my mouth shut and tried to assume the bored look of a person who had taken this trip often. Dmitri led me down a narrow passage with half open doors to berths on our left and windows to our right until we came to our *coupe*. Dmitri slid the heavy metal door back and we peeked inside. It was empty.

"This is very good," said Dmitri as he closed the door. He explained the arrangements. We would take the bunks on the right, which faced the direction of our travel. Up above was a metal deck with a pair of mattresses and pillows. The conductor would bring us sheets and blankets for which he would collect a fee. A small netted rack hung above the top bunk where personal items could be put. Clothes hooks were available for both bunks.

Dmitri showed me where to store our bags. The bottom bunk swung up to reveal a luggage compartment. He would sleep on the bottom bunk. I would have the top. A small fold-down metal table projected from the window side. I sat near the window and Dmitri by the door. Opposite us was the same arrangement. Up above, the muddy colored ceiling looked old. It was fitted with ancient looking light fixtures. I was surprised that everything worked. Dmitri showed me the light switches. A radio speaker attached to the wall was silent. Dmitri told me that it would come on after the train started. It had a volume control knob but no on-off switch and no tuner.

Nobody had shown up yet, so Dmitri was pleased by the situation. He had a chance to show me the ropes, and we could put our bags away before our companions arrived. The train started to rumble as the engines started. The radio came on at the same time, playing Russian pop music. It could not be turned off, but the volume could be adjusted. Whoever was coming were taking their time arriving. I began to wonder if we would have the place to ourselves. I pulled out a book (*The Structure of Value*) that Pomeroy had given me to help us with the project. I began to settle in for what I thought would be a fruitful discussion with Dmitri about the theoretical background of the HVP test. I noticed that he was a little edgy as we began our discussion.

The train lurched forward. As it began to slowly pull out of the station, I started to relax. Just at this moment, the first man made his appearance. He was tall and lanky with slicked-back black hair outlining a darkly tanned square face with an impish grin. His grin made me think that he was "pulling a fast one" on us. I guessed he was approximately my age, maybe younger. He disappeared as quickly as he appeared. Dmitri turned to me and said, wondering, "Only one?" We went back to our book. I hoped that maybe the stranger had gone away for good.

I got nervous again when the same man returned with another similar but shorter and stockier man wearing a baseball cap. They were definitely not Russian, being perhaps from the Caucuses. They appeared to be street wise. These men were traveling light; each of them had an expensive looking knapsack. They both wore matching black tee-shirts with the stenciled word, "Paris," long, pleated gray slacks, and loafers. "Trouble," I thought, "dull company at best." Dmitri immediately began speaking in Russian with the taller man. I nervously fingered my book and looked out the window at the moonlit landscape rolling by the train. I knew ignoring the strangers was not possible.

The shorter man sitting opposite me peered at me with an almost silly look on his face. I noticed that he seemed older than his companion. Nervous, I tried to avoid looking at him and watched the younger man speaking with Dmitri. I sensed that Dmitri was doing his best to diffuse the tense situation. When the first man arrived, we had been speaking half in English and half in Russian—I did not let my guard down and was trying to use every Russian word I knew.

A knock on the door interrupted the conversation. The young conductor who had checked our tickets when we boarded the train appeared. He had the rest of the bedding. Dmitri paid for our share. The boy checked our tickets again and asked if any of us wanted coffee.

After the conductor went away, Dmitri explained that our companions were from Azerbaijan. They lived in the *Kharabakh*, a forested region that was undergoing a civil war. The American media referred to the place as Nagorno-Kharabakh. This added to the intrigue of meeting these men. They told us that they were brothers: The shorter, older looking one, seated across from me, needed an operation for a stomach ailment. They were traveling to Riga to a hospital in which the operation could be performed. Dmitri asked them why they were traveling with so little luggage for such a long journey. They explained that they stayed with friends in Moscow from where they just came. Traveling to Leningrad first was the best way of getting a train to the Baltic.

The conductor brought us coffee served in glasses with metallic mug-like holders. Before departing with his payment, he told us we would arrive in Riga at eight in the morning. The conversation resumed. It turned out they both spoke a little English. That made it easier for me to understand what they were saying. The man sitting across from me was "Frank," his younger, taller brother was "Tony." They told us that, when they first showed up, they had correctly surmised that we were not both Russians and that one of us was an American, but, since Dmitri had been speaking more in English, they mistook me for the Russian. The revelation of this little mix-up broke the ice.

Combining the facts that Nagorno-Kharabakh contains a high percentage of Armenians, that the men had Christian names, and that Azerbaijanis are

Muslim while Armenians are mostly Christian, yields the conclusion that these men were most likely Armenians.

Tony was curious about me, especially my country, and asked many questions. Only about four months had passed since the war with Iraq, which he referred to as the "Winter War." He wanted to know what people in the United States thought of this war. I told him that most people were happy that it was over and that the United States won with a minimum of American casualties, but that the decision to go to war had by no means been unanimous; the country had been deeply divided over it, and bitter feelings remained. I told him that I had opposed going to war and did not relish the thought of my country being responsible for the death of thousands of Iraqis. This was a bit of a revelation to him because he had the impression that all Americans had been for the war. He then commented that the United States would not have gone to war if oil had not been an issue. I agreed. He shook his head and muttered that he thought so.

Frank joined the conversation. He wanted to know what Americans thought about Azerbaijan. I told him that we did not know much about his country except about the civil war in Nagorno-Kharabakh where he lived. They both agreed that this was a big problem but did not say much else. I then asked them how my country was perceived. They responded that they regarded my country as being full of "sportsmen." I thought about this for a second and asked them if they saw President George Bush on television. Yes, they did. Then I realized how strong an impression a country's leader can make about the nature of his country. Bush was often seen in the U. S. news giving impromptu press conferences in a yacht while fishing or out on a golf course.

Tony had a question: Is it true that many cars are available on the market in the United States? "Yes," I replied, "just about every family has one, some have more than one." Do I have one? Yes, I do. What kind is it? I named the model for him. He was not familiar with it. Then he named some of the car lines he knew. I said that we have these and many more; not only are American-produced cars available but many foreign imports as well. I started to name a few of them. Tony turned to Dmitri, and Dmitri explained that Tony wanted to know if I would write down all the models available in the United States. I laughed and said that it would take all night to do this, and I probably would not remember all of them anyway. "Do best you can," was the interpreted reply. Paper and pen were produced. I got to work and produced an incomplete list, but Tony was satisfied.

The hour was quite late. Dmitri turned to me, said that he was going to use the bathroom to get ready for sleep, and told me to stay put. I remained with the two men from Azerbaijan momentarily. They discussed something between themselves. Dmitri popped back into the compartment. The line for the bathroom was lengthy. He asked Tony if he wanted to have a smoke with him. Then he and Tony went outside to the corridor to smoke. People obey an unwritten rule about smoking on Russian trains. Even though no-smoking signs are not evident, they do not smoke in the compartments, only in the vestibules at each end of a car, and, on overnight trains such as this, in the corridors. I stayed with Frank. We did not speak much, but at one point he asked me to name my sport. I told him it was tennis, making a half swinging motion with my right hand. He told me his was boxing, imitating a boxer's defensive position with hands raised and his head weaving.

Dmitri returned and told me he would get the bedding ready while I used the bathroom. I had my stuff ready and went outside. Tony was there, looking out a half open window. I saw a line waiting for the bathroom and offered him a cigarette. He accepted, and we smoked together with no conversation. Staring out into the darkness while blurred images flashed by and wind blew in through the window, I saw only forest vegetation interrupted by an occasional shack or lighted train platform. Tony turned to go back to the compartment, leaving me by myself.

In a moment of tired absent-mindedness, I stuck my head out the port side window to get a better look around and get a sense of the rate we were traveling. Cold air hit my face and whipped my hair around. I could see the curve of the train bearing off to the right, its front obscured. The sharp sound of a train whistle came from the direction of the unseen locomotive. I judged we were going close to sixty miles per hour. I pulled back away from the window. Only a few moments passed when a train hurtled by in the opposite direction, its lighted windows rushing past quite close to us. Startled, I decided not to try this again.

I had to wait a short while. Some men and women were horsing around and smoking cigarettes in a vestibule at the end of the car. One of the men said hello in English. Did everyone speak English here? Finally, I got to use the bathroom. It was constructed entirely out of metal. I managed to use it despite the constant swaying motion and the occasional jolt and bump.

When I came back, Tony was getting his bedding ready. The others were in bed. I climbed up to the bunk above Dmitri's. The radio was silent, and the overhead lights were off. I flipped a reading light on and tried to read. Tony went out and returned some time later, getting into the upper bunk opposite mine.

Although the other reading lights were off, I kept mine on but could not read. Too many thoughts were whirling around in my head. I contemplated the little dance we had just performed with both parties leaving one man behind in the compartment at all times. Despite all our talk, mutual suspicion remained.

I turned the light off and lay on my side in the darkness, restless and unable to sleep. The shade had been drawn. By holding it back a little, I could look out the window. I could not see much, just a moonlit field with an occasional small building or clump of trees. I turned away from the window and lay on my back. I did not feel drowsy. The train rocked and clanged, with a constant tap-dance of the wheels below us. I was able to forget the conversation and the strangers lying near us, and, as my mind wandered, images of the city we were leaving behind entered my mind.

Lasting impressions of Leningrad had been formed by my initial glimpses of it by night. The spectacular sunset by the river Neva; the way the otherwise dull colors of the palaces glowed in the faded light of the eternal twilight; the fantastic sculptures, designed by artists with a taste for strong lines and an ability to fashion stone so it looked supple—all these things had combined to establish a charm inside of me. This charm was later wiped out by the grime and dirt of Leningrad and the reality of Dmitri and Alisa's tiny, musty apartment. It was replaced by disillusionment: Leningrad was dead. Only memories of an earlier glory remained as an outdoor museum in its heart.

Now, bumping along at the dead of night, with the train putting distance between us and the city, I began to form a different concept of Leningrad. I knew that this harsh, burly, industrial city, marred by sprawling, squalid suburbs, broken, empty side streets, and an unreliable water system, was hard on its inhabitants. Still, it had a clean efficient subway system, broad avenues, magnificent architecture, pleasant parks and canals, panoramic river-front views, and the lingering White Nights, which transformed Leningrad's center into a city from a legend. It was not a desolate city, nor was it charming—it was romantic and enigmatic. Leningrad was like a hardened laborer with roots of noble lineage. Somewhere in its past, a tragedy had befallen the aristocratic family that left its heirs in poverty.

A. Riga

After a long time, I fell asleep. I woke up to the sound of announcements being broadcast over the radio, feeling groggy from insufficient sleep. The train would be arriving in twenty minutes. The conductor knocked on our door five minutes later to announce the same thing just in case we had not heard. Music was back on the radio. Tony and Frank were already awake and busy getting ready to depart. Dmitri was still lying in the bunk below. Still half asleep, I struggled to pull my pants on, while Dmitri got up. He asked me if I wanted to use the bathroom, rushing off after I told him to go ahead. Tony and Frank were out in the corridor waiting to get off the train. I finished dressing and gathered our stuff together. Dmitri had already retrieved our bags. When Dmitri returned, I made my own dash to the bathroom after shaking hands with the men from Azerbaijan. This was the last time I saw them. The coach was empty when I returned. I ran down the corridor to catch up with Dmitri.

We stepped out on to the platform wading into the milling crowd, which was slowly drifting away from the train. The sky was overcast, but filtered sunlight bathed the train station with soft light. Dmitri was craning his neck trying to spot Alisa. She soon showed up, and we set off into Riga.

Heading into a strange town more or less as equals—after all none of us lived here—leveled the playing field for what was going to turn into a joust for control of the second half of my stay in the Soviet Union. The contest took place amidst the backdrop of the medieval city, Riga. By the time we reached Riga, the stakes had been set.

The issue of money was on everybody's mind. I had promised to pay Alisa in Riga. We had finished our negotiations before leaving Leningrad and reached an exact figure—a compromise, but, in my opinion, still an exorbitant amount (300 US dollars). This was also where Dmitri had promised to collect data for the Russian version of the HVP profile. Little did I suspect that fate would play an unexpected role. Given what ended up occurring, in an ironic way, it became appropriate that this place was given as my official city of "destination" on my visa.

Though subconsciously the seeds of rebellion were sown in my mind even before we left for Riga, I presently had no energy to contemplate wresting control of my mission from the grip that Alisa and Dmitri currently enjoyed. The hard tense train ride had taken a toll on my endurance. I needed some time to recover from the journey.

I had a typically American reaction to the situation. Americans, when confronted by what they perceive to be arbitrary authority, tend to question and challenge it. I had remained passive during the first week of my trip, letting my hosts have the initiative. This was not a conscious policy, only the results of my initial disorientation. As my anxiety grew, I realized that if this trip was to lead to better things, I could not let it turn into my holiday and their pay day. At this point, paying them what they wanted was a certainty, but getting my money's worth was not.

As we trudged into the greenery and architecture of a city quite different from the one we had left behind, I felt too weary to enjoy a little park with fountains, bronze statues of nymphs, and small ponds littered with flowers. One sight caught my eye, a geometric mobile hanging from thin wires, which made it seem to be suspended in mid-air. I photographed this against the backdrop of northern European style row houses, a collage of cubes, angled planes, and pastels. My spirits were temporarily lifted by the refreshing differences in style here, and their familiarity. Unlike Leningrad, which was at its best in twilight and at night, Riga shone during the day. Also, unlike Leningrad, the architecture was less gargantuan. I took a photograph of one of the bronze nymphs.

Our first destination was the Hotel Riga, a broad granite block carved into an elegant hotel with an austere facade facing the park we had just traversed. It was painted entirely in a pale yellow, which softened its appearance.

I waited for what seemed an eternity while Dmitri and Alisa chatted with the front desk clerk in the spacious marble lobby. At a money exchange in one corner, I asked about my traveler's checks. I found that they could be converted into Latvian "rubles" or Russian rubles but not dollars. I was told to try the local shops, or, if I wished, I could pay for a meal in the hotel restaurant, which would gladly accept my American money. I decided to wait.

We were eventually led to the fifth floor where we were ushered into a waiting room—a couple of sofas, a coffee table, a television, and a bathroom. The style was modern and severe. The red carpeting was stained and worn. A window looked out onto a wall. After another long wait, "Nelly," a perky, smartly dressed woman in her forties, came to talk with us. She was a representative of the Latvian Managers Club. Nelly spoke a little English and greeted me. She conferred with Dmitri and Alisa in Russian. After their chat was over, Dmitri explained to me that a room was being arranged for me at this hotel but it was not ready yet. Meanwhile Dmitri and Alisa would be staying in the Latvian Hotel across the park. They had reserved a room there before I arrived. It was now full. If I wished, I could leave my bag in the waiting room while we walked over to their hotel to see about Dmitri and Alisa's room. I did not want to have to drag my heavy bag all over town but was hesitant to leave it. They convinced me that the bag would be safe. So I left it behind.

Dmitri took us along the edge of the older part of Riga just behind the hotel. This part contained old churches and other late medieval period structures, some dating back to the thirteenth century. Other more contemporary structures were there. The entire area was characterized by narrow streets and small squares. It ended at the broad Daugava River, which intersected the city. We turned up a narrow street in the general direction of midtown away from the river. The street was abutted by austere granite facades and overhung with quaint shop signs.

As we walked along, I noticed that, whereas I was trying to relax, Dmitri and Alisa were tense and purposeful. I snapped a picture of Dmitri in a pale blue windbreaker as he walked in front of me, hunched under the weight of a large shoulder bag. The sky had grown darker and threatened rain. Elegant, stylish couples passed us. Some younger women wore miniskirts, giving Riga a cosmopolitan look.

Dmitri was taking a roundabout way. He wanted to stop at a commercial exchange office to ask about my traveler's checks. As we walked in the place, I noticed a military vehicle parked nearby with some uniformed men huddled inside. Dmitri commented that they were Soviet and preferred to keep a low profile. I waited inside in the bleak office while Dmitri tried to solicit some attention. A door to a back room was hanging partly open. I glimpsed a table covered by stacked rifles. Someone came out of the room and closed the door. I wondered why guns were kept in what was purported to be a financial establishment.

When Dmitri finally got a clerk's attention, the man asked to see my checks. I handed one to Dmitri. Then they had a short discussion, after which I got my check back. Dmitri seemed satisfied and we left. He told me we had to go to a hard currency store. These stores dealt with U. S. dollars, German marks, and other internationally traded currencies popular in the Soviet Union.

After a long walk, we reached the Latvian Hotel—a Soviet style skyscraper with a skin of light blue glass, ribbed by concrete balconies. Its otherwise pristine appearance was marred by blemishes—an occasional boarded window or discolored balcony. Over twenty stories high, it loomed above the surrounding older, more stately buildings like an embarrassed giant teenager among adults of average height. Once inside its vast lobbies and concourses, Dmitri and Alisa went to work securing their room. I waited in the lobby. There, some newspapers were available. I purchased one. It contained articles pertaining to the current crisis in the Baltics.

A general movement toward independence was underway in the three Baltic nations, Estonia, Latvia, and Lithuania. Earlier that year a much publicized violent action by Soviet forces occurred against a Lithuanian television station in the capital, Vilnius. More than a dozen Lithuanians died defending it (Lieven, 1994, p. 251). Later, the Latvian Interior Ministry was attacked by OMON (special police forces), and seven people were killed (Lieven, 1994, p. 254). The push toward independence accelerated after that, punctuated by clashes between Baltic customs officials (border police) and OMON forces (Lieven, 1994, p. 254).

If a problem existed here, I had yet to see visible evidence of it. At the time, things were relatively quiet, and any substantial Soviet military presence was kept out of sight. I had asked back in Leningrad, but Dmitri seemed to be only mildly concerned about the political situation here, keeping his comments to an opinion that, by separating from the Soviet Union, the Baltic countries would be shooting themselves in the foot, since they were so heavily dependent on the Soviet infrastructure for necessities such as petroleum and other raw materials.

After finishing the checking-in process, Dmitri and Alisa went up to their room by themselves, leaving me in the lobby to wait for them. I got a sense of the layout of the place. A large restaurant was on the left. Near it were stairs descending to a "hard currency" bar and grill. A corridor on the right led to another entrance where taxis and buses were discharging passengers and waiting to pick up new ones. I was sitting within sight of the check-in area. The entrance to a large boulevard separated me from the check-in counters. Beyond the check-in area was a small glass-enclosed shop and near it a bank of elevators.

It did not take long for Dmitri and Alisa to return. I was promptly informed by Dmitri and Alisa that hard currency (dollars) stores were near the hotel. Would I be so kind as to exchange my checks for dollars? I said that I would give it a try. We left the hotel, walked a short way on the large boulevard adjacent to it, and found a large store selling a wide range of items, including souvenirs, cigarettes, candies, clothing, and electrical appliances. This was the first time I purchased something in the Soviet Union at a retail outlet. My other purchases had been at street markets.

An elaborate process was involved. Instead of bringing the item you wished to purchase to the cashier, you had to ask first for the item from one of the many female sales clerks standing behind counters. Then the clerk would hand you a small ticket for the item, which stated its cost. At this point, you would take the ticket to the cashier, pay the stated price, and return to the clerk with the cash receipt for your purchase. Hoping to avoid all this, Dmitri and I asked the cashier if she would simply cash the check, but she refused. I had to purchase something. The cashier used an abacus to total bills, something I had noticed in Leningrad. This throwback to the past and legacy from the East disappeared in 1993.

Having finished my purchase and collected my change, I realized that I would have to go through this process several times before I would have enough to pay them. Dmitri and Alisa wanted me to make another purchase so as to change another check. I told them trying again was fruitless. Only one cashier was in the store, and she would remember me. To satisfy them, I tried again, and, as I expected, the cashier refused to cash a second check because I already had dollars. I told Dmitri I would try this store again tomorrow, hoping a different cashier would be there.

We wandered about for a little while looking for another hard currency store, but none were in the immediate area. Along the way we passed a curiosity—a large section of a concrete barrier was perched upright on the side of the broad sidewalk that ran to the Latvian hotel. It was covered with graffiti. One cut-off word read "slavery." The word read "SLAVER." I assumed the missing letter was a "Y" and that the entire word had been painted on the complete barrier of which this was a piece. Something was familiar about the barrier. Then I recognized what it was.

In 1989, Americans saw images of East Germans taking hammer and chisel to the Berlin Wall only moments after freedom to pass through had been granted. Reportedly, pieces of the wall became souvenirs. Someone had carried this section here. It was appropriate as a symbol of the current Latvian resistance to Soviet rule. Because its presence on an open boulevard was tolerated, some acquiescence by the Soviet authorities must have existed. I could not be certain that this was truly from the Berlin wall, but when I discussed it with Dmitri he agreed with my assessment. This was the first piece of physical evidence that a political crisis existed in Latvia.

Dmitri had too much on his mind to be in the mood for political discussion. Alisa seemed anxious. Lunchtime was approaching, and I had barely started to collect the money for the necessary payment. I tried to assure them that I had every intention of paying them, but that I was exhausted. I had not slept well on the train, I had nothing to eat except a small snack while waiting for them to make arrangements at the Hotel Riga, and I did not like being pressured. I told Dmitri that I would like to have a chance to rest and recoup my energy before searching for other hard currency stores. This was still our first day here; could they be patient? As we headed for his hotel, Dmitri told me that we would continue the discussion after lunch. He asked me to wait while he and Alisa went to see about lunch arrangements. I sat patiently in the lobby as Alisa and Dmitri went into the large restaurant on the ground floor of the hotel.

Dmitri eventually returned and explained the lunch plan. The restaurant staff had arranged a private meal for us in a small out of the way section of the restaurant. Though some of the conference participants had already arrived, the first conference-sponsored meal would be a dinner later that day. Alisa was waiting for us at a table that had been set for us. We had lunch, some bland tasting meat and mashed potatoes with a few vegetables. The ice cream for dessert was not bad.

The well-groomed waiter disappeared, and the china was cleared away. As we sipped mineral water, Alisa made a blunt request: I had to come up with some more money, or I would not get a hotel room. She had the key to the room and the cabinet where my bag was stored. I would not see that again until payment was received. Again, I was caught off guard. Who the hell did they think I was, some bandit? They already saw that I agreed to pay them and that I had begun to cash my checks. They also knew that the process was not exactly convenient. Also, why was so much pressure being put on me now? I was furious inside and could have easily exploded over their heavy handed treatment of me. Still, I kept quiet and told them I was sad and disappointed by the situation. Dmitri shook his head over my reaction. Alisa remained impassive and stony faced. What shocked me the most was that they seemed to have no inkling that they were treating me inappropriately. Apparently in their eyes, I was behaving badly. Since I was slow to comply with the agreement reached in Leningrad, I was being treated like a "Russian." (They had counted on having my money in hand already by the time they got to Latvia. Since I had not paid them yet, they had to improvise—promise the hotel money until they collected it from me.)

I surmised that I was dealing with someone who was used to getting her way regardless of methods and that this woman had served Dmitri's career nicely. I felt a growing need to put some distance between myself and them. Because I had a task to accomplish, I had to be patient. I told Alisa flatly that I would come up with one third of what I promised to pay, but I could not spend the entire day locating hard currency stores and making purchases. The rest of the money I would gather the next day after a good night's sleep. I also reminded Dmitri about his promise to gather HVP samples for Pomeroy.

So an agreement was reached. I located a store quickly enough. It turned out that the hotel shop I had noticed before in the lobby accepted hard currency. We browsed a bit before I asked if they would accept my checks. Alisa had been eyeing a VCR that was on display. She noted that the price was about what I had promised to pay her and suggested that I buy that for them instead. I considered it for a moment. Then, I remembered that their Soviet television set was an older variety probably not compatible with a VCR. So, I refused. Instead, I bought a few packs of cigarettes and got my change. Since the store was so tiny, the sales clerk took care of everything. I had succeeded in gathering sufficient U. S. currency to make my first payment. We headed back to my hotel.

Dmitri took a direct route along the main boulevard past a domed Russian cathedral and a tall white obelisk that was topped with a green statue of a woman holding three golden stars over her head with arms raised to the sky. The monument was erected to commemorate Latvia's freedom from the late Russian Empire in the early 1920s (Liberty Monument). I noticed the pretty flowers arranged at its base and wondered to whom they were dedicated. At a small street market on our way back, red and white flowers were being sold. It added a festive counter-point to what had turned out to be a dreary day. We crossed the park into the hotel. By now, the sky promised rain, so they felt an extra urgency to get the matter at hand finished.

Up on the fifth floor, my bag was retrieved, and a staff member of the Managers Club showed me to my room. It was spacious and carpeted, with a nice view of the park. The clean lines of Scandinavian style furniture evoked order and efficiency. The green-tiled bathroom looked modern and clean. Alisa followed me into the room, and the exchange was made. I paid the agreed amount with dollars and a few rubles. In return, I had her sign a hastily improvised receipt. After the deal was done, Dmitri came to discuss the plans for the evening. Dinner would be at the Hotel Latvia, followed by a reception at another location. I was to be at the hotel by such and such time. As usual, I was having trouble understanding all of Dmitri's English. It drove home my situation of being alone and practically at the mercy of hosts who seemed to have no sense of tact.

From out of nowhere, I heard a melodic voice speaking English, an English so refined that I first thought another American tourist had entered the room. I turned around and saw a young pretty lady, thin with a pale complexion and long brown hair, standing in front of me, probably in her early twenties. I was introduced to Eva, a Latvian. She explained that she had been provided for me as an interpreter. The transition from feeling trampled on to being treated as a foreign dignitary left me stupefied. I felt as if I was alone with her and hardly noticed Dmitri's presence. Alisa came back to the room. They had to get back to their hotel.

Eva was on Anatol's staff. She had recently graduated from a business college. She wanted to know if I had any points of interest that I wished to visit. I explained to her that I was an anthropology student studying the Soviet Union. She suggested a visit to the outdoor ethnographic museum, which was located at the outskirts of the city. We could go the next day. Before leaving, she gave me the room number where she could be found, the staff office of the Managers Club.

I had a couple of hours to myself. Now, I could take a bath, rest, read, write, in short, do whatever I pleased. I was slightly disappointed when I turned on the tap in the bath and the water turned out to be as yellow as in Leningrad. The tub itself was clean and stain free. The shower apparatus was a little different from those back home. Instead of consisting of a fixed shower head projecting from the wall above, it consisted of a shower head attached to a flexible metallic hose that emanated from the tap end of the tub.

After my bath, I slowly began to unwind. I lay on the bed and tried to take a nap, but I was still too tense. I thought about going for a walk, but rain had started. I had to walk to the hotel anyway, so I decided to stay in my room until then.

I took photos of the park with the Hotel Latvia looming in the distance. Off to the left, the distinctive Liberty monument was just beyond the tree line of the park. To the right was what appeared to be a government building in Renaissance style architecture. A little dome was perched on its top, and just above it, the red and white flag of Latvia. Low-hanging, bluish-gray clouds hovered above, accenting its Soviet gray color. Two pale lemon-colored buildings flanked it, further contrasting it from the more cheerful surroundings.

I wrote in my notebook a little, and thought about things. Meeting Eva and having some time to myself helped me get over the earlier confrontation with Alisa and Dmitri. My relationship with Dmitri had been developing around our many discussions. Like our discussions, it was a superficial, theoretical relationship. When anything of consequence came up, no bond existed between us. My relationship with Alisa was even more tenuous. I could only guess what they had in store for me that evening. I was not sure what exactly I would be doing in Riga. Besides making sure Dmitri collected data for Pomeroy, I had no direct interest in a business seminar. Staying in an international hotel did not fit my image of anthropology. Still, I was curious about the ethnographic park, and Riga itself was worth exploring. I hoped that, with Dmitri and Alisa being busy, I would have more freedom of movement.

From an anthropological point of view, I would have been better off getting myself more directly involved with Dmitri's work, as I did later with some of my subsequent Russian hosts. At the time, I had not yet developed the participant side of the traditional participant-observer approach of an anthropologist. I stayed around the edges of my host's activity. Ironically, my lack of experience on this trip helped me in the long run in an unintended way. Because I was not so attached to Dmitri, I projected a sense of being independent enough to encourage other Soviet scientists to approach me. This led to a new relationship that would prove to be quite beneficial to my long range goal of doing doctoral level research in Russia.

The time came for me to go to the other hotel. The rain had not let up, so I went to the room of the Managers Club to borrow an umbrella. It was a busy place—two adjoining rooms had been converted into a spacious office. Nelly was there along with some other women. They were all pretty and smartly dressed. Flowers decorated parts of the room. The atmosphere was bustling and lively. Eva was not there—she had gone off on an assignment. I noticed that there was no sign of the boss. I had not met Anatol yet and wondered what he was like. Nelly found an umbrella for me and gave me directions to the hotel, which I did not think I would need.

I made my way over to the other hotel via the park. I soon found that the trees obscured it, and becoming disoriented on the winding paths was easy. I was glad I had some street names with me in case I lost my way. I ended up on a street slightly wide of my mark. It had a statue of Vladimir Ilyich Lenin, one arm raised, chest forward, giving a speech to the passing traffic. I spotted the blue tower I was looking for and soon reached it. Dmitri was waiting for me outside. We went straight to the restaurant where Alisa was waiting for us. A waiter showed us to our table, one of many arranged in long rectangles forming a border around individual tables. The restaurant was full of conference participants. Dmitri was eager to meet them, and he already seemed to know a few.

Dmitri discussed the conference with me. He would be working all the next day. I told him that I planned to visit the ethnographic museum with Eva the next morning. I agreed to meet him at his seminar when I returned. He introduced me to some men he had met from Moscow. They did not speak English, and when Dmitri became engaged in an animated discussion with them, I was left alone with my thoughts. I looked at Alisa to see what her mood was. She was cheerful, with no trace of animosity from our earlier confrontation.

After dinner, I followed Dmitri and Alisa onto the elevator up to their room. Given that the hotel was so large on the outside, their room turned out to be surprisingly small. It had a nice view, and I took photographs of the city from the window. I could see the tops of the lush green trees of the broad park facing the hotel. Beyond it was the silvery domed shape of the Russian Orthodox cathedral we had passed earlier, and, beyond that to its left, the pale shape of the Hotel Riga. Way off in the distance behind the hotel was the long dark spire of St. Peter's, a landmark of the old town. To the right of the Orthodox cathedral was an assortment of modern buildings, beyond them more church spires of the old section, and even further back to the right, a huge futuristic-looking tower, shaped like Paris's Eiffel tower. The rain let up, and the sky was a bit brighter now, but the light would soon fade.

At dusk, they took me to the old town. We crossed the park, ending up on cobble stoned streets and eventually at the entrance to what appeared to be an ancient chateau. Its massive wooden door with iron handles swung inward to reveal a dimly lit hall with a plank floor. A staircase, made from worn white marble, led to the second floor. They took me upstairs into another smaller hall with some seating. Beyond it was a ballroom or auditorium where I could see many of the same people I had noticed at the hotel dinner. A little light filtered through its stained glass windows. Its polished pine floor was littered with folding metal chairs, which were being hastily arranged into rows by some workers. Up in front, an area was left clear with a microphone at its center. I also saw speakers being set up and what appeared to be sound equipment. I noticed Nelly and wondered if Eva might show up, but she was not there. Lights went on in the hall giving it a little more illumination, but I found it hard to see anyway. We took our seats.

I sat in the front row with Dmitri. Alisa sat directly behind us. Dmitri provided me with some interpretation. Nelly was the "master of ceremonies" and addressed the assembled gathering of about a hundred. She apologized that Anatol could not be with us that evening; he was away on business and would return tomorrow. This opening meeting of the conference would be a chance for the participants to introduce themselves and get to know each other.

Dmitri tells me right from the start that I will be introducing myself along with the others. I am glad that he has waited until the last minute to tell me, otherwise I would have spent many nervous minutes anxious over a stage appearance and probably would have over prepared. As it is, I hardly have time to get nervous. While Nelly is speaking, Dmitri explains that the rule of the introduction program is for each participant to name a city after finishing his or her remarks. Anyone from the named city can stand up and be next. Nelly chooses Dmitri (probably prearranged) as the first participant to step up to the microphone to introduce himself. He finishes to polite applause and names New York. I have to go on stage.

I stand up in front of the large audience, strangers barely visible in the weak light, give my speech in English, only daring to use one Russian word, "*spasiba*" (thank you), say "*Moskva*" (Moscow) to solicit the next participant and sit down. Dmitri translates my remarks after I finish speaking: I am an anthropology graduate student of the State University of New York, doing research with a scientist in New York City. With Dmitri's help, we are developing and evaluating a Russian language version of a psychological stress test based on *formal axiology* which is a new theory about the human capability to value the internal and external. This is part of an overall project comparing test results across different nations. This is my first time in the Soviet Union, and I hope to visit more of your enormous, complex country.

After I sat down feeling glad I had gotten it over with, I thought that the project I described would mean little to the other participants. These were businessmen and women interested in practical, readily applicable methods. What use was some obscure theoretical test to them?

The audience eventually completed the introductions. Nelly then closed the formal part of the meeting and announced that music would be provided for dancing. A small stereo had been set up near the sound equipment. Nelly flipped a switch, and the dance hall was filled with waltzes, polkas, and soft rock. The chairs were put against the walls, and couples soon started to dance. Some refreshments were served. Dmitri spotted an Asian beauty and danced with her. Alisa asked me to dance. I thought, "Why not?" Curiously, I found myself dancing with the "enemy," with all thoughts of the earlier battle erased.

The evening turned the day upside down. I looked at Dmitri's wife, dressed in white, looking elegant, and Dmitri in his tan suit with his partner in blue. Alisa spun me around the floor. I was glad I wore a nice shirt and slacks for such an occasion. I did not know how to dance well, but I did not stick out from the crowd.

One dance was enough for me. Alisa seemed pleased. I excused myself and drifted away from the dancers with a drink in my hand into an anteroom outside the auditorium-turned-ballroom. Small pockets of people were gathering there. I smoked and waited awhile, not talking to anyone. Then Dmitri appeared. He wanted me to stay put. He was going to introduce me to some people. Dmitri disappeared, and in his place a couple came into the room. A tall slender man with a graying beard and glasses introduced himself. He looked Western European. His female companion was also slender and tall, with long wavy hair. Together they made a distinguished pair.

At first, I thought they were the people Dmitri wanted me to meet. They spoke in perfect English, with an unfamiliar accent. My first impression was that they were from England. I asked them if they were connected with Dmitri. They said no: Their names were "Andrey" and "Anya." They were "scientists" from Leningrad. They heard my remarks and were interested in the "stress test." Could we discuss it the next day? I suggested we meet at the conference luncheon.

Dmitri came by at that point, trailing a group of people behind him. He took me aside and asked me to whom I was speaking. I said that the couple approached me; I had never seen them before. They were interested in my research. A worried expression crossed Dmitri's face for a moment and just as quickly passed.

Dmitri turned me in the direction of the small group he had assembled. I spent the rest of the evening chatting with a series of men from all over the Soviet Union. None of them expressed interest in my HVP project. Instead, they all had business propositions for me. I was not interested in any of their proposals. One man who looked Chinese had a Russian name—"Mikhail." He came from Tuva, a region near Mongolia. He was trading animal skins. Another man, "Sergey," a Russian from Moscow, sold rare books. Would I be interested? Sergey did not speak English. Dmitri told me Sergey was honest. Puzzled, I looked at Dmitri wondering if this was a clumsy attempt to endorse the man. How did he expect me to conduct business with a man with whom I had no common language?

Exhausted, having fended off the "businessmen," and feeling satisfied that I made fortuitous contact with what appeared to be Soviet scientists genuinely interested in my project, I felt anxious to get back to my room. Outside, it was quite dark when Dmitri, Alisa, and I left the chateau. The place was empty. We were the last to leave, ushered out by a worker as the massive door was shut behind us.

B. The Ethnographic Open Air Museum

Eva took me to the ethnographic open air museum the next morning (Wednesday, 17 July). We got an early start. This day was also overcast. We took a twenty minute bus ride to the northeastern end of town. From there, the museum was a short walk. Set in a large park, it turned out to be closed to tourists that day, but Eva spoke with an attendant, and we were given permission to look around. No guides or activities were available, but I did not care. Being able to see it was enough.

Set in a thickly wooded forest, the park contained the recreation of a peasant village. Its structures reflected an evolving architecture from the seventeenth to nineteenth centuries (Veveris and Kupais, 1989). Its features included a Lutheran church, a plain wooden structure on the outside but intricately decorated on the inside with a mostly blue ceiling mural—complete with angels and clouds, and an ornate altar with sculpted brass decoration. The museum park also displayed several spacious log cabin houses with thatched roofs; a mill with its original machinery; a carriage house that held carts, wagons, carriages, and sleighs; a shed containing farming tools, including pitchforks fashioned from tree limbs; and a bathhouse, a plain wooden structure with a bench and a stove over which water was poured and turned into steam. Near the church were stocks used to punish wrongdoers.

Some of the larger buildings had roofs constructed from wooden shingles. They seemed to have served as common areas. One of these buildings, a long structure, served as a pub with many chambers. Clients were divided by social position (Veveris and Kupais 1989, p. 196). Another building was marked by what appeared to be an "African mask" carved in wood in front of its entrance. Inside, despite the dim light, I photographed a set of similar wooden carvings, depicting what best could be described as gargoyles. Eva told me that they were the heads of unpopular landlords done in caricature. They were assembled into an exhibition by the museum. Originally, they were displayed surreptitiously when the landlord was away.

The rain drizzled intermittently. Fortunately, we had been smart enough to carry umbrellas. I took more photos as we meandered through the wet grasses, sandy paths, and dirt roads. Eva was generally quiet, only speaking occasionally to describe something, taking her time to read the signs posted on the buildings, and then interpreting them for me. Sometimes she would look up a word in a book she brought. At one point, she gave me permission to photograph her near one of the common buildings. I spotted some large stones that had been hollowed out lying at the foot of one of the structures. I could not make any sense of them—how they had been hollowed out, or what purpose they served. Eva did not know. I mentioned that they reminded me of grinding stones used by Southwestern Indians in the United States to grind corn. Eva was interested by this. She told me that she had a book about North American Pueblo Indians. Later, we looked at a painted wooden religious figure encased in glass on a post. She told me that Latvia had three religions: Lutheran, Russian Orthodox, and Roman Catholic.

Eva seemed to like me, but also maintained some reserve. I managed to find out a little about her during our walk. She was working for Anatol that summer. She had studied business and English at school, but was not sure yet which career to pursue. Her mother was single, having divorced her father some years back. He had disappeared from their lives. When Eva had time, she would go home to stay with her mother in her home town outside of Riga, usually on the weekends. Otherwise, she stayed at the hotel in a room provided by Anatol for some of his staff. Anatol's staff, as far as I could tell, consisted of women only. I imagined that he was perhaps a "father figure" to all of them. Whatever the case, they all seemed to be cheerful workers.

We ended our walk at the inlet of a large lake (Lake Jugla), a popular swimming spot. On this day, it was unused. Without taking off her sandals, Eva dipped one foot into the water, telling me it was warm. I asked her if she might like anything from America. She said "a book." Apparently, books in English were hard to come by. I said that perhaps I could mail her one. She was delighted by this. Then, she laughed and said by the time I mailed her the book the name of the street she lived on ("Lenin Street") would probably have changed.

I asked her about the Soviet Union. She told me that she felt that many of its officials and policies were stupid, and that they had made Riga ugly with industrial pollution and grotesque architecture. I asked her if she would enjoy an independent, freer country. She said that it would be nice if Latvia was independent of the Soviet Union. Our discussion led to the idea of freedom and free will. Eva seemed unsure about the idea of freedom. I told her that I believed that having a choice about what sort of life you can have is crucial. Eva was not disrespectful, but let on that this was not her philosophy. She believed in fate.

Eva's comment left me with a stab of disappointment: The Soviet Union was modeled on a philosophical system that promoted historical destiny. If Eva was typical, then it is little wonder that she lived under a system in which she half-believed. She (and others like her) just did not like the outcome.

We left the park, having seen only a portion of it, and headed back to catch a bus. On the way to the bus stop, I photographed buildings I had spotted earlier. Several houses that reminded me of American suburban homes interested me. They were all masonry structures. One, colored rose and orange and set behind a wooden picket fence, was in a garden with fruit trees and a shed. Another, painted a mustard color and almost obscured by shrubbery, was behind a hedge. The third, a larger more complex structure painted bright pink, amidst a mix of evergreen and deciduous trees, lay near the main highway. An official looking blue truck was parked in a driveway. I was struck by these structures, because I had not seen any like them in Leningrad. The one thing linking them to Leningrad was the rugged blue truck. (Such structures, serving a similar purpose, did exist in and around Leningrad. I had not seen enough of it yet.)

A bus came, and we got on. The morning began to change. The sun had come out. The bus was hot. On the way to the park, Eva and I sat together. Now, the bus was much more crowded. I offered her the one empty seat. She refused, telling me to sit—the trip would take a while. I would be tired. I said that I was afraid that she would be tired. She told me that she was used to standing. As we headed back, I watched Eva standing near me in her long printed dress and gray jacket, one arm stretched out, her hand grasping a metal pole, the other hand clutching her book and purse. This young woman, who had at first appeared to be thin and frail, stood on the swaying bus for ten kilometers, waiting patiently each time the bus stopped, never changing her position, like a tree rooted in the ground.

C. Dmitri's Seminar

We got back to the city before the morning was over. Eva deposited me near the front of the Hotel Riga with directions to the conference center. I asked her if she would meet me for lunch later. She seemed to change her mind, and she decided to take me to the center, a short walk. The place was located in the same neighborhood as the old chateau but, unlike that one, it was a totally modern structure. We went inside where Dmitri's seminar was already in session.

About two dozen people were sitting around two tables. More were standing or coming and going. I had brought my tape recorder and immediately began recording the events. Dmitri was lecturing. Alisa was there also. Eva began to do some interpretation for me. Dmitri was explaining the format of his next exercise. He would be conducting it in the adjoining room. Meanwhile, Alisa was fiddling with a hand held video camera. A partition separated the meeting area from the rest of the large room. When she was not working on the camera or shuffling through some papers, Alisa stood up to let people in and out through an opening in the partition.

Apparently, Eva could not interpret all the activity for me. She seemed anxious to get back to the hotel. I sensed this and told her that she did not have to stick around. Eva spoke to Alisa for a minute and left the room. I followed her out into the entrance area and asked her if she could give me a summary of what was going on. She obliged and then said she must hurry back. I thanked her for the ethnographic park excursion and told her I hoped to see her at lunch.

I rejoined the group. The initial part of the meeting had ended, and the participants were moving into the larger portion of the room where some chairs were set up. Alisa gave the video camera to Dmitri who tested it in different corners of the room.

Soon, the next portion of the seminar was underway. I was able to piece together what they were doing from Eva's earlier interpretation and summary and from a few comments that I was able to snatch from Dmitri during the session. Dmitri was using a calculation puzzle to test participants' abilities to persuade and to cooperate in problem solving. He used the video camera to record the session. The video was used later for follow up instruction.

I observed awhile to catch on to the exercise. Occasionally, I understood a Russian word. The participants were given a problem in selling and buying. A pair of men "on stage" sat in two chairs side by side. Dmitri was filming them. One of the men was apparently trying to convince the other man about something having to do with the puzzle. The next pair included Andrey sitting side by side with another man. Andrey was taking notes. His partner had the task of convincing Andrey of his solution to Dmitri's puzzle. This man was making an explanation, gesturing as he spoke. Dmitri intently scrutinized both with the video camera. The argument turned out to be convincing. Next up was the third pair of men. One was a social psychologist who was to do the convincing. Like Andrey he wore glasses and had a quiet tone of voice. Unlike the man who had convinced Andrey, he had his chair turned to the side so he could face his partner more directly.

When I got a chance to speak with Dmitri, he sketched out the problem. The task was to determine the profit from the following sequence of transactions. You buy a horse at six thousand rubles, sell it for seven, buy it again for eight, and resell it for nine. A story was attached but Dmitri had no time to go through it with me. Being familiar with this sort of puzzle, I quickly worked out the solution: The profit was two thousand rubles.

Confusion was caused by the story—the purchaser had to "borrow" 1,000 at one point since he entered the second transaction short of the second purchase price. Many calculated the net profit accurately and then made the mistake of subtracting the borrowed 1,000, not realizing that it had already been accounted for when they calculated that profit. The gross profit was 3,000. Subtracting 1,000 yielded 2,000. I used algebra to turn the problem into a single solution formula based on total purchases and total sales. Once I had calculated the answer, I did not worry about the "borrowing" portion of it, since the algebra showed only one answer was possible.

Another way to look at the problem is to assume you start off with a bank roll of 10,000 rubles. When you first purchase the horse, you will have 4,000 (10,000 minus 6,000) plus the horse. After you sell the horse the first time, you will have 4,000 plus 7,000, yielding 11,000. When you purchase the horse the second time at a cost of 8,000, you will have 3,000 and the horse. When you sell the horse again, you will have 3,000 plus 9,000, yielding 12,000. Since you started with 10,000, your net profit is 2,000.

Once sure of the correct answer, a participant tried to convince the other of the correctness of his calculations. Those that were quicker at doing the calculation tended to be the ones to do the convincing. Occasionally, neither side knew the right answer, and the results became hilarious.

The social psychologist was still up there and was speaking more loudly; his hands were moving quickly. The conversation was getting increasingly heated. Dmitri called a time out. The social psychologist had failed to convince his partner.

Next up were a man and a woman. She claimed the profit was 2,000. The man did not believe her. Dmitri was busy filming them. He was kneeling on the floor, quite close to them. He then changed camera position. I started to think Dmitri's shifting around might influence them. Then the woman believed the profit to be zero. Finally, they agreed on a figure of 1,000 as a "compromise." They had arrived at a political "solution" to the problem.

Andrey was up there again—this time trying to do the persuading. He was having trouble convincing his male partner. Andrey spoke with him quietly, almost confidentially, as if he were letting the man in on a big secret. The man remained stubborn as a mule.

At some point, I realized that Anya was absent. Maybe she was at a different seminar. That Dmitri's seminar was attended by only a portion of the total number of people I had seen the night before was evident. I was not sure about the overall structure of the conference. As it turned out, the conference consisted of a series of seminars, some of which ran concurrently. Some recreational activity was going on at the same time. Like me, the participants may have been taking time to see some of the city. The whole conference lasted two weeks. Many participants did not arrive until later.

I left the seminar before it broke up for lunch to get some fresh air and to have a chance to take a leisurely stroll through the park before lunch. I was supposed to be gathering dollars, so I went back to the first hard currency store that I had visited the day before. It was nearby. I had no luck there. The cashier remembered me and felt annoyed by my use of her shop to change checks. Disillusioned, I forsook trying the other smaller shop in the hotel, afraid I would have the same problem there

I arrived at the Latvia Hotel before most of the other seminar participants. Eva was there with a woman friend named "Lolita." Dmitri and Alisa were not there yet. Eva had brought her Latvian-English dictionary with her, a book she always carried when with me. I asked to look at it. I was unfamiliar with her language. I copied down the book's author, editor, and so on. I hoped to find one back home. I was fascinated by the unusual language, which the natives spoke so melodically, making Russian sound rough by comparison. Eva let on that she was turned off by Russian. It had many "*nya*" and "*zha*" sounds, which were ugly to her.

As we ate, I noticed that Eva was eating little. Conference participants were arriving all the time; the place was filling up. After the soup course had been served, Eva told me she had to go back to work, and she informed me that Anatol wanted to speak with me later that evening at nine o'clock. I thanked her for coming, and I wondered what Anatol would be like, as well as what he would have to say. Lolita stayed behind, and I finished my lunch with her.

After Lolita left, I spotted Andrey and Anya in the restaurant and joined them. This meeting was a turning point. Not that our dinner together was any sort of social success, far from it. Anya ("Please call me Ann") was in a foul mood. First, I made the mistake of referring to her as Andrey's wife. I had assumed they were married. "Ann" bluntly told me that she was not Andrey's wife. At one point, she snapped at my clumsy attempts to speak Russian. Later, she left the table. Andrey told me to "never mind" her—that she was in a bad mood for other reasons. This helped explain Ann's absence when I arrived at the seminar. Much later, I found out that those reasons were related to Dmitri. Ann had felt mistreated by him during a portion of the seminar that I missed when I took my trip to the ethnographic museum.

Andrey got down to business. He asked for my itinerary in order to arrange a meeting with me back in Leningrad. Andrey wanted to have a chance to review my project. Doing it in Latvia would be awkward. I had left material back in Leningrad that would be useful for our discussion. We had good reasons to talk in Leningrad. Unfortunately, he would not be back in

Leningrad until the last few days of my trip. Dmitri planned a second trip to Riga at that time. Given that he had already insisted that I go everywhere that he went, I would have to part ways with him before his second trip and stay in another place in Leningrad. Andrey said that he could make arrangements for me. I decided not to tell Dmitri about this yet.

Andrey, a mathematician with experience in computer methods, was the deputy chair of a retraining center at the main university in Leningrad, which had Soviet officials as clients. Administrators of the retraining process were interested in reducing the stress associated with career changes and in new educational techniques.

Andrey offered me some inducements: First, an official letter of invitation could be extended by his department to me and "my chief" (Pomeroy) for an official visit—it would be a scientific exchange. The "Atomic University" (Upgrade Center) in Leningrad was well suited for foreigners. Could my chief give a seminar there? Some payment could be arranged, and a good dormitory was there. In addition, Andrey offered to collect a sample suitable to Pomeroy's needs when we came. Pomeroy's standard national sample is 200 college students. Andrey also would try to get me a smaller sample of about twenty before I left.

Andrey wanted to check out our project a little more before the deal was finalized. I agreed. I thought that if things did not work out with Dmitri, this would be a backup plan. Addresses, phone numbers, and other information were exchanged, and our meeting was over. I also gave Andrey a copy of Pomeroy's test in English as a gesture of trust. In little more than half an hour, I had taken a decisive step toward gaining some control over my Soviet research. With Andrey, I had the sense that I was dealing with someone who was focused on my needs rather than being sucked into someone else's agenda.

Before I left the hotel, I ran into a man from the conference who spoke English. He was carrying a tennis racket. Since I played tennis, we had a mutual interest. He told me that an excursion to Jurmala, a beach resort, had been planned. He was planned to play there. We agreed to try to play sometime if he could find me a tennis racket.

Outside the Hotel Latvia, I ran into Dmitri who was on his way to lunch. I expected him to bring up the money issue again, but he did not. He was excited about his seminar. He thought it was going well. He also had some good news for me. He had found someone to help with Pomeroy's test: A printed version of the test had been produced. He showed me a copy—two sheets, one for each part of the test. I noticed that no instructions were on it. He told me that he would give the instructions when he administered the test. I asked him when he was planning to conduct the test and if could he get enough copies made for forty samples. He was not sure yet. Before we parted ways, Dmitri told me that Eva and I looked good together. I thanked him and replied that she was charming.

I strolled to a small shop selling postcards that I had noticed the day before. I bought a few with a dollar, getting a few unusual coins in change. The woman clerk, who was having trouble understanding my Russian, asked me if I was German. I just shook my head "no" and smiled. Germans, who had once dominated Riga, left in droves during World War II, and now they were a minority.

I knew that I should get busy again gathering money. I found a hard currency store near the Hotel Riga, bought a souvenir, and began to gather more dollars to pay Alisa. Given my earlier experience, I thought that I would have to comb the entire town for new hard currency stores. I was making progress.

I dropped in for a few minutes on Dmitri's seminar. He had divided people into two groups. More were listening than taking part. Dmitri was conducting another exercise. I did not have the energy to try to decipher a new exercise, and I was unsure about trying to get Dmitri to answer my inquiries. I did not want Dmitri to accuse me of bothering him during his seminar. Alisa was there and seemed to be annoyed when I appeared. Feeling uncomfortable, I left.

Outside, a group of people, including Andrey and the tennis man, were taking a break; and I joined them in conversation. Suddenly Dmitri burst out the door, yelling at me: "It is not honor! It is not honor!" It could only mean one thing. Alisa had informed him that I had not paid her yet. Feeling embarrassed, I excused myself and went to speak with Dmitri. I told him that he would have his money by dinner time but that I wanted a copy of our Russian translation of the HVP. He obliged.

I went back to the Latvia Hotel to try my luck at the shop there. The sales clerk had been friendlier than the one at the store that had turned me down. It was worth a try. I needed to cash two checks to garner the necessary money. This time I explained more of the situation and what I needed to the clerk. She was cooperative and said that, if I purchased enough, she would be willing to cash however many checks I needed. So after a little negotiation, I purchased more cigarettes and several rolls of film and got a substantial amount of U. S. dollars.

Mission accomplished, I went to the restaurant feeling confident. On my way, Andrey called to me in the lobby. He had seen my heated exchange with Dmitri. Did I have time to show him and Ann the Russian version of the test? Yes, I did. So we went up to his room.

Andrey's roommate turned out to be Sergey, the "rare book dealer." This man hung around watching us. He hardly spoke any English. I wondered if he understood what was going on.

Andrey explained to me that Ann was a philologist and wanted to check the Russian translation Dmitri had produced. She had already been working on translating the English version of Pomeroy's test into Russian. This was a delightful turn of events for me. Pomeroy wanted me to get a second opinion on Dmitri's translation while in the Soviet Union, and now, by a series of coincidences, I had a chance to do it. So, not minding the possible ramifications of this, I gave the go-ahead.

I found it odd that this clandestine meeting would take place in front of a man who obviously knew Dmitri and could warn him that we had met, even if he did not understand exactly what we were discussing. As it turned out, Andrey was aware of this and solved the problem partially. Ann would not join us there. Instead, Andrey took me out of the room, leaving Sergey there, and we went up a floor to another room where Ann was waiting for us.

Once inside, I handed them two sheets of paper that contained the test. As Ann scanned Dmitri's version, she started to chuckle. Apparently it had several errors; she showed me a couple of them. Asking Dmitri to make changes was not possible at this point. To make matters worse, a conflict of interest was starting to emerge. Andrey and Ann mentioned that Dmitri had been doing his best behind my back to try to keep them away from me, but they asked me not to reveal our meeting to Dmitri. I agreed.

With the good news that I had gathered more dollars, I met Dmitri and Alisa in the restaurant. Dmitri immediately sent Alisa with me to make the exchange. They were avoiding doing it in front of everybody. Up in their hotel room, I counted out the U. S. currency, stopping a little short of the agreed amount. I was holding back some dollars to keep for myself. I showed Alisa that I had plenty of rubles to make up the difference. She accepted. Again, a hastily improvised receipt was drawn up, which I had Alisa sign.

My obligation met, I was anxious to get back to Dmitri. I realized that, despite our differences, I was in Riga under Dmitri's auspices, and a public rift with him should be repaired as soon as possible. I wanted to make sure that the same people who had seen Dmitri blow up in front of me would see Dmitri and me together again, having a friendly chat over lunch. Alisa seemed to have other plans. When I started to go back downstairs, she announced that she was not hungry. I did not understand enough Russian to know what her plans were, but I thought it was pretty obvious that I was not planning to skip lunch, so I excused myself. I went back to the restaurant and rejoined Dmitri. He asked me if the payment had been made. I assured him it had, but Alisa was not hungry, so she was not coming to lunch. Alisa did show up a little later but did not stay long. Something seemed to be bothering her again. I assumed it had nothing to do with me since I had paid her.

D. Anatol

Dmitri said little during our dinner, other than passing on the word that I was taking too much of Eva's time—someone had complained. Apparently, once the ethnographic tour had been over, so had Eva's assignment to me for that day. Dmitri's earlier enthusiasm over our "relationship" had been replaced by scolding. I remembered what Andrey said about Dmitri's reaction to their intrusion, and decided that Dmitri was using psychology to reassert control.

Dmitri wanted to get ready for our talk with Anatol. I asked him what the meeting was going to be about, but he was vague and said he did not know, maybe "some discussion and negotiation." He told me that we should get going. The meeting was to be at nine but the clock had not yet reached eight. We had time. Dmitri asserted that Anatol would not have time after nine. We had to hurry.

Around eight o'clock, we walked over to the Hotel Riga and up to the Managers Club. Eva was there and explained that Anatol had not arrived yet. The hour was not yet nine p.m., the time for my meeting as she had told me. Dmitri said Anatol would not have time after nine p.m., so I was puzzled. Why was I being told two different things? I waited in my room until nine and returned. Anatol was not there. Eva apologized, and I made arrangements for her to call me when Anatol arrived. Keeping a client waiting is a familiar tactic among Soviet elite.

I waited almost two hours before Anatol came. Dmitri spent some of this time with me, but he did not shed much light on the upcoming meeting. I reminded him that he had promised to get samples for Pomeroy and me and that he had only one day left to do this. He told me not to worry. During my time alone, I thought about what I could possibly discuss with Anatol and took stock of the situation. I decided that Riga was intriguing enough for me to stay longer to make an investigation. I had paid Dmitri and Alisa and was feeling less obliged to them. I had an opportunity to have a mini-vacation before resuming work in Leningrad, so I was contemplating how to go about it. My meeting with Anatol left me feeling determined to make this a reality.

At last, Anatol arrived. We went to a separate room. Dmitri came with us to help with translation if necessary. Anatol's English turned out to be quite good, and except at the initial awkward beginning, Dmitri spent most of the time listening. I sensed he was tense around Anatol. I imagined that Anatol to him was a more important person than most.

Anatol was a tall, elegant man, with just a hint of strong authority underneath his genteel veneer. It gave him an intimidating, almost cruel aura. He was quite direct, asking me to explain my business in Leningrad and Riga. I was too nervous to be articulate, and Dmitri had not prepared me at all for this meeting. I suspected that Dmitri knew more about what Anatol would want to know than he let on.

Despite the difficulties, Anatol grasped what I was doing in the Soviet Union and asked if I would like some help with my research. After all, "Latvia is an interesting country, too." He proposed developing a Latvian version of Pomeroy's test. I thought that this was a splendid idea. Then I said that there would not be enough time. I was leaving tomorrow with Dmitri. "But, you're returning later aren't you?" I told him I was not sure. I did not want to be out of Leningrad so close to my plane flight home. Since Dmitri was there, I did not want to pursue the idea and reveal my change in plans to him more fully. Finally, I asked Anatol if I could speak with him about this more the next day. Anatol then presented the reciprocal portion of the exchange he had in mind.

Anatol ran a commercial business school. He would appreciate help with teaching his students practical psychology. Could Pomeroy teach a course? He also had an adult education program in mind, a one year program. For the younger students, perhaps a fourth year course was appropriate. Our meeting was turning into something like the discussion I had with Pavel deep in Karelia, but this time the ideas being entertained were closer to what Pomeroy and I were doing. Finally, Anatol said almost winking at me, "We can work out the details tomorrow." With that, the meeting was over.

Dmitri was annoyed with me. Never mentioning my possible change in plans, he went on for some time about how I had not presented my research correctly. I was not "business-like." Perhaps he was right, but I thought his comments were besides the point. I sensed he was starting to get nervous and felt he was being squeezed out. I was much more in control of the situation at that point, and that made him uncomfortable. I defended myself, pointing out that I solicited his help prior to the meeting but he had remained mostly silent. We parted company in an uneasy mood. I went to sleep that night satisfied but also knowing that, if I did not take action in the morning, the momentum I had gained would be squandered.

The tourist guide *Fodor's* informed its readers that in the Soviet Union, once a plan was set, no attempt should be made to change it. Soviet tourism was based on plans and itineraries written in concrete. Thursday would turn out to be a day I broke this rule.

When I got up the next day, I had a talk with Anatol to ask him if he could make arrangements for me to stay a few extra days in Riga. I told him that I preferred not to wait until the end of my stay in the Soviet Union to return to Riga, and that I had other plans for that time. I was interested in cooperating with him immediately since it would save me unnecessary traveling. He agreed.

In the course of our conversation, I discovered that Dmitri was exploiting a two-tiered pricing system. He was paying domestic prices in rubles for transportation and accommodations, while charging me tourist prices. For example, a room in the Riga Hotel cost eighty dollars a night for a foreigner; it cost Dmitri eighty rubles. The exchange rate being roughly thirty rubles to the dollar, Dmitri was paying greatly reduced prices for everything. This double tiered pricing system was in effect throughout the Soviet Union. This explained why Dmitri had me travel "as a Russian" on the train. If I had actually paid the full Intourist fare, it would have diverted money away from his pocket into Intourist's pocket.

Anatol offered to help me find alternative transportation back to Leningrad and to make arrangements for a place to stay at ruble prices. Since the Hotel Riga was full due to the conference, which would last several more days, to stay on at this hotel would be impossible for me. He thought my best bet for transportation would be a flight. Train tickets were hard to come by on short notice. That was fine by me. I was uncomfortable with the idea of a train journey alone, but I was concerned about the cost of a plane ticket. The offer seemed reasonable, so I accepted it. I noticed that Anatol was treating me more warmly than he had the night before. I no longer felt intimidated by him.

I wanted to check for myself. Down in the lobby I found a hotel office where I inquired into prices and room availability. The information I got corroborated what Anatol told me. I headed to the Latvian Hotel. I was familiar with the layout of its lobby and was confident that an Aeroflot ticket office was located there.

At the Latvian Hotel, I located the Aeroflot counter. I noticed a VISA sign. I had a VISA credit card. Since I was running short of cash funds, this would be a way around that problem. I inquired into the availability of tickets. Flights and tickets were available. I asked if I could reserve and pay later. That was not possible. I advised the ticket agent that I might return, and was told the office would close at two p.m. Now I knew that I had a fallback position if Anatol did not come through. Still, at that point, I had little reason to believe that his staff would not come through. He had put Eva, who was efficient, on the case.

After lunch, I went back to the Managers Club. I wanted to check on the status of the arrangements being made for me. Eva greeted me and told me that, while room arrangements were possible, unfortunately no plane tickets were available. She was apologetic, even slightly sympathetic, but her tone was firm. I realized I had run into a dead end. I had seen little of Alisa after I paid her. I suspected that she was at the heart of "behind the scenes" maneuvering. I calmly told Eva to please not cancel any room arrangements; I would be back.

I hurried back to the giant blue edifice containing the airline office that was my last chance. The hour was close to two. If I did not get there soon, I would be out of luck. I knew that without a ticket in my hand, all my clout would disappear. On the way there, some conference participants caught up with me. I recognized a few of them as acquaintances of Dmitri. To my amazement, they tried to talk me out of staying in Riga. I told them that it was not their decision. I got to the ticket counter with little time to spare, exhausted from running back and forth between the two hotels.

I took out the one weapon that neither Dmitri nor Alisa had—a credit card. With my VISA card, I secured a one-way flight back to Leningrad (seventy-five U. S. dollars). My trip was beginning to run over budget, but it did not matter just then. With ticket in hand, I again ran into the same group of people. In a much more relaxed mood, I chatted with them as some of them followed me. They were amazed that I had been successful; that I was acting as an independent agent.

When I reached the Managers Club, Nelly was there along with Eva. I showed them the ticket. I was scheduled to leave Riga on Sunday morning. Today was Thursday. Could they secure me inexpensive lodging for three nights? Nelly, who had taken over the assignment, said "yes." I was to come back in a couple of hours. They would take care of it. I had to pack my things and move them into their office. With that done, I went back to the business convention.

E. Clara

I wanted to see Dmitri administer the test. I got to the conference building where Dmitri's seminar was in session. He had just shown a videotape of activities that he recorded earlier. His group was having a round-table discussion. They were attentive, displaying much emotion; different individuals kept standing up. During a short break, I asked Dmitri if he had given the test. He told me to be patient.

After the break, Dmitri's class divided into three groups. One of the groups included Andrey and a woman named Clara. Clara had been part of the group that I ran into when I went to buy the plane ticket. She spoke some English and had been asking me questions about my trip. A gentleman friend of hers with a beard as thick as Dmitri's was in another group. This second group included the "Sergey" who had tried to sell me rare books and was sharing a room with Andrey. His silent presence was everywhere. I noticed that Ann was participating this day. She was in a third group that included an artist.

They all sat around small tables discussing what Dmitri had explained was a "scarce resource" problem. He confidently predicted that the groups would fail to cooperate among themselves. I noticed that the seating arrangements were not equitable in terms of light. The second group, which was nearest the lobby, had poor light to work in, while Ann's group, which was closest to the projector, had excellent light. Andrey's group, which was seated near a sculpted figure, had medium light. Was this an intentional ploy on Dmitri's part or just happenstance?

I went outside. I was getting anxious about the test. Dmitri and Alisa's train would leave before five p.m. Little time was left. Then I noticed some of the participants were coming out of the building to get some fresh air, stretch their legs, or have a smoke. It was a break—the last one before the session for that day would end. I went inside and noticed people hunched over papers. It was the HVP test in Russian. I was relieved. Dmitri came over to talk with me. He explained that he could not find a way to include the test formally in his seminar. So he was having them take it during the break. I inquired as to the number of copies, and was told that he had passed out no less than forty. I had to tell Dmitri that I was going to stay in Latvia a few more days. The news did not surprise him. Apparently, he had already found out. With that I went outside again.

Clara was there. She wanted to know if I could do her a favor. Could I deliver a letter for her in the United States? She did not trust the Soviet postal system and thought having it mailed for her in the United States would ensure its delivery. She would give me some rubles to cover the postage. I assumed she was asking me now because she thought I would be leaving that day. I told her I was planning to stay awhile longer. She seemed pleased by this. I asked her how she liked the HVP test. She told me that she had not turned it in yet because she had a question about it. She showed me the test form—a single page. I realized that she was holding only half of the two-page profile that made up the test.

A little more conversation revealed that Dmitri had been handing out only part of the test to each person. Some of them got part 1; others got part 2. Shocked, I hurried back inside. A pile of paper was growing in front of Dmitri. A few people were still taking the HVP test. The rest had already finished. I asked Dmitri to show me what he had collected so far before making any accusations. Sure enough, each person had gotten a single sheet, not a pair. I asked Dmitri what he had done. Dmitri said that he could only get twenty copies of each part of the test produced. So he had gotten the forty samples by giving only one part of the test to each participant.

This was, to say the least, a curious development, and I was at a loss as to what to do. I knew that Dmitri and I had had plenty of discussions prior to this about Pomeroy's test. He should have fully understood that a valid sample required both parts of the test to be filled out by each respondent. I shared part of the blame, since I had been too lax about supervising the test. I should have insisted on being present at all times to make sure the test was being administered properly.

I told Dmitri he should have come to me first. Twenty good samples were far better than forty useless ones. Was it not obvious? A little time was still left. Could he re-instruct the participants? Perhaps half the filled sheets could be reused. Reorganizing it so the sample could be salvaged would take some doing. Dmitri flatly refused. He had given the test. I had my forty samples. No more time was left, and no more copies were available—too bad.

Though my buoyant mood had been undermined by this latest twist, I was still hoping that some use could be made of these "samples." As far as Pomeroy's research was concerned, the samples were useless since he was doing cross-national statistical comparisons that required the same structure for each sample produced. To do the comparisons properly, individuals from each national group have to take the same two part test, the only difference being the language.

Dmitri had let me down. I was left alone to lick my wounds while he distributed rolled up posters as parting presents to the participants in his seminar. Alisa was there carrying some bags. She had been getting their stuff ready for their departure. Before I got angry or tried to speak with Dmitri again, Andrey buttonholed me. He told me that he could arrange a room for rubles or a private flat for me to stay at during our discussions in Leningrad. This follow through on his part gave me more confidence that things would work out. It lifted my spirits. I told him what had happened. Andrey said that he and Ann had realized pretty quickly what was going on but did not see me there and did not feel they should interfere. He told me not to worry about it. He would get me some samples back in Leningrad.

It would be a better sample. The Russian version Dmitri had given was pretty flawed. The group he had given it to were not all Russians. Andrey was right. They did not represent one city as well. Pomeroy wanted to sample students from a single city. A variety of business persons of all ages from all over the Soviet Union was not exactly what he was after. Still, I would have preferred to have the data in hand. I thanked Andrey and told him that I was planning to stay longer in Riga, so we would have a chance to talk again.

Then Clara buttonholed me. She wanted me to follow her. She had a plan. Did I know that today was Dmitri's birthday? No, that came as a surprise to me as well. Dmitri had not mentioned anything to me. She wanted to get Dmitri and Alisa some flowers—a birthday gift for Dmitri and a going-away present for Alisa. I was not exactly feeling generous toward them at the time. Regardless, Clara's mood was so infectious that I went along with the plan. I also decided it would be prudent to see them off; I wanted to make sure that Dmitri knew when to expect me back. I had already exchanged information with him but, given his recent demonstration of absentminded behavior, I did not want to take a chance. I had no key to his flat. If he was not home when I called him from the airport, then he would not be able to come and meet me. I had asked him to meet me, but he told me to call him instead, as domestic airline flights were notorious for being off schedule.

Clara and I went to a large market located in and around some large buildings. Clara was in a big hurry, so I did not have a chance to observe, take photos, or absorb the atmosphere. At an ice cream stand, Clara bought several ice cream bars. She handed me one. Then we found a flower stand. She liked some purple ones—they had a semi-tropical look to them with delicate fluted petals. I helped her pay for the flowers, and we dashed to the train station to look for Dmitri and Alisa.

We arrived as a crowd was milling around a waiting train. I had no idea how Clara was planning to find them amidst hundreds of people. The train was long but Clara knew where to go. She told me that the spare ticket created by my change of plans had been given to the son of one of her friends; so she was aware of the arrangements. Nothing was wasted in the Soviet Union, a train ticket especially. The scarcity of resources such as train tickets were caused by a contracting economy. Russians developed an extensive use of social networks to distribute these resources using a market-like system that involved cash, preferably hard currency, information, and favors.

Clara knew the number of the coach Dmitri and Alisa would be riding. Sure enough, we found them. They were saying goodbye to the father of the son who would be going. I was a little nervous about meeting them. Earlier, sometime after I had purchased my plane ticket, a friend of Dmitri's told me that when Alisa found out that I had secured a plane ticket, she was surprised and annoyed by the development. I guessed she was bewildered as to how, after paying her with the last of my cashed U. S. currency, I had managed to purchase a plane ticket, which by their standards was quite expensive. Ironically, before the trip to Latvia I had shown Dmitri and her my VISA card and tried to explain to them the function of the odd-looking piece of plastic. At the time they did not appear to understand what I was talking about. Consumer credit cards did not exist in Russia, and students, including graduate students, were notoriously poor. To think that a student far away from home could access hundreds of dollars with a piece of plastic was beyond their imagination.

The parting turned out to be lively and elaborate. It was truly a Russian farewell, Clara told me afterwards. Dmitri was visibly happy when we presented him with flowers. Alisa also received some flowers and was in a good mood. Referring to me, she shouted "*libertadt*" (you have your liberty now). I wished Dmitri a happy birthday and reminded him again of when I would be returning to Leningrad. A lot of hugging and kissing marked the occasion. This was the first time I had seen the traditional Russian bear hugging and cheek pecking. We walked away with Dmitri and Alisa waving from the entrance to their coach.

Clara walked me back to the Hotel Riga. I helped her finish the rest of the ice cream on the way. It had melted too much to be a present for anyone. Before parting, we discussed a letter that she wanted to send with me. Now that she knew I was going to be there a little bit longer, she wanted to add a few more lines to it. We could meet tomorrow. I suggested we meet at the conference luncheon or dinner. We also discussed the test she took. I answered the question she had about it. I told her she could take some extra time to finish it, just to give it to me along with the letter.

As I entered the hotel, I realized that I was alone and would be for the next few days. I would be dependent on Anatol and his staff to some extent, but as they had over a hundred people to deal with, I was sure they would not be hovering over me as Dmitri and Alisa had. I tried not to think about what rejoining Dmitri and Alisa would be like. We had a lot of unfinished business. They had the money I agreed to pay. They should be content with that for a while. Some of my things were at their flat. I still trusted them enough to feel confident that they would not go into my stuff. I also had a little bit of insurance. Pomeroy would be calling in the middle of the week. So, if anything was amiss, he would hear about it. He would have to be told by me about the insistence on cash payment, about Dmitri's failure to secure a proper sample, and about my failure to ensure that he did. Still, the dark clouds on the horizon had a silver lining, namely the unexpected, and potentially fruitful, association with Andrey and Ann.

F. A Working Holiday

After parting with Clara, I made my way up the five floors to the Managers Club using the broad staircases inside the hotel. I enjoyed the exercise and did not like to wait for the slow moving elevator. Besides, I felt a sense of exhilaration, being alone and unencumbered by the constant presence of

Dmitri, Alisa, or their spies. That solitude here carried a price had not sunk in yet.

Traveling alone in the Soviet Union was not recommended. Intourist was used to dealing with foreigners as groups. Individual foreign visitors were not catered to or welcome. A group was easier to manage. Individuals were more likely to follow their curiosity and get into trouble. Groups tended to stick together and reinforce the rules and guidelines laid down by their tour leaders. Groups stuck out by their numbers. Individuals might blend into the crowd and, if they looked Russian, might even go undetected for some time.

I had been closely supervised by Dmitri and Alisa up until then, largely as a part of this Soviet institution of monitoring citizens and foreigners alike. Yet, I had managed somehow to wiggle out of this snare, albeit for a time only. Still, it was a unique opportunity for me, but; as I was soon to find out, my general lack of experience with the country, its languages, and how to make use of its facilities would hamper my mobility. I lacked the savvy and confidence to get much further than tickling the surface. The next seventy-two hours would transform me from someone who had become accustomed to being handled into someone who refused to tolerate it for long.

My break from Dmitri had been visceral. Now, I had an opportunity to become more consciously aware of the reasons and motivations behind my gut reaction. I was inspired to some extent by the prospect of a few days of rest among people who seemed to like me in a place that had some more familiar sign posts, things considered mundane back home, like credit cards, suburban houses, and people who acted with something resembling initiative and independence. I placed myself in a different set of hands, not interested so much in handling and exploiting me, as in being responsible for my accommodations and comfort for a reasonable price, and other than that, leaving me alone. Latvia now represented a kind of "half-way house" in which I could do a little bit of growing up in terms of the culture of the Soviet Union.

As I entered the office of the Managers Club, I tried to spot the flower I had given to Eva when I knew that I would be staying longer, but I could not see it. Nelly and Eva were there and told me that arrangements had been made for me to stay two nights at a hotel in Jurmala, the beach resort on the shores of the Baltic. They told me the cost, fifty U. S. dollars. On my last night (Saturday, 20 July) I would be a guest of the Club back in the Hotel Riga.

The arrangement sounded good to me, but the cost was higher than I expected. Anatol had mentioned a hotel for rubles not dollars, but the price was not outrageous because it included hotel meals and taxi shuttles between Jurmala and Riga. I would get to see the place that I had heard about and read a little bit about in my *Fodor's* guide. Nelly and Eva would accompany me that evening to introduce me to the manager of the hotel and work out details, but I had a slight problem. I only had half the dollars necessary for the payment. I inquired if I could get a discount, mentioning that the price was higher than I expected. Nelly told me not to worry about it. When I sensed that a solution may be imminent, as a gesture of good will, I suggested to her that I go look for a hard currency store. Disregarding my suggestion, she asked me to wait because Anatol was coming to meet me.

Anatol showed up a little later. He told me that we would be starting work on a Latvian version of the HVP right away, but since he had a lot of pressing matters, he was going to turn the task over to his daughter, Ruta. She showed up a short while later, casually dressed in fashionable clothes, a pleasant young woman about Eva's age, smart, and with her dark hair cut short. Ruta took only a few minutes to discuss some logistical matters with me after I presented her with a copy of Pomeroy's test in English.

After our discussion, I said that I should go look for a hard currency store. Ruta suggested we go together. We left under the partly stern and partly amused look of her father. Ruta promised him we would be back shortly. Our walk was brief. The stores were closed, and the tall buildings blocked out the sinking sun, leaving us in shadows. We talked about nothing in particular. The situation felt like being with a college buddy. During our walk, I observed that young women in Riga, if Ruta was a representative example, were keenly interested in being fashionable and dressing well. Compared with Alisa, Ruta wore clothes much closer to the fashions of Western Europe and the United States in color and skirt length. Obviously, she had access to a wider selection of clothes. Russians like Alisa had to make do with whatever was available.

Ruta instructed me to call her that evening from the hotel in Jurmala, for what reason, I was not quite sure. The next day, I was to be back at the Managers Club for a follow-up meeting with her and Anatol around noon.

After Ruta left, Nelly, without comment, handed me twenty-five dollars to cover the rest of the payment. I wondered how she had come up with the money. I was not sure if this money was a loan or their round about way of giving me the discount I asked for. Nelly did not say. She did not speak English to any great extent, and Sandra was not there. I decided to stay silent and hope for the best. For the time being, I was just happy to have secured accommodations.

Nelly, Eva, and I left for Jurmala at twilight. A taxi took us all the way there. Expensive, I thought, since Jurmala was about forty-five minutes away, and the same taxi would bring Nelly and Eva back. Then again everything was priced in rubles, so the cost was probably relatively cheap. The Managers Club made arrangements with the taxi company for several trips and got a discounted price.

We left the city heading west and crossed a bridge that spanned the Daugava River. As soon as we left the city outskirts, I could see just how flat the countryside was. It reminded me of Jutland in Denmark, a long, green, flat stretch. Just enough light was left for me to make out the horizon. The taxi driver, dressed in a leather jacket, drove fast through the city. As we entered the long straight section of road that would take us directly to the coast, he began to slow down. He let the car coast for quite a way, until it was barely moving. Then he slowly accelerated the car to a good pace and let it coast again. I turned and asked Eva, who was in back, what he was doing. She asked the driver and translated that he was conserving gasoline.

We came to a little village after dark, a cluster of buildings illuminated by a single light. The road wound through the village and then hit an empty stretch. I could not see water but I could sense it was there. After a time, we pulled into a gravel parking lot in front of a small hotel surrounded by dark shapes suggesting trees.

The driver waited for us outside, as Nelly, Eva, and I went into the building. The proprietor, an Alexander R., was expecting us. He was a shorter and slightly rougher version of Anatol. Nelly explained to me that he wanted us to have a little supper with him, assuring me that he was a "good man."

The proprietor took us through a lobby and into a small restaurant. I found it hard to see as he led us to the right and toward the back, past some scattered dinner tables. The uneven lighting illuminated table surfaces but left the patrons huddled in shadows. We found an empty table down a few steps, tucked into a corner, partially hidden behind a low wall. The light was better in this back portion of the restaurant.

Upon on our arrival, a white linen tablecloth was laid over the table, and seats were drawn up to it by restaurant bus boys. Four people had just room enough to sit facing each other, two to a side. I sat with Nelly, looking up at the dimly lit tables we had just passed, set slightly above us beyond the partition; the proprietor and Eva sat opposite us with their backs to the partition.

A waiter appeared, and Alexander R. gave him some instructions. The waiter disappeared through the entrance to a kitchen on my right. Nelly immediately began an animated conversation with Alexander. The food began arriving pretty quickly. It turned out to be a sumptuous supper. I started wondering about the poor taxi driver waiting outside. I had not expected to be sitting down with the proprietor for a meal as part of the check-in process.

The meal included meat, salads, bread, cheeses, and caviar. Dessert consisted of almonds and fresh slightly under-ripe apricots. I noticed again that Eva ate little. I asked her about it. She said she had to watch her weight, which surprised me. Eva wore clothes that accented the long lines of her body. I noticed that Alexander seemed to be as charmed by Eva as I had been.

Eva was quieter than usual, her cheerfulness and frequent laughter held in check. Nelly was now doing most of the talking, most of it with Alexander. She enjoyed it.

The supper was lingering on longer than necessary when Nelly suddenly remembered the taxi driver. With a gasp, she realized how caught up she had gotten in the occasion. She made her excuses with Alexander as Eva told me what I was to do. Alexander would see me to my room. The following morning I was to go to his office and pay him the agreed price. She would come to fetch me at such and such time in the morning.

The room, modest in size, was decorated nicely, and it had a small refrigerator, a television, and a phone made from bright red plastic. Like my room at the Hotel Riga, this room seemed clean and, though the bathroom was a bit Spartan, comfortable enough.

Upon settling in, I dialed Ruta's number, and she answered. "You have arrived?" Ruta's staccato voice cut through a faint static. The phone connection was a little fuzzy, but not bad. I told her that I was at my hotel in Jurmala and that Eva and Nelly were on their way back. I asked her how she was doing with the translation. I expected her to have one or two questions, remembering my marathon sessions with Dmitri, but she had no questions and abruptly wished me a good night. "Okay, good night" I stammered, disappointed we could not chat for a moment or two. To hear her voice had been nice. Perhaps, the call was Anatol's way of making sure I had arrived in good shape. After a shower, I lay in bed alone, lonely, thinking about home for a long time.

I awoke early to bright sunlight streaming in through a curtained window. I opened the window to let in air that was cool and fresh. Tall pine trees blocked my view of the Baltic (Gulf of Riga). The night before had been too dark to notice that the hotel was set in a sandy forest of pine trees.

I spent a few minutes writing in my journal. I knew that I had to pay the proprietor, so I went in search of him without much delay. I felt awkward since I knew almost no Latvian, and the director spoke no English or Russian. I found him in the lobby. He immediately took me to his office. I presented him with the money, and he gave me his business card as a "receipt." We shook hands, and that was it. Not a word was exchanged. Dmitri had told me that some Baltic people were noted for their reticence, but this was more than I expected.

A little time was still left before Eva came, and I took the time to walk around outside and snap a few pictures. An open-air patio caught my attention. It had little red plastic tables with red plastic chairs under differently colored umbrellas (orange and blue, red and blue, green and white) set on a tiled patio bordered by a black iron railing. Beyond, grand columns of giant pines rose into the sky. Their gray and pink colored bark contrasted nicely with the artificial colors on the patio. The setting was a melange of different shades of green foliage and sandy paths. The hotel resembled a hunting lodge set in a pleasant, shady, wooded spot of earth that seemed never to have known an irritating noise. Though a sea was nearby, it was the rustling breeze that filled the air with sound. Jurmala was a retreat specially craved by those who suffered from hypertension.

Eva came. She was all business, immediately making sure I had paid the proprietor. I noticed that her voice sounded huskier when she discussed business. She took me to the waiting taxi, and we went back to Riga. Along the way, I noticed little cottages lining the road near Jurmala. One was so cheerful that I asked her to stop the taxi so I could take a picture. It had a view of the sea, was tiny and rose colored, set behind a picket fence, and surrounded by greenery.

The road took us in sight of blue patches of water, but trees mostly blocked the view. I would have to wait until the next day to get a good look at the Baltic. We passed through the village. I wanted to get out again, but I realized by Eva's mood that she was in a hurry. As we headed down the long flat part of the road, I noticed some structures in the distance and asked her about them. They were part of a vast state farm. As we passed green fields and stretches of naked brown earth, I was not quite sure what was being grown.

Eva asked me if I had had time to go to the beach near my hotel. I said that I had not but that I wanted to. "You have to make sure to do so tomorrow," Eva admonished me. She asked if I had been fed; I could eat at the Latvia Hotel and have dinner there too. That sounded fine to me. She reminded me that a pipe organ concert would be given at St. Mary's Cathedral that evening. I thought about asking her to accompany me, but only asked if she was planning to go. Before Eva deposited me at the Latvia Hotel so I could have a meal, I asked her if she would have dinner with me later. Her eyes lit up momentarily—perhaps it would be possible.

After brunch, I went back to the Managers Club. On my way into the hotel, the doorman tried to stop me. I had seen this man before. I supposed he knew I had come with Dmitri. He had never questioned my coming and going before. Today he did. I did not stop and said the only thing that came to mind, "*piatava etadge*" (fifth floor), and he let me by. The best way to deal with minor authorities in the Soviet Union was to act as if you owned the place. I wondered how the man knew I was no longer a guest there. Hundreds of people walked in and out. I never saw him checking hotel passes.

One of the first things I noticed as I entered the office on the fifth floor was the flower I had given to Eva. Eva was preoccupied with some paper work. Anatol brought a new helper with him, a woman named Iveta. She was involved in publishing and wanted to know if "my chief" was interested in becoming published. I was not sure what exactly she had in mind, but I said that I would relay the message to him. As it turned out, Iveta was doing some work in international affairs that involved "conflict resolution." I knew Pomeroy was interested in the subject, and I just happened to have a couple of copies of an article he had written about it (Pomeroy, 1985). So I gave her one. This seemed to please her, and we got to work.

Anatol brought news that Ruta made only marginal progress in translating the test into Latvian. The task turned out to be harder than she expected. He had found Iveta who was competent in Russian, Latvian, and English. She and I were to work together on the translation that afternoon. Then he discussed some logistics involved in gathering a sample. Since Pomeroy wanted students to take the test, Anatol proposed waiting until September to begin data collection. On my part, I reassured him that I would relay his interest in a psychology course to Pomeroy.

With that done, Anatol left us alone to work while he got busy with other matters. Iveta then asked to see the Russian and English HVPs. She felt that it would be easier to get a more accurate Latvian version that way, by a process of "triangulation." This sounded ingenious to me. We worked together for a couple of hours. Along the way, she made some corrections to the Russian test. Finally, she had a translation with which she was satisfied. She would have it typed up, and I would get a printed copy the next day. Meanwhile I started to make my own written copy. Under Anatol's direction, and with the help of his daughter and Iveta, we had produced a Latvian version of the HVP. Ruta had my instructions for how to administer the test and what kind of sample to collect. Iveta had done an excellent job translating it. In return they had acquired a possible American connection to further their enterprises.

Before Iveta left, I made one more request: I wanted to get a back translation of the test. I knew Pomeroy's standard of doing this with all the foreign versions of his test. I figured that finding a Latvian speaker back in the United States would be difficult, so I improvised. Iveta and I worked together, and she produced a nearly perfect back translation, but our way of doing it was not perfect. An independent party would have been preferable.

I reflected on this turn of events. In just about a day, I had an excellent version of a Latvian HVP. It had taken over a week to get a pretty rough translation of the HVP into Russian from Dmitri. True, Anatol's people had two versions of it to work from, the original test in English, and Dmitri's Russian translation, with a few corrections by Ann. Still, the performance on their part was impressive, and unlike my experiences in Russia with Dmitri, I was enjoying myself here. I started to regret that my research was based in Russia instead of Latvia.

Anatol, who was in charge of this operation, demonstrated a mastery of social networks to get the job done. Through his connections he had produced results that Dmitri, who tried to do the same thing alone, was not able to match. Future experiences in Russia would reinforce this idea. I tended to get things done with the help of those who skillfully manipulated social networks. Those who had few contacts tended to mark time, and I would have to separate myself from them.

After Iveta departed, a woman named Valentina came to see me, a buxom woman with cherubic cheeks, faint Oriental features, and a swarthy complexion. She was from Siberia, her dress was fashionable, and she wore a lot of make up and jewelry. Valentina had heard I was an American. She spoke some English. Her visit was for the sole purpose of having a chance to practice her English. We had a short chat, and she left.

I sat in the office alone. I contemplated going for a walk, but I was not yet in the mood. I had been planning a walking tour of the city to photograph some things that had caught my eye. I knew my time was running out. Unlike Jurmala, Riga was overcast, and though rain was not certain, it was a possibility. The next day, Saturday, would be my last in Latvia. My flight on Sunday was scheduled to leave early in the morning. Half of Saturday would be spent in Jurmala. Eva would come fetch me after lunch. If it rained Saturday afternoon, then my last photo opportunity would be gone, but this was my last chance for a dinner with Eva. If I took off now, I was afraid Anatol would send her off on a mission somewhere else.

So, I waited. I wrote in my journal, and I waited some more. Eva seemed to be endlessly busy. So, I gave up. She was talking to a young man in Russian when I was about to leave. I sensed he was interested in her. I told Eva I was going to go for a walk to take some pictures. I would meet her at the restaurant, if she were coming. She was surprised, and for the first and only time I felt she was disappointed that I was not waiting around for her.

My walking tour yielded some of my best photos of Riga. I was eager to get pictures of further evidence of political activity. This included the green statue of Lenin I saw earlier, some barricades I spotted down a side street, and a graffiti covered wall, which blocked another side street. "Red Army go home" and some other colorful phrases in English marked this wall. After years of hearing the catch phrase "Yankee go home" in Latin America, seeing the Soviet version as ironic. The most poignant scene was of the liberty monument. I took a photo of the flowers strewn over its base. They were in commemoration of fallen Latvian victims to Soviet injustice.

My walking tour lasted over an hour. I tried to notice details and photograph areas away from the tourist centers, as well as taking photos of the park, flower market, and some grand looking structures in the old district. Not far from the Latvia Hotel, a bearded priest, who I guessed was Russian Orthodox, hurried past me dressed in a black and purple vestment. He looked like a throwback to a time long past. He was a startling sight in a city doing its best to look modern.

I tried to get a sense of the place by comparing it to Leningrad. I noticed that the automobiles were the same general type found in Leningrad, boxy Fiat style cars that looked dated. The phone booths were more modern in appearance, looking almost futuristic; and, unlike Leningrad, they appeared to be in good condition. People, for the most part, wore casual clothes even though the day was a workday. The only sign of work activity was the speed at which some of them moved. Leningrad seemed lethargic by comparison. Here, many more people were in a hurry.

For people to be in a hurry, they need something of value to hurry to. Latvians were experiencing a more enriched life than Russians. After 1991, new values, material and spiritual, poured into Russia. By 1993, everyone was in a hurry in Leningrad.

Riga was a kaleidoscope of styles cluttered together. Building fronts adorned by rounded columns and statues were thrown together with rows of unadorned facades with peeling paint. Sharply sloped tiled roofs mixed with flat roofs, domes, and spires. Unlike Leningrad, Riga had no open panoramas and no unifying theme. Its features tangled together and obscured each other. Trees hid skyscrapers, hotels hid churches, and the broad Daugava River was out of sight from everywhere except a dusty tramway line and some warehouses. The chaotically arranged streets of the old town made spotting landmarks difficult and lent Riga an air of claustrophobia. The central park, which divided the city in half, was that way too. Pedestrians were bound to encounter its thickly wooded grounds and winding paths at some point in their journeys.

Once encountered, individual sites were charming or highly symbolic. The city was organized into niches. You could gaze at neo-classical architecture, a modern skyscraper, and a medieval church in one leisurely stroll. Somehow, none of them seemed out of place. Set on a broad avenue, Lenin's statue, the most prominent reminder that this was the Soviet Union, was only fifteen minutes away from a wall containing graffiti that expressed a desire that the same Soviet Union disappear. Riga also paid tribute to different religious styles: Romanesque churches, the narrow spires of Protestant churches, and domed Russian Orthodox churches all vied for attention.

My tour ended at dinnertime. I hurried back to the hotel restaurant where I had shared so many meals with other participants. I found Lolita waiting there with a message from Eva that she was sorry, but she could not make it. Lolita also brought a letter and a message from Clara, which included the completed test. I had not seen Clara all day. She, like Eva, had been too busy to meet me. I ate dinner alone. My walking tour and photographs had come at a price.

This was the first time I ate alone in the big restaurant. I felt uncomfortable and self-conscious. No one else was there to join. Andrey and Ann were not there. Dmitri and Alisa were long gone. Lolita departed after delivering her messages. Not to be sharing a meal with someone felt odd. Companionship was something I had become accustomed to without realizing it. I tried to read, but I could not concentrate. The waiter came by often with different dishes each time I said "*spaseeba*" (thank you). A few Russian women were at the next table. I could overhear them mocking the way I pronounced the word. Then one of them asked me for a light for her cigarette, which I provided. "Zankyou" was the way she pronounced "thank you." I could only smile to myself. They were as clumsy as I was with an unfamiliar language.

The situation drove home that I needed to change some things about myself if my overall Russian research venture was to succeed. I had a chance to measure myself and found that I was far away from standards I needed to achieve, namely competence with the Russian language and development of solid social connections in Russia. I improved these as time went on, and, by 1993, I achieved a measure of competence in both areas.

I got over my loneliness, finished my dinner, and walked to the cathedral where the pipe organ concert was to take place. A crowd was outside. I hoped Eva might show up at the concert, but I saw no sign of her. I spotted Andrey and Ann and joined them. They were happy to see me, and we watched the concert together. This was a chance for us to be together socially. Other than a reminder by Andrey about when to call him at Leningrad, no business was discussed between us. Spending leisure time together cemented our relationship.

An odd incident occurred at the concert in St. Mary's, otherwise known as the Dom Cathedral. Located in the old town, it was of Gothic design and noted for its huge pipe organ. The music soared to the high vaulted ceiling. The audience sat in pews. We were in a church, but the occasion was secular. When the first break in the music was reached, hesitant scattered applause started. I joined it immediately. Just after it died out, I felt someone shoving my right shoulder from behind. I turned to see a dignified looking old man, probably Latvian, scowling at me. Had I committed some indiscretion? If so, it was either one of two things. Sometimes classical music has pauses in the middle of an opus where clapping is inappropriate. I thought that this was not the case since others had clapped. Regardless, I did not deserve a shove. Second, and this I suspected more strongly, people do not clap in church. Still, this was not a mass; it was a secular concert. As far as I knew, applause was appropriate. Whatever it was, I did not take kindly to the gentleman's gesture. At the next break, I heard the applause begin again, this time louder and longer. I joined it enthusiastically. Andrey and Ann were applauding this time along with me; my whole row was. I turned around and calmly stared at the old man. I must have gotten my message across because a short while later he stalked out of the church—another curiosity to add to my list.

Public admonitions of perceived improper behavior were common in the Soviet Union. A milder version of the same thing occurred to me in the Polish Catholic Church, when my chess set made noise as I sat in a pew. Once, during a train journey in Russia in 1993, I saw an argument break out between strangers, an elderly couple and some teenagers, over the teenagers' deportment.

After the concert, I said good bye to Andrey and Ann. I wondered if I would see them again. I remembered my experience with Eileen—how we had failed to meet. Plans just seemed to melt. Nothing seemed stable in this land of growing mystery. I went back to the Managers Club to find Eva.

When I got back, Nelly had a little treat for all of us, fresh cantaloupe. Fruit of any kind had been a rarity during my trip. Now, I had it two days in a row. The melon was delicious. I watched Eva eating some, obviously enjoying it. She was standing. Below her long skirt, her ankles turned in slightly. I asked her what had happened. It turned out that she had been given an assignment at the last minute. Another conference participant needed some logistical help. She had just gotten back.

Some time was still left before we had to go. Eva took me to the old district. The fading light made everything bluish gray, almost ghostly. We walked among ancient ruins and reached a little cobblestone square lit by lamps that once held gas lights. The setting fitted her. She had an air of the past about her. Unlike, the more fashionable Latvian women her age, Eva did not wear her hair or her skirts short.

A couple stopped us. They turned out to be American tourists; the first I had seen. They wanted me to snap their picture. In return they would take ours. The whole process lasted a minute. Afterwards, Eva told me that she was not used to how quickly and decisively Americans acted. Latvians took a long time to think things over before acting. This was the same thing that Dmitri told me about the way Russians did business. Latvians were reserved. Clara told me that her people were generally closed; compared to them, Russians were extroverted. Latvians suffered much under foreign regimes and were cautious about revealing themselves. Earlier that day, I noticed how the architecture of Riga, with its nooks, crannies, and peekaboo vistas, also reflected a kind of closeted existence.

We took a taxi later on. As we left our hotel, our driver sped off so fast he almost hit a woman crossing the street in front of him. He did not slow down as he made his turn. I just caught a glimpse of the woman leaping onto the sidewalk, clutching her handbag, her skirt flying up around her legs. She did not yell at him. Apparently, he had the right of way, and that was all there was to it.

Before going to Jurmala, we had to stop at the bus station, where Eva dashed off to retrieve another traveler, a young man. His name was Alois. He was Latvian, and he was beautiful—dark, handsome, with delicate features, and black wavy hair. He, like Eva, seemed to be a throw-back to another time. He spoke no English. Eva told me he had come on business. I noticed how courteous he was with her. I felt jealous and realized I had developed a crush on Eva.

Again, I was riding into the Baltic night. About half way to the village that marked the beginning of Jurmala, Eva fell asleep. So did the boy. My day had been too easy—I was wide-awake.

As we wound through the village, I saw a young couple kissing, or rather, a young man kissing a young woman. The woman was standing straight and stiff with her arms at her sides and her feet turned slightly inward, almost like a wooden doll, while the man held and kissed her, his head buried in her shoulder. This scene was lit by a flash of illumination, and just as quickly we passed into darkness.

The ride seemed to take an eternity. We had left later than the day before. The last half of the ride was in pitch black, there being few highway lamps along the road. By the time we reached the hotel, I was tired. I noted how Alois helped Eva out of the cab, extending his hand, and how she took it demurely to get out. His manner suggested that he was an expert at this sort of courtesy. Eva took her time depositing each of us at our rooms and left. I was alone again at the end of the world. Somehow it had lost its mystery to me. I was to have the next morning to myself and would finally get to see the Baltic.

I got up early and decided to go for a walk to find the sea. A few of the hotel guests were walking the grounds. I smiled at them but did not attempt to engage them. I was feeling my solitude again—an American so far away from home in a communist country. I felt awkward and shy, knowing almost no Latvian. I realized that I had grown used to Latvians who spoke English or Russian. I longed to be back in Riga.

Alois was not around. Eva was to come and fetch him in the morning. She would be back for me later in the afternoon. I was to have brunch at midday. They assumed that I would sleep late. I slept well and got up early. A cooling spell made the air conducive to sleeping. The temperature dropped enough overnight for me to use one of the wool blankets provided in my room. That morning, I felt calmer and more rested than I felt in a long time. I did not feel hungry. So a late brunch would be fine. The woods near the hotel were enveloped in a thin mist that was slowly being burnt off by veiled sunlight, which made the sky white.

Since clouds obscured the sun, I had trouble orienting myself at first and did not know which way to go. Eventually, I found a promising path that I felt confident headed west in the direction of the sea, a narrow dirt trail that cut through a grassy knoll and went under the overhanging branches of pine trees. The path began to descend until it reached a sandy spot, where a dune interrupted the path. Underbrush on the dune partially hid the sea. All I could make out was a white patch framed by green leaves. I stepped through the gap, ducking my head to avoid some branches.

I felt like I had stepped through a portal between worlds. The scene in front of me was surreal. I had been expecting to see water. My memory of the first sight of oceans, gulfs, seas, even lakes, is patterned: I will see a flat stretch of a body of water, blue, green, perhaps gray, or even asphalt in color, depending on the conditions. Waves might be breaking on the shoreline. I will always see a horizon between the water and the sky. Here I saw a beach with a white void beyond. I could not tell what it was. Logic told me that this had to be the Baltic Sea (Gulf of Riga). My senses did not register that. I might as well have been on the side of a mountain looking into a white cloud. The light gray sand had a subtle pink glow to it. A straggly line of dark green grasses marked the beginning of the beach. Instead of sloping down to in-rushing surf, the beach just faded away out of sight, melting into a blank space beyond. Because I perceived no horizon, I had no way to tell what was water and what was sky. I could not hear the sound of pounding surf, just stillness.

I had to walk out onto the beach before my senses began to unravel the mystery. I could now see the curve of the narrow strip of sand forming a concave line to my left and right. The edge of the forest was just behind the beach and stretched uninterrupted beyond the sand out into the white mist on either side of me. My eyes started to discern the vague outline of clouds, which slowly gained definition as my eyes, traveled up to the zenith. The bottoms of these clouds were lost in a grayish white mist that rose from the surface of placid, limp water, which had the same color as the sky. The clouds were lost somewhere in the water, and the water was lost somewhere in the clouds. I thought I had stumbled into some place out of a legend—the place where clouds are born.

As time passed, I could see the sky becoming bluer and the clouds darker. The beach looked more ordinary now. Yet the placidity of the sea and the absence of people still left a residue of strangeness. The temperature was not warm or cool. A little breeze moved the grasses at the beach's edge. The beach, being empty, should have been a vacationer's dream. Still, something was unsettling about it.

Eventually, I saw signs of life. A group of young boys and girls, some wearing jogging suits, others with tee-shirts and shorts, came running along the edge of the water from the north. They were far enough away so I was not of any concern to them. They passed in front of me, turned around, and headed back north. They repeated this process. They must have been training. Eventually they stopped and horsed around with each other. I did not see any of them go in the water. I started to wonder about this when I saw a man approaching. He stopped nearby, put a towel on the sand, and stripped down to his bathing suit. I watched him go into the water. It was shallow. He had to walk out quite far until he could swim.

I took some pictures of the beach. Then I found a piece of driftwood to sit on and watched the sky turning a little bluer with each passing minute. Some white gulls hovered near the beach. A family had come by wearing street clothes. They had some food for the birds. I watched them as the gulls wheeled and dove around them, fighting for the scraps of food.

Soon the time came to head back. I watched the man return from the water, dry off, put his clothes back on, and walk away. The family finished with the birds and also disappeared. Other people were trickling on to the beach. I went to the edge of the water to test its temperature. It felt cold, but that did not matter to me. I had not planned to go swimming, as I had no bathing suit. The heavy clouds dispersed, and the sunlight brightened, though the sky was still hazy. When I left, the beach seemed ordinary enough.

Back in my hotel room, a tall blonde woman brought me a meal. She smiled as she set the tray laden with food on the little table by the window. The meal included meat served with a tomato, a couple of thick slices of white bread, and a large white porcelain tureen containing vegetable broth with small pieces of chicken. I ladled out some of the soup and ate it with the cutlet. I had some watery juice to drink as well. I finished as much as I could and wrote in my notebook until Eva came to fetch me. As we set off, she asked me if I had a good rest. I told her that I spent the morning at the beach. A concerned look crossed her face:

"Oh my God, I forgot! You didn't go in the water did you?"

"No. Is there something wrong with it?"

"I forgot to tell you. It's polluted."

"Really? But, I saw a man go swimming."

"Suicide."

Poor man, I thought, but I was puzzled. Why would he have not known about it? He did not appear to be a tourist. As for me, I had not read my *Fodor's* guide carefully enough. If I had, I would have known that the Baltic was quite polluted and that swimming was not recommended. I had not gone swimming because I had not brought a bathing suit. That saved me from possibly getting sick. The Baltic was polluted by effluents from the mining of shale oil, phosphorous, and limestone (Smith 1992, 162). I had been at the Gulf of Riga, which was part of the Baltic. I wondered if the polluted nature of the water had contributed to the strange effect I saw on the beach.

On the way back, I saw my first auto accident in the Soviet Union. At a crossroads with no traffic control, a light truck and a small car side swiped each other. "This should be interesting," I thought. Instead of a scene developing as it inevitably does in America, the two drivers went their separate ways after the accident. The man in the truck got out to check the rear, which had a sizable dent. The driver of the other vehicle waited, not even bothering to get out to inspect the damage to his car. After seeing that the other was not hurt, they each took off, a kind of hit-and-run by mutual consent. I noticed that Eva showed no interest in the situation. I turned and asked if she had seen that. She told me to stop getting excited; it was no big deal. This would be the first of my many observations of the flat affect among Soviet citizens that Polish journalist Ryszard Kapuscinski also noted during his travels in the Soviet Union (Kapuscinski, 1994, 143–146).

The cause of this lack of reaction is not easy to determine. Dmitri and Alisa could get quite animated on occasion, such as when the canoe sprang a leak, or when they were afraid I would not pay. Yet they had no reaction to the fighter jet that buzzed us. Russian friends that I knew later also exhibited this dichotomy of behavior. I noticed that, more or less, the typical reaction to a public event such as an accident or loud noise would be that of nonchalance, while private behavior could be more emotional.

Two factors most likely contributed to this. First, Russians had experienced several wars, where sudden violence was a matter of course. Second, during Josef Stalin's reign, public openness was avoided to ensure your safety. A third, psychological, factor also may have been at play. The closed nature of society and a grinding existence contributed to individual neuroses such as depression.

Flat responses are characteristic of an individual suffering from depression. This last factor is problematic, as psychological characteristics have to be taken on a case by case basis. As an anthropologist, I am more interested in cultural characteristics, those features that individuals share as part of a group, as opposed to features that individuals possess by themselves. When I visited Russia in 2000, I noticed that Russian public behavior had changed to resemble that of a Western European country.

We got back to the hotel. This time Eva was with me when we went past the doorman. She spoke with him briefly, explaining my situation so he knew that I belonged there. I was to spend the last night at the Riga Hotel as a guest of the Managers Club. In the evening, I would be able to use the spare room, the same one where we first met Nelly and where my bag was held hostage by Alisa. In the interim, I was able to hang out in the extra room that adjoined the main room of the Managers Club.

The rest of the afternoon included a visit by Alois to the club office. He brought a box of chocolates as a gift for the staff. I envied his inbred chivalry and the obvious impression he made on Eva. I also wondered why, after Eva had told me the day before that he was there on a "serious business trip," he was spending so much time entertaining Anatol's staff. Gift giving was a part of business in the Soviet Union, something I had yet to learn in all its complexity.

Whenever I spoke with Eva in English, I noticed that Alois would sit quietly, and though he said nothing, he was paying attention. Finally, I asked about this and found that he did not speak English because he was not confident enough to do so, but he understood quite a bit of it. This struck me as being borderline duplicity. I put a blunt question to him: "So, Alois are you here on business or pleasure?" He understood the question without it being translated for him. He gave his answer to Eva in Latvian. I asked her what he had said. She told me that she would tell me after he had left. He did leave not long thereafter.

When he left, Eva told me his reply: "Both." Eva found it amusing. I considered it to be a cliché and noted, "Alois is quite the gentleman, isn't he?" Eva and Nelly agreed, but the tone of their agreement gave me the impression that they found him slightly intimidating. Eva appeared more relaxed after he was gone and spent some time with me. She showed me her book on the Pueblo Indians. As I handled it, I noticed that she started to get a little anxious. She was quite possessive of this book. Books in English were a rare treat in the Soviet Union. I teased her about it: "Don't worry Eva, I won't swipe your book!"

I had been wondering about where I was going to eat later. This being the weekend, the restaurant at the Latvia Hotel was not providing meals for the participants. Besides I was no longer officially a conference participant. That had ended on Thursday when Dmitri and Alisa left. The Managers Club had seen to it that my meal privileges continued through Friday. I asked Eva if she could recommend a restaurant. She discussed it with Nelly and told me to come back a little later. They would provide a meal for me in the evening.

I took my last walk in Riga. I wanted to take some photos of some places not quite so charming and a little run down to get a more balanced record of the city. The day was again overcast but without rain. I found a promising side street that had buildings with exposed brick and rusting garages. Near a dirty wall with billboards, I noticed a public phone that looked more like the ones in Leningrad, the traditional steel and glass phone booth. Like one of the posters on the wall, it was a little askew, and most of the glass was missing. This was a reminder that even the most charming spots in the Soviet Union had their scars.

When I returned to my hotel, Nelly and Eva had a little surprise for me. They had put together a tea for me. The tea was served with some of the chocolates that Alois had brought, along with some tea biscuits and fresh fruit. This was not the sort of meal that I had been expecting, but I enjoyed it. When we were finished, Nelly presented me with a coffee table book about the open-air museum I had seen with Eva (*In the Latvian Ethnographic Open-air*

Museum [Veveris and Kupais, 1989]). It was a delightful book with many color photographs and text in Latvian, Russian, and English. I was touched by their generosity.

As we chatted, I started to reflect on my trip, which was in its twilight hour, and some of things Eva told me during the course of my stay came back to me. I thought about these people's generosity of spirit. Long under suppression, they had come through as a resilient culture. Yet, their language was threatened with extinction because so many Latvians chose to speak Russian or German. Latvians were a strong and energetic people, living in an enchanted land where the Church had a difficult time stamping out witchcraft and paganism. Now these people wrestled with the giant Soviet Union for independence.

Five

NEGOTIATING LIFE: LENINGRAD, RUSSIA

1. Overview

This portion of the narrative covers one week of my 1991 trip, including my return to Dmitri's flat in Leningrad and events after my return. These include a reunion with my friend Eileen, Leon Pomeroy's overseas phone call, and a trip to Petrodvorets, a town south of Leningrad. Several revealing incidents occur that shed more light on how Alisa and Dmitri negotiated life in Russia.

Continuing the themes begun in the first part of the narrative, my problems with Alisa come to a head and are resolved. I discover that Dmitri has more resources than first meet the eye. Still, he keeps me away from some of his most basic resources such as his primary work place (a technical and educational institute) and his side of the family. His parents, I am told, do not live in town, are not interested in meeting me, and are in principle opposed to Dmitri's involvement with an American. Up until now, I have seen Dmitri apply his craft of psychology to others, such as Pavel. When he starts to pay more attention to me, I become uncomfortable with his probing. I also witness more of Russia's struggle with its problems, including Eileen's account of the state of nursing care. Dmitri opens up to me more during this period, and, since the HVP work is temporarily abandoned, I concentrate more on ethnographic aspects of research.

The narrative picks up where it left off in Chapter Four: I was spending Saturday night (20 July), the night before my flight to Leningrad, in a guest room of the Hotel Riga in Latvia. I would soon get a taste of how much you needed to know before you could survive in a place like Leningrad.

Dmitri was on vacation between his summer seminars. So, he was more relaxed and in no mood to work hard. This effectively brought an end to his cooperation with Pomeroy. Still, he remained willing to show me more of Leningrad and its immediate environment. He was a good guide and was willing to teach me more about how Russians valued social networks.

2. Returning to Leningrad (20 – 21 July)

Latvians were not typical Europeans, judging from the way they did business: Money was handled differently here. I was still puzzled by the roundabout way the man in Jurmala had been paid with some of the money coming from the Managers Club. Late at night, I was trying to sleep, but some mosquitoes kept annoying me, and the well-worn spare room seemed a little stuffy and uncomfortable. I had to be at the airport early in the morning. A thought kept nagging me. Perhaps I had not understood the payment process properly. A chance existed that I owed them money, but the subject was not mentioned, and I forgot about it until this most inconvenient time.

Early the next morning, I got a wake-up call from Eva. I was still half-asleep as I dressed. Eva came to my room fifteen minutes later and helped me with my bags. Lolita was with her. Together, they took me to the airport in a taxi. I had wanted to speak with Nelly, but she was not around.

We got to the airport fairly quickly. It turned out to be ordinary enough, but its condition and the manner of its patrons reminded me more of a bus station than an airport. The terminal had no shops selling magazines and souvenirs and no bars where people could watch television and sip drinks. Still drowsy, I constantly checked to make sure I had brought everything, my camera and film, my notebooks, my passport and ticket. Eva found a small airport restaurant selling cokes but no coffee. We had about five minutes.

By now, I was feeling embarrassed about bringing up the subject of payment. I had not gone to a hard currency store; I had nothing to pay them with if I owed money. I just had a few rubles and my remaining uncashed traveler's checks. I expected that Eva would bring it up at any moment, but she did not. Finally, I decided not to mention it. In America, the custom of "buyers beware" applies to both parties in a transaction. Each party to a transaction is responsible for making sure that the amount of moneys and goods received is what was expected. In a supermarket, a careful shopper knows to check the receipt because with so many items being checked through by the cashier mistakes are bound to occur. I knew Dmitri was planning to return to Riga, so if it turned out I owed them money, I would have him take it back. I did not know how I would cash a check in Leningrad, but hard currency stores or hotels had to be there that could do such a thing.

By leaving this little matter of the money hanging I was making a social mistake, but I did not understand that Eva may have been embarrassed to mention it. I was not correctly assessing the nature of social ties in the Soviet union. Though their connections were largely informal, and they each worked for separate official institutions, Alisa and Nelly were effectively on the same team. Loyalty to a network was stronger than loyalty to an institution. My transaction with Nelly was not separate from my transactions with Alisa. Given my history with Alisa, I was taking a big chance that Alisa would take an interest and, if I owed money, react as ruthlessly as she had done before.

By the time Eva and I finished our cokes, I had put the matter out of my mind. I started to feel nervous about the upcoming flight. Aeroflot had a bad reputation when it came to domestic flights. My flight might be delayed, an occurrence all too common. Who knew when I might arrive in Leningrad? I faced the prospect of being entirely alone for the next few hours. I might be viewed with suspicion as a foreigner traveling alone. If I ran into snags, I had no one to help me, and my Russian was lacking as well.

Lolita and Eva took me to the gate where my flight would board. A line was forming. Lolita left us to go find an airport official to see about how to handle me. I thought this was unnecessary. Why could I not just get on line with the other passengers? Lolita returned with a flight attendant. I said goodbye to Eva and Lolita, thanking them for all their help. I was taken upstairs to a small waiting area, and the attendant asked to see my documents and ticket. She returned a minute later and escorted me through another room, down some stairs, and out through a small door to the tarmac, where a small passenger jet was waiting. It seated less than a hundred passengers. The attendant handed me my ticket and my passport with the little visa stapled inside, wishing me a pleasant flight. I walked to the plane and boarded. A stewardess told me to sit anywhere. The plane was empty. I was the first one aboard besides the stewardess. I took a seat to the left near a window about halfway down the aisle.

This was nice, I thought. I was getting the royal treatment. In reality, I had only gotten half of the foreign traveler treatment. About a minute later, a policeman—I thought since I had seen similar uniforms in Leningrad, light blue with red trim—boarded the plane. The way he approached me gave me the feeling that he was going to arrest me. My heart started to beat faster. "*Bee-lyette ee passaport*!" He barked. I handed them to him, looking anxious. "*Spasiba*." He handed them back to me, scowling. Then the passengers boarded. The cop was friendly with them, as if he was an old pal with all of them. I had gotten a little taste of Soviet authority and disdain for outsiders. He exited the plane shortly before the cabin door was closed. He was KGB. The experience left me feeling isolated and marked as a foreigner.

As the plane taxied to take off, my heart sank. I was leaving Latvia and Eva. I had not realized how attached I had become to them. The prospect of going back to Dmitri's dingy apartment saddened me. I did not want to think about what faced me back in Leningrad.

The flight was short and uneventful. I gazed down at the green fields and forests of Latvia until our plane went into some clouds. Then I saw more forests and lakes. The passengers all had brought food with them. I made do with the pitiful bag of peanuts and some flat soda that the waitresses served. Fortunately, I had saved a granola bar for my trip. I brought granola bars from home for these kinds of occasions. It would have to serve as breakfast. Our plane soon landed in light drizzle under a flat gray sky. Then I had to face the airport in Leningrad alone and without breakfast or lunch.

Getting off the plane and into the terminal was easy enough. I did not see the ubiquitous presence of men in uniform that I had seen during my arrival in Leningrad. We landed at the Pulkovo 1 section of the airport. Pulkovo 2 was the international terminal. The walk from the plane to the terminal building was short, which was good because rain was falling harder. As I entered the circular steel and glass cage that was located across the concrete tarmac, I felt like I was walking into an urban bus station. This part of the voyage was free and easy. I soon found myself lost in a maze of corridors with passengers coming and going. I was glad I had carried my luggage on board so I did not have to find it. I was also surprised that none of it had been examined at any point.

A few minutes later, by following the general flow of passengers, I was able to locate a street entrance, where I saw a bus pass. A waiting area with some seats was nearby. I sat down and waited for a while. I had the crazy idea in my head that perhaps Dmitri would be there to meet me. I started to rack my brains to try to remember what exactly Dmitri had told me during the hectic parting of ways at the Riga railroad station. I had not written it down. I had not considered the possibility that a domestic flight would take me to an entirely different terminal. So nothing was familiar. This terminal was much larger and had multiple entrances and exits. I vaguely remembered Dmitri telling me that, instead of him, Alisa would be coming to meet me. I was not even positive if they were waiting for my call or one of them was supposed to show up without the necessity of a call. For that, a prearranged meeting spot would have been selected, but I was sure that it had not been mentioned.

I sat in my seat for a long time in a daze. I was suffering from lack of sleep and proper nutrition. After a while, I knew that nobody was coming to fetch me. I now faced the daunting prospect of having to use a public phone, something I had no experience with, though I had seen Dmitri use one.

I was under great stress, and my behavior became bizarre. I started to act like a traveler waiting for something, perhaps a party coming to pick me up or a departing flight. The terminal seemed like a place that was constantly busy, and I probably could have stayed there indefinitely. Airports in the Soviet Union were notorious for long waits, and many people "camped" in them. Now that the Soviet Union is gone, and competition has entered the airline industry in Russia, the waits are not as long.

I took out my gift from Eva and Nelly—the book about the open-air museum—and thumbed through it as if I had time to kill. Memories of Riga and Eva came back. I started to cry like a little kid who had become lost. I eventually got a hold of myself and began to focus on a task that would require all of my energy and gumption.

I was experiencing stress common to fieldwork and the necessity of negotiating an unfamiliar culture. In this case, the unfamiliarity did not lie in the level of civilization, for this was an urban culture, and I had experience with my urban culture. The unfamiliarity lay in the language and in the kind of technical organization that I had to negotiate.

I dug some ruble bills out of my pocket and went in search of a place to change them into *kopecki* (coins). I found a *kiosk* (an enclosed, steel and glass stall used to sell merchandise), managed to find the Russian word for "change" in my pocket Russian-English dictionary, and got some change that I guessed was appropriate. I fortunately remembered what Dmitri had told me about using public phones. I then went in search of them. I found some soon enough.

Just as I thought I was getting a handle on the situation, I hit a snag. I knew the basics in operating a Soviet public phone: Put the coin in the slot, pick up the phone, dial the number, and let it ring. If the party answered, the coin would drop through the slot. Once the coin dropped through the slot, you had no way of retrieving it. I found Dmitri's number in my notebook and followed the procedure. For some reason, the coin dropped through before I could complete dialing the number. Someone who sounded like a woman came on the line speaking Russian. I could barely hear whoever it was, let alone understand any of it. I tried again, and the same thing happened. I tried several times. I tried switching phones. Some phones just gave me a busy signal; others had the same indiscernible voice or just static. I went through all my coins and had to return to the *kiosk* to get some more. This time I got more change and of different sorts. I noticed that these phones, unlike the one that Dmitri had shown me, contained slots for other denominations. I tried to use different coins this time. Nothing happened. Totally frustrated, I decided to inquire at the kiosk. The lady turned out to know a tiny bit of English and, after she understood that I was trying to reach a number in Leningrad, pointed out some other phones. They looked more like the ones Dmitri had used. Before I left, I handed the lady a quarter, explaining it was an American coin, a souvenir for her.

As I found out later, I had been trying to use an "international" phone to make a local call—a scene suitable for a Woody Allen movie. The comedy had barely begun. I rang Dmitri's number, and nobody answered. I tried again, thinking that perhaps I had dialed it wrong. I was experiencing a rising panic. Perhaps nobody was home, and I was not going to reach them. Then I heard Alisa's voice. I never thought I would be glad to hear it. I struggled with my Russian to try to explain to her where I was. I did not understand what she was saying. I was starting to wonder why she just did not put Dmitri on the line. Perhaps he was not at home. I was about to tell her to put Dmitri on the line when we were cut off. My time had expired. I put another coin in and dialed again.

This time Dmitri answered: "Allo, Gaaree."

"Dmitri! I'm at the airport. Near the buses. Is Alisa coming to pick me up?"

"Where are you?"

I started to try to explain where I was, but Dmitri cut me off: "Take bus 39."

"What? Isn't Alisa coming to meet me?"

"She does not want to."

"Why not? Can you come?"

"No. I don't feel well. Take bus 39."

"All right, okay. Where do I get this bus?"

"It is there. Near door."

"Are you sure?"

"Yes I know it. Go to metro. Two stops."

"Okay. Then what?"

"You know where buses...."

We were cut off. Again I dialed.

"Dmitri?"

"Yes"

"Where do I go on metro?"

"To where buses for home."

I realized that he meant the bus depot near the Finland Train Station: "Okay, what bus number?" He gave me a number, or it sounded like that, but I was not quite sure what he had said. Then he blurted out: "Finnish station!"

"You mean Finland Station, yes? What number?"

"Finnish station. Call me from station."

We were cut off again. I was not going to call again. I was exhausted just from speaking with him. I kept a couple of kopeck coins for the next call I would make from the Finland Station bus depot to ask him what bus to take. I went outside onto the rain-soaked sidewalk, heaving my overstuffed bags over my shoulder. I stood under an overhang. A little way down, I noticed a knot of people waiting by a bus sign. I never thought to look for a taxi. I had never been in one in Leningrad since the first day. I did not feel confident enough to give the proper directions, and the address I had was not written with Cyrillic. Besides, I did not have many rubles with me and only a couple of dollars in cash. So, I patiently waited for a bus to come, while digging through my bags for the *Fodor's* guide, thinking it had a metro map.

I knew better than to take a taxi from the airport terminal since they were likely to charge me a high price. I could have walked away from the airport to look for one on the streets but my Russian was poor. Chances were I would not find a taxi driver that spoke any English. Recognizing a passing taxi on the street was not easy. Few marked official taxis existed. Many gypsy taxis handled most of the business, but they were unmarked. The only way to get one was to make it obvious you were looking for a taxi and hope one would appear. These informal taxis constituted a gray market. Though not officially sanctioned, they filled a void, so the authorities looked the other way.

The bus came before I could locate my guidebook. I hopped on. A little way into the ride, I realized I had no bus tickets. I had to chance it. Unlike America, in the city, the bus driver was not responsible for collecting fares. Occasionally, a ticket inspector would come onto the bus. If you could not show him a punched ticket or a metro pass, you would get fined on the spot. I did not relish the idea of such an event, but I feared getting off the bus before my stop even more. Fortunately, no ticket inspector appeared. I reached my stop and got off. The first leg of the journey, the shortest, had been successfully negotiated.

I found the metro entrance soon enough and headed for the token booth. Five years of riding the New York City subway paid off. So, even though I hardly paid attention when I was in the metro before because I was being led around, I was familiar in general with the features of a subway. I could recognize token booths, turnstiles, and direction signs. I purchased a token. Then I took some time to find my *Fodor's* guide, but it contained no metro map. This leg of my journey was going to be rough.

I could not hang around the token booth long. The metro entrance was too crowded, and I was in the way. I figured that the token booth cashier probably spoke no English. I decided to go ahead, go into the metro, and chance that by trial and error I would find the right way to go. So I went through the turnstile and down the long escalator along with dozens of people. For some reason, in the metro, Leningraders were in much more of a hurry than they were on the streets. The pace of the pedestrian traffic added to my confusion. Standing in one spot to try to make out a Russian sign in Cyrillic with hundreds of people passing in every direction was difficult. The trains from both directions seemed to arrive almost constantly. Each time one left, I felt like I was missing *my* train. I was trying to find the name of the station associated with the Finland Railroad Station. I remembered only that it had something to do with "Lenin."

I kept my orientation, so I knew which train headed uptown, the direction I needed to go. I could not see any name that looked familiar on the directory posted on a wall. So I got on the next metro train. It would take me in the general direction I needed to go. As the train pulled out, I noticed that on the station wall next to the train was a map of the line I was on. Each time the train pulled into a station, I would look for this map on the wall and study it a little more. Eventually, I determined what the markings for a connecting station were and, when the train reached the first one, I got off. I was right where several corridors intersected. I wandered around looking for another sign and found one. There it was, the *Ploschad Lenina.* Then to my horror, there was another one with the name "*Leninsky Prospect.*" By the time I found the second sign, I lost my sense of direction. I was thinking about trying a direction, and if it did not work, heading for the other one. The stations were both on the same line. I then had what I thought was a bright idea. Why not just head for the street now? I could already be at a place that looked familiar on the street. If I was, I could walk to the Finland Railroad Station. So I headed for the outbound escalator.

I was at the *Tekhnologichesky Institut* station. The name sounded familiar. Dmitri mentioned once that he worked for a technological institute. When I reached the street, I saw the Institute. It might as well have been the moon. It was not going to help me get home. I was still south of Nevsky Prospect and the Neva River. With no familiar landmarks to guide me, I stood there at a corner, feeling stupid, clutching my bags, and watching some young, tough looking characters watching me. Rain still fell, not hard, but enough to make me uncomfortable. A little market was down one of the streets. I found a bench and sat down. I had to think quickly. I did not want to hang around this place too long. It looked dangerous. The market vendors seemed different from other Russians, darker and more hardened. They carried themselves like men I had seen in pool halls back home. I had planned to walk, but three things dissuaded me from this plan, the rain, the lack of familiar landmarks, and my bags, which seemed to be getting heavier. The overcast sky made telling east from west impossible. Afternoon would soon pass into evening. I lugged my bags and myself back into the metro.

Back underground, I decided to pick a station at random. It turned out to be the wrong one. I went to *Leninsky Prospect.* I got out onto the street, and my heart sank. Nothing looked familiar here. I surmised that I had headed south. I was making progress since I had eliminated one direction. I was glad that tokens were cheap because otherwise I could have run out of rubles. As I boarded the train heading north, I spotted a seat. Up to now, I had to stand on the metro. I rushed for it and nearly fell down trying to get it. My bags swung wildly around me while people looked at me suspiciously to see if I was drunk. I sat on the metro heading to what I hoped would at last be the right station, watching the maps on each wall attentively.

I got off the train and went up the escalator. There he was. I never thought I would be glad to see Lenin as I passed through the exit to the park in front of the Finland Station. The rain had stopped. I knew where the cluster of bus stops and the phones were. I even found a *kiosk* selling bus tickets and purchased some. I called Dmitri.

"Dmitri?"

"Gaaree! Where are you?"

"I'm at the Finland Station. What bus number do I need?"

"Finnish Station."

"Yes, Dmitri. I'm at the Finnish station. What number? The number *Poozhaloosta* (please), Dmitri. The number."

"116. Finnish Station!"

"116?"

"*Da, da*"

"Okay, *harasho* (good), I'll see you soon."

I could not understand why he kept repeating "Finnish Station." By now, I did not care; I was on my way home, feeling just a little bit proud of myself. The bus came. I punched my paper tickets like I had seen Dmitri do. I punched about twice as many as necessary without realizing it. I sat on the bus watching the familiar route unfold—the narrow streets near some factories, the shopping areas, a broad avenue with the store that displayed children's toys, a couple of small parks, and some tall apartment buildings. I even remembered the right stop.

As I climbed the dusty stairs up to Dmitri's flat, I heard a door open above. I reached the fifth floor. Dmitri was standing there, looking at me curiously.

"Hello, Dmitri how are you?"

"Allo, Garee. Where Alisa?"

"Huh?"

"Alisa. Finish station. You not see Alisa?"

"No. Was she supposed to meet me at the bus stop?"

By now I was in his kitchen. My bags had been deposited in the little entrance hall. I was wearing my *tapochkee* (indoor slippers). After some discussion, I finally found out what happened. Alisa was supposed to have met me at the airport. Since she had a cold, the rainy weather dissuaded her from making the journey. Dmitri was not feeling well either. They waited for my call. Dmitri tried to tell me to meet her at the nearby railway station, the one we used to go to Karelia, which was the last stop the bus made. That is what he meant by "finish station." I started to laugh and explained to him that I thought he was talking about the Finland Station. "Finnish," "finish," the words sounded the same. The phone rang. Alisa was on the line. Dmitri told her that I had arrived.

3. Lenin and the Meaning of Gifts (21 – 26 July)

Alisa returned from the train station, and Dmitri explained to her what had happened. I greeted her with an uneasy smile, feeling that in her eyes I had been a bad boy by going my way in Riga. She put a kettle on the stove to boil water, filled a teapot with the loose black tea Dmitri could not get enough of, laid out some cups, saucers, and little ring shaped tea biscuits, and excused herself. She went to lie on the couch in the living room. Dmitri told me to wash, while he finished preparing the tea. This was a ritual I had seen repeated many times already. Usually, Alisa stuck around for a while before leaving to watch TV. Sometimes Alisa prepared the tea by herself. If she were out, Dmitri would do it. Today they shared the task. It was a dull routine, and I had lost interest in it pretty quickly, but this day it had a reassuring quality. After the excitement in Latvia, I felt like I was like coming home to a pacifying repast after a stressful day at work.

I sat at the tiny kitchen table. The window was open, and flies, trying to escape the chill outside, kept buzzing into the kitchen. Dmitri paid little attention to them. In the initial relief and exhilaration of being home again at last, I failed to notice that Dmitri was dressed in a rumpled flannel bathrobe, suitable to a man who is spending the day at home resting. His outfit was complemented by his oversized slippers, which made a shuffling sound as he walked. I watched as Dmitri poured the tea from the teapot, a thick brew that was diluted by adding hot water according to taste. Dmitri liked his tea strong. I preferred mine relatively weak.

I plunged into my story about my travails. I told him about the phones at the airport, about the confusing metro experience, and about not understanding what he meant by "finish station." Dmitri, whose mood had been subdued when I arrived, became animated as he sipped his tea. He followed the twists and turns of my story as if he was reliving it himself. Several times he stood up, as if he was too agitated to sit. He alternated between groans and blurting out the word "*oy*," half-shouting, shaking his head. I could hardly keep from laughing at his antics and my story. I could not tell if he was serious in his behavior or putting on a dramatic act. At one point he asked to see the bus tickets I had used. I showed him the punched tickets proudly. Just then his fist crashed down on the table: "You use too much, too much!" I told Dmitri to calm down. Then I burst out laughing. I told him not to worry, because my first bus ride had been free. The number of rubles I had spent getting home from the airport was minuscule compared to what I had given him and his wife in dollars, what I had just spent on the plane flight, and what the last couple of days in Riga had cost. That he was making a big deal about some kopecki struck me as being hilarious.

Alisa had come back into the kitchen by now, curious about Dmitri's excitement. She too had changed into a bathrobe. Still dressed in a sweater and slacks, I felt like I had intruded on a rest home. Dmitri calmed down and told her my story in Russian. Alisa chuckled and followed Dmitri's story attentively as he rolled his eyes during the highlights of my ineptness at negotiating Leningrad. Alisa shuffled back into the other room, and I heard the television being flipped on.

The relief of telling my story brought back my appetite. I had been running on adrenaline all day and had not thought much about eating. I started to munch on the biscuits and spoon jam into my tea. Dmitri got up and began to pull some items for dinner out of his tiny refrigerator. I had felt the temperature inside this contraption—which had no interior light—sometime before and had noticed it was barely cold. No wonder bottles of milk never sat in it for long. An endless stream of kasha dishes cooked in milk soaked up the contents of the few bottles that made it in there. I asked Dmitri to close the window because of the flies. Together we swatted at the few that remained inside. I used the ever-present kitchen fly swatter—a plastic and metal implement that resembled those back home. He used a rolled up newspaper. We managed to kill or expel all of them.

Dmitri began to get supper ready, and Alisa dozed off in front of the television set. I sat at the kitchen table, finishing my tea and watching Dmitri slice one of the giant squashes that served as a staple for our diet. The slices would be fried with potatoes. There might be some *bifstek* or *kolbasa* to go along with the vegetables.

No special "welcome back" dinner was prepared for me that day. I started to suspect that, since they already had my payment, they no longer had a need to impress me. I gathered that in his mind Dmitri felt that he had already fulfilled his end of the bargain. He had not collected the sample properly, but it never came up. At that point, I did not know how to broach the subject and suspected he never would unless I did first. My stay would last until they went back to Riga at the end of the month. After that, Dmitri would begin preparing the courses he would teach at Leningrad's Polytechnical Institute that fall. The last remaining days of summery weather were ahead; with August came the rains as the days got shorter and cooler rapidly. Dmitri seemed set to enjoy the rest of the warm weather. A call from Pomeroy was expected. He was bound to ask questions about our progress. Yet, I detected no anxiety over this on Dmitri's part. Another matter was on Dmitri's mind, but he would wait until the next day to broach it.

After watching Dmitri fiddle with the stove and shuffle around the kitchen for a while, I decided the time had come to unpack and take inventory. I went to my room with my bags and closed the sliding partition so I could be alone. I went through my bags, checking to see if everything was there. By this time, I had gone through most of my clean clothes and was wondering about how to get the dirty ones washed. I had turned one of my bags into a laundry repository. The inside of my clothes bag was dusted with white powder and flakes from a packet of instant oatmeal that had burst during the trip to Latvia. I had not made use of the remaining packets yet and was thinking of handing them over to Alisa before another one burst. I anticipated getting a kick out of trying to show her how to prepare the contents.

I had miscellaneous things to keep track of, including lots of gum and some cheap retracting pens. I even found a couple of granola bars that had gotten lost amidst the items in another bag. I checked four rolls of exposed film left under some clothes out of sight. Two rolls remained. I counted my unused traveler's checks and put them, along with my passport, in the special wallet that I kept tied around my chest under my shirt.

I had saved the sugar packet and unused plastic spoon that had been handed out on the flight. I thought about handing the sugar over to Dmitri but decided against it. I received a troubling reaction to my first attempt to give them the left over stuff from my original flight to Leningrad. They had grudgingly accepted the items with what almost seemed like chagrin. Having heard Dmitri and Alisa complain about the lack of basic staples like salt and sugar, I gave them the packets of sugar, salt, pepper, and jelly that had come with the flight. This was just a gesture that I thought they would understand. Back home, I sometimes did it when visiting friends after a flight, giving them the little things I did not want to go to waste. At home, after returning from a flight, such things were usually thrown into a container with similar items.

When I completed my inventory, I took out a clean notebook. I checked how many clean pages were left in the pale blue compact notebook that I had been writing in since the beginning of my sojourn to Russia. It had a few more clean pages remaining, so I put the new notebook aside for the time being. I wrote for an hour. Writing helped calm me down and get my bearings for the next part of my stay.

When I began to write, I noticed that the room was stuffy and slightly damp. The last part of July (this was the 21st) started off with rain and would be a little rainier and more humid than the beginning of the month. I opened the window. The air was remarkably cool for a July evening. The days were becoming shorter. This night was a bit more like a summer night back home, with darkness coming sometime between nine and ten o'clock. I noticed that now with the cooler weather more people were out on the street making noise that I found distracting.

I also found that the mosquito population had increased. During my first week in Leningrad, I had no need of the "Off" bug repellent that I was advised to bring. Even camping in Karelia had not been so bad. I decided to keep the spray handy. The Russian mosquitoes were slow. They were easy to kill if I saw them, but late at night or early in the morning, with little light, they were harder to spot. The whining sound they made when they passed close to my ears was itself enough to keep me awake.

Dmitri called me in for supper. Alisa had made herself some kasha and was again lying in front of the television. I thought about how hard finding a place to be alone in this tiny apartment was for her. I had the only spare room. Since tension still existed between us, this added inconvenience only aggravated the existing stress. The balcony, a place of last resort, was unusable today because she had to stay warm. Dmitri did not eat much. He explained that they had had their main meal before, and he was not feeling well enough to eat a lot. He excused himself and went to watch television with Alisa.

Eating alone and bored, I wandered in to see what they were watching. The news was on featuring a report about Iraq. Apparently, Saddam Hussein had violated one of the United Nations sanctions on his country, increasing tension between Iraq and the United States. I was worried about this. Armed conflict again loomed. If fighting started again, would I be safe in the Soviet Union? My fear was not baseless. Muslim radicals who had been suppressed during the Stalin years in the Soviet Union were starting to cause problems in southern Russia. The conflict in Nagorno-Kharabakh, which was discussed by our companions on the train to Latvia, was but one example. Problems also existed in the Soviet State of Georgia and in the Russian republic of Chechnya. During the post-Soviet years, these problems would grow worse. Islamic-terrorist-sponsored bombings, kidnappings, and ambushes plagued the Russian Federation in major cities and remote provinces.

After supper, Dmitri and I smoked on his balcony. I decided that I was too tired to have a long discussion with him as was sometimes our habit after supper. He did not seem in the mood to talk much either. I told Dmitri I was worried about the crisis in Iraq and that I was glad that Pomeroy was supposed to call soon because I wanted to ask him about the news from my country. By bringing up the crisis in Iraq and Pomeroy's impending call, I was able to remind Dmitri about the joint project and his promise to help me collect (usable) data. I questioned Dmitri about the news report. Besides his description of it as a "dangerous" situation, I got little in the way of details from him. The balcony conversation ended as the patch of sky visible above the surrounding apartment blocks, still overcast, darkened considerably. Alisa had already unfolded the couch into a bed and turned the light out in the living room. I tiptoed past her to my room after saying good night to Dmitri, who was back in the kitchen, cleaning up.

I had been up since early that morning. Sunday had been stressful. I was glad to be getting to sleep early. This night, I sprayed myself with Off. I did not want to worry about having to stay awake to swat mosquitoes.

A. Eileen Resurfaces

On Monday morning (22 July), I got a call from Eileen, which was a delightful surprise because we had a chance to compare notes and share our separate experiences. I relished the chance to get out of the apartment and to be with a friend. We barely knew each other, having only spent a couple of hours together on the flight from Shannon to Leningrad and another hour at the airport. Nevertheless, the circumstances—for each of us, this was our first time in the Soviet Union—pushed us together, and an implicit bond had formed. Eileen had been in and around Leningrad for a longer time than I had by then, since I had spent more time out of the city and its immediate environs. So she knew the best place to meet, the *Dom Knigi* (House of Books). Dmitri had taken me past this place a couple of times on our outings.

Dom Knigi is a book store of three floors located in a big six-story building that once served as the headquarters of the Singer Sewing Machine Company in Russia (before the revolutions of 1917). The building has an unmistakable conical roof decoration topped by a giant ball, which makes it stand out among the nearby buildings of Nevsky Prospect. On the opposite side of the prospect is the gigantic "Kazan Cathedral" with its bizarre facade consisting of a concave double row of enormous Corinthian columns.. On the other side of the Dom Knigi is an entrance to the metro, one of four that can be found on this portion of Nevsky.

At the time, Dom Knigi was a popular spot for street musicians to play to curious crowds Tour buses left from the front of the Kazan Cathedral. All in all, this spot was a gathering point for tourists and Leningraders alike.

Eileen wanted to visit the Hermitage. I had heard about this world-famous art museum, housed in the former Winter Palace. With that piece of good news, I had enough energy to get to work on several projects. The Russian translation of Pomeroy's test had some flaws. So I spent some time cleaning it up. I also completed my hand-written copy of the Latvian test. I had decided to compile the results of Dmitri's sample. Though I did not have complete results, I did have a pile of results for part one and a pile of results for part two. I decided to compile these on the chance that Pomeroy would find some use for them. He never did, ultimately deciding to throw out Dmitri's entire sample. I also had postcards to write and gifts to purchase for my wife, family, and friends back home. I spent some time deciding whom to include, and making a list.

Alisa spent little time with us that day. She was busy preparing to go visit her mother and spent a large part of the day shopping. Dmitri and I watched "Donahue" on television. Phil Donahue's show, long a mainstay on American TV, had made it to the Soviet Union. This episode had something to do with sexual mores. I did not pay much attention. I was not a big fan of talk shows. Besides, the heavy-handed Russian dubbing made it impossible to understand. The dubbing—I had seen this done in Mexico—consisted of lowering the volume of the show's original sound and laying it over with a single voice interpreting everything into Russian. Dmitri found the show stimulating. I found it annoying. Dmitri was fascinated by the concept of people speaking so openly. I told him it was *normalna* (routine) for the United States.

B. Clearing the Air

Sometime later in the same day, Dmitri invited me into the kitchen for "a discussion." I sat down to see what Dmitri had in mind. Dmitri wanted to let me know that my insistence on staying longer in Riga put him in a "difficult situation." He did not elaborate much on his theme, so I was not sure exactly why my decision caused him any more trouble than having an extra train ticket to dispose of. I rather expected that he and Alisa would appreciate not having me on their hands for a couple of days. I only gathered from the discussion that a "number of people" had been upset by my "unpredictable" behavior. I did not know, besides Dmitri and Alisa, who they were. Instead of pressing Dmitri on this, I mentioned that Anatol had been flexible about my change of plans, and that he had turned the new situation to his benefit. I explained that Anatol was interested in a Latvian test. Dmitri said that he already knew that—he had been there when the subject first came up. Dmitri still was upset over the way my initial talk with Anatol had gone, claiming I had been too reticent and inarticulate. I reminded him that he had not prepared me well for the meeting.

Dmitri's concern of leaving me by myself was real. As my host, he was responsible for me throughout my time in the Soviet Union. A mitigating factor did exist: My invitation had been extended officially by Anatol who felt comfortable assuming authority over me in Latvia.

I did not want to discuss much about my further interaction with Anatol and his helpers. I just told Dmitri that I had a good rest and worked a little with Anatol. If Dmitri had taken a different approach, one less prying, I would have probably mentioned the odd payment arrangement in Jurmala to him. I did not feel comfortable enough to bring it up because I felt alienated by his scolding. I was being reticent again. This was a continuation of the dynamics that evolved from a new set of entangling relationships, which had acquired a complexity I still had little confidence in negotiating openly. My introduction to Andrey and Ann generated potential conflicts. During my extended stay in Latvia, they were pleased to have me around to shore up their plans. I did not mention this to Dmitri. Judging by my earlier secret meeting with Andrey and Ann at the Latvia Hotel, I knew that competitiveness existed between them and Dmitri when it came to me.

Andrey and Ann were outside of Dmitri's circles. In Soviet Russia, competition existed not between corporations, which did not exist there at the time in the form found in the United States, but between social groupings of interconnected individuals. Though individuals were attached to official Soviet institutions, such as government bureaucracies or state-run universities, these attachments were transcended by individuals' loyalties to their informal groups.

Anatol was a third player in this scenario, partly independent of both of them, yet also connected with them in another sense. I definitely knew that the two were linked because Anatol had arranged my visa for Dmitri. Judging by Dmitri's sensitivity to Anatol's reaction to me, Anatol seemed to hold more power than Dmitri. Andrey was more of an equal, an outsider with his own power base, who was skillfully playing for a separate relationship with me and "my chief" (Pomeroy), and perhaps also with Anatol. I based that on Andrey's presence at Anatol's conference, his impressive credentials, and his cultured behavior, including his diplomacy when it came to dealing with Dmitri.

Dmitri was reacting to what he did not know, namely what had gone on in Riga between me and Andrey after he left. Maybe he was digging for information. Since Dmitri was closed about the details of just how I had put him in "a difficult situation," I did not feel like opening up and discussing my budding relationship with Andrey in detail. I did tell him of my plans to stay on in Leningrad to have "discussions" with Andrey when Dmitri returned to Riga. This additional change in my plans did not surprise Dmitri. Given the way other information had seemed to flow to him and Alisa when we were in Riga, I suspected they got wind of it before they left town.

In our discussion, I took the attitude of "so be it." I rocked the boat because I generally did that. I was not a conformist by nature; I often differed from norms and expectations. By risking trouble, I also brought about circumstances that revealed characteristics of the cultural and social behavior among differing types of Soviet citizenry. I saw Soviets fighting over access to an American. It showed me how they craved any contact with the West. It also revealed how Soviets formed associations to compete for scarce resources. Still, I thought, perhaps I could find a less volatile way of going about my research, and I should not make a habit of rocking boats.

I was sure of one thing: I had been patient so far with regard to our conflicts over money. After my dealings with the Latvian Managers Club, I knew that the problem with Dmitri was not that he had asked me to pay him for my accommodations but the manner in which he and Alisa went about doing it. If I had been told up front, before setting foot in Russia, that (and how much) I would have to pay (which I expected), I would not have been reluctant to do so when it came up after I got to Leningrad. If I had not been metaphorically grabbed by the ankles and hung upside down to have the money shaken out of my pockets, I may have been quicker about completing my promised payment when we were in Latvia. Also, I became suspicious about the amount of the payment, which had initially seemed reasonable by American standards. Since I knew more about the cost of things, the exchange rate, and the quality of room and board, I felt that I had overpaid by Soviet standards. Having a convenient way of cashing my checks would have helped also. Subsequent trips to Russia bore this out. Payment arrangements, though not always smooth, never proved to be so sticky as on this trip.

I told Dmitri that I may have put him in a fix—a "difficult situation" as he put it—although I was not sure what sort of fix, but that he was ultimately not responsible for my behavior. Anatol understood this, why could he not? Dmitri thought that this was "very interesting," yet I could not tell if he got the point. Like many of our previous conflicts, it remained unresolved.

For a country founded on Marxism, which abhorred the trappings of capitalism, namely economic competition, I found the Soviet citizenry to be engaged in a fierce form of it. I grew more curious about my hosts' exact relationship to the ideal of communism.

C. The Communist

Later on Monday when Alisa was out, I opened a subject that had been in the back of my mind. I was sitting with Dmitri on the living room couch. Something on TV interested him. I did not pay any attention to it. I was lost in thought about the program I saw Dmitri and Alisa watching sometime earlier in my trip.

I barely paid attention to Soviet TV when I first arrived, although I occasionally sat down to watch the news, once even getting into an animated discussion with Dmitri about Soviet coverage of the conflict in Yugoslavia, which was in its early stages. Dmitri claimed that only Soviet reporters were allowed near the front lines. I told him that this was nonsense. I had seen American reporters and European journalists covering the war near the front. Perhaps this contradiction was due to which front lines were accessible to America, Europe, and the Soviet Union. The Soviets were covering the story from the Serbian side.

Other than the news, we saw movies and many musical variety shows, none of which I understood unless Dmitri translated for me. One night was different. I was sitting alone in the kitchen writing. Dmitri was in the living room longer than usual. He had a habit of dividing his time between me and Alisa, going back and forth between the two rooms. This time he stayed in the living room. Curious to know what was preoccupying him, I got up to peek into the living room. There on the television, I saw arresting images of a man I should have known but did not recognize at first—an intense, demonic looking figure, speaking with great force and animation. It was obviously an old film of a historic event. It turned out to be a documentary about Lenin. I remembered mentioning to Dmitri that Lenin seemed to be a "serious man" who was not apt to tell funny stories or laugh at jokes. Dmitri had replied, "very serious."

I was thinking about this incident, about Lenin, and about his impact on Russia. I had heard the Soviet Union being called "Latin America with nuclear weapons by pundits back home. The way the "Donahue" show was dubbed reminded me of Mexico. The hot water problem—I still had not taken a proper shower or bath in Dmitri's flat, making do with occasional cold sponge baths—also reminded me of Mexico and of Ecuador. Drinking the tap water was impossible, a problem also found in Mexico. These problems had a cumulative effect, producing a backdrop of unpredictability and crudity that might be found in a third world country.

Added to this was a sense that the transactions we regarded as routine back home had an entirely different meaning here. Dmitri's frequent discussions of "difficult" or "dangerous" situations plus his stifling attempts to handle me, squeeze me, present me, and make a trophy out of me in Karelia and then Latvia left a bitter taste in my mouth. In America, you do business in the market place. If a transaction goes sour, you can take your business to dozens of alternative spots. You have general freedom of movement; you are not watched all the time. If a problem is serious enough, you can take it to court.

In Russia, I became keenly aware that which group you belonged to made more of a difference than any sort of market or court system. Dmitri wanted me in his group. Andrey was trying to get me into his. Anatol was also bidding for my attention, as had the kayak man in Karelia. I got the impression that I could not belong to all these groups at the same time. If I was to do business with one group, I had to forgo the others.

The movie about Lenin reminded me that a different kind of group held more power than all others—the Communist Party. Despite my thin background in things Russian and Soviet, I already knew that Russia was not "converted" to communism *en masse*. Some people joined the Party. Others did not. Those who did so enjoyed an advantage at the price of having a hand in the misery the Communists perpetrated on those outside the Party as well as within. I now wondered if Dmitri was a member of the Communist Party. So I asked him.

"No, Alisa is," was Dmitri's terse reply implying that, to be in a social position good enough to entertain an American, one of them had to be a member.

He did not seem startled by my question, which had come out of the blue. By now, I gathered that Soviets in general did not like to reveal shock or surprise if it had anything to do with serious issues. They could emote over day-to-day stuff, be sentimental or raucous in social occasions with friends, but if something had to do with politics, an accident, or being seriously startled, they generally did not register much emotion. A psychologist might call this "flat affect."

After jumping into the subject of communism, I pressed on: A little more discussion revealed that Alisa was, to some extent, a "believer." Some people joined the Party out of cynical greed, amoral types who saw it as a way up into better circumstances and only paid lip service to the ideology. Dmitri insisted that Alisa joined out of a real belief.

Alisa knew no English, and thus we had no discussion about something like this. Our interactions were based almost entirely around "negotiations" with Dmitri interpreting. Other than this, Dmitri translated almost nothing else that his wife had said. In Karelia she found the idea of public parks "noble," but this was only a vague indicator of her beliefs. Most Americans would have agreed with her assessment.

Dmitri's revelation shed light on Alisa's character and actions, especially her utter ruthlessness when it came to negotiations. Since no established market in the Soviet Union existed for the kind of transactions we were making, she simply tried to take me for everything I had. In my mind, communism and banditry were closely associated due to my familiarity with the Communist habit of "nationalizing" private property, something I had read about long before setting foot in the Soviet Union. I was troubled because I failed to apply this concept to my situation beforehand. After all, I was "bourgeois" and thus a target for Communists. I should have armed myself with caution and probed this question earlier. I should have been more assertive about negotiating instead of merely reacting to each twist and turn. I naively trusted what Pomeroy had told me about Dmitri: "They'll treat you like a baby." I took Pomeroy's comment to mean that Dmitri was a rich, powerful scientist who would pamper me and treat me nicely to impress us. Culture shock did the rest. While my energy was being spent familiarizing myself with new cultural and social markers, they maneuvered me into a position where I could be exploited.

The revelation also resolved another curiosity: Alisa's behavior at the police station when my visa was processed. She ignored the long line and went into the same office that people were waiting to get into as if she worked there.

I pressed a little more: "Alisa helps you, yes?"

"Yes," Dmitri said with a characteristic way he had of laughing when he was nervous. He did not seem interested in pursuing the topic.

A convenient setup for Dmitri, I thought. He could keep his hands clean of the consequences of being a Communist, and consequences loomed on the horizon in 1991. Academician Andrei Sakharov had already challenged the supreme authority of the Communist Party. He wanted its monopoly on power written out of the Soviet constitution. After his death in 1989, Article Six of the Soviet Constitution, which guaranteed all power to the Communist Party, was repealed in early 1990 (Dunlop, 1993, p. 155). More recently, the newly elected president of the Russian Soviet Federated Socialist Republic, Boris Yeltsin, proposed banning Communist cells in factories. If the Communists lost more power, they could become targets for revenge. It had already happened in Romania. At the same time, Dmitri had an intimate partner who could open doors for him. I wondered if this imbalance in the relationship affected it negatively; perhaps theirs was a marriage of convenience. (In 2000, when I met Dmitri again, they were still married, but Alisa had turned to religion with an obsession that worried Dmitri.)

This would have been a good opportunity for me to open a related discussion I had previously thought of opening: I wanted to dig into what Dmitri himself thought about communism. He talked almost from day one about "Gomilev" (L. N. Gumilev), a historian and scientist whose father had been shot and mother persecuted by the Soviet authorities. Gumilev was a hero of Dmitri's. This was not a position an ideological Communist should be in. What did this say about Dmitri and, for that matter, Alisa who must have been aware of Dmitri's interest in Gumilev? Still, I did not feel comfortable broaching this subject. I had strong opinions about communism, almost completely negative ones. I would have found it difficult to take a neutral position (as an ethnographer should) in such a discussion. So I kept silent about it and wrote the paradox off as a consequence of *glasnost* (openness) and *perestroika* (restructuring). Under Mikhail Gorbachev's grand social experiment in civil freedom and economic reform, official tolerance of heretofore unacceptable ideas was becoming normal.

After our brief exchange, I felt apprehensive and a little intrigued. I was not just staying with Russian Soviet citizens, but with a Communist and a Communist "sympathizer." They were part of the elite, not because Dmitri was a noteworthy scientist, but because they had standing in the official culture. However, the future of the official culture was becoming less sure with the passing weeks. All of my information about the situation in the Soviet Union, except for the revelations on the trip to Latvia, was gathered before I left. I had not watched and understood enough of the Russian news reports or seen any English language newspapers or magazines in Russia that would have told me more details of the impending crisis. True to form, Dmitri kept silent about the developments occurring during July. For instance, an appeal had appeared this month in a prominent newspaper. Written by so called "conservatives," those who supported the rigid structures inherited from Stalin, it called for the salvation of the Soviet Union, which they feared was in mortal danger (Dunlop, 1993, p. 163–165).

Alisa returned later. She had acquired a new aura as far as I was concerned that simultaneously made her more intriguing and repelled me. Again we watched the news, and again it had a report about Iraq. Pomeroy was scheduled to call Wednesday early morning or Wednesday night (Thursday early morning). I was more anxious than ever about his call. Since today was Monday, I had to be patient one or two more days.

Alisa left after an early supper. Enough light was left for the half-hour trip to her mother's home town, where we had picked up Ilya on the way to Karelia. Dmitri left me alone in the apartment for a few minutes, as he wanted to see Alisa off at the nearby train station. I noticed that Alisa's bag seemed a little large for an overnight stay.

When Dmitri returned, he wanted to stay up late to have more discussions. I told him that I wanted to be rested for the next day. I was more anxious than ever to have some sympathetic company. I started getting the sense that Alisa was becoming more preoccupied with other matters, and that I was mainly Dmitri's problem now.

Before going to sleep, Dmitri buttonholed me into one more discussion. This one had to do with what he felt was a generally unfriendly attitude on my part during the first half of my trip. I had been remarkably reticent as far as he was concerned. He also wondered about the time on the train going to Karelia when I got up and moved to another seat. I decided to be frank with him: I reminded Dmitri that I was not used to being in Russia. It was my first time. In many situations, I did not want to stick out as a tourist, especially when we traveled away from Leningrad to Karelia, so I kept my mouth shut. About the incident on the train, I told him that I was uncomfortable being squeezed so closely next to him on a hot and stuffy train, and that I had found his breath hard to take.

Dmitri was not terribly upset by this and not affected by my last remark. Instead, he seemed glad to be getting some information from me that he was not aware of before. He used the occasion to introduce a psychological concept he was interested in: "comfort zones." He explained to me that people all have a "space" that they feel comfortable operating in. Going outside this space entails risk. He felt that a basic component of psychological growth involved the creation of a new and larger zone of comfortable space. Dmitri urged me to increase my comfort zone in the Soviet Union, by being less reticent in all situations. Our theoretical discussion turned into a "therapy session."

I appreciated Dmitri's theoretical discussions but did not like his playing therapist with me, probably because of its ineffectiveness. Instead of empathizing with me to get me to open up, he was using my personal dilemma as meat for the grinder of his different theories. The whole effect left me feeling unsettled, but Dmitri seemed satisfied with our talk, which had cleared the air as far as he was concerned. Before I went to my room, he left me with the admonition: "Now you must repair [your] relationship with Alisa." I did not sleep for a while, fretting over this remark.

D. The Hermitage

Tuesday morning (23 July) was bright and sunny. If being back in Leningrad, had an advantage, it was the nice weather. Sunday had been overcast, Monday not much better. I started to suspect that the almost perpetual cloudiness in Latvia had followed me back to Leningrad. This day the clouds cleared, and conditions became much less humid.

Having forgotten the blanket coverage Dmitri gave me before the Latvian excursion, I assumed that I would be going to meet Eileen by myself. I had become accustomed to being on my own during my stay in Latvia and thought I had enough familiarity with Leningrad to find Dom Knigi. So when Dmitri told me he would be going with me, I started getting nervous.

Getting to Dom Knigi entailed a running argument between me and Dmitri that started before we left: "Dmitri, please let me go by myself. I know how to find my way. She's my friend. We only have one afternoon. She's going home at the end of this week."

Dmitri insisted that being on my own was too dangerous and persisted in accompanying me. Finally, he half-promised just to make sure I made it to my rendezvous. When we got to the Finland Station, he insisted on going with me on the metro to the Nevsky stop, telling me I would get lost without his help.

When we reached Dom Knigi, I tried to say good-bye to Dmitri: "Dmitri, *dosvedanya*. You don't need to stay. I can meet her by myself."

Dmitri refused to leave, insisting that leaving me alone was "too dangerous." He pointed out some youths nearby, sitting on the ledge of a stone wall: "You see those men? Those not good men. Trouble with such men."

I told Dmitri that I was familiar with big cities and that I did not get involved with strangers, but to no avail. We waited at the corner near the bookstore under bright sunlight. Eileen came more or less on time, her big round face and big eyes beaming, her skin red from the sun, and her unruly hair bleached to a golden color. She gave me a hug. I told her how glad I was to see her and introduced her to Dmitri, embarrassed that he was there. She had no "chaperone" with her, unlike me. Instead, a friend had come along, another young woman, Mary, a hospital volunteer like her who knew some Russian. Dmitri was immediately interested in Eileen's companion. I thought that perhaps this might work out with someone to keep Dmitri occupied.

We walked to the museum together. Eileen and I tried to do some catching up on the way. I explained to her that I wanted to come alone, but Dmitri insisted on hanging around. She listened with a knowing look on her face and replied, "Don't worry, Mary can accompany him." I felt reassured. Eileen had grown in confidence from the anxious, modest girl I had met on the plane.

Eileen described some of her experiences to me: She was taken to Petrodvorets the day we were to meet at the church. She was taken to other parks as well. She showed me her sunburned arms covered with insect bites, explaining that she had forgotten to bring insect repellent—the parks had been mosquito havens. I told her I tried to call her with no luck. She explained that her host, "Aleksiy," had been protective of her in the beginning, shielding her from any calls from strangers. Dmitri had gotten her number amidst other numbers he garnered on that frustrating day, but when he had called it, Aleksiy answered and acted like he never heard of Eileen.

Eileen started to describe how her volunteer work went but our conversation was cut short. We were at the entrance to the Hermitage. The blue Neva gleamed in the sunlight just across the road that ran between it and the palace. I left my camera home, an oversight in my rush to get going that morning. Eileen had hers with her. I had read that they did not allow camera usage inside the museum, but this was not going to deter her.

Dmitri, whom I had almost forgotten, suddenly announced that he was not going to stick around, but he was going to do us a favor. I was glad and felt obliged to Mary. She must have gotten through to Dmitri in a way I had not been able to. Mary had plans to meet a friend at the museum, so Dmitri would have been a fifth wheel. Dmitri announced that he was going to buy the tickets for us. I started to try to talk him out of it but relented. Eileen explained to me that Russian tickets were a lot cheaper than tickets for foreigners. At the time, the attendants only checked the tickets and did not try to guess if the patrons were foreign unless it was obvious, so Dmitri was able to do the trick for us. On later trips, I found that you needed more savvy to slip through as a "Russian." Mary handed Dmitri some rubles, but Dmitri insisted on treating all of us. He was a wealthy man at this time.

I watched Dmitri wait in a short line to purchase tickets. He did not want us near him when he did. The lobby was too crowded and the museum ushers too busy to notice our transaction. If we had gone with Dmitri to the ticket booth, the cashier could have spotted what was going on and refused to sell Dmitri the tickets. When Dmitri came back, I shook his hand and told him that I appreciated what he was doing. He asked me to call him from the bus station before eight, so he would not worry about me. I felt like I had a parent looking after me. Still, I had taken a step away from being led by the hand like a toddler all the time.

Dmitri watched us go in. Mary, who knew the most Russian, would give the attendant the tickets. We were all to keep as silent as possible and walk in nonchalantly. Our ploy worked. The attendants were much more preoccupied with another group trying to get in. We were lucky. I looked a little Russian with my beard and glasses. Mary's dark hair and Russian vocabulary helped her. Eileen did not look Russian, even after hiding her hair under a shawl, but the ticket collectors hardly paid us any attention. We waved goodbye to Dmitri and headed toward the museum shop located just before the white marble staircase that led up to the art treasures.

The shop was just a row of tables end to end, displaying books, postcards, and souvenirs. Eileen wanted to buy a book about Leningrad—*Leningrad: A Guide* (Kann, 1990). It looked like a nice book, and I figured it would cost about ten dollars (or the ruble equivalent). It turned out to cost forty rubles, which was less than two dollars! I bought one too. I was starting to like this place.

Meanwhile, Mary met her friend, a young man, who was waiting for her at the shop. We made our way up the grand white marble staircase, which was carpeted with a plush red runner, graced by white statues, and decorated with gilded moldings. On the way, Eileen showed me how she had hidden her camera under an over-shirt. The museum was cool, so she did not have to take off this extra garment, which made it easier for her to conceal the camera.

The museum was vast and richly complex. I had not had an experience like it since the first time I went into the Metropolitan Museum of Art in New York City. I was impressed by the beautiful and huge, silver and gold objects of art under glass—prizes of the Russian nobility—sparkling chandeliers, polished floors of rare woods or stone mosaic, all varieties of marble and malachite, as well as paintings of famous generals, tsars, and battle scenes from Russian history. What struck me the most was the wealth of Western art in the museum. All the masters were represented, from Rembrandt and da Vinci to VanGogh and Picasso. The Russian Museum—a separate museum located in the former Mikhalovsky Palace in another part of Leningrad—was devoted to the works by Russian masters such as Ilya Repin, Victor Vasnetsov, and Ivan Shishkin.

Eileen and I resumed our discussion in one of the larger rooms of the museum. You could see out onto the river and across to the Peter and Paul Fortress through windows set in deep niches. As we wandered from painting to painting, I asked her about her hosts and accommodations. After comparing notes, I found to my chagrin that I had been overcharged by Dmitri and Alisa because the sums Eileen and I had paid were hardly comparable. To top it off, it sounded like Eileen's hosts—a married couple perhaps a little older than Dmitri and Alisa and probably more well-to-do—had given her much better food to eat than I had gotten, including cakes and pastries. Eileen tried to make me not worry too much about it; after all, I had been taken to Latvia; perhaps that had been an expensive venture. I thought that the trip to Latvia could not have been expensive enough to account for the difference. Besides, she had been taken to parks south of the city. I was staying a week longer than Eileen, but even this additional factor would hardly account for the difference. I joked that her gift of green apples must have been the key to unlock the "bargain" she had gotten. Her hosts had loved them. Eileen had paid forty dollars for a three-week stay. I had paid 100 dollars for a four-week stay plus an additional 200 dollars for the Latvian excursion, according to Alisa, who had broken down the payment for me during our negotiations. This did not include the money I spent for accommodations on my own in Latvia. I did not know what to make of this difference, but I felt exploited.

Eileen and I got lost on the top floor where the Impressionists were on display. We were in the museum a long time. Eileen snapped many clandestine pictures. Nobody bothered us about this. By then, the museum was closing, and we could not find our way out of it. Finally, a nice *babushka* (literally, "grandmother," used here to mean "old lady"), one of the many attendants dotting different portions of the museum, seeing our confusion, pointed the way out.

Downstairs, among the people gathering at the cloak rooms, we rejoined Mary and her companion, who had gone their own way early in our tour of the museum. We had a short discussion. Eileen and I wanted to find a café so we could continue to talk about our experiences over a cup of coffee. Mary's companion, who I had guessed was Russian, had a different agenda. So we parted company with Mary and her friend.

Out on the central square behind the Winter Palace, we walked across the cobble stones toward the canal-lined street that led to Nevsky Prospect. A couple of hours remained before I was supposed to call Dmitri. I was in a good mood, confident that, with a little effort, we would find a nice place to sit and chat. I was under the mistaken assumption that Leningrad would, after some trial and error, turn out to be like New York City, a place where coffee shops and cheap restaurants were not hard to find. As the minutes passed and Eileen and I battled through thick crowds looking for a suitable place on Nevsky Prospect, my spirit began to sag. This was going to take longer than I thought. Evening had already started. Eileen, like me, had promised her host that she would be back well before dark.

We expended a lot of energy just trying to get through the crowds while stumbling over crumbling sidewalks. Little kids bothered us for gum or a pen. Unlike the museum ushers, they had a sharp eye for tourists. Leningrad swirled its dust around us. Young men stared at Eileen with eyes that reflected the general hunger of the city. I put a protective arm near her shoulder when we passed them. Heading east, we walked all the way to the faded red walls of the nineteenth-century Baroque-style Beloselsky-Belozersky Palace—at the time, occupied by the local branch of the Communist Party (Humphreys and Richardson, 1994, p. 58), it now houses a municipal cultural center (*Saint Petersburg Encyclopaedia*, 2007[www.encspb.ru]) —occasionally stopping to look at my *Fodor's* guide, which turned out to be useless for locating a cafe.

We had walked well past the palace when we gave up heading east and crossed the boulevard to walk back toward the west on the other side. We never found a place to sit and enjoy some coffee. The hard currency restaurants and hotel restaurants all seemed intimidating, and I did not have a lot of dollars. Neither of us knew of a place to go. The little cafe at the Peter and Paul Fortress that Dmitri took me to earlier in my trip was far away. When, finally, we spotted a promising place, a little hole in the wall that resembled a coffee shop, the few tables inside were all occupied. Most of the patrons were standing at counters and tall tables without chairs. No coffee or tea was available, only an overly sweet fruit drink and some equally sugary pastries. Eileen could not finish her drink. We left the place pretty quickly since it was too noisy to hold a conversation. Though we thought it nice to get in off the streets for a bit, standing at a counter crowded with strangers was not what we had had in mind when we set off to find a cafe.

Outside on a corner, we talked some more. I wanted to know about her volunteer work. The horror story, related in bits and snatches before we reached the cafe, was now told all at once: She had been assigned to an old age home. I had heard pretty terrible things about nursing homes back home, but they paled in comparison to what she told me. Some of the patients she attended had not been bathed for months. They were neglected by their relatives as well as the nurses. When she bathed them, they were so grateful they wanted to pay her. She often found their food covered with flies or infested by bugs. Her work also took her to the apartments of elderly shut ins, where the conditions were equally horrendous. The nurses assigned to care for these old people were hard and had a callous attitude toward the patients, often mistreating them. In short, the conditions were awful, so awful that Eileen often wished she had not volunteered for the work. These conditions affected Eileen negatively, sometimes throwing her into depression. She would not soon forget the experience. The Soviets extracted a different sort of price from her than from me. Maybe I had not been so unfortunate.

Before we parted ways, I learned more about how Eileen dealt with her "overprotective" host. She confronted Aleksiy after he was overly solicitous, as Dmitri had been with me. Aleksiy did not give her much space in the beginning. She felt smothered and rebelled, insisting that he leave her alone, let her go out of the apartment alone, let her have time to herself at the apartment, and let her find her way to work. She did this fairly early in her stay. As a result, she had developed the skills I was only just beginning to develop, the skills necessary for navigating Leningrad on her own. As a sign of her independence, she told me that Aleksiy had given her a set of keys to the flat. This left an impression on me. I too wanted more freedom.

I said good-bye to Eileen inside the Nevsky Metro Station. She gave me a quick lesson in how to read the signs and where the connections were in the station. I thanked her and asked her to call me before she left for Ireland.

E. No Time for Science

Back home, Dmitri was glad to see me. I asked if he had been worried, half teasing him. "Just little bit," was his reply. He seemed relieved when I had called him from the bus station. I noted that Alisa was not around. I asked Dmitri if she was still visiting her mother. He replied that he did not know. Dmitri had prepared a supper for me. As we ate, I told him about my day. He only half listened and seemed preoccupied. At one point, some noise came from the street, and he darted over to the kitchen window to see if it might be Alisa. He was worried about her. Dmitri's concern grew as the evening progressed and she did not return. I thought Dmitri might ring her mother's flat, but he decided to wait until the morning. Perhaps she had missed the evening train.

In the gathering gloom of late evening, while we smoked leaning on the balcony railing, Dmitri started an informal interview with me about my training in psychology. He was surprised and concerned about my lack of psychology courses. I felt that Dmitri misunderstood the field I was in. I tried to explain that psychological anthropology was derived from cultural anthropology, not academic psychology. I assured him that, as my study and experience in the field grew, I would probably become more familiar with the psychological disciplines he had mastered.

The next morning brought out my concerns. Dmitri and I had waited for Pomeroy's call until one a.m. the night before to no avail. I was feeling urgency about speaking to him. Meanwhile, Dmitri wanted to resume our previous talks, which initially revolved around Pomeroy's test and the theory behind it, and then expanded beyond that to topics that interested Dmitri. Before we started, Dmitri called Alisa's mother's flat. Apparently, Alisa departed early that morning, had other errands to run, and was expected home at any time. With that out of the way, Dmitri and I became absorbed in our discussions.

I wanted to practice speaking Russian with him. So together we went over some Russian words and phrases that I had heard Dmitri use frequently: "*ochin apasno*" (quite dangerous situation); "*eto horosho*" (it is okay); "*Ya seechas abisnyou*" (I explain); "*ochin horosho*" (very good); "*sechaz*" (now); "*ochin interesnaya situatsiya*" (quite interesting moment); "*ochin ni obuichna*" (quite unusual); "*neechyevo*" or "*poostyakyi*" (never mind, nothing); "*obschaya*" (general).

Then came Dmitri's turn to solicit help: He wanted me to assist him with some paper work concerning his courses and a simple value test he had designed. Before we got around to this, we picked up a running discussion about formal axiology, the philosophical model that supported the theory behind Pomeroy's test. Dmitri was interested in loose connections between axiology and psychological issues. Our discussion took on a rambling character full of free associations.

Robert S. Hartman, the founder of formal axiology, was fond of using an analogy between values and optics. In his writings, he often referred to "value vision." Dmitri showed me a book about perceptual psychology (*Algebra of Conscience* by V.A. Lefebvre). He saw a connection between two different perceptual limitations identified in the book and "keenness of vision values" as discussed by Hartman.

Full of boyish enthusiasm, Dmitri proceeded to elaborate: "Value astigmatism," connected by Hartman to difficulty with concentration on value issues, was related to perceptual astigmatism, a general dimness of perceptual awareness. Astigmatism could be bifurcated into its component parts—focus and drift. General difficulty with concentration involved an inability to maintain focus. Its opposite, drift, was behind dimness, a lack of keen vision. The book about perception could be used to modify and enhance Hartman's optical analogy.

Dmitri pressed on. He picked up another book, this one by E.I. Lacatosse—*Falsification and the Methodology of Scientific Research Programmes: Criticism and the Growth of Knowledge.* In it was a discussion of Gestalt. I associated this word with internal psychological states, but Dmitri preferred to think of it as referring to outside conditions. I struggled to see where Dmitri was taking the discussion. He turned back to the original book to bring up the second perceptual limitation: strobism, the inability of the right and left eyes to work together—"*kosoglasya*"—one becomes cross-eyed. He related astigmatism and strobism to the basic components of formal axiology as applied in the HVP. Four measures in the test underlie its other measures:

Diff – overall health of value vision
Dim – imbalance or balance of value vision
Int – capability of seeing the relevant
Diss – value confusion

Dmitri saw a rough connection between *Dim* scores and strobism and a rough connection between *Int* scores and astigmatism. Gestalt concerns the overall or *Diff* score that accounts for astigmatism and strobism of value. *Diss*, a related score, measures value confusion. A poor *Diss* score could be caused by poor *Dim* or poor *Int* scores.

Dmitri introduced another book (*Ecological Optics* by perceptual psychologist J. J. Gibson) that discussed perceptual systems. I felt he was taking the discussion too far afield, turning it into intellectual over-indulgence. Then Dmitri suddenly switched gears and made it relevant in a surprising twist. Putting aside the books, he made the flat statement that in the present day Soviet Union, people do not think about books, only food. He told me that the day before he had not gone home immediately after leaving me at the Hermitage. Instead he spent time downtown, standing in line for one hour on a hot day in order to buy six kilograms of *sahar* (sugar) to take it home. This sounded like a lot to me (over thirteen pounds of sugar). Dmitri told me that having to do this was normal for scientists and intellectuals because all citizens had to buy as much sugar as possible whenever it was available or they would have forgo it. The Soviet economy was plagued by shortages of goods whose abundance was taken for granted in the United States.

The net effect of the "show and tell session" I had wandered into, thinking that I would be having our usual heady discussion *sans* practical relevance, was to bring up many questions in my mind. Dmitri skillfully set me up for his punch line. He plunged us both into a theoretical discussion, only to impetuously trash it at the end, slamming home the point that this theoretical talk was useless under current conditions. Food had value, books did not. What else was Dmitri trying to tell me? I recalled sharply how, in an earlier conversation, he related a story about the time a large library in Leningrad burnt to the ground. Thousands of books, many irreplaceable, had been lost. Dmitri witnessed it and cried like a baby. This happened some time ago. Had Dmitri experienced a value shift since then? Would he cry now over such a tragedy?

Perhaps Dmitri was laying out some priorities for me through this unexpected juxtaposition. Scientists, after all, have to eat. I began to think that Dmitri's fondness for theoretical discussions was a habit with him, an indulgence to be satisfied only after the more essential work of procuring necessities was accomplished. Though Alisa and Dmitri were busy, they had more time on their hands than a comparable American couple would have. A shortage of available work contributed to this. Yet, theory, in a way, was still Dmitri's bread and butter. He had to teach for a living—a seminar in Riga or his courses at the Technological Institute (*Tekhnologichesky Institut*). His teaching required him to master different theories.

The theme of practical relevance was not entirely new. During our initial work on the translation of Pomeroy's test, Dmitri brought up the subject of finding practical uses for it throughout the discussions. He also steered me in the direction of business people eager to make a deal with me. I got the sense after a while that his cooperation with me and Pomeroy had an ulterior motive behind it—to hook one of his contacts up with us in an unrelated venture and perhaps act as the "middleman" for it. Dmitri was looking to go outside his profession into some kind of money making venture, and we happened to be a convenient lever that he wanted to use while I was around. Even if nothing panned out, just being associated with "American scientists" would make Dmitri's acquaintances remember and respect him.

On a more mundane level, I also wanted to know how Dmitri was able to purchase so much sugar. He did not lack the money to do so, since with my payment he could afford such a purchase. Yet, with the current system of rationing and coupons, which he and Alisa had taken great pains to describe, how was he able to access such a large quantity? By asking this question I was beginning to understand a fundamental aspect of Russian culture during Soviet times. Having inside information was crucial during periods of shortages.

Dmitri wanted to smoke after making his point. We stood outside watching people coming home on another sunny and windy day. I began to wonder about Alisa. The day was well into the afternoon, and she still was not home. Had Dmitri forgotten her during our talks?

After our break, Dmitri opened a new discussion. He was interested in game playing with groups. He liked working with groups, had done so in Riga, and did so during the academic year in Leningrad. He wanted to explore a way of using "Hartman values" in his group work. He thought he could use the test as an index to select group members and as a way to teach adaptation and learning skills. The test could provide feedback, which was obvious, but it could also be used for "exchange." I was not sure what he meant by that, but I did not pursue it. I was burnt out by the discussions, which had already consumed half the day.

F. The Confrontation

Later, Dmitri became anxious again, jumping up to look out the window several times. He was seriously concerned over the whereabouts of Alisa. Forty-eight hours had passed since we last saw her. Dmitri called Vasili to find out if she had happened to call there. When he got off the phone, he asked me if I wanted to have a hot shower. I said that was agreeable to me. So we went to Vasili's apartment, where Dmitri shared his concerns with Vasili and Sonia. As before, I gave Vasili a pack of Camels. Sonia got a postcard from Riga. Having a shower and seeing them again was nice, but the mood was subdued that evening as we kept a vigil for Alisa's return. We did not see or hear from her.

Vasili walked us back to our flat. A short while later, the phone rang. For a second, I thought it might be Pomeroy. Much to Dmitri's relief, Alisa was on the line. Something had held up her return. She would explain when she got home. By the time Alisa got back, an impromptu party had been arranged. Sonia came over, and the four of us greeted her. We celebrated in the tiny kitchen with a little vodka and cognac. I went back to my room to sleep before the party ended. Pomeroy had not called. It was just as well since I was too tired to speak with him.

The next morning (Thursday, 25 July), I woke up late. We all did. The party had broken up late, and I was asleep when Sonia and Vasili departed. Dmitri seemed quite pleased to have Alisa back. I wanted to find out what had happened, but the subject did not come up over breakfast. After Dmitri had said to me shortly after she left that I had to "repair my relationship with her," I felt apprehensive about her return. Now that she was back, I felt awkward asking about what caused her to disappear for a while.

After breakfast, Dmitri and I were taking a break on his balcony when I heard the phone ring. Since Pomeroy had not called yet, I was wondering if it might be him every time the phone rang. Alisa picked it up. I could hear her sharp, high voice rising in intensity as she talked on the phone. Something was amiss. I had a gut reaction as to what it might be—the money situation with the Managers Club—and braced myself for the worst. Dmitri went inside to see what was going on and came back to tell me that Alisa wanted to discuss something with me. I was prepared to discuss openly what had happened, to take whatever blame was necessary, and to rectify the situation. I was not prepared for the fury I encountered. Alisa had been called by Nelly who discovered that the money she loaned me had not been collected by Eva before my departure.

I had hardly sat on the couch next to them when Alisa launched into a ferocious diatribe. Dmitri, as was his custom, translated the words and the tone of voice: "Why you not pay? Why you not pay?" This was not exactly true; I did pay, but I was not sure if the money Nelly gave me was a loan or a reduction of my payment. The matter was never brought up again. I tried to explain this, but I could not get a word in edgewise. Alisa was going on and on, her face turning red. Dmitri stopped translating. I did not like this situation at all. It felt like a police interrogation. I had paid these people many times what Eileen paid her hosts. At that moment, as far as I was concerned, they could pay the loan back themselves.

The tension that was building over the course of two and a half weeks came to a full boil. I was fed up and named the thing that was bothering me the most at that moment:

"I refuse to be interrogated by a member of the Communist Party!" I shouted leaping up from the couch.

Dmitri stared at me, his eyes bulging. Alisa abruptly stopped lambasting me and had a stunned look on her face. They had never seen me get angry before. Alisa turned to look at Dmitri, who was shaking his head. He was not going to translate what I was saying.

My gut reaction was not far from the mark. Alisa as an active member of the Communist Party was trying to use its authority on me by assuming the tone of a police interrogator. From Alisa's point of view, I had put her relationship with Nelly and, more importantly, Anatol in jeopardy. The situation escalated from a dispute between buyer and seller to that of Soviet versus American. By naming it, I brought it to a halt. I am still proud of my stand, however tactless it was.

Furious, I was out of words and could only repeat, "No way! No way!" I was talking out loud to myself, wondering all the time if my remarks would touch off a larger conflict. In effect, I had breached diplomatic normalcy and declared war. Dmitri calmed down and said something to the effect that he thought he understood what I said but was not sure. He acknowledged that I had used "strong language." I felt he was dissembling and understood exactly what I had said.

Meanwhile, not to be outdone, Alisa disappeared into the kitchen and returned flinging some things onto the couch. Looking closer, I saw the items from the plane I had given to them. Under any other circumstances, I would have burst out laughing. This was too ridiculous. They considered them to be "presents," like Eileen's bag of green apples was for her hosts. I suddenly felt sad for my hosts. This misunderstanding was a catalyst in my mind. If they misunderstood this, what else had I done that they misunderstood? The situation reverted back to its original form: It was now a business dispute. I had not followed Russian customs properly when I showed up without a sizable gift for my hosts on the first day.

Dmitri retreated to the balcony, stood there blowing jets of smoke, and avoided looking at me. I joined him, having no idea what to say to Alisa, who was still hovering over the couch. So far, I had limited myself to one cigarette per break. Now, I started to chain smoke.

I lit up the first cigarette, taking a few puffs, and then explained that I compared payments with Eileen and had been upset when I found that I had paid Alisa a lot more than Eileen paid her hosts. Dmitri looked at me: "Gary, I am only scientist. This is not my business." I did not know how to react to this. Why was he always bailing out of these money discussions? He was taking no responsibility, which was not helping the situation.

Alisa was still inside, now sitting on the couch. I went to the balcony door, cigarette in hand, turned to her, and exclaimed in my broken Russian: "*Bolshoy! Bolshoy! Ochin bolshoy. Ya platit ochin bolshoy!*" (I paid a very big amount)! She started to say something in Russian. I turned back to Dmitri, asked him to please translate for us, crushed out the half smoked cigarette in one of the tin can ashtrays on the balcony, and lit a second cigarette. Dmitri refused. He wanted to have nothing to do with this meltdown.

I stared at Dmitri. He finished his cigarette and was watching me smoke my second one. I finally decided that this scene was pointless. Besides, they were not the ones who needed the money. Nelly did. I did not want her to suffer because of this ridiculous situation. I told Dmitri that I accepted that I owed Nelly money and would pay it, but I wanted him to understand that I did not feel good about the amount I paid him and Alisa. Dmitri visibly relaxed and went inside to relate this to Alisa.

When he came back onto the porch Dmitri said that Alisa understood. The immediate crisis passed. Further discussion revealed that Nelly made the call. I asked them to call Nelly back. I wanted to make sure that she heard it from me that she would get her money, that a misunderstanding had occurred. I was on the third cigarette by now, trying to get my jangled nerves back in order. Dmitri commented on how "strong a smoker I [was]." I told him that these were "very unusual circumstances." Did he not think so? Besides, we had work to do—this was no time for his observation. Dmitri told me that Nelly gave me her own money, and it was the only U.S. currency she had. Of this, I was not aware, and it would have made a difference.

Calling Nelly turned into a painful experience, but not because Nelly was upset. On the contrary, she was glad to hear from me and to get my reassurances that she would have her money. She wanted to know if I would like to speak with Eva as well. (Nelly was making her usual fuss over Eva: Was she not pretty; was she not charming?) Yes, I did, but felt some ambiguity over it. Eva was not so enthusiastic during our chat. I apparently had put her in a difficult situation. She felt responsible for forgetting to secure the money before I left. This was a responsibility she would not have had to bear if I had brought the subject up myself. She may have been embarrassed to ask someone to repay a loan.

So now I had to come up with twenty-five U. S. dollars. I had never encountered a country before where a foreign currency was more trusted and valued than its own. The desirability of the U. S. dollar proved to be a constant theme throughout my trips to Russia. I told Dmitri and Alisa that I would go immediately downtown to try to secure it. Dmitri wanted to come with me, but Alisa stopped him. Grateful for her insight, I thanked her. Then she told me not to compare my payment with Eileen's—"different situation." She may have been right about this. Eileen's hosts were acting through an institution (Smolny) that may have been providing some compensation to them, in effect subsidizing Eileen's trip. My trip was subsidized through my stipend from a research fellowship. I also had private funding. Spending the funds was up to me. Psychologically, I took a long time to make the adjustment from the illusion of being sponsored by a Soviet scientist to the reality of being sponsored by myself.

G. Getting It Right

Before I left the flat, Dmitri handed me a small paper map of the metro system if I should need it. The morning's histrionics had produced one tangible compensation: I had gained another small measure of independence.

I needed to find a hard currency store. I knew of one good place to try, the Leningrad Hotel. I sheepishly retrieved my unintended "gifts" from the living room couch and deposited them back in my room. I decided that more than a restitution of Nelly's money was necessary to smooth relations with Dmitri and Alisa. Presents were in order as well. I was in Dmitri's court—I should have known that substantial gifts were necessary when visiting a foreign potentate. So a hard currency store would serve a twofold purpose.

Getting downtown by bus was easy. When I reached the bus depot, I took notice of an open air market loosely organized near the Finland Station. Peddlers had set up wooden crates, selling a motley assortment of items: potatoes, giant wild mushrooms, flowers wrapped in paper or cellophane, some vegetables, items most likely carried in by the peddlers themselves. Some peddlers with no stalls hung around the entrance to the train station, selling gum and *papiros* (Russian style cigarettes). Since no metro stopped there, I walked to the Leningrad Hotel. The long walk involved going along a busy street near the river by which several military trucks passed. I did not want to try a bus or a tram, afraid I would make a mistake.

The weather was mild and comfortable for walking, though the streets were a bit dusty. I reached the large concrete patio in front of the massive glass and steel structure in good shape, passing the ground floor entrance to the hotel restaurant. I stopped to peek inside and saw no activity. I went up to the main entrance. A doorman asked to see my hotel pass. I mentioned "*pochta*" (post office), and he let me in. I found the post office on the ground floor and got directions to the hard currency store (*beryozka*) from the clerk who spoke a little English. The store, located near the hotel, had a separate entrance, so I had to go outside again. It was a fashionable shop that, besides leather goods and electronic items, included a wide assortment of liquors, teas, coffees, sweets, and drinks. I found spring water, an item that I needed for myself, the tap water being undrinkable. It would be refreshing change from Dmitri's black tea. I found some Earl Gray tea, imported from England, a substantial quantity in a fancy container. I thought it would make an adequate and safe present. I knew they both liked to drink tea.

This hard currency store used the "official" ruble currency, which was different from "street" rubles—the rate being two rubles on the dollar. Street rubles could be purchased legally as I had done at the exchange office for about thirty rubles to the dollar and illegally from speculators for substantially higher rates, according to Dmitri. These hard currency stores were designed to deal with dollars *via* an artificially controlled exchange rate and dealt strictly in imported items considered to be fashionable and a sign of status.

I cashed a check, made my purchases, and left the shop. I then went back into the hotel, made my way to the foreign exchange counter on the second floor of the hotel, and cashed another check there for rubles. Now, I had plenty of rubles and dollars. Feeling pretty good about things, I contemplated having a drink at the hard currency cash bar on the first floor. I noticed a patio outside where some seats were available amidst a few potted ferns. The view from this beer garden overlooked the calm Neva and would have made a fine subject for a work of art. If I had not been on a mission, I would have bought myself a beer and had a relaxing time. I decided not to dawdle, to save this for another time.

As I swung through the open air market near the bus depot, I noticed a lone woman standing with a bunch of small red roses for sale. A closer inspection showed that the roses were a bit old. I took the cellophane wrapped roses from the woman, handing her some rubles. The price had been far less than I would have paid back home for so many roses. In this way, I added a little more insurance to my gift selection; even if the tea turned out to be a dud, the roses could not be. I did not like Alisa much. Still, I had forced myself to overcome this in order to repair the busted fences. Back on the rattling bus that was taking me home, I struggled to keep the roses from getting crushed.

When I reached their flat, I found Alisa and Dmitri waiting for me. I immediately presented Alisa with the flowers. She took them with an almost embarrassed shyness. For a moment, she was transformed back to how she had appeared the first day—when I was a complete stranger—as Dmitri's "shy bride." While Alisa was finding a container for the flowers, I gave Dmitri the money for Nelly and showed him the English tea, another present, this one for both of them. Dmitri hurried inside the kitchen to show Alisa. I had taken a risk, and it paid off. They both seemed genuinely touched by the gifts. I was proud of myself since I had finally been freed to traverse the city streets alone, and I had accomplished my mission.

H. Shopping Russian Style

My mission accomplished, a tentative air of normalcy returned to the flat. Over a small tea, Dmitri and Alisa asked me if I was interested in seeing a state food shop. Up until then, I had been largely in the dark as to mundane things such as food shopping. I had seen nothing resembling a supermarket. I had seen street markets where some items were sold and a few lines standing outside food stores downtown. One of these shops on Nevsky Prospect featured a stylized decoration of fish on its window and a pyramid of cans of fish stacked neatly as a display near the window. Inside was the familiar strong smell of fresh or thawed fish for sale. The prospect of seeing some of the places where Alisa went shopping every day intrigued me.

The shop was located within a comfortable walking distance from the flat. We reached it shortly before it closed, and I followed Dmitri inside. Only a few customers were in the store. It was a small place with glass cases, two juxtaposed wooden counters, and sawdust on the floor. Dmitri stood in line to get some margarine that was being sliced into slabs from a large block behind one of the counters and wrapped in plain paper. Dmitri also purchased a couple of bottles of milk. When Dmitri finished his purchase at one counter, he turned toward the other. I turned around to see where he wanted to go next. Noticing another customer trying to get ahead of us, Dmitri pushed me from behind and shouted for me to hurry so I would reach the counter first. Then he slipped in front of me to make his purchase.

I did not know what was being sold at this counter, as the glass case was empty. The clerk turned and reached for something out of sight through a partition behind him—a long piece of *kolbasa* (sausage). Dmitri told him how much to slice off. Dmitri wanted to complete his purchases by buying some bread, which was also available at the shop. Since the store was closing, the remaining bread was not for sale. Dmitri paid for everything at a cashier near the door. Before we left the shop, I noticed that onions, garlic, large cucumbers, watermelons, and bottled water were also on sale. Dmitri put all his items into his synthetic fish net bag that he brought with him.

On the way back, Dmitri asked if I wanted to see a supermarket (*universam*). I liked the idea, and he took me on a tour. The Soviet supermarket had many of the features of an American one: check out lines, metal shopping baskets (not carts), and aisles of food organized into sections. The similarities soon broke down. A dearth of variety marked this supermarket. One aisle consisted of almost entirely of cardboard box after cardboard box of giant cucumbers, which by now appeared to be a Russian staple as ubiquitous as potatoes and bread. Some other vegetables were in boxes, including potatoes. Another aisle contained large bottles of compote, jam, olives, and soda water. Pepsi, stacked neatly in plastic crates, was on sale too.

Dmitri showed me some flavored sugar water artificially colored bright green, yellow, purple, or orange. Dmitri wanted to know if I wanted to try one. I said, "Why not?" So he bought a bright yellow one. It turned out to be a concentrate of some sort. Dmitri bought some of the soda water to act as a mixer for the colorful sugary concoction. We were like two kids in the supermarket, eager to try anything that looked interesting.

Watermelons—two kinds, one with a yellow rind and the other with the more familiar green marbled rind—were stacked on one of the end aisles. I noticed some of the grass-like salad greens (including dill) that Alisa often used laid out much like lettuce and other leafy vegetables would be in an American supermarket. At the opposite end of the store, a variety of freshly baked bread was for sale, stored in wooden bins. Dmitri wanted to get some because he had no luck in the other store. He showed me the different varieties of *khleb* (bread)—rye and white square loafs, flat round bread from Georgia, as well as oval shaped black and white breads that Dmitri preferred.

The front check out area was different from an American supermarket. Instead of the moving rubber-topped conveyor used to advance groceries, only a flat metal surface was available. An unusual system used to conserve shopping baskets held my attention. The metal baskets the shoppers used were not to be taken out of the store (as shopping carts can be in America). Instead, they were deposited at the end of a conveyor that sent the baskets round and round, much like luggage is at the airport, to be picked up at the other end by newly arriving customers. The other difference, sometimes found in frugal American supermarkets, was that here we had to bag our own groceries. While I waited for Dmitri to pay for his purchases, I noticed that the floor of the establishment was dusty and dirt stained. It was probably cleaned only once a day and never polished. Laden with goodies, we hurried home. Alisa scolded Dmitri for some of his more frivolous purchases, but the overall mood was positive.

I. The Phone Call

Later, while waiting again for Pomeroy to call, Dmitri involved me in yet another discussion. It began with our earlier discussion of psychological comfort zones. I watched as Dmitri drew some circles on a piece of paper. He described the differences between human beings' comfort zones. Individual comfort zones varied in size. Those with larger comfort zones took more risks. Risk involved the possibility of making mistakes and feeling bad. The plus side of risk was success. Success had two dimensions. The first was the immediate reward of the risk taking action, perhaps a new friend or lover, perhaps a raise, or maybe prestige. The second and, in Dmitri's mind, the true goal of risk taking behavior was the expansion of the individual's comfort zone. The flip side of risk was avoidance behavior, which guaranteed the individual's comfort zone stayed the same. Dmitri thought that human beings were constantly faced with these two choices: take a chance, or avoid the chance. It constituted a paradox in human life. More comfort involved more risk. Dmitri complimented me on the risk I took that day by buying them presents, especially the roses for Alisa, since my situation was such that avoiding Alisa might have been preferable to presenting her with such a gift. I felt that Dmitri was right to an extent; giving her a gift under those circumstances went against my nature. I also felt that in some way my back was against the wall. I noticed that my risk-taking had benefits for him as well. Perhaps, he was encouraging me to buy them more gifts. Still, my feelings told me that it did not matter. I was far more relaxed than I had been the previous night.

I had not felt this at ease with Dmitri for some time. I turned the discussion to a subject I had avoided since my return from Riga—the collection of Russian data for Pomeroy's test. I had given up on the idea of securing any viable data from Dmitri before I left, but I hoped that Andrey would come through on this matter. Because getting Dmitri to collect data from his regular students still was possible, I reminded Dmitri that Pomeroy ideally wanted a sample of 200 Russians in order to validate the Russia version of his test. Validation involves producing a sample that, while being unique to the country in question, nevertheless produces a pattern that falls inside a statistically expected norm. Testing in other nations revealed some statistically significant consistencies that cross national boundaries.

Dmitri discussed his overall schedule. On 1 September, the children would return to school, and the academic year would begin for everybody. Dmitri would get his first group of college-age students sometime in early September. He worked with each set of students for one month. Each month, he got a new set of students. He estimated that the average size of each group was about fourteen students. He worked until July first, so he had ten sets of students. If Dmitri tested every individual in each group, he could accumulate about 140 test results. It was not quite what Pomeroy wanted but maybe it would do. Besides, he had already collected forty. I reminded Dmitri that in all likelihood that sample would be rejected by Pomeroy as unusable for his purposes. Dmitri then suggested that the following summer he might be able to collect the balance. I asked Dmitri if he could try again when he went back to Riga at the end of July. Dmitri was not sure. He did not want to promise anything. I was not going to return with him because I did not want a repeat of the first experience. I was gambling that Andrey would get me some data after I parted company with Dmitri.

By now, I felt pretty sure that Pomeroy was not going to be pleased by the developments because the initial sample was botched and he liked to get his samples all at once. He wanted a group of 200 assembled, the test distributed, and the results collected in the same place, preferably at the same time. Having the process dragged out for months was not going to please him. Still, I felt that I could do little about it. Besides, my major responsibilities were overseeing the translation of the test and collecting a pilot sample. Pomeroy had to hash out the logistics of the larger sample with Dmitri.

Dmitri turned the discussion to the subject of his version of a stress test. He was interested in using a modified version of one of the scales in Pomeroy's test. We continued our talk with an increasing number of breaks as we grew more tired until Pomeroy called.

Alisa stayed up as well as Dmitri. An air of tension was in the flat as the minutes passed. By now, I was mentally prepared to speak with Pomeroy. I still felt some of the aftereffects of the day's earlier explosion, feeling ashamed that it had happened, but also self-righteous about it. I had to take some kind of stand at some point. Life is messy. Standing up for yourself is not something that can be scripted.

Sometime after one in the morning, the phone rang. Pomeroy was on the line. Breathless, I got the phone from Dmitri. This was my chance to talk to someone back home. The phone connection from overseas was not good. Though I could hear Pomeroy, and he could hear me, a constant annoying echo made it seem like everything was being said twice, words tumbled into each other, overlapping. I could see why it had been such a struggle for Pomeroy to communicate with Dmitri by phone. Our conversation lasted for several minutes. Dmitri and Alisa sat and watched me. I did my best to concentrate.

"Hello Leon!," I shouted into the phone, hearing an answering echo, followed by a momentary pause.

"Gary-gar, eets-is good-ood to ta hear-er your-ur voice-ves. How-ow are-er you-oo?" ("Gary, it's good to hear your voice. How are you?") Leon's familiar calm voice came on the line sounding strangely distorted due to the echoes.

With that, the much anticipated discussion began. After a minute or so, I got used to the echo effects. Leon explained that he was not able to get through the previous night: the switchboards were clogged. I decided to get the issue of Iraq out of the way first. Leon reassured me that the situation with

Iraq was not serious enough for me to get overly worried: "Saddam's dragging his heels."

Apparently, Saddam Hussein, reluctant to meet some weapons inspection requirements, faced diplomatic pressure. Despite some saber rattling, an outbreak of renewed fighting was not likely.

I asked him to communicate my love to my wife and that I was missing her. "So, the Russian women are not so interesting," Leon joked. Then I told him about the unexpected request for payment, how much it was, and how I thought they had gouged me. "There's been an exchange of money," Leon noted before promising to split the cost with me: He felt partly responsible for the situation. This offer on his part gave me great relief. I felt like he was giving me the support that I needed, financial and moral.

When he asked about the progress of our "joint project," I told him as much of the situation as I could. He confirmed that he received Dmitri's preliminary translation of his test, but he found it lacking. I assured him that this translation was prepared before my arrival and that we made substantial progress since then. I also told him that I met a linguist (Ann) who helped improve the translation. I started to tell him more about Ann and especially about Andrey and his proposal. Naturally, Leon was more concerned over my work with Dmitri. I told him candidly that the sample we collected at the business conference in Latvia, which included many Russians, was improperly administered. He asked me to have Dmitri try again. I told him that this would be difficult according to Dmitri. Besides, I was planning to stay with Andrey when Dmitri went back to Latvia, so I could not directly oversee a second effort. Leon wanted me to take Dmitri and Alisa to a restaurant and to give them gifts to try to get them to cooperate. "Use your credit card. We'll split the cost." By the time the phone call was over, I had a pretty good idea where things stood.

Pomeroy did not understand that going to a restaurant was not an easy thing for me to do. Dmitri had previously resisted the idea as being too complicated. Restaurants in the Soviet Union were pricey by his standards and often controlled by gangs. Getting in was reserved for elite Russians. Tourists with hard currency had an easier time, since they were outside the status system.

Apparently, Pomeroy would have taken a different approach to Dmitri than I. His words constituted a "half-time pep talk" that would have served our purposes better at the beginning, but the phone conversation put me into a better mood. I felt that the remainder of my stay with Dmitri had a sense of purpose. I was a little disappointed that Pomeroy had little reaction to my finding Andrey and Ann. I figured that he would pay attention only after getting some tangible results from them

Alisa and Dmitri were anxious to know what Pomeroy had to say. For the first time, I sensed that Dmitri was truly concerned about the state of our project. I told them that everything was *horosho* (well) and that Pomeroy had offered to cover some of my costs. This relieved them as well. I also noticed a look of dawning awareness on Dmitri's part, but I was not sure to what it referred. I later found out that Dmitri initially thought that my trip was being funded by my government. This was yet another misunderstanding plaguing our relationship. I told Dmitri that Pomeroy wanted Dmitri to get a good sample before I left. Dmitri remained reticent about this.

They were surprised that Pomeroy had not spoken longer with me. Dmitri wanted to know why he always seemed so intense during these calls and in a big hurry. I told them that Pomeroy was spending a lot of money per minute on these calls, they could not be long, or else they would be quite expensive. Dmitri told me that, after Pomeroy's first call, he was nervous during the subsequent calls because of the pressure Pomeroy put him under to get on with the conversations. This probably made Dmitri's already broken English even worse, which in turn made the conversations more difficult.

Dmitri and Alisa believed Pomeroy to be a wealthy man, making so many calls to the Soviet Union. I said that he was not rich—he was a psychologist like Dmitri. I let on that in his apartment in New York City Pomeroy had no more room than they had in their flat—not mentioning that Pomeroy had turned half of his apartment into a library, and that the apartment was in a secured complex with a parking garage in the basement where he kept his luxury automobile. I mentioned that Pomeroy had a second flat. Upon hearing that, Dmitri revealed that he kept another flat as well—near the center. He managed to retain his original flat after he married Alisa. Dmitri offered to take me there sometime. I commented that Dmitri and Pomeroy were quite similar. I did not tell them that Pomeroy also had a house in Pennsylvania. I did not want them to think that he was fabulously wealthy. They may have pressed me for more things, knowing that he was willing to help me with costs.

Before I went to sleep that night, I had another chat with Dmitri. He wanted to know if perhaps Pomeroy might come to the Soviet Union himself sometime. I told him that this would depend on future circumstances. I was trying to drop the hint that Dmitri's future performance would influence Pomeroy. Since subtlety did not take well with Dmitri, I should have made the blunt suggestion that a visit would be linked closely to a collection of useful data.

I asked Dmitri how he had happened to possess two flats. I heard that apartments were hard to come by in the Soviet Union. Dmitri revealed to me that the flat I currently shared with them, which I assumed belonged to him, was originally Alisa's. Normally they, being married, would be allowed to have only one flat. Dmitri's other flat was too small for a married couple, but this one was not. He had managed to hold onto the other flat through some "arrangements." What exactly they were I did not find out. Manipulating the Soviet system of distribution of resources was key to success in the Soviet Union.

J. Petrodvorets

Friday came at last. It was a long week as far as I was concerned. Even though Alisa and Dmitri seemed not to have a regular Monday to Friday work schedule, their weekly rhythm differentiated between weekdays and weekends. I knew Vasili worked in a factory during the week and spent time at his "garage" on the weekends, working on his car. I had read that the general weekly pattern here was similar to the one back in the States. So, by associating with weekday workers like Vasili, Dmitri and Alisa kept a familiar working rhythm.

Alisa was preoccupied with domestic matters, doing most of the cooking and cleaning as well as most of the shopping. Dmitri pitched in on occasion. Alisa also had Ilya to look after. I was not sure who was taking care of Dmitri's other son or even where he was.

Dmitri never seemed to have work to do except one time shortly before our trip to Latvia when he scolded me for being too inquisitive about a short outing he made: Did I not know people had to work for a living? His comment was odd. His preparations for the seminar had taken half a day. I got the impression that he winged most of it. I reminded myself that this was the summer. I knew that this was the holiday season, which was more rigidly followed by Europeans than Americans. I found that Russians followed it as well.

Eileen had not called me as promised. She was due to leave the next day. So I called her. A woman answered the phone and put Eileen on the line immediately. Apparently, I was known and approved by now, so I encountered no stonewalling. We had a short chat. I thanked her for her company and wished her luck back in Ireland. I asked her if she would ever return to the Soviet Union, telling her at the same time that I was being invited back by another party. She said that she probably would not. For her first international volunteer experience, she should have chosen a less difficult place. She wished me luck in completing my research. The finality of parting with Eileen left me in a slightly melancholic mood for the rest of the day.

The day developed slowly. Dmitri seemed to be in no hurry to do anything. Alisa busily poured sugar from a large jar into smaller jars. I assumed she was getting ready to take the sugar to someone. Dmitri mentioned that Alisa was taking it to her mother, but she was filling more than one jar. Evidently, someone else would be getting sugar, but who?

Three possibilities come to mind. Perhaps she found it easier to carry it this way. But since the weight would increase with the addition of jars, this possibility made little sense. The second possibility was that she planned to visit another party besides her mother. But nothing was mentioned about another party. The third possibility was that, once received, the sugar would be further divided. Alisa was providing not only the commodity but a means of further distribution.

Alisa was probably not just making a social call. More likely, she was going on a business trip. Further evidence of this came later when Dmitri revealed to me that Alisa was an expert shopper, and that they decided that she would spend most of her time on the acquisition and distribution of goods. I did not understand at the time what profession she may have been assigned by the state, nor did I know when she performed these duties. I was beginning to discover that Alisa was a marketer in a communist country. In an ironic sense, those who joined the Communist Party could engage in a crude form of capitalism. I had the feeling that her status allowed her to do this. (At one point in her career, Alisa had worked for Intourist, the large state monopoly for tourism.)

Dmitri wanted to know if I would like to go to the center. Sure, why not? Nothing was on my agenda. Andrey was not planning to be back until the following week. The call from Pomeroy was over and done with. Eileen was out of the picture. So, besides flattering Dmitri and Alisa, filling my notebooks, and shopping for presents for an ever expanding list of people, I had nothing to do.

The day turned out to be one of the best during my journey to the Soviet Union. It consisted of a whimsical decision and things falling into place. Time stood still, and I wished the day would linger on and on, because of the mood it created inside me, being the one time I felt at peace with myself and Dmitri.

Dmitri's immediate destination was the Dom Knigi. He was scouting for a book. The crowds outside the bookstore were thick as usual. I noticed the ever present clusters of uniformed men on the street: men in blue uniforms with red trim, men in brown uniforms with black trim, men in aqua-marine uniforms with blue trim. They all seemed to be heading somewhere, but not necessarily on duty.

We walked into the busy book store, passing through its swinging wooden doors, bumping into people trying to get out. The place was packed. People squeezed past each other through narrow openings between book islands. Wider and emptier spots where you could stand and peruse a book were hard to find. Dmitri took a long time searching for a book. In some ways, the place reminded me of the hard currency store in Latvia. Women clerks stood behind counters showing books to patrons on request. People hung over the counters with squinting eyes, trying to read the titles of books stacked along the wall behind the clerks, pointing to the ones they wanted to see. Some books were on display under glass. Others you could look at yourself in self-serve islands. They were all in Cyrillic. I could not see any foreign books, including any in English.

The ground floor of the book store followed no pattern. A cash register was in a corner with a long line in front of it. Behind some book shelves were some stairs going up to the next floor. The ground floor was devoted to selling books and some souvenir items, which included the popular *matrioshka* dolls from the Ukraine—hollow wooden dolls, nested one inside the other, usually a colorfully painted peasant woman in different sizes, sometimes famous historical figures such as Russian leaders, receding in size with each doll representing a step back into the past. A big bronze bust of Lenin, prominent at one end of the floor, oversaw the entire operation.

I knew more of the store was left to see, but Dmitri was not interested in the upstairs portions. He took his time scrutinizing some books. I wandered around trying to translate the titles to see if I could recognize what they might be about. A few covered economics and some other technical subjects. Dmitri asked me if I might want to purchase a book. Though I had not intended to, I decided a book would make a nice souvenir even if I never deciphered any of it. I spotted a paperback about ancient history, something to do with Central Asia. I thought that showing it to my friends back home might be fun. It only cost a few rubles. Most Russian books were incredibly inexpensive compared to American books. I told Dmitri that I wanted to purchase this one if he would help me with the purchasing process. He asked me if I was sure with an amazed look on his face. I said, "yes, of course," wondering what the big deal was.

When we got out of the store, Dmitri, who hemmed and hawed over several books and, in the end, bought nothing, was almost in shock that I selected a book so quickly and, hardly looking at it, purchased it on the spot. He told me that, for him, selecting a book was serious business and the process could take many days before he decided to buy it or not. I told him that the book did not cost so much (the equivalent of a few cents), so I was not worried that I might not like it. Something beyond the cost made Dmitri fussier about books than I. For him, purchasing books carried more weight, as if it was a religious decision.

I looked at my new souvenir—*Zapad Tsentralnoy Aziyi* (Western Central Asia) by L.A. Borovkova (Borovkova, 1989). In back was a table of contents in English. The rest of the book was entirely in Russian. Inside were some maps of regions in the Soviet Union near China. I flipped through the pages of Cyrillic text like a kid with an exotic toy. Dmitri was still shaking his head over my impulsive buy.

While we stood in front of the book store, I wondered what would be next. Dmitri was mulling over something. He led me across the street to a sort of car park near the Kazan Cathedral. A kiosk was there, where he made some inquiries. He told me that we were in luck, that a bus would be coming soon. I asked him what he had in mind. He told me that tours to Petrodvorets (Peterhof) left from here. Was I interested? Yes, I was interested. Eileen highly recommended seeing it, and I had already seen impressive photographs of its palatial estate in travel brochures.

Soon a coach showed up, and we got on. It was a fairly modern bus with an ancient intercom system that buzzed and crackled. The seats, with little white cloth head rests, were comfortable, and the bus was air conditioned. We rode along the streets of Leningrad heading south and west, the bus's improved suspension absorbing the shock of pot holes and tram tracks, leaving us in relative comfort. Dmitri occasionally translated the running tour lecture being given by a blue uniformed tour guide sitting at the front near the driver. Dmitri especially wanted to point out a large factory located near the western end of the south bank of the Neva. Dmitri claimed it was the largest factory in all of the Soviet Union. Its specialty was tanks and other military equipment.

Not long after, we found ourselves in shaded suburban roads somewhere between the outskirts of the city and the beginnings of the town of Petrodvorets (named after the palace). Dmitri explained to me that he wanted us to go our way after the bus reached its destination. We were in effect hitching a ride with the tour group but had no intention of remaining with it all afternoon.

The bus terminus was at the eastern edge of a large wooded park. Dmitri and I separated from the rest of the group when we disembarked. We walked through a gate along a path through trees until we reached an open space. Beyond was a plaza, complete with a manicured garden. Beyond that was the "*Petrod Vorets*" (Peter's Palace), which was what this place was all about. It was a broad, lemon-yellow structure, trimmed in white. It was flanked by large gilded, tulip-shaped domes, topped by golden crosses, on squat structures, strawberry pink in color. The whole ensemble looked like a gigantic and elaborate gourmet cake. In the center was a large pond with fountains and white statues. Sandy paths lined by decorative trees went around the pond and led to this palace (the Grand Palace). Dmitri and I stood there under a perfect summer day's sky, gazing at the splendor left behind by Russian tsars. I took photos.

Dmitri and I debated whether to go back and join the tour group, which would be heading to see the inside of the palace first, or to save this tour for later and see the park grounds first. I let Dmitri decide. He chose to see the grounds first, ensuring our complete disengagement from the tour. He was not worried about getting back to Leningrad with the tour group since he had another way home in mind. We could stay at the park as long as we pleased without feeling rushed. I liked this idea.

Dmitri found another gate near the corner of the right side of the Grand Palace. There, women attendants were collecting or checking tickets of people headed into the area we were leaving. Past this check point, the ground sloped down to a short flat plain. Beyond that was the sea. The flat plain was an intricately landscaped and quite large garden full of a wide variety of fountains. The main fountain, which I had seen so many times in pictures, had been shut off for repairs and was now surrounded by a large exposed pit containing construction equipment, makeshift supports, and workers, which was reminiscent of the state of a large number of tourist attractions in Leningrad. They were all under repair. I was exploring a museum that seemed to be not ready for its "grand opening" yet. Scaffolding was the most prominent architectural feature of the city and its suburban surroundings. Despite this, the rest of the Petrodvorets park fountains were operational.

The park, a forest of trees and fountains, was cut in two by a long straight canal stretching from the palace to the sea. Dmitri and I wandered around the grounds looking at the fountains. At one point, he took me to see an elaborate staircase decorated with a wide checkerboard patterned railing with dragons spewing water, sending it cascading down the railing. A man was selling posters of a fabulously rich staircase, done in a green motif with plenty of gilding. It was the grand staircase of the Grand Palace, which we had yet to see. Dmitri purchased all of the posters from the man. I helped Dmitri roll them up.

I wanted to see the interior of the palace. We climbed up one of the staircases to the upper level of the park to the narrow opening we passed through earlier. Dmitri spoke to the attendants, showing them our ticket stubs. Unfortunately, since we technically left the upper park, we effectively used our tickets already, and they would not let us back in to go see the palace. To get back in, we would have to purchase new tickets. We also had to be part of a group to see the interior of the palace. We abandoned our original group long before. Faced with this dilemma, we decided to forgo the palace tour. I did not mind since Dmitri assured me that we could find other places to see, and the weather could not have been better for strolling through the grounds.

We descended to the lower level of the park again. I took the time to photograph a portion of a staircase that was flanked with "Greek-like" white marble statues of half nude women. This time, Dmitri led me to a square pond in the center of the lower park. Between this pond and the gulf was a lonely tangerine-colored building surrounded by a small moat. The building, called the Hermitage (retreat), was a different structure from its namesake in Leningrad. This small, two-story building served as a dining hall. A tour of the building was available for a small fee. We had found something to do.

Visiting this small museum involved an unusual procedure. To enter the building, we first had to don oversized slippers (*tapochkee*), which were tied over our shoes. The *tapochkee* were designed to protect the ancient wooden floors of the museum from scuffing and also helped polish them. The museum provided a few benches and a large bin where the *tapochkee* were thrown in at random. Finding a matching pair that fit was a bit of a chore. Some time passed before I tied a pair of "floor buffers" over my sneakers and we were ready to proceed.

The (little) Hermitage was designed to be a self-sufficient dining room for about a dozen people. The dining area, located on the second floor, had a view of the Gulf of Finland as well as of the grounds. The kitchen was located on the ground floor. A large, round table had been specially designed to ensure the Tsar and his guests complete privacy. A system of pulleys lowered large plates through openings in the table to the kitchen below, where the kitchen staff would refill the plates and raise them back to the table on the floor above. If the guests grew tired of gazing at the sea or gardens outside, they could turn their attention to a large collection of oil paintings on the walls of the dining area, depicting a wide range of subjects from portraits to naval engagements.

Dmitri was fascinated by the novel table. I was caught up in the art work. Peter the Great and his heirs left behind a rich heritage of art for contemporary Russians and other citizens of the Soviet Union, as well as tourists, to enjoy. I was just starting to learn a little about the history of this palace and soon found out that the art I was gazing at this day was almost lost during World War II.

Peter had wanted a residence that could be enjoyed in the summer away from the center of St. Petersburg (as Leningrad was then called). He chose this spot on the south shore of the gulf located to the west of Leningrad. Many additions were added to Peter's original residence by his successors. The main feature of the entire palatial estate was its water works. A system of canals fed by a river located uphill of the site led the water downhill to the palace grounds where water pressure worked the fountains. The water eventually ended up in the gulf.

When Germans blockaded Leningrad during World War II, they overran Petrodvorets, looted many of its treasures, and destroyed most of the rest. The Russians managed to hide some of the art work and museum pieces before the Germans arrived. After the war was over, a costly project of restoration was begun (Selby, 1996, p. 296; Humphreys and Richardson, 1994, p. 281; Kann, 1990, p. 282). The architecture was meticulously restored, and the art work that was hidden from the Germans was now available to all for a small fee. The Soviet government did well in preserving the splendor of Russia's imperial heritage This positive feature, in contrast to so many negatives in the history of the Soviet Union, was one of the few signs that the government here cared about its people.

That the Soviets spent so much time and used many resources to preserve these historical artifacts was revealing. First, it showed that the Soviet Union's leaders considered tourism to be crucial for economic development. Besides a commercial interest, the restoration suggested something deeper. It signaled a concession by communism to a failed cultural policy. When the Bolsheviks (communist revolutionaries) took over the defunct Russian Empire, their first impulse was to destroy the old culture, ruin the former aristocracy, suppress the Russian Orthodox Church, and dismantle the Tsarist landmarks. I had seen a small sign of this when Dmitri told me about the missing crowns on the bridge near the Peter and Paul fortress. The ubiquitous statues of Lenin that dotted Soviet cities represented an attempt to create a new Soviet iconolatry. But the new forms did not take hold. Russian Orthodoxy was making a come back. Symbols of Tsarist Russia such as Petrodvorets were being displayed proudly. In Eastern Europe, the infamous Berlin Wall had come down. Signs that the clock was being turned back to Russia's imperial cultural heritage foreshadowed nation-changing events that would occur a short time after I left the Soviet Union in 1991.

Dmitri and I had eaten on the bus, so we were not hungry when we reached the park. We enjoyed the lingering afternoon without having to bother with a meal. A lot of the day was now gone. The bus that originally brought us had left an hour ago. We had gotten our fill of strolling the shady paths and gazing out onto the waters of the gulf. Time had come for us to decide on how we would make our way home.

Dmitri decided to purchase tickets for a boat ride back to Leningrad. Little time was left before the last of the boats would leave for the city that day. I waited for him on a bench, under a small clump of trees situated at the end of the long canal that ran all the way to the Grand palace, while he went to the nearby kiosk selling tickets. Some families were waiting for tickets. They occupied part of my bench as well as two others. Being next to the gulf unsheltered from the wind was chilly. I got my rolled-up windbreaker out of my nylon bag and put it on. Some boys playing nearby eyed me curiously and seemed to be making noise to attract my attention.

I was hungry again and pulled a leftover sandwich, wrapped in some plain white paper, from my bag. It was part of a stack of *booterbrod* (open faced sandwiches) that Dmitri brought along for the trip. Dmitri liked to stack them together to make them easier to carry. The sandwich consisted of a Spam-like meat garnished with cucumbers on *bulka*.

I munched on my sandwich, waiting for Dmitri to come back with the tickets. The sun went behind some clouds, and the nippy wind coming off the sea made the early summer evening feel more like the late afternoon of an autumn day. I spotted Dmitri standing near the front of a long ragged line waiting in front of the kiosk. The customer ahead of Dmitri was taking a long time to purchase his tickets. I started to feel slightly anxious. Dmitri had been worried that the boat rides might sell out. Momentarily distracted by an outburst from the children playing nearby, I missed when Dmitri's turn came. When I looked up, Dmitri was hurrying over to me, holding some papers in his hand. He managed to get us tickets on the last of the boats for the day. Dmitri seemed quite pleased with himself and wanted me to follow him immediately to the docks, even though the boat was not scheduled to leave for another thirty minutes. He explained to me that seating was limited on these boats and a crowd would be waiting to pile on—best to get there early.

We went around the square shaped dock area where some people were already waiting. Dmitri explained to me that we would be taking a "rapid boat" back to the center of Leningrad. The sun came out from behind the clouds and warmed us up a bit. I watched an odd couple conversing. I was attracted by the sound of English. A man in a business suit was speaking with a girl about half his age. She seemed to be quiet mostly and spoke only a few words of English at a time with a Russian accent. He was saying something about his wife, referring to her in the third person. I guessed at the situation and spoke with Dmitri about it. He confirmed my suspicion. This was an American businessman with his Russian girlfriend: "They sometimes come here and stay long time. Man lonely. She interested in someone who maybe buy her things, take her to restaurant, maybe clothes." I was not surprised, until Dmitri mentioned that these situations were all too common.

Our boat came a little earlier than I expected. It was a remarkable sight. The hydro-foil, sleek, silver, and white, slowed down as it approached us. This was not what I expected, having only seen the slower ferry boats on the Neva used for tourist operations. We watched as the hydro-foil (called a *rokyeta*) slipped into the pier. A stream of passengers filed out of the boat. I asked Dmitri how they expected to get home. He told me trains left the Old Peterhof (Petrodvorets) station in the evening.

A crowd had gathered by now, waiting to get on board. We filed onto the craft while it bobbed up and down. Its powerful engines, having been throttled down, idled with a throaty pulsing sound. Two main seating areas were available, one to the front and another to the rear. I told Dmitri that I was interested in taking pictures. He told me to be patient; I would have a good opportunity once the boat started. The boat slipped out of the dock area and motored out at normal speed for the first hundred yards, the engines barely changing pitch. Then I felt the pulsing beneath the hull increase its tempo. The engines began to roar. The craft increased its speed, and, as it did so, started to rise up, like a sprinter rising from the starting blocks. Soon we were skimming over choppy waves. After a few seconds of this, Dmitri motioned to me to follow him. I followed him to the central portion of the boat where a set of stairs went up.

We emerged out of an opening onto a small, uncovered observation deck in the middle of the boat. Salty water sprayed our faces, and wind whipped our hair back. The view was amazing. Inside the boat felt like you were watching the seascape go by on television. Outside felt wild and cold with nothing but sea and sky. The grounds of Petrodvorets, already in miniature, receded rapidly behind us. Ahead, above the slate blue sea, I could see a thin white line that was the barely discernible beginnings of a cityscape.

Dmitri tapped me on the shoulder. He wanted me to see something on the other side of the boat. To our port side and back a ways was a tiny gray island obscured by haze. "Kronstadt?" I asked. Dmitri nodded. Kronstadt was the tiny island where sailors mutinied against the Bolshevik government in 1921. Later, it became a military base, off limits to tourists and the general population.

I knew that taking pictures was not a good idea. Anything the Soviet government considered sensitive, especially military, was not to be photographed. I decided to take photos as discretely as possible and make sure that I did not photograph anything that looked remotely military, and I figured that included the boat we were on. I noticed the glass enclosed bridge just ahead and wondered if the crew was noticing me. There was not much in the way of pictures to take just yet. I took the time to observe the boat. The hydro-foil, which looked modern from a distance, close up revealed its construction to be not of a single piece, like a fiber glass boat might be, but of large plates of heavy metal riveted together. Nevertheless, it was an impressive boat.

The first discernible cityscape approached ahead. As the boat swung to its port side, the cityscape passed by our right. The setting sun brilliantly illuminated a row of apartment houses so their white facades shone. As we got closer, I could make out distinct shapes, including giant cranes towering over portions of the coastline. The long continuous line of buildings was broken into discernible clusters. Our boat began to slow down as the buildings came closer. Two identical apartment blocks, tan and white, rolled slowly past. Giant cumulus clouds hovered above them. A thin, uneven strip of trees separated the blocks from a golden sand shoreline. The boat headed for a narrow opening and soon began to slow down. We were heading into one of the major branches of the Neva (*Malaya Neva*).

At this point, I stopped taking photos. In front of me, appearing apparently from nowhere, was a large futuristic looking craft, blue-gray with large white numbers stenciled on its side. Obviously a military boat, it looked like an oversized swamp boat—the kind propelled by an air propeller in back and meant for shallow water. This one had three giant propellers in back. Next, we passed a similarly colored navy boat that looked like a light destroyer.

Once we passed the navy ships, I resumed taking pictures. We passed through an ever narrowing channel and under a low bridge. The hydro-foil slowed to a crawl, putting it low in the water to ease an under bridge crossing. On our right was a long pastel pink building topped by a white dome. Behind it rose the narrower dome of St. Catherine's Orthodox Cathedral. A little further on the channel opened up, and to the right I saw the dark red *Rostral* columns (naval beacons) that mark the edge of the *Strelka,* an architectural ensemble that includes the pre-Revolutionary stock exchange building with its classical facade of Greek columns. We were fast approaching the bridge that connects Vasilevsky Island on the right to the Peter and Paul Fortress on the left. Further in the distance to our left was the golden dome of St. Isaac's Cathedral. To its left, I saw the golden spire of the Admiralty building.

My heart beat a little faster. The feeling was something akin to seeing the skyline of Manhattan. Despite its panoramic views from land, the only way to enjoy and appreciate the total scope of Leningrad's architecture is from its rivers.

We went under the second low bridge. On the other side was the main (*Bolshoya*) Neva, and in it was another navy ship, perhaps a cruiser, larger still than those I saw in the channel. Careful to avoid photographing it, I again crossed to the port side of our craft and took a photo of the Peter and Paul Fortress. It was mostly in shadows; the sun only illuminated a ruddy outer wall and the eighteenth century church inside its yard. The hydro-foil swung around, keeping the cruiser to its starboard side, as I took a photo of the Winter Palace's river front facade. The green, gold, and white motifs were sharply etched against a deep blue sky. Giant, dark green figures, frozen in time, staunchly guarded its roof. I stopped taking photos and stared at the sailors lined up on the navy ship as our boat slipped into the covered pier located just in front of the palace. The ride was over.

The day came to an end, and a long evening began. I did not speak to Dmitri much, except to ask him about the navy ships. He explained that "Navy Day" (an annual city holiday) would be held that weekend. Preparations were underway for a celebration of Leningrad's seafaring tradition. The navy display boats, which would soon line the Neva, were just beginning to arrive. I felt grateful to Dmitri. The day was by far our best together. We grew to understand each other, and I did not use up nervous energy trying to cope with misunderstandings. Unfortunately, now that the day's activity was over, the melancholia that had affected me earlier began to come back. The charm of Peter's "suburban" retreat was only a memory. Only Dmitri's lonely flat awaited us.

When we got off the bus that took us back to the flat, Dmitri led me through a short cut we often took. There was a saloon there, tucked into an obscure corner away from the street, that Dmitri had sternly warned me not to enter—it was apparently a criminal "hang out." This day it was not open. The alley in which we were was deserted. I told Dmitri that I felt sad and just a little lonely.

Dmitri gave me a puzzled look, "What [do] you mean, lonely?"

"I mean, I feel I am by myself now; alone."

Dmitri shook his head, "This [is] not possible."

"What do you mean?" I inquired as my self pity vanished and curiosity took its place.

"No one is alone in the Soviet Union. It [is] not possible [to] live [as] one."

I did not know what to make of Dmitri's last remark. Maybe I had inadvertently insulted him, since he kept me company all day. I wanted to explain that my mood began earlier that day, when I knew that I would not see Eileen again. Other than her, I knew no one who could see things from my point of view.

Dmitri cut me off: "Later. We discuss later."

We arrived back home. In spite of the day's general lightness and a repaired relationship with Dmitri, my mood grew somber. I had a general sense that during the remaining days I would only kill time until I got in touch with Andrey.

Six

VALUES AND THEIR COST: RUSSIA'S HIDDEN SIDE

1. Overview

This chapter ends the narrative taken from my 1991 trip. This period of time ended when I heard from Andrey who became instrumental in the rest of my research. In the last chapter, I traveled with Dmitri to Petrodvorets. In this chapter, I travel with him and Alisa to Pushkin (Tsarskoye Selo), another tourist attraction south of Leningrad.

Dmitri was on vacation between his summer seminars. He wanted to show me more of Leningrad and its immediate environment. This was part of his services. As I learned later, Alisa and he were in the business of entertaining foreign scientists in return for different forms of compensation. They were trying out different activities, including trips to tourist sites and camping visits to other cities. They used my trip as a prototype. With subsequent clients, they stuck to things that worked well with me and eliminated those that did not. I was a test case for them, something neither Leon Pomeroy nor I knew. This helps explain some of the things I found puzzling early on, such as why Alisa seemed so concerned about being compensated and not spending much on meals, why Dmitri had me pretend to be Russian on the train to Riga, and why they took me to visit tourist areas after they received payment.

Continuing the themes begun in the preceding chapter, I discover that Dmitri has more resources than first meet the eye. He shows me his studio, located in a room that technically he should have given up when he married Alisa. In the previous chapter, Dmitri began to apply his craft of psychology to me. Uncomfortable with his probing, I turn the conversations, which had progressively grown more theoretical, to topics that interest me. These include Russia's current problems—I experience a power outage on the state electric rail system during our outing to Pushkin—and other topics such as the use of informal friendship networks to cope with chronic shortages, the concepts of values and stress in the study of society, and the role of status in Soviet society.

I get to see more of Russian private life in the Soviet context. This includes family relationships, resources hidden from view, and the ritual of the Russian bath, an event that is public and private.

The narrative picks up where it left off in Chapter 5: Dmitri and I had just arrived at his home after a day-long outing to the suburban retreat of Petrodvorets.

2. No One is Alone in the Soviet Union (26 – 28 July)

Dmitri's response to my revelation of loneliness puzzled me, but we did not discuss it over supper. Instead, most of the talk centered on our visit to Petrodvorets. Dmitri announced that we would be visiting another park the next day, Pushkin, another palatial retreat south of Leningrad. Dmitri seemed determined to show me a good time before I left. Perhaps my tirade about how much I paid them made them feel a little guilty, and this was their way of compensating. I did not know.

One thing seemed certain though. I knew that any further collaboration on our joint project during my stay was at an end. Even if Dmitri showed an inclination to find test subjects, he seemed to be able to do little about it. Dmitri taught at the Leningrad Polytechnical Institute, but he had nothing to do with it while I was there. He and Alisa seemed to live their life in Leningrad independent of any institutions. By contrast, Andrey seemed to live at his place of work year round. In 1992 and 1993, I would discover this, and it was Andrey's involvement with his institutions that made him successful at the task Pomeroy needed done.

Another thing puzzled me: Although I saw evidence of extended families living together, as in the case of Dmitri's friend Vasili, I did not see any of Dmitri or his wife's relatives (besides Ilya). Dmitri commented that his parents were not inclined to meet me and that they disapproved of Dmitri having me as his guest. Besides a few brief remarks, I got no more information from Dmitri about his relatives. For instance, I never found out if Dmitri had any brothers or sisters, let alone aunts, uncles, nephews, nieces, or cousins. I got the impression that, apart from Vasili's family and the long distance connection with Anatol's staff, Dmitri and Alisa were isolated. Since I was not with them for long, temporary circumstances may have led to this impression.

My experience in the Soviet Union was unusual. Though I found the country to have some third-world characteristics, a sharp contrast existed between my personal interaction with Soviets and people I met in Latin American third-world countries. In Mexico and Ecuador, I was freely introduced to a multitude of the relatives and friends of my immediate contacts. In Ecuador, I was taken miles away from my host's home to visit his relatives. During 1991, my Russian hosts were reluctant to have me meet a large number of their relatives or friends. Most of the people I met through Dmitri were related to him superficially. Besides a small portion of the business people Dmitri introduced me to in Latvia, the majority of them were virtually strangers to Dmitri as well as myself. I suspected that whom I met was carefully controlled according to criteria I did not understand.

In later trips, this trend began to reverse itself. In some cases, I was introduced to different relatives. This happened with Andrey's family and later with Lena's family. On these trips, I was more experienced and had more time to get to know the families.

Separation from my home, my wife, and my colleagues, added to a sense of a carefully monitored social life, left me feeling lonely. Being in Russia dropped a veil over my eyes. I found it hard to remember how things felt, sounded, and looked back home. The first day after my project with Dmitri was over—the first day Dmitri could just hang out with me—he chose to show me things instead of have me meet people. Not that I minded, because I knew that meeting new people was not necessarily a good thing. For instance, my experiences meeting my host's relatives in Ecuador were not pleasant and included boredom, disgust, exhaustion, frustration, and illness. By contrast, the leisure time spent with Dmitri was pleasant, but also monotonous because I saw the same faces repeatedly.

Later on that evening after supper was over, Dmitri and I smoked cigarettes on his balcony. I told Dmitri that I was homesick and missed the familiar things back home. I tried to communicate my emotions by quoting from a song by Phil Collins, the rock singer. The song tells the story of a man who has traveled the world and seen more than his share of exotic places: "Please, take me home, 'cause I don't remember." Dmitri, unsettled by my words, tried to talk me out of my melancholy.

He did little to dispel my mood, more or less told me to snap out of it, and placed too much importance on Eileen's role in my current state of mind. I needed moral support, and it was not forthcoming. I knew how I felt, Dmitri did not, so analytical discussion was pointless. Dmitri seemed to lack a component necessary to successful psychotherapy, the ability to relate to the client emotionally. In my case, I could not tell if I was a friend, a colleague, a client, or a customer to Dmitri.

Soon silence enveloped the balcony. As the *lastochikh* (swallows) whirled around us in the fading light, I smoked another cigarette and gazed at the lights from a distant high rise. When I turned to go back inside, I noticed that Dmitri was staring into the darkness himself, lost in his thoughts.

A. Pushkin

Saturday (27 July) promised to be a fine day. Alisa would accompany us to the park in Pushkin—another town on the so-called "necklace" of towns including Petrodvorets, which lay to the south of Leningrad. She had the day off, but from what I could not tell. Alisa, unlike most Soviet wives, did not seem to have a job. However, from some things Dmitri mentioned to me, as well as subsequent experiences in Russia, I can surmise that Alisa did have an official job that she did not perform. Spending her workdays shopping was more economical for her family. This often involved standing in long lines and taking care of matters that would have taken Dmitri's time. Their marriage had a strong division of tasks.

I watched Dmitri make the stack of *booterbrod* that was our staple that day. He carefully wrapped it in paper and then foil. I rarely saw him or Alisa use aluminum foil. They made other preparations as well. Alisa packed a knapsack with the *booterbrod* as well as some *compote*. I rummaged through my things looking for insect repellent. Although I had found no use for it on the trip to Petrodvorets, I knew that Pushkin was located away from the Gulf of Finland and the winds that kept the insects at bay. I also brought anti-diarrhea medicine. I learned from previous outings that public toilet facilities in and around Leningrad were primitive, and I did not relish the thought of getting a bout of intestinal problems far away from Dmitri's flat.

Our trip, which lasted about an hour and a half, required three modes of transport—bus, metro, and electric train. We took the bus to the Finland Station. From there, we took the underground to the Pushkinskaya metro station. Just outside the station, a small band played brass instruments. I did not recognize the music, which closely resembled march tunes. The station was located next to the Vitebsk Railroad Terminal, the preferred line to Pushkin according to Dmitri. We took a not too crowded electric train south to Pushkin. Once in the town of Pushkin, another bus was required to get us to the park.

The first portion of the trip was smooth, almost dull. While waiting at the Vitebsk terminal in Leningrad, I noticed that the sky was overcast and rain was possible. When we got off at the station in Pushkin, the sky was clear and the sun strong. Dmitri and Alisa led me to a bus depot, a semi-circular drive located just outside the train station describing a half moon shape around a small park. Streets radiated out from this drive to different parts of Pushkin. Several bus stops lined the drive. Buses came frequently, but some time passed before the one we needed arrived.

From the railroad station to Pushkin park, the ride took an unusually long time as we took what seemed to be a zigzagging route through most of the town. The town was a mixture of neo-classical buildings and ugly Soviet apartment blocks. The ubiquitous alder tree, used for public decoration in Leningrad, along with oaks, birches, and pines helped soften the otherwise hard-looking streets and facades. Dust and heat prevailed and seemed to be the theme song for Pushkin's buses in July. Every time we passed a shady avenue, I longed to be off the crowded bus, walking on the tree-lined path where I imagined the temperature must be several degrees cooler.

As we got closer to Pushkin park, I noticed private gardens along the side of the road, not far from the park entrance. When they first appeared, they looked like neglected plots of land with overgrown vegetation behind storm fencing. Only the green-sided shacks topped with tar roofs hinted that something other than an abandoned lot lay behind the fencing. Dmitri told me that these lots were popular, and every inch inside them was put to use. Sometimes the occupant tried to convert the shack, meant to be a tool shed, into a livable dwelling. As we came closer, I saw that some of the small trees and thick bushes were speckled with bright colors suggesting that they were laden with fruit.

You did not own these properties in the sense you might in the United States. Instead, each Soviet citizen was given the opportunity to acquire a small plot of land through a distribution system that was usually handled through the citizen's state employer. The use of a plot of land was supervised by the state, and some rules applied to what could and could not be done with it. Apparently a plot of land could be bought or sold, according to my Russian friend Lena, but this involved a lot of time and heavy state regulation.

We got off the bus, and, sure enough, the street was cooler. The park entrance was a short walk up a hill and around a bend to our left. Some vendors sold trinkets from makeshift stalls set up near the gates. A couple of vendors had ice cream. We avoided these temptations.

We entered the park and stepped into another world, leaving behind the dust and squalor of Pushkin's streets and buses. The magnificent Catherine Palace, an imposing aquamarine and snow-white structure set on the side of a small rise, dominated Pushkin park. Gilded copulas that looked more golden than the sun topped the palace. I saw evidence that the facade once had more gilding. The entire front facade had at one time been covered with gilded decorations, but the gilding had been removed when it prematurely tarnished (Humphreys and Richardson, 1994, p. 296). Mocha-brown paint covered the formerly gilded moldings. I wondered if the restoration process was complete yet and thought more gilding would be added. However, I saw no evidence of scaffolding, the sure sign that restoration was in progress.

The palace towered over a luxurious verdant garden with clay paths that described a complex geometric design. At one corner of the park, just a few yards away from the baroque facade of the Catherine Palace, was a small shady square bordered by dark green benches and tall oak trees. Park visitors could sit there and absorb the sounds of eighteenth century tunes played by court musicians dressed in period clothes.

The scene had a kind of irony. Communists had wrecked the former aristocracy only to preserve some of its traditions and make them available to a public that otherwise endured a grinding existence. So, at a price and for a little while, the Soviet public at large could enjoy the status of royalty—a token reward for being a good citizen of a nation destined to be the "shining model" for the world. Exactly when this destiny would be achieved, no one knew.

After a little exploring, we found an empty bench and had our lunch. After an indecisive start, the weather turned out to be pleasant enough, and you could not beat the setting—manicured lawns, shade trees, and a rectangular, concrete pool of glassy smooth water, which reflected the sky like a mirror. Dmitri and Alisa discussed something among themselves while I finished my portion of the *booterbrod*. When I finished, Dmitri asked me if I would like to go see the palace. I had no objections. After the disappointment at Petrodvorets, I was eager to see the interior of one of these royal residences.

One snag remained. Only tour groups were being allowed into the museum. Despite this, Alisa and Dmitri were determined to get us in. Alisa disappeared for a while to talk with someone and came back. I do not know which strings were pulled or what sort of story they concocted, but we got inside. This practice of getting favors turned out to be a specialty of several of my subsequent Russian hosts. They had status and influence without the apparent wealth associated with these things in the United States.

Dmitri told me to speak English with him as we entered the palace. He also wanted us to keep close to one of the tour groups that was getting its tour in German and English. The situation put me under a lot of stress, and I felt hurried throughout the tour. I preferred a slow pace and did not like to be rushed through a museum as if we had something better to do afterwards. Dmitri insisted on keeping close to this group that, from my viewpoint, was getting a whirlwind tour of the palace.

The tour was over before it started as far as I was concerned. I got only a fleeting glimpse of an outstanding display of wealth beyond imagination. I had seen house museums of the so called "robber barons" of the United States, but their money and opulence paled in comparison to this. I wondered how many backs were broken by the royal family to distill these riches from Russia, for this wealth was ultimately derived from slaves (Russian serfs) and conquests.

The dark side, hidden from view, that made these riches possible involved a moral inversion that placed material possessions over human life. Russia's experiment with communism was supposed to reverse this injustice. However, the experiment only succeeded in replacing the aristocratic elite with a new more base elite. The common Russian remained a slave for all practical purposes. Nostalgia for the past remained strong. The past held an aesthetic experience that the modern industrial state could not match.

Amidst all the art work, decoration, gilding, chandeliers, rare woods, and priceless antiques, one thing stayed in my mind—a single room that spanned the width of the palace. It was aptly called the "Picture Hall," because its walls were covered almost entirely by a mosaic of different size canvases by masters of the European schools of the seventeenth and eighteenth centuries. The paintings were from the era of Rembrandt and Vermeer. So they were meticulously representational with special attention given by the artists to the interplay of shadows, light, and color. They were dark, somber, and heroic in subject matter. In the center of the mosaic of canvases rose a tall narrow stove used to heat the room. Supported by short fluted golden legs, the stove was made out of delicately patterned blue and white porcelain and must have been worth a fortune. On opposite ends of each side of the room lay two entry ways smothered by gold relief that formed a sort of crest over and around double doors. The doors were painted in a satiny, translucent color that was not quite light blue, or pale green or off-white but something in the vicinity of such colors. The gold and translucent satin color theme was repeated across the room under the mosaic of paintings interrupted only by the stove. Chairs that matched the walls in color were set on both sides of the stove. They seemed to melt into the wall. This motif went around the entire room. The floor, which we polished with our *tapochki* (shoe covers provided at the entrance), was made out of teak, mahogany, and other expensive tropical woods that had been inlaid in an elaborate geometric design that had some of the quality of a M. C. Escher painting. I wanted to spend an hour in the Picture Hall and was disappointed that I only had a few minutes. I spent them looking at two canvases depicting scenes from famous Russian military battles.

This fabulous wealth and richness of material culture contrasted strongly with the dismal conditions Russians faced outside these well-kept museums. You can only wonder what effect this contrast had upon the spirit of those Russians fortunate enough to be able to see these splendid riches. Those Russians who could travel to the West brought home a similar comparison. Russia was relatively poor in relationship to its past and to its European neighbors. In this case, economic conditions affected the spirit of the nation. Hence the look of weary resignation on so many of the faces of the older generation. Had they struggled so hard to become poor?

We spent about an hour going through the entire museum. By the time we were two thirds of the way through, I had an upset stomach. By the time we finished, I needed a bathroom. The stress or the food had gotten to me. Dmitri located the rest rooms and I made it just in time.

Outside the museum in the fresh air, I was able to relax and regain some intestinal fortitude. I did not want to wait for another attack. I had fortunately remembered to bring my pills and only needed some liquid with which to take them. So I asked Dmitri to get me something, anything to drink. I waited on a bench in the garden in front of the palace with Alisa and contemplated how a simple thing like clean drinking water, so taken for granted back home, would have been a godsend at that moment. Dmitri returned after what seemed to be an interminable period of time with paper cups full of "lemonade," a fizzy, yellow-colored soft drink that only faintly resembled the real thing. I used the lemonade to wash down two of the green pills I hoped would cure my condition.

Then we all had a rest. Dmitri and Alisa sat quietly while I wrote in my notebook. At one point, Dmitri asked if I would like them to take another bench so I would have more privacy and quiet for writing. I sensed that they thought I might be writing about them and were getting self-conscious. I assured Dmitri that I was not writing about the immediate moment and asked him to stay put.

The fizzy water and pills helped my stomach. After a while, I felt strong enough to take some photographs. While I took photos, Dmitri and Alisa walked to a different spot where they could sit on a bench and look at a small lake located near the palace. Near the edge of the lake to their left was a white grotto that had a small shop in it where Dmitri had purchased the drinks. In the middle of the lake was a tiny tree-covered island. By walking along the edge of the lake in the direction of the grotto, I could make out a marble column rising behind this island. The grass bordering the shoreline of the lake was tall, and more shade trees were there. Unlike the area closer to the palace, there was no visible pattern to this part of the park. Dmitri explained that this was the so-called "English" garden, marked by its more irregular and natural features in contrast to the "French" garden immediately in front of the palace with its carefully manicured lawns and shrubs and its regular geometrical patterning. Here was a demonstration of aristocratic Russia's knowledge of outside cultures giving the former imperial society a sense of openness.

At the time of my visit, Russia was striving to reach out to other cultures in order to open the stagnant Soviet society to fresh cultural currents. This spirit of reform was moral therapy for the nation, long in a state of malaise. *Perestroika* and *glasnost* were Mikhail Gorbachev's ambitious programs to open a closed society. The moral inversion that this involved, in effect undoing Stalin's steel-like hold over Russia that lingered even in the late twentieth century, was akin to turning a giant rusty wheel, according to Boris Yeltsin. A new generation of Russian political leadership ignoring Gorbachev's later hesitation pressed forward. Today, Russia is a much more open and mobile nation than it was in the 1970s and 1980s, bringing its people more opportunities.

I took a photograph of Dmitri and Alisa sitting on the bench. Dmitri turned his head and leaned over the back of the bench to smile at me. Alisa, head half turned, was smiling too. They seemed much more relaxed than when I had taken photos of them earlier. I spent some time alone after this, exploring other areas of the park nearby and discovered that the entire park was a collection of niches, each with its architectural features.

Now that I was feeling better, Dmitri asked me if I would like to visit the museum shop located inside the palace. It was a good place for souvenirs. I was intrigued by a collection of hand painted wooden eggs and found the cost to be remarkably low. I bought about a dozen, thinking they would make nice gifts. The museum shop also sold sets of colorful postcards depicting the palatial parks south of Leningrad. I bought a few of these, including those that showed the destruction wreaked by the Nazis in the Great Patriotic War (World War II) to most of these parks. The Soviets were proud of the job they had done restoring these parks to their former glory and splendor. The restoration begun by Stalin in order to restore Russian national pride continues to this day with the more practical purpose of attracting tourists, bringing much needed currency.

We left soon after visiting the museum shop. As we made our way back to the entrance of the park, I began to feel ill again and wondered if I would make it home without the need for another bathroom stop. We passed under an arch that connected the right side of the palace to a structure set at right angles to it. This was the "Lyceum," a place where the famous nineteenth century Russian poet Alexander Pushkin studied. The town, originally called "*Tsarskoye Selo*" (Tsar's village), was renamed to Pushkin in honor of this learned man who did so much to bring Russian literature from obscurity into worldwide recognition and helped inspire a generation of Russian literary giants.

Near the edge of the park, Dmitri showed me a bronze statue of Pushkin as a student, half reclining on a bench, lost in thought, perhaps contemplating his next opus. I did not feel well enough to spend more than several seconds contemplating this Russian hero. I asked Dmitri if perhaps one of the kiosks I spotted on the way out might have some milk for sale. He doubted it, but we set off to try. We found no milk available, but some ice cream was for sale there. I thought that it was worth a try. The ice cream did not help my stomach, but it did not hurt it either. The persistent queasy feeling that nagged me got no worse.

Before setting off on our journey back home, Alisa took Dmitri aside and had a short chat with him. Dmitri came back to tell me that Alisa wanted us to go ahead to the train station. She wanted to do some shopping and needed to use a different bus line than the one we used to get to the park. We would rendezvous at the train station.

Dmitri and I set off by ourselves. As we were walking to the bus stop, I realized that the light exercise was helping me feel better. I wanted to take photos of the private vegetable and fruit gardens that we saw from the bus earlier that day. Since I did not want to take the photos from a moving bus, I asked Dmitri if we could walk to the place and then catch a bus. I also thought the exercise would do me some good.

The weather had turned again. The sky was completely overcast. Rain seemed imminent. Dmitri chose a compromise. Instead of walking all the way to the location of the gardens, he suggested we take a bus there. So we did. Luckily, we reached the spot before the rain came. I took photos of the private gardens and also took pictures of an apartment complex just across the street because I wanted to capture the setting more fully.

The apartment complex was ugly. In an attempt to break up the monotony of its overall squat and blocky shape, the architect or architects had concocted an unusual three-tone color scheme designed to give it a "painterly" quality, that is, to highlight instead of mask the components of its construction. An irregular combination of white, red, and tan was used to show how the blocks had been assembled by piecing together horizontally oriented slabs of concrete. The overall result was not pleasing to the eye and left the viewer wondering if the construction crew had run out of materials more than once before the job was done and, as a result, substituted materials of different colors to complete it. The grounds around the apartment block followed no pattern and looked more like an abandoned lot with wild grasses and weeds overrunning dirt pathways. Having just come from viewing a wealth of esthetic objects, I was startled to see something so ugly.

You have to be careful when passing a subjective judgment on the product of a foreign culture. For example, my assessment of the unkempt landscaping around these projects reflected a taste cultivated by my American background with its suburban ideal of well-kept lawns. According to Lena, Russians did not seem to mind some wildness amidst civilization because it reminded them of their beloved countryside. The Soviet architecture and its decaying nature left me feeling unsettled. I felt it to be akin to an act of vandalism after witnessing the beauty of the imperial architecture.

The sharp contrast was symbolic of Soviet Russia's break from its aristocratic past and the ruin of Soviet life. The great equalizing principle that was the idea behind communism had not succeeded in making everyone equal for economic disparities still existed throughout the Soviet Union. An entire class known as the *nomenklatura* (those named on the list), having access to scarce goods, were much better off than the average Soviet citizen. However, the communist ideal did succeed in driving most Russians below the equivalent of the American poverty line. Vast public housing projects all over Leningrad (and all over the Soviet Union) attested to this.

Just after we caught the next bus on the same line, the rain came. We had to stand because this bus, unlike the first one we were on, was quite crowded. Once the rains came, the pedestrian-filled streets rapidly emptied into buses.

Our bus followed a slightly different route going back to the train station, which included stopping at an apartment complex located on the edge of town. Dmitri and I stood all the way in the back. We waited there while some of the apartment dwellers trickled out of the apartment block, trying to dodge raindrops on their way to the bus. Only a few had umbrellas. Getting impatient about having to wait standing up, I asked Dmitri what the delay was. He told me that the driver was on a break. The apartment dwellers who knew this took their time getting on the bus. They boarded it in little groups and clusters. The bus was almost full since not enough people got off to make room for those boarding.

Some teenagers tumbled into the bus, laughing and talking among themselves. To pass the time, I tried to figure out how these people were related to each other. Two young girls and a young man made up the party. One of the girls was striking, even though she was wearing too much makeup, and the boy obviously was attracted to her. The boy seemed to be treating the other girl more like a sister than a girlfriend. The girls seemed to be good friends or close sisters. Whatever the truth was, they were obviously enjoying themselves and seemed to be anticipating a night on the town in Leningrad, perhaps to one of the many night clubs that were springing up at the time (Paulsen, 1991, pp. 8, 26–29, 35). Despite the general poverty of the Soviet Union and its overtly repressive regime, the energy and enthusiasm of youth rose above the conditions. Amidst the decay, an optimism existed for the future among the youth.

When we finally reached the train station, the rain stopped and the sun came out through a gap in the clouds low in the western sky. I was not anxious to get home, my illness abated, and I felt tired. This day, unlike the one before, had not been a light one. I enjoyed seeing the park and the inside of the palace, but I did not feel relaxed. I was looking forward to sitting on the train and perhaps relaxing then. This, as it turned out, was wishful thinking.

The events of the next couple of hours formed a deep impression on how I remembered Russia, for I had an unexpected opportunity to get a glimpse of the Soviet Union coming apart at the seams in the form of a public transportation breakdown.

When our bus pulled up to the *vogzal* (train station) and emptied its load of passengers eager to catch the next train, I noticed that a lot more people were around the train station than were there when we came into Pushkin. I did not want to plunge into the crowd just yet. Dmitri, sensing my anxiety, told me not to worry. He would go and check out the situation. He suggested we find a bench in the little square just in front of the station. Alisa planned to meet us at this spot. One of us had to be there.

As I waited alone on the park bench on the square next to the railroad station (*Detskoe Selo*), I fantasized I was in a scene from Carlos Castaneda's tales. Carlos would wait, usually at dusk, for Don Juan (his ethnographic informant) on a bench in a park square like this one. The sun was slowly setting. The faded yellow buildings, crumbling curbs, colonial looking architecture, old buses, and dated cars reminded me of Mexico City. The diminishing light and sound of foreign tongues added to this impression.

While waiting for Dmitri to show up, I noticed an unusual looking bus coming up to the front of the station. It was light in color, shorter and more squat looking than other buses I saw. As the driver pulled up, waiting passengers ran toward the bus. He stopped short and angrily waved them back. Then he slowly brought the bus to the loading point, and many passengers streamed into it. One man ran around the front to ask the bus driver a question and then took his family into the bus. This bus did not accommodate all of the waiting crowd, and only a portion of the people waiting managed to get on it.

Dmitri reappeared. I could tell that he was nervous, and he immediately told me "no train." Then he said that this was the first time in his life that he had seen this kind of problem. Normally in the former Soviet Union, the electric trains were religiously on time; when such a train failed to be punctual, something was seriously wrong. I suspected that something was amiss by the way the people behaved around the bus. So this revelation did not come as a shock.

We waited for Alisa and smoked. I was not worried. Having worked in New York City and experienced nasty public transportation breakdowns before, I figured the problem would be straightened out eventually. Alisa showed up, and we drank *moloko* (milk) and ate *khleb* that she bought in a shop in Pushkin. I had not drunk milk in weeks, and it never tasted so good to me. Dmitri went back to the station to find out about buses. While we waited, I thought of asking Alisa where she found milk that tasted so naturally sweet. The bread was warm and fresh. I began to appreciate her talent for shopping.

When Dmitri returned, he was even more excited. I was drinking my third glass of *moloko* at this time and feeling much better. In Russia, you had a lot or nothing at all. Dmitri told us we had to get moving: "New information. Three minutes for train. There is train, no stop, to Leningrad."

We hurriedly packed our things, ran to the *vogzal* (train station) entrance, went under the tracks via a tunnel, and ran up some steps to the opposite platform where a nervous crowd waited for the train headed north. Dmitri explained to me that electrical power had been lost on the rail line from Pavlosk a few miles to the south all the way north to Leningrad. A train pulled up coming from Leningrad on the opposite side. Next, a freight train came lumbering toward Leningrad on our side. Close behind came the train we expected, pulled by a diesel locomotive and nearly full. With so many people trying to get on, and some lesser number trying to get off, things quickly got chaotic.

I wanted to wait, but Dmitri and Alisa were determined to board the train. Who knew when the next one would arrive. So I had little choice but to enter the noisy mass of humanity near the open doors. In the car we were initially trying to enter, we noticed that the second door leading from the boarding compartment to the passenger compartment was closed. This left no room for any more people, unless somebody opened that door, and we were not going to wait to find out.

A crowd surged behind us trying to push us toward the train. Dmitri shouted something to Alisa who occasionally shouted something back. We quickly turned toward the other car and pushed our way to the edge of the platform. A chance existed to squeeze into this one. Alisa, who did most of the shouting at this time, urged me to get on first. I hesitated before getting on the train and looked back to my left at Dmitri. He mouthed and nodded "yes," so I jumped on in front of Alisa, and they followed me inside.

The crowd was jammed tight in the vestibule. People yelled, and angry tones filled the air. The smell of sweat and perspiration odor was unbearable. My bag was crushed against many people, and I was worried that I might lose it. Alisa and Dmitri pushed forward into the crowd, Alisa all the while shouting to open the door into the passenger compartment and for people inside to move to let others inside. By now, even though I could not understand what Alisa said word for word, I picked up the overall meaning of many of her utterances. I was compelled to focus by the force of their combined characters. Dmitri and Alisa used forceful behavior to deal with the chaotic situation. I was witnessing a measure of their cultural competence.

As we stood there waiting for the train to move, inching our way forward into the passenger compartment, I felt the weight of the heat and humidity. I had kept my mouth shut so far, but I finally said something in English to Dmitri as people tried to push past to get off the train. Immediately, a man dressed in matching military-green shirt and pants, with a haircut to go with the military look of his outfit, caught my attention. He was packed in the same crowded space that we were in, separated from us by only a few people. He began talking rapidly and excitedly to no one in particular but loud enough so we could all hear. Amidst his Russian, I could make out something about an "*Amerikanski.*" I was afraid this was not a good situation. Sure enough, Dmitri said to me that he was an aggressive man and commented that the situation must be interesting for me. This man was upset that an American was taking up valuable space on a Russian train!

Dmitri would explain the situation in more detail to me when we got off the train. At that moment, I felt I was encountering xenophobia. As an American I had no cultural value in Russia according to this man. Fortunately, the woman who was with him got him to calm down, and a few tense moments later they got off the train. Dmitri explained the situation to a second young man in a red checkered shirt who smiled and said something to me. I smiled back, and, even though I did not understand what he had said, I nodded my head in agreement and turned around. I wanted to stay silent and get through this.

Meanwhile, Alisa managed to get us near the door that led to the passenger compartment by pushing away the people in front of it. Others joined in the attempt to get into the passenger compartment. The door slid open, and, after several shouts, people who stood near the door inside the passenger compartment edged away from it to allow the little knot of people we were in through the door.

Once inside the main compartment, Dmitri quietly told me that he would explain more about the situation when we got off the train. I listened and said little. I did not want a repeat of the previous incident.

Our luck got better when some more people got off the train. Things became easier as we edged our way toward a window and stood near one of the hard wooden seats. The windows were open, and some fresh air came in occasionally. The situation improved slightly for everybody, and spirits seemed to be better. The metal door that led to the loading compartment was unlatched and occasionally slid open when the train swayed on the tracks, yielding intermittent glimpses of some young men laughing and talking excitedly in the outer area. Two young girls stood near me. I had not noticed them before. Somehow, I felt protected standing near them. Even though I saw the man in green get off the train, I was still afraid that he would reappear, so I kept sneaking peeks in the direction of the unlatched door.

The train began to move slowly but the normal twenty minute ride took an hour. As the train moved, I saw many fields and vegetable patches. Occasionally, I saw a human figure huddled over a strip of land. In the background stood the smoke stacks of the factories that marked the edges of Leningrad. Dmitri explained to me that these lands contained the only soil around the city available for growing food. I found the juxtaposition of heavy industry and farming land somewhat disconcerting, fearing the food grown there might be contaminated.

The train made an unscheduled stop in the middle of a field, and someone got off the train without using a platform. We waited awhile, and the train continued. This happened a few times. Waiting for the whistle signaling that the train would start again became routine. All the while, discussion continued concerning the schedule of stops and who might be blamed for the electrical power failure that precipitated the current mess. I heard Gorbachev's and Yeltsin's names being mentioned. As we got closer to Leningrad, we approached a train station. Our train was not on the regular train track and did not approach the platform.

Near the Leningrad outskirts, we saw more and more trains stopped at each station we passed. Soon we approached one that had more tracks and more trains waiting on them than any we had reached so far. The electrical power had gone out for the trains leaving Leningrad from the south bound lines of the station. I saw people on foot, who I assumed abandoned their journeys south, heading back toward the city on paths along the side of the tracks. I also saw some people walking directly on the tracks. This was not exactly safe, since later on some diesel locomotives went whizzing by from the direction that the people were heading. I got a scare when one of these trains went whistling by unexpectedly; the force of the wind generated by the passing train was enough to make our train shudder.

When we arrived at this station, our train stopped in a field before reaching the platform. The doors opened, and half of the passengers spilled out onto the ground. Some people jumped off the train through the exits by themselves and helped others not so bold or lithe down from the cars. This occurred up and down the entire train. I saw other heads stuck out like mine witnessing this spectacle. I saw the young man in the checkered shirt who had smiled at me and the two young girls that had stood near me. I saw old people and middle-aged people making the precarious jump, some struggling onto the platform just a few yards ahead of the first cars, others walking along the tracks.

I hoped our terminus would not be the same. It was not. We ended up stopping at a platform. We were able to sit for the rest of the trip. The passengers visibly relaxed and laughed at the engineer's comments over the intercom system. Like a taxi driver, he was taking requests for stops.

When the train finally let us off at the Vitebsk terminal, things seemed to be back to normal. Whatever the extent of the power outage might be, Leningrad was not experiencing a blackout as we had first feared. We still had a little bit of daylight left to see by as we walked from the train station into an unfamiliar part of town. Some of the city lights were already relit.

An electrical malfunction led to a breakdown of the transportation system. The ensuing commuter chaos had left our little entourage shaken but intact. Though I saw Russians coping with this situation with fortitude and aplomb, I still got the sense that they were wondering what else might go wrong. This systemic crack hinted at deeper fissures in the state of the Soviet Union.

Once we were on the street, Dmitri elaborated that the angry man on the train not only had been upset that an American was on a public train, but was claiming that "American Jews come to Russia and don't use car but take train" to save money. He thought that I was Jewish because "only Jews go on train"—do not ride around in taxis or tour buses like normal tourists. Dmitri found the incident to be amusing, but I did not. I felt thankful that the man's female companion got him to calm down. I had been relieved to see him exit the train.

According to numerous Russian sources, including my social contacts in Russia, religious and ethnic discrimination was endemic in the Soviet Union (as it is in the United States). Being subjected to this experience was decidedly uncomfortable. At the time, I was rolling with the punches and did not become angry with my hosts though I had a good reason to do so. The man, despite his crudity and religious slur, had a point behind his annoyance. The Soviet state subsidized public transportation for its citizens, train rides in Russia being so cheap at the time. (The price of rail travel has gone up since the early 1990s.) I was perceived as a foreigner taking advantage of another country's welfare system, much in the same way as some foreigners come to the United States to take advantage of its welfare system. Our country has passed laws that at times prohibits this kind of behavior.

The man had no business making his comment since he had no information about my arrangement with my Russian hosts. I had already paid for the ride by paying them. They had chosen the cheapest means of travel to maximize a profit. If they had chosen a more expensive and more comfortable way of traveling such as a tour bus, we would have all been spared a lot of discomfort. In the long run, they would have benefited from more good will from me, and indirectly from Pomeroy.

B. Dmitri's Treasure

After walking for a few minutes, lost in unsettling thoughts and trying to absorb all that had just happened, I realized that we were not retracing our steps back home. Alisa and Dmitri seemed to have other plans. Dmitri asked me if I was interested in seeing his other flat, which was located nearby. Though I should have, I did not feel exhausted. The eventful train ride home got my blood pumping. The milk and bread Alisa fed me gave me some energy. I did not feel ill anymore, and my earlier lethargy went away. So, curious and glad to be distracted from my troubled mood, I said, "Let's go!"

Dmitri's second flat was located in a large communal apartment located somewhere near the *Sennaya Ploschad* (Hay Square—or in Fyodor Dostoyevsky's time, the "Haymarket"). I followed Alisa and him through the squalid looking interior courtyard of a four-story apartment house. I stopped to take a picture of soot stained walls and exposed bricks. Dmitri frowned at me in disapproval, and I quickly put my camera away. We ended up at an entrance tucked near a corner of the courtyard.

We climbed into an unlit corridor carefully stepping over the broken stones of a threshold. Once inside the darkened corridor, I had trouble seeing. Dmitri, who knew the place well, quickly guided us up some cracked stairs, past wet mildew stained walls to a second floor. There, a large pair of wooden doors and two smaller doors on either side faced us. A single naked bulb lighted this small entrance hall. The tiled floor was filthy.

Dmitri took out a skeleton key and slipped it into one of the keyholes. He swung the heavy, creaking door open and let Alisa and me in behind him. Again we were in darkness. My eyes took a moment to adjust to the dim light. We were in another corridor. This one was narrower but warmer than the one downstairs. It had a high ceiling. Dmitri led me part way down the hall, opened another door, and led me into a small room. He flipped on a light. I found myself standing in a storage room with magazines, books, and newspapers stacked on either side of me. In front of me was a yellow-orange curtain suspended from a wire that extended from opposite walls that separated the storage area from the rest of a larger room.

Dmitri pushed the curtain aside and let me into the larger portion of the room. It looked like a writer's den with cases and shelves everywhere, all crammed with books. A few of the bookcases had glass doors and looked like antiques. The rest were plain. Some of them divided the room from the small storage area through which we had entered. Dmitri had a desk tucked into one corner of the room and a cot placed near its sole window. Night had fallen so no light came through the curtained window, which looked out at a back alley. While not an aesthetic masterpiece, the room made a comfortable study. This was Dmitri's treasure, a room that technically he was not supposed to have. It was crammed with objects to please an intellectual interested in travel and travelers.

A ruin of a building held hidden wealth. I could sense Dmitri's pride in this place as he showed me around. I was glad that Dmitri showed me his retreat. I got a sense after all the nasty surprises of dealing with him and his wife that this couple valued something on a more than pragmatic level. They, especially Dmitri, valued this room intrinsically, that is, for the joy and beauty it brought to their lives.

Alisa, who disappeared when Dmitri first let me in the room, came back and began helping Dmitri rearrange a few things. I started to look around the place, noticing the pale, orange wallpaper and all the little knickknacks and dolls, an occasional decorative ceramic, and some lamps. However, the dominant theme of the room was books. I noticed some art books. Seeing my interest, Dmitri proudly showed them off to me and brought out more that he had stored. Many contained photos of ancient Russian architecture, including dozens of pictures of Orthodox churches in northern regions of Russia. Some of the landscapes of these regions were breathtaking.

I wondered how Dmitri could afford these books and asked him about it. He told me that they were not so expensive. A few of the art books were foreign but most were published in the Soviet Union. I also noticed some scholarly works, including books in German and English, some with impressive price tags. Dmitri told me they were "gifts." Dmitri had a robust collection, and I had only skimmed the surface.

Dmitri did not want me to spend all my time looking at his books. He wanted to show me the rest of the communal apartment before we left. Out in the narrow corridor again, Dmitri took me further down the hall. One of the doors was open, leading into a dark, empty, narrow room. Dmitri told me that a family of five had once lived in this room. Years had passed since Dmitri lived here. When he was younger, more families resided in the communal apartment. We passed a bathroom with its door half open. A light illuminated the translucent glass pane above the door, and a wedge of light covered the floor in front of the door. Inside, I saw a man in an undershirt and dark pants bending over a bathtub washing some laundry. The man did not look up as we passed. We went by the water closet then a few more shut doors. The windows above each door were dark except one that presumably belonged to the man we had just seen. No other sign of life existed. The place was eerily quiet. Besides us, only this man seemed to be in the place at the time.

We reached an opening at the end of the corridor, through which appeared a large room with a high ceiling, its features hidden in deep shadows. Dmitri switched on an overhead light that provided sufficient light to reveal a spacious kitchen. On one side of the kitchen were four small gas stoves, one per family. On the other side were three refrigerators, items harder to obtain.

I asked Dmitri how many families currently used this kitchen. He was not sure about the current situation since he spent only a few hours working in his room each week and often did not even venture into the kitchen. He assured me that when he lived in this communal apartment, the kitchen was a bustling place, with all four stoves going at the same time. In the middle of the room stood a large table used mainly for food preparation. People did not use the kitchen to eat as a rule. Meals were taken back to the individual rooms.

This was a glimpse into the recent Soviet past—families sharing one apartment. The large apartments that formerly belonged to (pre-Revolution) Russian middle class families had been subdivided into communal arrangements. Dmitri's family had at one point all lived crammed into the little room that was now his study. Later, I met several families that still lived in such places, and they were not necessarily poor. However, they had more than one room. Andrey's family, coming from the Soviet elite, had succeeded in buying out several families to acquire an entire apartment for themselves.

After my little tour of the place, we had a tea prepared by Alisa, using an electric hot plate back in Dmitri's room. Then we headed home. That night, I was too tired to write in my notebook. I wrote about the day's adventures the next morning.

C. Ilya Visits

Sunday morning (28 July) brought about another change. Alisa went out early in the morning. When she returned, Ilya was with her. I had not seen him since the camping trip. He brought a board game with him that he wanted me to play. It had a geographical theme to it. When we played, I noticed that the game was expensive and probably was purchased with the funds I provided to Dmitri and Alisa.

Later, Dmitri took me aside and said that playing and interacting with me helped Ilya practice his English and get out of his shell. Apparently, Ilya was an unusually reticent boy by Dmitri's standards. Dmitri also told me that his teachers found Ilya to be bright but excessively shy. I told Dmitri that I enjoyed playing with his son and found him to be an intelligent boy. Dmitri liked the attention I gave to his son.

Dmitri and I had planned to do some work that day. I wanted to tape record a conversation with Dmitri and was making preparations for our session when Ilya came into the den from the kitchen curious to see what I was doing. Then Dmitri came in and seemed preoccupied with something so I decided to leave him alone with his son.

I went to my room and returned with my notebook. Ilya was watching TV with Dmitri. Alisa was busy in the bathroom and the hall between the den and kitchen, getting some stuff together. I thought the balcony might be a good place to write. Dmitri kept a comfortable folding canvas chair there. I asked him to show me how unfold it.

I spent some time writing in my notebook under a clear sky and a hot sun. I could hear the TV blaring inside. Occasionally, I got up to stretch and look through the glass panes of the balcony door. A cartoon was playing. The voices sounded several pitches lower than the usual cartoon voices back in the States, as if all the characters talked with gravel in their mouths. Ilya stared at the television, transfixed by the action on the screen.

Later in the day, when I was taking a break back in my room, Dmitri came by. He wanted to know if I was interested in taking a bath. I hesitated. I had bathed one time in their tub, not a hygienic experience, the water being almost brown.

"No, not here. Real bath. Russian bath." Dmitri explained, seeing my initial reluctance.

I hesitated some more. "You mean at a public bathhouse?"

"Yes of course," Dmitri drawled.

The closest I had ever been to a bath house was the steam room in a university gymnasium. I suffered an attack of shyness.

"Well. I don't know."

"We go, yes? You like, no?"

"Oh, all right," I gulped.

"*Atleechna*!" (Wonderful)

A Russian bathhouse—why pass up the chance? This was where half of working Russia was supposed to go if they felt like playing hooky from their jobs. Too bad it would be a Sunday evening when we would be going—only legitimate bathers then. I tried not to think about being naked in front of a lot of strangers who would be naked too.

I soon found out that it had been Vasili's suggestion. He and Sonia would be going as well as Dmitri and Alisa. The bathhouse had separate baths for men and women. Ilya would be left with Vasili's mother.

The bath was to be that evening, so a whole afternoon was left for my talk with Dmitri. Since Dmitri was not ready yet and Ilya was still watching TV, our talk had to wait until after lunch. I spent another half hour writing on the balcony, with the TV blaring in the background. Occasionally, I looked inside where I could see Alisa collecting some items for the bath and putting them into large plastic bags.

D. A Theoretical Discussion Concerning Values and Stress

When Dmitri was finally ready to talk with me, Ilya was cleared out of the living room, and we had the place to ourselves for a while. Dmitri had expressed an interest in helping me formulate a research proposal that I needed to write eventually to secure grant money to do follow up research in the Soviet Union. I wanted to talk to him about it. I also wanted to probe what Dmitri meant by the comment that it was "not possible to be lonely in [the] Soviet Union."

Dmitri scanned the research proposal I prepared for my current field trip and asked me questions about it. He thought it "lacked conclusions." Puzzled, I said that conclusions could only come afterwards when the research was done. Dmitri told me to put my proposal aside and start from scratch. I thought that was fine and agreed; I did not want to waste the afternoon arguing with Dmitri about a previously approved proposal anyway.

We proceeded to have a two hour conversation that was satisfying. Dmitri had a way of formulating concepts by talking about things simply, using a rudimentary vocabulary, probably partly due to the necessity of translating everything to English. Yet he wove together a huge number of these simple ideas into a complex whole that was quite sophisticated. I recalled that Pomeroy was not impressed by Dmitri's knowledge. Much of this was due to fact that Pomeroy, being a native English speaker, was comfortable using a richer English vocabulary. Listening to Dmitri discuss science gave me the sense that I was speaking with a poet—a poet of science—and I enjoyed it.

I wondered why Pomeroy bothered becoming acquainted with Dmitri, who was obviously of different temperament. I concluded that Pomeroy's priority was to make contact with *any* Russian scientist who was willing to help him with his international research. Since Dmitri and Pomeroy were both interested in the topic of stress, they had formed a working relationship that eventually led to my trip to stay and collaborate with Dmitri. Since my collaboration with Pomeroy and Dmitri was based on this topic, one of the central topics of my research proposal was the examination of the stress concept through anthropological field work. My preliminary focus was to see if generating discussions around the topic of stress was possible. Systemization of research would come later with more experience and a wider set of research methods. Dmitri and I held several discussions relating to the stress concept. This day we had our lengthiest and deepest involvement with it.

The concept of stress, beginning as a medical model, evolved into a subtopic of several social sciences. My background in anthropology introduced me to the empirical and theoretical work of cultural anthropologists interested in stress. Pomeroy opened up new horizons in the field for me, introducing me to conceptual links between stress, values, the self, and the world. I was keenly interested in finding out what a Russian psychologist had to say about it.

Dmitri and I began the discussion by reviewing some topics in stress research. Then we plunged into the heart of the conversation: how to link the stress concept with cultural anthropology. Dmitri began going over the differences between traditional or structural anthropology and the more recent studies of dynamics in anthropology, which included the study of psychological anthropology. I added my observations whenever I could.

Under the model of traditional anthropology, human behavior is considered to be predictable and society stable. Behavior is predictable because it never changes, only repeats itself over hundreds, even thousands of years. Once the structure of behavior is uncovered and the details are fleshed out, different aspects of society can be explained—things such as marriage, child rearing, and other customs. Dmitri referred to this kind of anthropology alternately as "explanation science" or "description science." Since societal patterns do not change, they can be predicted simply by describing them. Traditional or structural anthropology only involves sociological research. Dmitri was ultimately interested in a "predictive science," one that could account for socio-cultural change.

Then came a new way of looking at things that Dmitri compared to linguistic hermeneutics, the study of the pragmatic meaning of language. Societies under the traditional approach are implicitly stress free. After all, what would you get stressed about if things were entirely predictable and routine? Obviously, societies like individuals suffer from stress. How do you account for this? Dmitri introduced the idea of a "dynamic society." A dynamic society is one in which people arise who have "intention." That is, differences in energy levels and psychological characteristics exist among members of a dynamic society. Some people are more active, some less. Some people are more dependent on others, some less.

Another way of looking at this involves considering society extrinsically, that is, for its practical value. Dmitri's "dynamic society" model takes this factor of human existence into account. Culture can no longer be viewed as a clockwork mechanism, ticking on for generations with little change.

The issue of values arises in the "dynamic society" model. Dmitri saw values as being an intersection of personal psychological characteristics and culture. An "activity person" (we would say "self-motivated") has values. Accompanying any value is the threat of the loss of that value. This is a psychological characteristic. The threat of loss can be linked to stress. The classic stress reaction is associated with the threat of the loss of life or a perception of such a threat. Here it is extended to include the threat of loss of those things valuable for life.

Dmitri took the discussion step by step from the simple beginnings of a static system and introduced dynamic characteristics that led inexorably to the concept of "stress" and related concepts of "value" and "loss." Then he explored the dynamics of stress, loss, and value a little further. He introduced the idea of "cost."

Every value has a cost. The cost can be measured by determining how meaningful the loss of this value would be. If the loss of something has little emotional impact, then it is not so valuable to begin with. Stress is the *emotional* impression over the loss of value "from [the] human side," as Dmitri put it. We had made a little system in which value, cost, stress, loss, and meaning were related to each other. The goal was to tie this system to the study of societies.

Next, Dmitri explored the emotional "work" involved with stress and the maintenance of values. He hunted for a word in Russian that captured this concept succinctly. He thought that there was no good English equivalent to it. The word had something to do with "extreme vivid emotional experience."

Finally, Dmitri came up with it: "*perezheevat.*"

This word—a verb—translates to "experience emotion." It can be associated with "endure," "suffer" or "worry." Dmitri lumped this under the term "work inside" (emotional work). "Cost" in Dmitri's scheme was a combination of value and work. As Dmitri saw it, value arises from the investment of mental work. Values are tied up with things such as worrying, enduring, suffering, all of which involve work "inside."

"*Perezheevania*"—the noun—is the same as the English rough equivalent "stress," or so I initially thought. Dmitri saw stress as being a more abstract concept than *perezheevania*. *Perezheevania* is something you experience. Stress is something you discuss. Dmitri wanted me to think about our topic as being more like *perezheevania* because it is a more concrete term. Stress as a concept is too general to be useful. It can mean many things depending on the circumstances.

Perezheevania involves work and is not merely reaction to external events. *Perezheevania* involves the anticipation of loss, which is the work of the imagination. You are "stressed" in the concrete sense when you anticipate loss. *Perezheevania* also involves daily "work" (mental energy expended) done to compensate for the routine loss of values, for instance figuring out how to replace spent money or consumed food. "*Ya nee pereezhil!*" is a Russian phrase commonly used to express frustration. For instance, if you lose a lot of money you might say this. It is the rough equivalent of saying: "I can't deal with this!" *Perezheevania* is related to our notion of "coping."

Perezheevania involves two concepts found in the social sciences. The first is the so-called stress response, fully documented by pioneer Hans Selye (Selye, 1984). The second is the role of human interpretation of events, a theory developed by Albert Ellis (Ellis, 1962). Selye defines stress as "the nonspecific response of the body to any demand" (Selye, 1984, p. 55). An adaptive element is contained in the stress response: "Stress is the common denominator of all adaptive reactions in the body" (Selye, 1984, p. 64). Selye relates stress to psychological as well as biological conditions. He shows how the first stage of stress, the alarm response, can occur in relation to a social event. Ellis gives us a more precise insight into the psychological connection between life events and human adaptive response. Drawing from the work of different philosophers, he arrives at the conclusion that how you interpret an event plays a larger role in the your emotional response than the event itself (Selye, 1962, p. 54). An emotional response has psychological and physiological consequences. Ellis ties in values with emotional response: "Both fleeting and sustained emotional responses have in common the element of 'What does this event that I am responding to mean to me?' " (Ellis, 1962, p. 46).

As our conversation continued, more concepts were tied into the stress response, including the relationship between stress and values. I only discovered this later upon reflection. At the time, I was swept up in the momentum of the conversation, and I had trouble grasping exactly what Dmitri meant. Dmitri explained that he wanted to distinguish between the routine meaning versus the scientific meaning of stress. People use the word "stress" to explain an entire range of experiences including those that are outside *perezheevania*. Dmitri was trying to make the conversation more precise, thus more scientific.

According to Dmitri, *perezheevania* involves emotional experience, loss, and dynamics. The introduction of dynamics opened new possibilities in anthropology because dynamics involves studying changes in values, their acquisition and loss, the crux of change in culture. Traditional anthropology did not account for values or an "exchanging society." Exchanges imply exchanges of value. Values are not lost or gained in "traditional society."

In reality, societies change and cultures change. The traditional model of a static society is insufficient to account for culture change, especially rapid culture change. Only people create much rapid change. Geographic change, climatic change—the global factors that pertain to cultural ecology—can account for incremental changes over long periods of time. Social drift may account for changes as well. However, these are all slow and gradual kinds of changes. Dmitri was talking about change that takes place over generations, not eons.

Though I could not grasp it then, Dmitri had provided me with a vital clue to a puzzle that still remains in cultural anthropology, namely, what exactly is culture? Tying culture with values is not always done by cultural theorists. Much of cultural anthropology looks at societies in a mechanistic way. Society is seen as roughly equivalent to a living mass with a collective will and an instinct for survival. Furious debates rage over whether a field such as psychological anthropology with its implied egoism and individualism is appropriate to have. Introducing the idea of the pursuit of values is a dangerous thing that threatens to upset the metaphoric apple cart, but much is to be gained and perhaps a few illusions swept away. A simple way of looking at what culture is exists, and it has everything to do with values.

Culture is the cultivation of value. Culture transcends society, which is only one of its manifestations. Culture comes from the individual's struggle to survive the wild and society too. But human beings see culture as giving them more than survival value, although that is at the core. If culture were not in the arena of value, we would have no such thing as civilization, or xenophobia for that matter.

Dmitri was concentrating on transition and change, not definitions. The overarching issue for him was one of structural change. In conjunction with this idea, I introduced the schema of Edward B. Tylor and Lewis H. Morgan, that of stages of cultural development (bands, tribes, chiefdoms, states). Dmitri, although the names Tylor and Morgan did not ring a bell with him, recognized the scheme. Karl Marx and Friedrich Engels, the founders of political state-level communism, adapted Morgan's schema. Their version of the progress of civilization has it progressing through the stages, feudalism, capitalism, and socialism, with communism as the highest possible level of civilization.

Dmitri agreed that Morgan had a valid scheme of structural change, but he wanted to focus on micro-change and the concurrent idea of dynamics. Turning back to his theme, Dmitri asked the question: "Why introduce value to classical (traditional) anthropology?" This amounted to asking the related question: "Why introduce psychology to classical anthropology?" I told Dmitri that this question was discussed by a variety of anthropologists, from a founding father of psychological anthropology, Franz Boas, to psychological anthropology specialist Philip Bock, and I mentioned their contributions. While Dmitri led the discussion, I acted as a foil and filled Dmitri in on relevant American and European anthropological personalities.

The sources we used concurred that anthropology without psychology becomes Skinnerian behaviorism, a psychology without "person" (personality in the sense of the mind, not of a complicated machine). This means "no personal reaction" and consequently no values. Skinnerian behaviorism does not deny the existence of human individuals; it denies the existence of spiritual and experiential characteristics that make each human individual unique. These character traits, born of the process of making choices in the world, account for the "personality" of an individual and obviate laboratory stimulus-response mechanisms. Humanistic psychology, by contrast, works at the level of individual idiosyncrasies and spiritual experience based on freedom of will.

Without values, accounting for changes in culture becomes impossible. The heart of social dynamics is change, and change is motivated by human goals that revolve around values and consequent priorities. Culture entails the process of growing value. The achievements of civilization, such as monumental architecture, attest to this. They involve the expenditure of energy over time, which is a kind of cost. They involve social change as well. As technology and art progress, new social forms come into being.

Dmitri then reiterated an earlier theme. Social scientists want to do more than explain; they want to be able to predict. Why have a science at all if you cannot predict? The introduction of dynamics, which involves accounting for things like "cost," "work," "value," "loss," and so on, helps us move from explanation to prediction.

We wound up this portion of our discussion by returning to the notion of stress. Dmitri believed that developed society is a reaction to stress. He went on to explain how stress is involved with society and culture.

Stress is related to a large host of socio-cultural issues including health and sickness, neurosis and abnormality, levels of aggression within and between societies, and levels of activity in economy and industry. Stress is also related to marriage patterns, divorce rates, and sexual practices.

At this point, our conversation about cultural anthropology and stress stopped. Dmitri wanted to change gears and discuss the relationship between axiology and stress. The discussion did not get far because we were both tired and ended up stuck over a term with which Dmitri was not familiar.

It was a technical term that came from the Hartman manual on the theory and application of the test that Pomeroy had adapted for use in psychology. The term, *atychal*, means a condition in which a person has a deep sensitivity of himself (herself) and a shallow sensitivity of the world, which leads to accident-proneness or social mishaps.

Dmitri, who seemed to be following a pattern of finding the simplest, most obvious interpretation of everything I had told him so far, was baffled. First, he got the concept confused with "introvert," a person who is more involved with him or her self than others. Then he thought the word was "atypical." His two-volume English-Russian dictionary did not have "atychal."

Making Dmitri understand the difference between someone who was "introverted" and someone who was "atychal" was hard. He understood the difference between self-involvement and self-sensitivity, but because he had apparently never encountered a condition in which a person is identified as having an "atychal" imbalance, he could not extend his understanding to account for such a person.

I had to look up the term in the manual, and show him the definition as well as the mathematical formula used to measure this condition. By working with the definition, I was able to steer the conversation to common ground. The definition of atychal as outlined in the manual was "problems in the capacity to handle the outside world." In this case, the person is significantly better in his self valuation than the evaluation of objective exterior situations. This can result in undeserved failure due to poor management of situations involving interpersonal behavior and other issues connected with the outside world. Such a person is prone to "bad luck." (Hartman, 1973a, p. 58).

At this point, Dmitri cut me off and asked me what I meant by "bad luck." After a little bit of explanation using concrete examples, Dmitri got it and threw the Russian term "*neoodachnik*" (bad-luck man) into the discussion. He had found the simple link between the complex set of concepts that made up "atychal" (which can be grouped into self-evaluation, world-evaluation, and balance-in-evaluation) and the conceptual world he understood. The term "atychal" has more to it than "bad luck," but this was irrelevant to Dmitri. Once he felt he had grasped a topic, he did not spend time exploring the details.

We wound up our discussion of axiology shortly after that because Dmitri wanted a break. We had coffee that Dmitri prepared. For a long time, Dmitri had been complaining about not having coffee, claiming that a long time ago Russians had drunk more coffee than tea. A popular misconception existed that Russians were primarily tea drinkers. This misconception had arisen as a result of coffee shortages. Now coffee had appeared in his household.

After our break, the subject of immigration arose. I was discussing the work of Ruth Benedict with Japanese immigrants (*Sword and the Chrysanthemum*), which I used as a reference in my first proposal, when Dmitri asked me why Japanese people immigrated to the United States. I said that they did because they wanted a better life. Dmitri asked if this was for economic reasons. I concurred. Dmitri concluded that the Japanese had different motivations to go to the United States than Russians, who went there primarily for political reasons (to escape persecution). Only recently had Russians gone for perhaps economic reasons. According to Dmitri, only "advanced" Russians, not simple Russians, emigrated from the Soviet Union. Simple Russians could not get cooperation from the Soviet government.

I was just warming up to a possible discussion about Soviet émigrés, when Dmitri asked me to stop the tape recorder. I figured the discussion was getting too sensitive to be recorded. After a pause, Dmitri asked me to continue, but with a new subject. I shrugged. I had not initiated the discussion of emigration and had only referred to it in passing. Dmitri seemed to have fallen into talking spontaneously about something he subsequently had second thoughts about bringing up at all.

E. The Russian Social Contract

We finally reached a good time for talking about the second topic I wanted to address, namely Dmitri's curious statement on Friday that nobody is lonely in the Soviet Union. Now that Dmitri wanted to start a new topic, I thought we should talk about the absence of "loneliness" in the Soviet Union.

I reminded Dmitri of the question: "For instance, yesterday, not yesterday, day before...when we went to [Petrodvorets]... I mentioned I'm lonely, and you [said] that it's not possible to be lonely in the Soviet Union."

Dmitri thought a moment and replied: "Yes, of course,...this is big difference in economic situation. In order [that] Soviet people [survive] in complicated economic situation[s], people have to [maintain] different relationships...in order to buy food, buy different commodity goods, and so on. [It is] very important for every Russian family. For example, Sonia knew where [to] buy sugar without coupons."

Sugar was scarce and was being rationed through a coupon system at this time. Many desirable commodities, such as coffee, sugar, good meat, fresh fruits, imported cigarettes, and cosmetics, were hard to find.

Dmitri continued: "Because, coupon...because buy sugar with coupons, it is very little. This is only example. But the same. I must connect with my friend from Baltic (Anatol) [to handle] different problems, for example, your problem."

"Your problem" was Dmitri's reference to his arranging an official invitation that made it possible for me to get a visa to travel to the Soviet Union. He had solicited Anatol's help with this. He was comparing this case to the one involving sugar, saying that they were two instances of the same sort of thing. Both involved informal relationships and connections.

I was getting interested. Dmitri went on: "It's not [possible], official way."

"I understand," I concurred, expressing curiosity.

"It's not official way. So, if I feel that..."

Dmitri was cut off by Alisa who needed his help in the kitchen. He returned shortly and tried to pick up where he left off: "...so in order to develop, we must [join] and [rejoin] many relationships...ah, friendly relationships, because...not friendly relationships very cost, very expensive. Unofficial..."

"Unofficial way?"

"Unofficial way, unofficial way..."

"Less expensive?"

"Not only less expensive...Unofficial way [is] the main...friendly way."

"Main, friendly. I see."

"Simply unofficial way, very expensive too...destroy law, unofficial way... Do you understand?"

"Not completely."

I was having trouble following Dmitri's broken English (which is cleaned up here). Dmitri decided the introduction of some Russian terms might help.

So, I learned two new Russian words, "*sviazi*" and "*blat.*" The first term means "informal relationships." The second term has the same meaning but is the slang form. According to Dmitri, for Soviet people, in everyday routine behavior, to live without *sviazi* was not possible. I was discovering a vast new landscape of the underground Russian economy, where favors were exchanged much like stocks are traded on Wall Street. Except it was done discreetly, but with the understanding that everyone did it, including those whose jobs were to prosecute illegal trade. I could only compare this activity to 1920s Prohibition America.

Dmitri had introduced me to a variety of situations that involved making choices about what was valuable and what price was paid for those values. The basic theme was social networking. Russians value social networking differently than Americans. To an American, a social contact may mean the difference between a good career and an average one. To a Russian, a social contact may mean the difference between life and death. Placing so much importance on friendship's practical value often involved destroying its intimate value. Russians ran the risk of prostituting friendship. The Soviet system could be blamed for this, as its insistence on central control of all economic aspects of life produced a weak economy.

Another side to this involved the subversion of some basic values such as law-abiding behavior and honesty. Unofficial contacts were technically illegal even if everybody had them to some extent. Having to conduct business this way produced a sense of lawlessness that became evident once the Soviet Union was gone. A Wild West atmosphere pervaded Russia in the early 1990s as the lid was lifted off of formerly subterranean activity. Andrey would lament to me in 1992 that the most horrible thing about communism was having to teach his children to lie.

We were interrupted when Dmitri went to help Alisa with something in the kitchen. The TV was on again. I flipped through the few channels available while waiting for Dmitri to return. When he came back, we talked about what was on TV for a little while. Since the interrupted talk about *sviazi* acquired a magnetic attraction, we soon were back on the topic.

"This is a very important value, this...*sviazi*?" I prompted.

"Yes, very important. But this is Russian word, very important for survival, for routine survival."

"For just ...biological survival, or maybe psychological survival too?"

"Interesting. Very interesting question. Maybe more...social survival."

"I see."

"Because, present moment, not problem biological survival. Present summer; it's not next winter."

Social survival was required for biological survival. Winters in the Soviet Union could still bring hard times. Preparing for winter had to be done by assuring oneself that one's contacts were in place to face hard times.

Dmitri stopped our conversation momentarily to bring my attention to a discussion about an art school for children that was on TV. The question was asked as to how a designated group of children could get into that school. They had talent but no "personal relationship" (between their parents and school administrators). Without connections, without *sviazi*, they had no chance. I told Dmitri that getting into a similar school without connections, while difficult, would be possible in the United States. He was not surprised.

I knew that connections and networking are not altogether foreign to my country. I told Dmitri about this. He dismissed it off hand: "Yes, of course, it's very international, but..."

"Maybe to get job maybe...in special education," I interrupted.

"Of course, I understand; very clear this. But Soviet Union, [there is] very much, very much."

"Yes, much more," I agreed, wondering what his point was.

"Because routine behavior."

"Because it's routine behavior." I was beginning to understand.

"Sugar for example. Sugar!" Dmitri was now on a roll: "It's not only for education, new job. No."

"But just for sugar. Yes, I see."

"Sugar. For example, ticket, simple ticket. Not possible to buy ticket for…"

" Ilya?" I asked because he had just come by train.

"So, it will be ticket yesterday...we have to plan many…"

"Of course [you] must plan ahead."

No doubt, in many countries social ties are crucial. Dmitri emphasized that number of things you needed a contact for was far greater in his country than in my country. This quantitative difference produced a qualitative difference in the way ordinary life was lived in the Soviet Union at that time.

At this point Ilya walked in, interrupting us. Perhaps he heard his name being mentioned. After a little discussion, Dmitri explained that he just wanted to listen. We continued the conversation about purchasing a ticket, sorting out some confusion that occurred due to Ilya's entrance and Dmitri's not understanding something I said. Eventually, Dmitri finished making his point: "... Personal relationship between cashier, for example [was required]; maybe different people [were needed] to allow to buy ticket, simple ticket."

Without knowing the cashier, no tickets would be available to purchase. Supply was limited not by demand but by social ties. The lack of a personal relationship could mean that getting a train ticket for Ilya, a practical concern, would be impossible.

I got the gist of it. In the Soviet Union, you needed all sorts of connections to get anything but the most rudimentary necessities of life. I did not know it at the time, but I had struck pay dirt in terms of a research theme. The last bit of our conversation had more impact on my research than all the previous abstract talk about stress and anthropology. Social networks, I found, played a major role in the daily routines of the Russians. The value of networking to Russians was priceless.

Our conversation wound down, and I stopped taping. Soon, we got going. Some light was still left, and a busy evening lay ahead. After the Russian bath, we planned to go watch a little bit of the "Navy Day" celebrations being held that evening. We also planned to have a midnight tea party at Vasili's place afterwards.

F. An Initiation

Ilya was dropped at Vasili's, and we headed off downtown in search of a public bath house. I carried the large plastic bag containing my soap, a sponge, and a cotton towel that Alisa gave me. I held Vasili's plastic bag, as well as a thermos he brought along. I noticed that Vasili's bag contained a ski cap and wondered what its purpose was.

The bathhouse was located on one of the side streets off eastern Nevsky Prospect in a part of town I had not seen before. The facades of the buildings were plain and worn. The area had the feeling of factories and warehouses about it, although none were in plain view.

Vasili parked his car on a broad street near the bathhouse. I wondered what to do with my wallet, thinking that maybe I should have left it at the flat. I did not want to take it into the bathhouse with me because I knew that I would have to part with it at some point. I decided to ask Vasili to keep it in his car. He took my wallet and put it inside an empty briefcase in the trunk of his car, closing the trunk lid with emphasis to assure me it would be safe.

We went inside the bustling bathhouse, up a central staircase, deposited the women on a lower floor, and climbed up to another level. The landing was empty. Through a swinging door, we encountered a desk with a sleepy attendant and a passage way that led to a locker room. I thought Dmitri would head straight for the desk, but he ignored the attendant, and we found some lockers first. Then Dmitri went back to the desk. While Vasili and I were undressing, he offered me some tea that was in the thermos he had brought along, suggesting I drink something before one of these baths. Still half undressed, I drank the weak, sugary, lukewarm tea.

Dmitri came back and announced that no towels were available. We brought our own, but those were for drying off after the bath. They could not also be used to sit in the steam room. I took off my glasses and hesitantly left them along with my clothes and towel in the locker. We all took our soap. In addition, Dmitri and Vasili had scrub brushes and natural sponges used for washing the back. After Vasili finished undressing, he put on the ski cap he had brought along. Before I could ask him, he told me that it was to protect his head from the heat.

I asked Dmitri if our stuff would be safe since the lockers had no locks. He told me not to worry about it—that one of the attendant's jobs was to see that people did not rummage through the lockers. Attendants also collected the bath fees and rented out towels.

We went past a small room with a closed door. "Sauna," Dmitri muttered as we passed it. "Maybe later." Another door appeared. A puff of steam came out as the door was opened. For a second, I thought we were heading into a steam room. It turned out to be the main "bathing" room.

Hot, but not uncomfortably so, the room was arranged into sections and a whole range of activities. It was crowded with naked men—old men, young men, teenagers, fat and skinny men, pale and swarthy men, all with skin glistening, dripping water. Some of them were flushed red from the heat. In a far corner was a door that led to the steam room. Nearer to us was a square concrete pool, about five feet high, with a ladder. I watched a couple of men jump off a small platform into the pool, hooting and hollering, splashing around like boys on a beach, then both disappearing under the water. They came out a few seconds later. More men were waiting to get in the pool.

Dmitri led me past a long trough-like basin full of spigots. Underneath were metal pans stacked together. The floors were wet, covered with streaks and little rivulets of soapy water, which was disappearing into drains at several spots on the floor. Long wooden benches, completely occupied by bathers, ran across the main room like pews in a church. Set along the walls were more benches. Dmitri led me to a far wall, where we found an unoccupied bench. He told me to stay put and hold the spot. He and Vasili returned shortly, carrying pans full of warm water. Dmitri showed me how to wash. I was to use half the water to soak myself, then wash with soap, then use the remaining water to rinse. If I wanted to wash my hair, I should use a separate pan of water for that. One more thing: wash, wash, wash. This was serious bathing. I got to work, washing myself methodically, while Dmitri and Vasili washed more quickly, repeating the process, several times. Eventually, I was off with my pan to get more water.

After washing myself this way three times and my hair twice, I waited for Dmitri and Vasili to finish. They were busy taking turns scrubbing each other's backs with the brushes and lufus sponges. I noticed that Vasili brought eucalyptus branches with him. These were soaking in a pan of water that he set aside. I could smell the fragrance, mingling with strong soap, and the occasional whiff of shampoo. I tried to take in more of the place. Off to my left was the entrance to the steam room, where pale men went in and ruddy men come out, along with puffs of steam. Some of them carried branches with the fragrant leaves. Closer was the pool, which some teenagers occupied. They seemed to be spending a long time there as if it were their pool. Some older men eventually persuaded them with angry words to leave. Off to my right was a set of shower stalls, which seemed to be perpetually occupied.

The whole scene was overwhelming. I felt completely vulnerable, yet somehow detached. The last thing I expected from my trip was to end up naked in a room full of naked Russian men with only white vapors between me and them. I felt Dmitri tugging on my arm telling me we should shower. Dmitri led me to the stalls and kicked out the teenagers in two of them with a few sharp words.

After showering, Dmitri suggested we go to the steam room. I followed him feeling slightly anxious. I did not know what to expect. The door to the "Russian" sauna opened, and a blast of hot air hit my face. It felt like a furnace. Dmitri urged me to follow him. I was reluctant to do so. I took a few tentative steps inside what seemed like a cave. It was gray inside with little light. Men were perched on niches, some with towels, most naked. I could hear some guttural rumblings of men being beat with branches. They sounded like bears telling jokes. I lasted about ten seconds inside before I felt suffocated by the heat. I panicked and ran outside. Dmitri ran out after me: "You must, Gary!" He was not giving me any leeway. After a few seconds of being harangued by Dmitri, I relented, and we went back inside.

Dmitri led me to one of the perches, and I sat with him for about a minute, concentrating hard on breathing. I was able to relax enough to see my surroundings. The size of the room was hard to judge. Everything seemed to be made out of black stone. I found it impossible to tell where the heat source was. The entire room seemed to be on fire. Wisps of gray steam curled around and partially obscured the occupants who were letting out occasional groans and what seemed like shouts of encouragement. I could not tell if they were enjoying themselves or enduring torture. I could hear the sound of skin being whipped by branches. For a wild second, I thought I had wandered into a scene from Dante's "Inferno."

Just as I was starting to feel comfortable, I was hit by another wave of heat. As the door opened and closed to the room, the sudden gust of cooler air followed by a return of the wet, scalding air created a sensation that made it feel like the room was getting even hotter. That was enough for me. I could barely get used to the hot air, I was feeling even hotter, and I was not going to be able to handle that psychologically. I told Dmitri that I had enough and left. Dmitri followed me outside. I had been in the "room from hell" less than two minutes.

Once I regained my composure, Dmitri suggested I cool off in the cold water pool. I said "no thanks" and headed for the locker room. I needed a break. I found Vasili waiting for me. He had finished his first round and was relaxing with some tea. He offered me some along with some tea biscuits he had stashed in his locker. So, for a minute or two, I sat with Vasili drinking tea and munching on hard biscuits.

I was starting to towel off and feel the first of the chilly air in the room when Dmitri joined us and told me that I should have completed the process. A cold water bath was necessary to close the skin pores, which were opened by the steam room. Getting clean involved opening the pores to let impurities out of the body, then closing them quickly so the impurities could not return. I thought that Dmitri was right but too late. I had already cooled off. The only solution was to repeat the process.

This time, before reentering the main bathing area, Vasili took me to the "Finnish" sauna, a small room with a wooden bench. The air was dry, quite dry. I sat with Vasili who had donned his ski cap. Another man was in there, also wearing a ski cap. He sat quietly with his head bowed in meditation.

The heat in this room did not hit me immediately like the steam had. Instead it crept up, warming me from the inside out. Soon I felt the heat on my skin and especially in my head. I was already too hot, sweating profusely. I got out. Vasili stayed behind, his head wisely protected by a knit cap.

I got into the bathing area and found Dmitri. He asked me if I was warm enough. I said that I was. Vasili joined us after a bit. Dmitri told me to wash a bit more. So I repeated the process of washing my body. Then Vasili gestured to me to ask if I want him to scrub my back. I supposed that it was part of the ritual too. So with my hands on the bench, leaning over, I let Vasili scrub my back. To finish off this "baptism" he smacked my back with the eucalyptus branches a couple of times. I was then deemed set by Dmitri, and after another trip to the shower, all three of us returned to the steam room. This time I stayed three minutes.

After this, I was considered fit for the final stage: the plunge into the icy cold water of the pool. I felt a little trepidation. Dmitri assured me that it would not feel cold. I did not care any more. I climbed the ladder and jumped in. He was right. It felt good, like jumping into a swimming pool on a hot summer day. I ducked my head under the water. My baptism was complete. While I was still in the pool, Vasili jumped in. Dmitri did not; he had gone back to begin another round of washing. I got out and left Vasili in the pool. Some other men were waiting to get in.

Feeling relaxed, I strolled out of the bathing room back to the lockers to dry off. I was there for quite a while. Apparently, Vasili had rejoined Dmitri for more washing. I slowly got dressed and helped myself to some more tea.

After we finished with the baths and collected Alisa and Sonia, we made our way back to the dusty streets and Vasili's car. My wallet was fortunately intact and right where we left it. Our mood was buoyant, like teenagers on our way to a party.

Night had come and along with it lights on the Neva. We approached the center of activity cautiously, Vasili threading his way through thick traffic on a roundabout route. We ended up at the *Strelka* (Point) on Vasilevsky Island. Vasili found a place to put the car but was nervous about leaving it there for a long time. As we got out of the car, Dmitri told me to speak English—this was another situation where he wanted to pose as tourists. A crowd was gathered in this park near the water. Some of them were looking out at the boats on the river. Others were looking up.

We were just in time to see a short fireworks display. The exploding rockets had an unusual quality: The colors of the star bursts were unlike any I had seen before. They had more pastel in them and the glittering sparkles that rained down as aftermath to the explosions looked like bits of colored tinsel. The display was also quieter than a typical American display, having a softer quality to it.

After viewing the fireworks, I took in the scene on the Neva. A succession of Soviet Navy ships were lined up near the far bank of the Neva. Each of them was lighted by a string of lanterns. Sailors stood on the decks lined in formation. I could see the crowds along the parapet on the river just in front of the Winter Palace.

We had not been there for more than five minutes when Vasili decided we had to get going. We removed ourselves from the crowd of tourists and headed by car across the Neva on a nearby bridge. Then we followed the southern bank heading west. I noticed the cars approaching us drove with lights that were dim, much dimmer than the lights on cars back home. They probably had worn out batteries, another scarce commodity.

As we passed each boat on display, Vasili described it to me with Dmitri's help: gunboat, patrol boat, nuclear sub, destroyer. Vasili told me that some of these ships could carry and launch nuclear tipped missiles. I was impressed. Some of the Soviet Union's military might was on display, and I was getting a first hand tour by one of its ex-officers.

The destructive power of the Soviet system was gained at the price of consumer comfort. You could say that the Soviet Union placed governmental or systemic considerations over its citizen's practical ones. This may not have been the intent of Soviet leadership. Perhaps it was an unintended consequence of their race for power.

Suddenly, Vasili stopped the car because an old man decided to cross the roadway against traffic. Fortunately, we were not traveling fast. The jaywalker waved his hands as if to show his disdain for the traffic. I had seen this happen before in the United States. There, this crazy behavior may have eventually gotten the old man locked up in a mental institution.

Vasili gave me a lesson in how to handle such people without "medical" intervention. He stopped the car next to the wayward man and proceeded to lecture him for several minutes. Vasili used his position as a retired Soviet navy captain to take an authoritative stance. The Soviet state was organized as a military institution. Everybody had an official job as a government employee and carried some authority.

I was stunned. Normally, the most attention someone like this would get back home would be a curse or horn honk and some dirty looks, provided the person did not get hit. Here, Vasili put us at risk, stopping on an uncontrolled section of road to have a chat with this old man to set him right. I imagined his parents should have given the man this sort of chat when he was a young boy. I was surprised to see someone show that much care or interest in a complete stranger.

We parted company with the old man. He made it to the other side safely and perhaps a little wiser. I commended Vasili on his actions. He told me the man was drunk, indicating this by touching his throat with the back of his middle finger. I suggested that the man may be a little crazy. Vasili was not sure but indicated that he had given him a piece of his mind and thought the shock might make the man a little more alert. He also wanted to make sure the man got across the road in one piece. I appreciated his show of compassion for a stranger.

Cultures differ according to the values they cultivate. Since time, saving it, is so highly prized in the United States, a wayward "crazy man" holding up traffic is especially annoying because no reason is evident for his behavior. But the primary concern in Russia was for public order. Everybody held a position in the vast state bureaucracy. Some Soviet bureaucrats seemed to specialize in putting up roadblocks to simple activities, such as entering a hotel. Others like Vasili (or the ladies in the Polish Church, the man at the church concert in Latvia, and the man on the train from Pushkin) were more keen on admonishing perceived incorrect behavior.

Before getting home, Dmitri invited Sonia and Vasili to come and see Dmitri's communal flat. I waited in the car with Alisa, sipping on some warm

Pepsi, which we stopped to purchase from a street vendor. Up to this point, I believed that Vasili and Dmitri had been friends for a while. However, if they were long time friends, Vasili would have seen Dmitri's flat long before this.

G. The Matriarch

We made it back to Vasili's flat where a midnight meal was prepared by Sonia and Valentina. While Dmitri and Alisa fussed over Ilya, Vasili took me into a different room to show me his collection of rock-and-roll records and tapes. He had an old phonograph that did not work and a tape player that did. He played me some "Rolling Stones" music that had been copied onto an audio cassette, perhaps from a radio station. It sounded awful, but it was recognizable. Vasili's room was plastered with paper posters of rock-and-roll stars, fancy cars, and women in bikinis. It reminded me of a college dorm room. The room had a bed, but I was not sure if this was where he and his wife slept. It did not seem to suit Sonia's aesthetic taste, which leaned toward pictures of Orthodox cathedrals and samovars.

I was interested in the contrast. Here, side-by-side, were two contrasting aspects of Soviet life. Sonia's posters and calendars reflected a nostalgia for the old aristocracy and ties to Russian Orthodoxy. Vasili's posters reflected the influx of flashy, cheap Western imports, the wave of the future. A flood of these would pour into Russia during the following years.

I was also disturbed by Vasili's obsession with rock-and-roll music and especially his taste in decorations that were more appropriate to a college dormitory. He was almost a middle-aged man. The system's cradle-to-grave social security and complete domination of economic life may have retarded maturity. But since this did not occur in every case, I could not come to any conclusion about this.

Before dinner started, Dmitri, Vasili, and I smoked together in one corner of the kitchen. I offered Vasili another pack of Camels as was my habit. This time he refused, explaining that he had plenty of cigarettes. What he wanted was a bottle of genuine American whiskey. I was surprised at his directness, but promised that I would see what I could do. I knew that the time I had to leave the Soviet Union was drawing near. Substantial presents would probably be expected by my hosts when I departed. I was grateful to have a chance to impress.

Sonia prepared a roast chicken dinner with marinated tomatoes and roasted potatoes. Valentina made her pickled watermelon. This time, we drank vodka with the meal instead of after. I was not used to eating a heavy meal at that time of night, and I started to feel ill and could not eat or drink much. I made my excuses, and fortunately they were heeded.

Vasili and Dmitri got into an animated conversation, little of which I could understand. When I was finally able to get Dmitri's attention, he told me that they were discussing "rope TV," a new kind of television being introduced to the Soviet Union. I did not know what he meant by it, and

Dmitri was reluctant to explain it further. Only later did I realize that they were discussing cable television technology. I supposed that comments on my part that this was nothing new in the United States may not have been appreciated. So perhaps that I did not understand until later was for the best.

At some point during the meal, the television set was turned on. It hung above us on a shelve tucked into a corner of the kitchen like a television in a tavern. I started to watch what was on. I recognized the face of the American "tough guy" actor Charles Bronson. He was in an off-beat Western where his main adversary was a Samurai warrior wandering through the Old West. The film was in English with Russian subtitles, but I could barely make out what they were saying above the din in the kitchen. Dmitri started to watch it with me. I explained to Dmitri who Charles Bronson was. I did not know who the Japanese man was or what a Samurai had to do with the Old West. Dmitri and I agreed that the two characters were both "very serious" men.

The warmth and intimacy of the Russian kitchen, the last refuge from an impersonal state and public life, was being invaded by Western imports such as cable television and American movies. Along with Vasili's preoccupation with pop music, these foreign cultural influences only hinted at a coming groundswell of populism that would soon sweep the old order away. Russia would take a wild swing to the West over the next eight years. Only at the end of the twentieth century would Russia begin to retreat into the ways of the East. The clumsy attempts at *laissez faire* capitalism, which had trouble taking hold in a land not culturally suited for it, would give way to a more careful approach at economic reform that was consistent with Russia's past. However, Russia would not go back to its pre-Yeltsin days.

At some point, Dmitri turned his attention to Ilya when the boy complained that he was not hungry and did not want to finish what was on his plate. Dmitri began to scold him. Alisa intervened and scolded Dmitri. They started to quarrel openly in front of me. Valentina intervened, scolding both of them. Order was restored.

This happened quickly, much like Ilya's tantrum at the camping ground in Karelia. After a little bit, Dmitri went back to watching the movie with me. Ilya was allowed to leave the table. Later, Vasili proposed another round of drinks and proposed a toast to every body's health: "*Na f'storovia*!" This broke the tension and the gay atmosphere resumed, albeit a little more subdued. Ultimately, women ruled in Soviet Russia, while men had ruled in the former aristocracy.

The normal intimacy and freedom of family life was undermined by tension. The source of this tension could have been many things. It may have been due to my presence, the strain of entertaining a guest. It may have been due to overall tension in Dmitri and Alisa's marriage. Whatever it was, a tension caused by the uncertainty of Russia's immediate future probably colored all of Russian life at that time.

3. Closing Comments

This ends the narrative portion of the book. The following day, Andrey called me to arrange a meeting for Thursday, 1 August. It opened a new chapter in my Russian journey. Once Dmitri knew for sure that I would be Andrey's guest, preparations began for my departure. A going-away party was given for me on the Wednesday of that week. Alisa, with Sonia's help, prepared a sumptuous feast, and many gifts were exchanged, including a bottle of whiskey for Vasili. By then, I gathered that gift giving and accepting was a social lubricant in Russia.

I spent my last few days with Dmitri wandering the city, seeing another art museum, the Russian Museum, and visiting the Summer Gardens. Dmitri indirectly implied that he knew that "I had been taken advantage of" but sought to mollify it by suggesting that he had mistakenly thought my trip was sponsored by a grant. He hoped I would not take it personally.

I never saw that money again. Nor for that matter did I see Dmitri, until years later when I returned to Russia in the year 2000. By then, the money was ancient history, and I was grateful that Dmitri gave me a chance to start my doctoral research in Russia.

I saw Vasili one more time in my 1991 trip. He drove Andrey and me to the airport on Saturday (3 August) so Andrey could see me off. The airport presented another chaotic scene reminiscent of the train journey from Pushkin. I managed to get through and get out "just in time" according to Pomeroy's wife, since the 19 August 1991 coup attempt was imminent.

Later, vacationing in Michigan, I sent Dmitri a postcard, the very day of the coup, but before I heard the news. This strange coincidence made me think of another one. Just before I left his flat, Dmitri asked me to advise Pomeroy to contact him before 19 August, as he was planning to make yet a third trip to Riga then. I coupled this coincidence with Alisa's mysterious disappearance and reappearance just ten days before I parted company with them, around the time the coup plotters were organizing. I remembered that Alisa was a member of the Communist Party. Could she have been given advance notice along with other Party cell members?

By the winter of 1991, I had a lot of work to do and was determined to get back to Russia. Andrey sent an official invitation to Pomeroy and me, and I negotiated a time and place for our seminar on the HVP. The 1992 trip would lead to a further trip in 1993.

I had gotten a taste of life in the former Soviet Union and had seen the conditions, the positive and the negative. I had seen Russians under stress, witnessed their sudden explosions, and I had been under stress myself. The whole region was in flux during this time. I was observing a society in transition, not a static arrangement.

Although Pomeroy and I decided not to contact Dmitri when we went to Russia in 1992, since we felt that the two groups, Dmitri's and Andrey's, involved with the HVP in my 1991 trip would conflict with each other, my association with Dmitri had a strong influence on my subsequent research. The most important concept he introduced to me, that of *blat*, would play a key role in my doctoral dissertation.

The next chapter introduces the theory of formal axiology and its connection to the HVP. My stressful encounters in the Soviet Union involved clashes of my values with those of my contacts. The encounters and my observations shed light on the nature of the values held by the Russians and Latvians I met. Formal axiology can help bring those values into focus.

Formal axiology revolves around three basic kinds of value introduced in this chapter through examples. To review, I talked about differences between the kinds of values and dis-values I found among my hosts and in the circumstances in Russia. Those things that Russians found priceless or brought joy to their lives, such as their children, social networks, and Dmitri's "treasure" (secret studio), have intrinsic value. Those things that concerned practical or pragmatic aspects of life, such as the shortage of some goods like coffee and sugar, or collecting money from an American have extrinsic value. The Soviet system of economic planning and political control and subordinates to it, such as the rail system near Leningrad, have systemic value. Objects may have more than one kind of value. For instance, social networks have practical value, and a train running on time has practical value.

These three value types can be treated formally. Once understood formally, they can be applied analytically to the entire narrative I presented in the previous chapters, which abound in examples of all three kinds of value and their combinations. In addition, the HVP that is derived from formal axiology can be applied to analyze the character of a human being. Thus, after some trial and error, I used the Russian HVP to gain insight into the value orientations of some of my Russian contacts.

This closes the second part of my book; the following three chapters constitute the final part. The next chapter discusses formal axiology and the construction of the HVP in some depth. The chapter after that demonstrates the power of the HVP in uncovering personality traits at their value roots. The final chapter is an application of formal axiology to the three weeks just described here.

Seven

THEORY AND METHOD: VALUES, AXIOLOGY, AND SOCIAL NETWORKS

1. Overview

In the dissertation on which this book is based (Gallopin, 1999), I used four different methodologies, including participant-observation, the Hartman Value Profile (HVP), self-disclosure for ethnographic elicitation (open-ended interviews and their structured analysis), and social network analysis. In this book, I focus on two of these methods, the HVP and its associated formal axiology and social network theory.

In this chapter, the HVP receives extensive theoretical treatment. It is new to the social sciences and potentially quite useful. The data collected by using the HVP-Pomeroy Interpretation Validation (HVP-PIV) is useful for giving insights into how the Russians I encountered structured their world of values. By cooperating with Leon Pomeroy in his cross-national comparisons with HVP-PIV data from other nations, I got a chance to see how Russians measured up against other parts of the world (Pomeroy and Gallopin, 1991; Pomeroy, *et al.*, 1992). Insights gained by trying to construct a valid test version of the HVP-PIV in Russia illuminated different aspects of Russian culture from language and conceptual differences to historical trends and social priorities.

For the book, I select individual HVP results and not group studies. My approach differs from that of Pomeroy, who did cross-national comparisons based on similar samples gathered in different countries. I was attached to his research, but a detailed discussion of it is not included here. My approach to the relationship between the individual and the group diverged from Pomeroy's. Instead of surveying arbitrarily selected groups, I investigated groups formed by personal connections between individuals. I wanted to focus in depth on a handful of individuals as opposed to statistically measuring larger groups.

Part of the original dissertation research involved conducting interviews. In order to collect interview material, I had to locate willing respondents. The process of arranging the interviews proved to be of interest in itself for it meant making creative use of my contacts and expanding my personal network at the same time. The strategies I used as I became more savvy in the ways of the culture often involved circumventing the more traditional institutions left over from the days of the Soviet Union by allying myself with members of the new class of Russian entrepreneurs. In this way, I gained knowledge in several different directions at the same time, including that of

Soviet institutions, of the new breed of entrepreneurs, of patronage, of the means and methods of exchange and barter, and of networks.

Network analysis allowed me to map the ever changing social structures that shaped and also gave meaning to the lives of the Russians I knew. This approach to studying the social context of people's lives is especially suited to Russia at the time I was there because it is designed to deal with change and complexity (Boissevain, 1973, pp. vii–xii). Russia was undergoing a culture shift. Traditional institutions were breaking down and new institutions were being formed. These days were a dynamic time and a time not given to the more traditional structural-functional approaches that are better suited for the study of more static societies.

2. Entrepreneurs: Focus of Study

In the original research, I used the anthropological technique of participant-observation that I discussed in the introduction. The observations I gained from employing this method form a "deep background" that guides my writing. For a more detailed account of those observations, see my dissertation (Gallopin, 1999).

For the purposes of this book, I concentrate on the activity that I observed during my 1991 field trip. Much of that activity was discussed in the earlier narrative portion (Chapters Three through Six). During 1991, I did not categorize what I was observing. In subsequent trips to Russia (1992, 1993, 2000), I had a much better I idea of what constituted entrepreneurial behavior and duly categorized it when encountered. I will draw on a few examples from those categorized activities to supplement my detailed observations from 1991.

This book concerns the role values have in the entrepreneurial activity of Russians. I discuss entrepreneurial activity generally here before moving on to the theoretical aspects of this chapter because understanding the concrete relevance of the theory that follows is crucial. When I speak of values, the ultimate source and application of those values lie with the entrepreneurs.

The entrepreneurs in Russia are the class of people who earn their living by working in the interstices of the remaining official social structure of the Soviet Union. The official structure did not evaporate when the red and yellow Soviet flag was lowered over the Kremlin and the new tri-color was raised in its stead on Christmas day of 1991. The bureaucrats hung on to power by changing the labels they carried from Communist Party *apparatchik* (Soviet civil servant or bureaucrat) to businessperson. Their way of doing business lingered.

Once the power of the state withdrew its stranglehold on economic life, the formerly suppressed and secretive aspects of the second Soviet economy came into the light of day. When the people saw what was possible, they took up arms in the new war to make a living. In January of 1992, Boris Yeltsin lifted the laws banning private trading for profit. Immediately the streets were full of private citizens selling everything from odds and ends of hardware to the family silver in order to make ends meet in a now uncertain and volatile economic environment. During this explosive period, Russian entrepreneurs began to emerge, some coming from the ranks of the formerly all powerful bureaucratic and professional corps, some coming from the faceless ranks of ordinary people, from engineers to day laborers. The new Russian entrepreneurs quickly learned that by operating in the ever widening gaps and cracks of the rapidly crumbling post-Stalin infrastructure they were free to maneuver and set up networks of friends and helpers to get things done much as the *apparatchiki* (Soviet bureaucrats) had done behind the scenes during the days before the Soviet Union began to fall apart.

Russian entrepreneurs have roots in the Soviet system, where a large black market was created as an unintended consequence of the state planned economy. The Mafia with which we are familiar targets illegal markets such as prostitution, narcotics, gambling, and money laundering, and restricted markets such as unionized trades and fixed-location small businesses. The province of the Soviet *mafiya* involved a much wider range of goods and services. To some extent, every Soviet citizen was involved in some kind of illegal or semi-legal activity due to the lack of a functioning free market (Pryce-Jones, 1995, p. 378). So it was difficult to isolate the *mafiya* in terms of the law. What set them apart from ordinary citizens and most officials was their use of violence. What made them so hard to ferret out of the culture was their entanglement with the *nomenklatura*—the Soviet ruling class. The modern post-Soviet *mafiya* deals with those items and activities we might currently find to be illegal in our country. The new class of entrepreneurs are generally out of this kind of activity.

The new entrepreneurs are not in narcotics, prostitution, or gambling, but they are in areas formerly forbidden, namely commerce that involves risk, calculation, and speculation. They do business with foreigners if they can because that is where a lot of the action is. They trade in hard currency, ideally dollars, and gold. They have an eye for the deal, but also have savvy when it comes to the properly placed gift.

They do not necessarily carry guns, but they know something about them and ways to protect their property. They do not pay all of their taxes and sometimes do not pay rent, but they know about the laws of taxes and rent. These new Russian entrepreneurs are keen to learn business techniques and technology and clamor for technical assistance from up-to-date computers to standard Western accounting systems. Many young ambitious men and women with a ability to adapt to change constitute this new breed of businessmen and women. They share some of the naive assumptions about America that their parents had but at the same time have turned their back on America as their only role model. Many of them embrace foreigners that come into contact with them as capital to be saved, spent, and invested according to circumstances. As the creative force driving Russia today, this emerging class deserves close attention.

The particular group of Russians I studied were largely in the academic world with some exceptions. That did not prevent them from doing business because they used the state resources found in the university to conduct business *na lyeva* (on the side). While their official business was routine and did not appear to take up much time (as a result of the state policy of over-employment), their side business was substantial.

Dmitri and Alisa belonged to this group. I met them at the seasonal height of their entrepreneurial activity and at the same time knew that one of them was officially in the academic world. From my description of them, we may gather that they were engaged in moonlighting during their summer vacation and that I represented far more than an academic acquaintance. To briefly sum up, Dmitri and Alisa managed to mix their business with ostensible pleasure trips and scientific exchanges. They used these trips to gain new contacts, always advancing the network of relationships crucial to their success in the Soviet Union. While the end of the Soviet Union would bring about the end of their Latvian outlet due to closing borders, they continued to entertain other foreign scientists after I left. I had served as a kind of prototype. They learned from their experiences with me to improve the way they entertained future guests. This helped them establish new contacts in a never ending search for those relationships that could bring them hard currency and other items coveted by Russians.

Their learning experience and mine revolved around the different value clashes in our brief relationship. In particular, Dmitri noted problems with the trips on which they took me well outside the environs of Leningrad. These were the experiences where I had been most guarded. In and around Leningrad, our experiences had been better, and I had been more relaxed.

While my Russian friends were interested in the practical aspects of the learning experience, I was interested in its scientific value. This book focuses on values as they applied to the world that Alisa and Dmitri negotiated on a daily basis. In order to lay the foundation for how values and society will be explored here, I turn to the theoretical foundations of formal axiology and its product, the HVP.

3. The Hartman Value Profile—Pomeroy Interpretation Validation

The HVP-PIV is used throughout the book. It played a major role in the fieldwork. The first part of my fieldwork involved developing a Russian version of the test and collecting a sample in order to examine its validity. Other parts of my research involved refining the translation, doing a back translation, and gathering additional samples. The presentation and evaluation of the test were also conducted in a formal way *via* a seminar that I co-presented with Pomeroy in Russia (Pomeroy and Gallopin, 1992) and *via* a congress paper (Pomeroy, *et al.*, 1993) and poster board that I co-presented with Andrey and his student worker, Yuri (a young linguistics student), at the *International Congress on Computer Systems and Applied Mathematics, 1993*

(CSAM '93), and in informal ways *via* individual interpretations and consultations. Pomeroy and I used the Russian version of the HVP-PIV to collect data for our joint and separate research projects. In addition to the overall collection of several hundred Russian samples, a Ukrainian version of the test was developed and a substantial sample set was drawn with the assistance of Glasha, a Ukrainian graduate student of journalism.

As recounted in the narrative, an attempt was also made to collect Latvian data. However, even though a Latvian version of the test was created, no samples were taken, and this possibility withered away once ties to my Latvian connections were severed due to a change of circumstances.

Russian samples drawn using the HVP-PIV were evaluated for reliability. Several portions of each sample taken had to be discarded after informal interviews of the Russian and Ukrainian assistants who collected the samples determined that some of the procedures used were not sound. The cleaned up samples were used by Pomeroy in his research, and I use several of them in the dissertation.

In addition to the problems associated with testing and sampling, several associated problems arose in conjunction with the collection of the data. Our Ukrainian assistant, Glasha, encountered mixed success in the securing of samples. The collection of the Ukrainian samples was ultimately more successful in an urban university setting and less successful in rural areas. In addition, Pomeroy and I ran into problems when attempting to collect Russian data in rural and urban settings.

The rest of this section will deal with formal aspects of the HVP-PIV. The book will directly employ the concepts outlined here as well as the test itself.

A. Theory Supporting the Test

The HVP-PIV is based on the *Hartman Value Profile* (Hartman and Cardenas, 1970; Hartman, 1973a) but with a different interpretation that arises from Pomeroy's work in clinical psychology. The Hartman Value Profile (HVP) is a two part test based on value formulas derived from philosopher Robert S. Hartman's formal axiology. Formal axiology is an attempt to isolate and elaborate value structures in life and in the mind. Three separate value types based on three kinds of concepts form the building stones of his theoretical structure. Each value type corresponds to its equivalent concept in the world of facts. The three kinds of concepts are *synthetic*, *analytic*, and *singular*.

A *synthetic* (Hartman, 1967, p. 31) or formal concept that refers to a mental construction (Hartman, 1973b, p. 35) or the name of an idea (Forrest, 1991, p. 132) is exact and limited, having a "finite and definite amount of properties" (Hartman, 1973b, p. 39). "Circle" is such a concept. A circle is the locus of all points equidistant from a single point. In geometry, a shape is a circle or it is not. Circles as such cannot exist in reality. They are constructs of the mind used to deal with reality in a formal way and belong to a formal system called geometry (Hartman, 1973b, p. 36). Synthetic concepts, because of their precision, are powerful ways of dealing with reality. However, the formal mental objects they refer to do not exist apart from the human mind. The referents of synthetic concepts exist inside the minds of the scientists and technical experts that manipulate and apply them. The validity of a synthetic concept depends on how well it maps reality, in other words, if it is of a system isomorphic to reality (Hartman, 1967, pp. 31–43).

An *analytic* or abstract concept is not as precise and so not as powerful as a synthetic concept, but in another sense, it is more closely linked to reality because it is directly derived from the objects and actions existing in reality. The dictionary definition of a chair is such a concept. A chair is a "knee high structure with a seat and a back" (Hartman, 1967, p. 31). Chairs can come in a variety of types, be made of different materials, and have different functions. *Singular* concepts, which will be discussed in more detail below, can deal with any individual existing chair. An analytic concept deals with classes of chairs. An analytic concept, unlike a synthetic concept, does not have a limited number of predicates in the *intension* (set of predicates; words or symbols) of its definition; nor does it correspond to a limited number of items in its *extension*, the set of objects it covers in reality.

The intension set of an analytic concept is countable, and the more predicates the intension set has the smaller is the extension set to which it refers. So, for example, while the number of predicates of the concept "easy chair" is greater than the number of predicates of the simpler definition given above, the extension set it refers to is smaller.

The last kind of concept, *singular*, refers to a single specific thing, event, or person. They are the least useful in terms of a formal science because of their idiosyncratic nature, but because they name actual entities, their referents are quite real. Concepts such as this may refer to things like the "Mona Lisa," the Renaissance, or Leonardo da Vinci. Such concepts denote things, events, or persons that are unique. While the extension of these kinds of concepts always consist of a set of one, the intension of a singular concept is infinite and uncountable. We could easily exhaust a life time trying to account for everything that makes up the Renaissance, Leonardo, or the "Mona Lisa" and would not come close to finishing. This idea could be equally applied to such mundane things, events, and people as your neighbors, their wedding, or the chair you are sitting on, because examined this way none of them is mundane.

Hartman transformed the three classes of concepts into value concepts. Using the work of G. E. Moore as a starting point, Hartman came up with a definition of "good" that he could use formally as an axiom for formal axiology. The axiom states that a good thing is one that fulfills its definition. Or, to put it another way, "a thing is good if it fulfills the intension of its concept" (Hartman, 1967, p. 103). Value can be measured in terms of how much a thing fulfills the concept of its class (Hartman, 1973b, p. 32). From this, Hartman deduced that values are based on concepts and must come in three varieties, those that correspond to singular, analytical, and synthetic concepts. Values turn the conceptual equation around. With values, the focus is on the definition and the exposition, the concept, and its intension as a set of predicates that corresponds to the properties of things in the universe. With facts, the focus is on the extension of a concept, the objects or events to which a concept refers. To evaluate something, we start with the thing and proceed to compare its properties to the concept that refers to it by conceptualizing the item in question in terms of its desirable properties. According to formal axiology, the thing is examined by comparing its individual concept as a member of a class of like objects to the definition and exposition of that class.

The definition of a class involves the minimum set of predicates that identifies the object in question thereby separating it from other kinds of objects in the universe. The exposition of a class includes predicates that are outside the minimum definition set but are at the same time possible and desirable for the object to possess. A car for example must possess wheels, an engine, a steering mechanism, a place to sit, a means of stopping, and so forth. It may also have a radio, air conditioning, and tinted glass, things that are not included in its definition yet are perfectly within what a car may have.

The thing in question is evaluated in terms of how well it conceptually fits its definition and exposition (Hartman, 1967, 103). For instance, a car with a broken engine is not a good car, because the concept of a car includes the property "engine that propels it" while the individual concept of this particular car has the property "engine that does not propel it." A car with more properties than the basic set may also not be good, for example, a car with a broken radio.

Keeping in mind that the above discussion is greatly simplified and leaves out a great deal of the conceptual details that Hartman had to lay out in order to make his value science fly, I turn now to the derived value concepts. Hartman defined three basic value types, an *intrinsic* type that corresponds to singular concepts, an *extrinsic* type that corresponds to analytic concepts, and a *systemic* type that corresponds to synthetic concepts. These three kinds of value can be considered to be concepts themselves. They are synthetic concepts because they are limited, precise, and have formally related predicates, and they are mental constructions. At the same time, like a geometrical definition or mathematical formula, they are constructs that can be applied to the value world, much in the same way that $E=MC^2$ can be applied to the natural world.

We can look at extrinsic, systemic, and intrinsic values in two ways, formally, as a set of formulas or, informally, as something occurring in the realm of ordinary reality. Informally, an extrinsic value refers to things that are practical or social. Economics studies the practical monetary value of individual objects. In the social world, connections between people, friendships, business relationships, marriages, and a variety of other relationships can be compared to each other in terms of practical value. Love and integrity may play a role in relationships as well. These qualities involve intrinsic value. Legal considerations may be applied to relationships. They involve systemic value. Some psychologists study the human mind from the point of view of an individual's practical functioning in nature and society. Axiologically, these psychologists study individual persons in terms of extrinsic value. Some schools of psychology, such as humanist psychology, study the individual's human potential in terms of intrinsic value. Sociologists examine extrinsic values with relation to groups of persons. They study the practical value of different classes of individuals such as bankers, fire fighters, and artists.

An intrinsic value refers to things that are unique. An artist is concerned with the aesthetic rendering of a unique object. The outstanding quality of a masterpiece such as the "Mona Lisa" is that it is one of a kind, never to be repeated. Top architects strive to make each new building truly new, based on its unique location, context, and function.

Intrinsic value deals with the continuous infinite. An individual human being is unique with qualities that are not countable. Love is an expression of the continuous infinite. Novelty or newness is also intrinsic. A new encounter or a new land seen for the first time fills up the senses. This should give some feeling for what is meant by intrinsic value.

A systemic value is all the way at the other end of the spectrum. Systems are carefully defined scientific objects or propositions. Laws have systemic value. A computer algorithm has systemic value. Technology can be summed up as the application of systemic value to the natural world. We use carefully defined formal concepts, formulas, scientific equations, and calculations to guide the creation of new objects from the substance of nature. A technical improvement can be summed up as a systemic value enhancing a pre-existing systemic value.

Systems may also disvalue things at times. When a cop gives you a ticket for speeding, you are being confronted with a systemic value—the system of laws that regulates the ways you can drive your automobile. The fine you receive is symbolic of the underlying value formula that is being applied. The formula states that the event that caused the ticket, driving too fast according to the rules of the road, is being disvalued by the system that the police officer represents. Real world events such as driving can be classified. Hence they represent extrinsic value. Any set of rules systematically applied are by definition systemic in nature. Reducing the formula to its essentials, what the police officer did was to disvalue systemically an extrinsic value.

Extrinsic, intrinsic, and systemic values can be looked at more formally. Formal axiology applies set theory to value concepts much in the same way that physics applies calculus to concepts of motion. Three basic different kinds of sets exist in set theory, countable finite sets, countable infinite sets, and uncountable (continuous) infinite sets. Countable finite sets can be used to denote systemic value. A systemic value is based on a synthetic concept, which has a limited discrete intension. An infinite number of ways to describe a circle in geometry do not exist. Its characteristics must be described by specific formulas (for example, $C=2\Pi r$). Systemic value refers to the objects or extensions of a synthetic definition. In the world of geometry, a shape is or is not a circle. Systemic value is either-or. Being a circle is the same as being a good circle.

An extrinsic value can be denoted by a countable infinite set. An extrinsic value is based on an analytic concept, which has a discrete intension that can potentially consist of an infinite number of predicates. To examine this, take a look at the concept of "chair." The intension of this concept can be extended to include an easy chair by adding more predicates such as "reclining," "soft," and so forth. Imagine how complex a chair is in a dentist's office. Analytic concepts can be extended indefinitely by adding more and more predicates. At the same time, the class of objects denoted by analytic concepts with larger predicate sets will shrink. The most complex chairs are the most rare.

Extrinsic value denotes those kinds of values that are characterized by a countable but potentially infinite set of conceptual properties. The goodness of an object in terms of its extrinsic value will depend on how many of the predicates of its definition and exposition are fulfilled. Thus a good sports car will have the properties: aerodynamic, light, maneuverable, compact, and having a powerful engine. If you take away some of these properties, you may have something less than a good sports car and something more than a good car. Hartman points out that the value of an object viewed analytically depends on the richness of its concept. Extrinsic value depends on a kind of concept that can be said to be analytical, which by definition has a countable but ultimately infinite set of predicates. The extrinsic value of an object is also countable and potentially infinite. Objects can be thought of as having extrinsic value when we view them in terms of classes. So an apple in terms of its extrinsic value must be thought of as part of the set of all apples. A specific apple, like the one you buy at the supermarket, call "your apple," and eat, as a separate distinct object, does not have extrinsic value. It has intrinsic value when seen this way and is the way an artist will typically view it.

The measure of the value is in the concept. We can say that extrinsic values based on concepts that are infinite but countable are richer than systemic values, which are also countable but not infinite. We may also say that intrinsic values are richer than both systemic and extrinsic values.

An intrinsic value can be denoted by an uncountable infinite set. Intrinsic value is based upon a singular concept, which has a continuous infinite intension. Concepts such as these are the names we assign to specific objects, events, or people. The extension set of a singular concept consists of one item. Questions regarding the goodness of the object of a singular concept, as noted above, are subtle and complex. For the purposes of this discussion, note that when the object of a singular concept fulfills its definition, its value can be measured by the richness of the concept. In this case, the concept has an uncountable and infinite intension set. Its value is correspondingly uncountable and infinite.

Hartman's proto-science, to make progress toward becoming a science, has to combine the dimensions of value and derive new values from the combinations. It also has to arrive at a measure of value by treating some kinds of value as better than others. Only in this manner can the theory of Hartman be applied to the reality of the realm of values. The whole purpose of a value science is to help humankind be more precise moralists just as natural science has helped us be more precise technicians.

Values are ranked according to the richness of their sets. Systemic values with finite sets are at the low end of the pole, and intrinsic values with continuous infinite sets are at the high end. Hartman's theory does have its own appeal. Common folk wisdom says that money, extrinsic value, cannot buy you love, intrinsic value. A lower value cannot gain a higher value. Hartman appears to be tuned in to the common person. We also have seen the horrors of systems turned against people such as systematic extermination factories known as Nazi death camps. People, such as Adolf Eichman, who planned and ran concentration camps, thought of transporting millions to these infernal places as nothing more than an engineering problem, in effect placing systemic considerations over human life (Pomeroy and Bishop, 1991, p. 302). Those who suspected the existence of such horrors but ignored the evidence because of the strategic requirements of Germany's war effort valued "the system" over "sentimentality" (Speer, 1970, pp. 446–447). Hartman also addresses the uncommon—a crisis situation perpetrated by unusually evil persons placing a lower value, a system, above a higher value, individual human life.

The combination of value types gives formal axiology its richness and potential for use. Combinations of values have been mentioned above. "A technical improvement," which is the systemic valuation of a systemic value, the technical system being improved by another systemic value, the technique used to improve it, can be represented as a systemic value raised to the power of a systemic value (S^S). Hartman uses this value formula to represent the enhancement of value and the diminution of it (Hartman, 1967, pp. 265–266, 275). He uses the arithmetical function of powers and mathematical set theory to show how values may jump into higher and higher levels of infinity, representing richer and richer levels of value:

N = (Finite),

$\mathbf{X}_0$ = (Infinite-Countable),

$\mathbf{X}_1$ = (Infinite-Uncountable; 2^{X_0}),

$\mathbf{X}_2$ = (2^{X_1}), etc.

So, a technical improvement (S^S) is represented by the mathematical formula $N^N = N$. N corresponds to the finite nature of a systemic value.

Combinations of values can also lead to disvaluation. For instance, "garbage" is the combination of two extrinsic values in such a way as to disvalue the values taken separately, for example, milk spilled on a floor. This disvaluing combination could be represented axiologically as (E_E) and represented mathematically as ($\mathbf{X}_0^{-X_0} = 1/\mathbf{X}_1$).

As you can see, words and phrases such as "garbage" and "technical improvement" can be used to represent axiological and corresponding mathematical formulas. The mathematical formulas can be ranked according to an increasing value of infiniteness (representing ever larger and ever more complex sets):

$$(1/\mathbf{X}_2 < 1/\mathbf{X}_1 < 1/\mathbf{X}_0 < 1/\mathrm{N} < \mathrm{N} < \mathbf{X}_0 < \mathbf{X}_1 < \mathbf{X}_2).$$

A test can be derived from this set of axiological formulas that tests a person's ability to see values as represented by phrases. By being asked to rank a set of phrases according to how valuable the things they represent are to each other, the person is asked to identify the values represented correctly and then correctly evaluate them relative to each other. Hartman derived a value inventory of eighteen phrases (Hartman, 1967: pp. 272–273; 1973a) that correspond to all the possible combinations of the three value types in sets of two, taking into account *compositions* (value enhancements) and *transpositions* (disvaluations).

The hierarchical ordering of the eighteen possible combinations is expressed in Table 1 with the best value on top and the worst on the bottom (Hartman, 1967, p. 275).

The table demonstrates that the set of possible value combinations produces mathematical ties. Hartman used his theory of axiology to break the ties. The three combinations at either end of the scale (each valued mathematically as $\mathbf{X}_2$ or $1/\mathbf{X}_2$) can be separated by the base of the value combination and ordered according to it. We run into a bit of difficulty with those four value combinations on either side of the middle of the scale (I^E, I^S, E^E, S^E). The order of all combinations except I^S can be separated by the base of the value combination, but where should we put the exception? Hartman placed it where it is because he emphasized the base portion of the value formulas (and I > E). The exponent can also be used to break ties. In that case, the correct ordering (in descending axiological value) would be (I^E, E^E, S^E, I^S).

B. The Test

The HVP-PIV is derived from the principles outlined above. The test has two parts. The first part measures a person's ability to value items drawn from the outside world. The second part measures a person's ability to value features of the self. Both involve the person's *General Capacity to Value* (GCV), a cognitive mechanism deeply rooted in the mind of every individual. Pomeroy and Hartman have described the GCV at length and consider it to be a universal aspect of human existence (Hartman, 1973a; Pomeroy and Ellis, 1991; Pomeroy and Bishop, 1991). For Hartman, this implied a world wide applicability of his test (Hartman, 1967, pp. 307–311; 1973a; 1973b). For Pomeroy, it means the basis for cross-cultural, cross-national comparisons (Pomeroy and Bishop, 1989, 1990a, 1990b, 1991; Pomeroy and Gallopin 1991; Pomeroy, *et al.*, 1992, 1997).

Table 1: *Hierarchical Ordering of Second Order Axiological Combinations*

Axiological Value Formula	*Mathematical Value*
(compositions)	
(I^I)	$\mathbf{X}_2$
(E^I)	$\mathbf{X}_2$
(S^I)	$\mathbf{X}_2$
(I^E)	$\mathbf{X}_1$
(I^S)	$\mathbf{X}_1$
(E^E)	$\mathbf{X}_1$
(S^E)	$\mathbf{X}_1$
(E^S)	$\mathbf{X}_0$
(S^S)	N
(transpositions)	
(S_S)	1/N
(E_S)	$1/\mathbf{X}_0$
(S_E)	$1/\mathbf{X}_1$
(E_E)	$1/\mathbf{X}_1$
(I_S)	$1/\mathbf{X}_1$
(I_E)	$1/\mathbf{X}_1$
(S_I)	$1/\mathbf{X}_2$
(E_I)	$1/\mathbf{X}_2$
(I_I)	$1/\mathbf{X}_2$

Each part of the HVP-PIV is based on a scrambled value inventory represented by phrases. Table 2 shows the ranked phrases for Part 1. Table 3 shows the ranked phrases for Part 2. Next to each phrase is the corresponding value formula. For Part 2, the value formulas shown are exponents of an intrinsic value, namely the person taking the test, because the phrases refer to the person. The full formulas are left out for the sake of brevity (Hartman, 1973a, pp. 35–36).

Table 4 shows the phrases in test order. The respondent to the test is asked to rank the first set of items according to how valuable they are and the second set of items according to how much he or she agrees with them.

The test evaluates the respondent's ability to value by comparing the responses to the normative order given by formal axiology. Differences are measured in a variety of ways for each part of the test and by combining both parts of the test. Each value dimension (I, E, S) is treated individually, and all three dimensions are evaluated collectively to give a series of scaled

Table 2: *HVP Part 1, Phrases Ranked Axiologically*

Phrase	Value Formula
A baby	I^I
Love of nature	E^I
Mathematical genius	S^I
"By this ring, I thee wed."	I^E
A devoted scientist	I^S
Good food	E^E
A uniform	S^E
An assembly line	E^S
A technical improvement	S^S
Nonsense	S_S
A fine	E_S
A short-circuit	S_E
A rubbish heap	E_E
A madman	I_S
Slavery	I_E
Burn a heretic at the stake	S_I
Blow up an airplane in flight	E_I
Torture a person in a concentration camp	I_I

measurements. These measurements are then evaluated according to a specific frame of reference. The basic frame of reference is axiological, but other frames of references can be applied. Hartman himself worked with a clinical (psychological) frame of reference (Hartman, 1973a) along with Maria Cardenas Trigos (Hartman and Cardenas, 1970). Pomeroy uses his own clinical psychology frame of reference derived from his own research.

C. Testing Procedures

Because the test produces raw numerical results, it can be applied to groups of people (Hartman, 1973a, p. 1). Pomeroy exploits this advantage in his cross-national and cross-cultural research (Pomeroy and Bishop, 1991; Pomeroy *et al.*, 1992).

As in the other countries where Pomeroy had already done cross-national psychology research using HVP-PIV samples (Japan, Mexico, Indonesia), doing work in Russia required that a native language version of the test be produced. The translation of the test into Russian required accuracy. Pomeroy felt that by obtaining a successful back translation of the test, he could achieve the confidence level necessary to trust the results of the test.

Table 3: *HVP Part 2 phrases ranked axiologically*

Phrase	Value Formula
"I enjoy being myself "	I^I
"I love my work"	E^I
"I love the beauty of the world"	S^I
"My work brings out the best in me"	I^E
"I feel at home in the world"	I^S
"I like my work—it does me good"	E^E
"My work adds to the beauty and harmony of the world"	S^E
"The more I understand my place in the world, the better I get in my work"	E^S
"The universe is a remarkably harmonious system"	S^S
"The world makes little sense to me"	S_S
"No matter how hard I work, I shall always feel frustrated"	E_S
"My work contributes nothing to the world"	S_E
"My working conditions are poor, and ruin my work"	E_E
"The lack of meaning in the universe disturbs me"	I_S
"My work makes me unhappy"	I_E
"My life is messing up the world"	S_I
"I hate my work"	E_I
"I curse the day I was born"	I_I

I have my reservations about this. Let me put my case succinctly. The original English version (and Spanish version) of the HVP makes assumptions about the nation, society, and culture in which it is framed and used. To translate the test successfully into another language for use in a different part of the world means examining those assumptions to see if they hold true for its new context. Each new language translation and place of testing will be a unique case and bring some idiosyncratic features of the new language, nation, society, and culture to bear. In my opinion, the most important thing that must be held constant is the set of value formulas that the phrases of the test represent. If this means tossing out some of the original English phrases entirely and replacing them with their axiological equivalent in the focus culture, then so be it. Retaining the underlying integrity of the test is better than maintaining perfect linguistic translations.

For purposes of the book, I selected three test respondents. Chapter Eight contains a discussion of the results of the tests they took and a brief description of the test conditions. My criteria differed from Pomeroy's in that

Table 4: *HVP-PIV, Part 1*

a) Good food
b) A technical improvement
c) Nonsense
d) A fine
e) A rubbish heap
f) A devoted scientist
g) Blow up an airplane in flight
h) Burn a heretic at the stake
i) A short-circuit
j) "By this ring, I thee wed."
k) A baby
l) Torture a person in a concentration camp
m) Love of nature
n) A madman
o) An assembly line
p) Slavery
q) A mathematical genius
r) A uniform

HVP-PIV, Part 2

a) I like my work—it does me good
b) The universe is a remarkably harmonious system
c) The world makes little sense to me
d) No matter how hard I work, I shall always feel frustrated
e) My working conditions are poor, and ruin my work
f) I feel at home in the world
g) I hate my work
h) My life is messing up the world
i) My work contributes nothing to the world
j) My work brings out the best in me
k) I enjoy being myself
l) I curse the day I was born
m) I love my work
n) The lack of meaning in the universe disturbs me
o) The more I understand my place in the world, the better I get in my work
p) My work makes me unhappy
q) I love the beauty of the world
r) My work adds to the beauty and harmony of the world

while he was looking for a similar structure of testing and similarly constituted test samples, I wanted close control over the test taking process to avoid misunderstandings and subterfuge. The narrative in Chapter Four exposes the possible pitfalls of not carefully monitoring the test-taking process.

D. Application of Formal Axiology

With the exception of Andrey and Ann, I was unable to get HVP test results for the principal Russian contacts I had during my 1991 trip, which is the focus of this book. I did get more test results during my 1992 and 1993 visits, but these results, though interesting (see Gallopin, 1999), involved Russians outside the main networks I encountered in 1991. In order to supplement the test results shown in the next chapter, I use a more general approach in the final chapter that involves the theoretical principles outlined above.

While individual test results can reveal characteristics of particular Russians, the focus in the final chapter is on the relationships in terms of value dynamics. No HVP test has been developed as of yet that can measure a relationship. Therefore, I use axiological analysis. Frank Forrest, a member of the R. S. Hartman Institute for Formal and Applied Axiology, is pioneering this kind of analysis (Forrest, 1994). Forrest applies Hartmanean Algebra, his extension of formal axiological theory, to everyday personal and professional ethical situations. In Chapter Nine, I refer to Forrest's manner of applying formal axiology in order to support my own application of formal axiology to the value rich and value poor situations I encountered in the former Soviet Union.

4. Network Analysis

Inspired by the suggestions of social anthropologist Norman E. Whitten (Whitten, 1970, pp. 398–402), I paid close attention to the formation of my personal network in Russia and elicited information concerning the personal networks of several of my contacts. Because my personal network naturally overlapped the personal networks of my contacts in the field, I was able to observe those portions of their networks with which I had contact.

My doctoral research interest in social networks went beyond sampling. I wanted to see how they were constructed, how they related to key concepts that I was exploring including values, stress, economics, markets, solidarity, and survival strategies. I also was interested in exploring what roles, if any, networks had in the culture shift that occurred during and around my time in the field. In this book, I am more interested in using network theory to help us model the social context in which exchanges of value take place.

The study of social networks and systematic network analyses has been established as a theoretically and methodologically valid tool for sociologists and anthropologists since the early 1970s (Boissevain and Mitchell, 1973;

Milford, 1987; Rogers and Vertovec, 1995; Whitten and Wolfe, 1973). The introduction of network analysis came about as a response to what was seen as the increasing inadequacy of the structural-functional framework (traditionally used to study more stable and less overtly dynamic, small, non-complex societies) to deal with the dynamics and complexities of larger heterogeneous groupings characteristic of civilizations and proto-civilizations (Boissevain, 1973, pp. vii–viii). Four assumptions made by the structural-functional framework,

a) that a social group can be appropriately mapped with models drawn from the natural sciences, the organic model of society,
b) that the functions of a group determine its characteristics, "my nose functions to support my glasses giving it its unique shape,"
c) that a social group may change only if its equilibrium is upset by an outside agent, and
d) that the appropriate unit of study is the group as a collective instead of the individuals that make up the group,

were all challenged by the founders of network analysis in the social sciences (Boissevain, 1973, pp. vii–viii; Noble, 1973, p. 4).

My discovery of network analysis as a potentially powerful means of modeling the urban society into which I had landed, initially to do cross-cultural psychology, came about by paying attention to what my first and most enigmatic informant (Dmitri) told me in 1991, that Russians lived by the network. Their daily existence was colored by network considerations in ways with which I was not familiar. This revelation by a member of a society that was superficially characterized as being "monolithic" and "regimented" opened my eyes to the truth that the Soviet Union was teeming with life and dynamics largely unseen and unrecorded by the media of the United States. Occasionally, a journalist who had spent some time there would put together a report on Russians that belied this carefully constructed mythology of the Cold War (Smith, 1981; Shippler, 1983). Most Americans remained unaware of how complicated a society the Soviet Union encased.

If anyone had walked the streets of Leningrad in the early summer of 1991, he or she would have believed the myth. The public life of Russians, though already officially changing according to the propaganda of *glasnost* and *perestroika*, was still of the gray color reported by Soviet observers. Walking the same streets one year later showed the change. The underground currents began to spring above ground and reshape the face of society. Dmitri had predicted this. The second summer I was in Russia, I witnessed the confirmation of a theory that was suggested to me the year before, not by an established Western social scientist, but by a native educator (informant).

So I owe a debt to Dmitri. Translating his suggestion into a working model, however, requires a more formal assessment of what he told me. The following is a summary of the way I applied network analysis to my research in Russia.

Networks constitute social phenomena and systemic models of such phenomena. Mathematically, networks are sets of interconnected points. As a phenomenon, a social network consists of individuals connected through social relationships. In formal axiology, a network is a systemic value. It is a mental construct used to map reality. It is perhaps a quite powerful construct because it is analyzable using established mathematical models, namely graphs and matrices. Matrix algebra and graph theory are well-established methods of modeling real world events and are used in a wide variety of applications from business to theoretical physics. Telecommunication companies and airline carriers use graph theory routinely to increase their efficiency.

A system of network analysis can be used to map the day-to-day interactions between members of a social group. Social scientists making use of the network model encounter the difficulties facing scientists in any discipline, that of clarity and precision. Questions concerning differences between groups, corporations, and networks on a practical level and a lack of models to account for change in networks hamper theoretical unification in the field (Boissevain, 1973, pp. x–xii).

A central consideration of social network analysts is the exchange that takes place between any two people linked together in a network. This is a central problem of anthropology, social anthropology in particular (Whitten and Wolfe, 1973, p. 726). Almost any item of cultural value can be exchanged such as money, barter objects, favors, gifts, information, different tokens, including tokens of love, of religion, of status, and of authority, and friendship, which includes a whole constellation of words, gestures, as well as the material tokens of friendship.

The network analyst must consider the nodes of the network, the points at which different lines intersect, and the links of the network, the connecting lines. In a social network, the nodes are individual human beings; the links are the exchanges that take place between those individuals who are connected in some fashion. A social network is a system of interpersonal relationships. Seen from the model of formal axiology, a network is a *systemic* valuation of a group of persons in terms of their relationships (Hartman, 1967, p. 310). It is to be distinguished from a social class, which is an *extrinsic* valuation of a group of persons, people as functions within social groups (Hartman, 1967, p. 307). It is also to be distinguished from a political movement, which is an *intrinsic* valuation of a group of persons, people in unique groupings deeply involved with symbols and institutions (Hartman, 1967, p. 309). A network is subject to formal laws. In an institution, these laws would be part of a legal framework. Modern institutions codify and document their laws. Networks that exist outside institutions and can be characterized as informal are part of a quasi-legal framework. The laws of an informal network are by definition informal themselves. They remain to be codified and documented.

Social network analysts study previously neglected kinds of relationships, those of informal social relationships (characterized sometimes as "friendships" or as "personal networks") in order to add a dynamic element to their analyses of society (Boissevain, 1973, p. viii, Whitten and Wolfe, 1973, pp. 720–725).

To do cumulative analyses, we must seek to isolate rules and laws of conduct in the interpersonal relationships that constitute a network. The interpersonal relationship can be analyzed as a play between all three value dimensions, the systemic in terms of prescribed roles, the extrinsic in terms of practical value, and the intrinsic in terms of intimacy. I seek to clarify what is implicit in the approach of network analysts, namely that the systemic dimension of valuation be combined with the three kinds of relationships (prescribed, practical, intimate) they have identified. We may formally model interpersonal relationships by considering them across the entire range of possible valuation.

In summation, what network analysts do is not strictly sociology, nor is it political analysis. It is a study of the laws of interpersonal relationships. What is new is that such relationships are not just considered in their legal sense as prescribed roles but also in their practical and intimate senses. Social network analysts include sociologists, social anthropologists, cultural anthropologists, and geographers. This interdisciplinary nature of social network analysis indicates that the technique is not the exclusive province of one social science discipline and that it is a new tool of analysis that has been derived from a marriage of social analysis to aspects of legal studies.

The social network is a crucial model used in the book to complement the formal axiology of Hartman. To clarify the model, we should understand what is meant by an "informal" network. In order to discriminate between different kinds of relationships, social network analysts coined the terms "non-group" and "informal" or "friendship network." They did so to distinguish what they were studying from what was studied before in terms of groups. Groups traditionally were treated as bounded and corporate in nature. This led to the traditional structural-functional approach discussed before. To distinguish their new mode of analyses, social network analysts employed new terms.

Social networks, especially informal networks, are groups just as corporations are. The world has reached a stage today where connectivity is the rule instead of the exception. Only one human network exists, that of the entire human population of the planet. Obviously, network analysts are interested in much smaller and more limited groups than that; the task of the network analyst is to describe formally the boundaries of the network that is under consideration. For example, lineage, a social structure often studied by anthropologists, is considered to be a "partial network" by network analysts because it includes a set of individuals limited by the tie of kinship (Whitten and Wolfe, 1973, p. 726).

For this book, I use what network analysts call "informal networks." I bound these informal networks in one of the ways accepted by network analysts, that of the personal network. A personal network is the informal network of friends and other significant acquaintances that the ego (central person) of the network knows personally (*first order* relationships). It does not normally include those persons that are only known to the ego indirectly, such as friends of friends. However, I have included such (*second order*) relationships if they are of sufficient importance to affect the workings of the personal network. The personal network also includes some links between those persons other than ego. Some of those known to ego will also know each other and will be linked in a network diagram, while others will not.

During two and half years of study of Russia, in the field and at the University of Buffalo, I mapped eight informal personal networks labeled by their respective "egos" or central personality. Most of these networks involve Russians I met after 1991. They are summarized here in Table 5 as examples. In Chapter Nine, the focus will be primarily on Dmitri's network.

Dmitri's network covered three areas, Leningrad, a summer retreat in Karelia, and Riga, Latvia. It was characterized by fluid institutional linkages, exhibited characteristics of patron-client relationships, and featured links in Japan and to the U.S. through Pomeroy (whom Dmitri met in Japan). Andrey's network was located primarily in Leningrad/St. Petersburg with partially obscure links in Privyetneskoye (a village along the north shore of the Gulf of Finland), Pavlosk, Riga, and Moscow. The network was heavily involved with two major institutions in Leningrad/St. Petersburg. It featured links in Eastern Europe and Sweden. These two rival networks naturally clashed because their characters differed.

Here are some relatively less important but equally interesting networks. Seryozha's network was located primarily in St. Petersburg. It was non-institutional, characterized by a creative combination of weak and strong links that extended their reach to Gatchina, Suida (a small village to the south), and areas around Lake Ladoga (located to the east of St. Petersburg), and featured an international link in Canada. Glasha's network had centers in St. Petersburg and her home town of Dnipropetrovsk, Ukraine. Like Seryozha's network, it was non-institutional. Like Dmitri's network, it was characterized by fluid and unstable links and peopled by creative entrepreneurs. Svetlana's network was one of the weakest I encountered, and I place it here for contrast. It was located primarily in Pushkin with links to St. Petersburg. It featured ambition for growth, but a lack of resources. Svetlana was energetic but not very attractive. Andrey found her to be abrasive.

These networks are fleshed out in my dissertation (Gallopin, 1999). The following three individuals were strong players during my 1993 extended stay in Russia, Nicholas, as my Russian companion/bodyguard, Liza, playing dual roles as my English student and Russian language instructor, and Fedya, a Russian more in the Soviet style of Pavel, who provided me room and board for three weeks.

Nicholas's network was located primarily in St. Petersburg with strong links to Moscow based on friendship. It was non-institutional, had potential

Table 5: *Informal Network Maps*

Ego	Years	Type	Locations
Dmitri	1991	*extensive*	Leningrad, Karelia, Riga, Japan, Odessa
Andrey	1991–1993	*intensive*	Leningrad, Pavlosk, Riga, Privyetneskoye, Moscow
Seryozha	1993	*mixed*	Leningrad, Gatchina, Suida, Lake Ladoga
Glasha	1992–1993	*extensive*	Leningrad, Dnipropetrovsk
Nicholas	1993	*mixed*	Leningrad, Moscow
Svetlana	1992-1993	*limited*	Leningrad, Pushkin
Liza	1993	*extensive*	Lenigrad, Novorossiysk
Fedya	1993	*intensive*	Leningrad, Moscow, Africa

extensive—having a wide geographical reach
intensive—having strong and numerous local ties
limited—not extensive or intensive
mixed—features of both with potential of becoming extensive or intensive

for growth, and featured resources and mobility that allowed for extensive travel. Nicholas, in contrast to Svetlana, was attractive but relatively less energetic. Andrey and Pavel did not think much of him. Nevertheless, he had access to a considerable range of resources and social connections. They just were not developed yet when I met him.

Liza's network was located primarily in St. Petersburg. It had familial links to Novorossiysk (southern Russia), and was characterized by kinship. Liza was still firmly ensconced in her wider family network. A process of differentiation was just getting started when I met her. Bright, personable, attractive, and ambitious, Liza would probably eventually break free of family to develop her own network.

Fedya's network was intensive in the present but had been extensive in the past, during the height of *apparatchik* (bureaucratic) Soviet power. He had been assigned overseas to Angola and Morocco, as an interpreter and translator. When I knew him, he was studying English so he could teach that language at the university, French being *passe*. Just before we parted ways, he received another chance to work abroad, once again in Morocco. His network was located primarily in St. Petersburg with patronage from Moscow, characterized by hierarchy and client-patron relationships.

The above thumbnail skeletal sketches of the networks I analyzed are not all-inclusive. For instance, Dmitri's and Andrey's networks could also be described as being involved with entrepreneur activity. Glasha's network did involve some linkages inside institutions. (I met Glasha, a graduate student of journalism, in 1992. In 1993, she helped me with my research.) I only included those characteristics that the networks emphasized.

I was interested in several aspects of these networks. I wanted to explore the different modes of exchange within each one in terms of psychological, social, and economic characteristics. I believed that by examining these interpersonal links in terms of their practical value, I would be able to deduce the laws that governed them. Directly asking the participants of these networks about any laws or rules that guided conduct proved to be fruitless. Directly eliciting information about practical aspects of these networks proved to be difficult. In both cases, I was told that these kinds of networks were "a thing of the past" or else I encountered blank looks or puzzled frowns encouraging me to change the subject. I often received little bits of information regarding the existence of a connection here and there that was used to get such and such item, "difficult to find in the stores." Sometimes, I was made the beneficiary of such a connection. Sometimes, I picked up bits of information about networks and friendship in a theoretical discussion. Generally, I made my own observations to discover how networks operated and who was connected to whom.

Surprisingly, I elicited more information about the intimate aspects of interpersonal relationships than the other aspects. One of my tasks was to integrate this knowledge with what I could uncover about the practical and systemic aspects of the networks I studied.

I did not conduct a methodical examination of the legal or systemic structure of the institutions that some of the networks intersected because it was not the focus of my study. I believe that though partially housed in institutions, such as St. Petersburg University, these networks operated outside of the legal structures of such universities. I took note whenever legal rules were applied to the participants of these informal networks. I was interested in the intersections of institution and informal network as opposed to a comprehensive study of the legal codes of the institutions.

Though quantitative methods are applicable to network analysis, I did not feel that I had a sufficiently large sample of networks to warrant quantitative techniques. I did gain enough information about each one to provide sketches of how they operated and the nature of exchanges within them. Bear in mind that one aim of my research was to provide a profile of the new entrepreneurial Russian. Network analyses provide an additional frame of reference to the study of this often misunderstood group. They are meant to complement the value-oriented techniques described earlier in this chapter.

A more theoretical aim of the book involves the development of a model that can account for the value shift occurring in the former Soviet Union during its last days and the early days of its main replacement, the Russian Federation. This model includes the continuously shifting social relationships at the local level that manifested themselves in broader movements in politics and economics. Individual Russians used networks to cope with institutional constraints during the days of the Soviet command economy and institutional chaos during the early days of Yeltsin's economic reforms. Coping strategies had to adapt to the sudden absence of clear official policies. Russians were already adept at using social networks when my study began. During the course of my study, many of them used this knowledge and skill in novel and resourceful ways for survival and profit.

The model I develop provides the foundation for future research and hypothesis testing. It includes insights into some of the underlying rules of network formation and manipulation. The model and rules uncovered can be applied to future studies of value change.

Eight

STRESS ANALYSIS: THE HVP IN THE FIELD

1. Overview

This chapter illustrates how I used the HVP in the field and extends the discussion of formal axiology started in Chapter Seven by focusing on data gathered using HVP analyses. It also focuses on the emotional aspects of Russian entrepreneurial coping activity.

Values and stress are associated concepts. They are associated through the concept of loss or cost. Values by their nature, concrete values such as a prized possession or a secure environment, entail the expenditure of energy, and their loss represents the loss of the energy invested. This kind of investment is basic to life. Stress is a biological and psychological condition associated with the threat of loss of acquired values and so the loss of a piece of life itself.

Russians experience stress (distress), anxiety, and possibly depression in the course of their lives as a result of unsuccessful decisions or unfortunate circumstances. They also experience positive stress called *eustress* (Selye, 1978, p. 74) as a result of successful decisions or fortunate circumstances. The stress reaction is not solely determined by failure. It is determined by situations created by socially interrelated decisions and responses to such situations—the interpretation of an event is the key component in the stress (or any emotional) reaction (Ellis, 1962, pp. 42–43; Folkman *et al.*, 1991, p. 240; Pomeroy and Ellis, 1991). Cognitive evaluations mediate bodily flight or fight responses. Such evaluations may elevate anxiety without the presence of a physical threat. So an event does not have to be life threatening to produce the stress response. Stress involves the polar ends of value, from the severely negative to the extremely positive (Selye, 1978, p. 74).

Stress is an inevitable consequence of life (Selye, 1978, p. xv; McElroy and Townsend, 1989, p. 242). It can be studied in two ways. The first involves studying the stress response itself and its mechanisms. The HVP can yield insights into the cognitive part of the stress response, as will be demonstrated here. The second involves studying what people do to deal with stress. Here and in the next chapter, I discuss the coping mechanisms used to deal with stress by the Russians I met and observed.

2. HVP Analysis

You can demonstrate that Russians felt stress from their predicament using results from the HVP testing. In order to make the testing a little more understandable, I will continue the formal discussion begun in Chapter Seven about the HVP. Since I already discussed the basic form of the test, some of its theoretical underpinnings, and a few of the translation problems, I can now demonstrate the application of the test to Russian subjects. For purposes of this study, I chose four tests drawn from three individuals. The first two individuals were tested during my first trip to Russia. Their results were taken from a small HVP data sample gathered by Andrey at the end of that trip. (Even though an earlier sample collection was attempted by Dmitri, as discussed in Chapter Four, the process was flawed. I could not evaluate these tests because of the incompleteness of the testing.) In addition, I use two tests drawn from a third individual, one during my second trip and one during my third trip to Russia. Even though some minor technical problems occurred, I successfully evaluated the test results of these three Russians.

Note that I do not include tests from my major Russian subjects in 1991, Dmitri, Alisa, Vasili, Sonia, Pavel, Andrey, and Ann. Except for two cases, these individuals never took the HVP test. To include only those individuals who did would have not provided a comprehensive analysis. Instead, I chose a different form of analysis from formal axiology to evaluate the people and events of 1991. This analysis appears in the next chapter.

A. First HVP Case Study

I begin by taking, as my first subject—I call him "Alex" here—the first person in Russia to take and get feedback from the HVP. The HVP- Russian version #2 can be found in my dissertation (Gallopin, 1999, pp. 625–626, 631–632).

First, I include a little background for Alex. Andrey worked with computer programmers. One of them was Alex. Since Alex was thirty years old, I assumed he was one of Andrey's equals (as a programmer) instead of a subordinate. Alex, much like others in Andrey's network, was a graduate student at the University. He was studying phonetics in the department of philology. Alex, along with most of his contemporaries, had been in the military. Russian men serve two years in the military as a matter of official policy. Those who can get into particular institutions of higher education are exempt from service.

I asked Alex if he did anything to relax because he smoked cigarettes, worried that it had become an addiction, and was trying to quit. After I evaluated his test, Andrey explained the results to him. I talked with Alex the following day. He told me that he had had a dream the previous night of smoking a cigarette that stretched to the horizon. As a result of this strange dream, he decided to give up trying to quit, a curious decision, which he did not want to elaborate upon. (I can only guess that Alex interpreted the dream to mean he was destined to smoke for a long time, and he thought that fighting his destiny was not worth it.) Alex did have other outlets such as Oriental mediation and Zen, and he also had tried acupuncture and various hobbies to control his stress.

Although Alex was not shy about talking with me, while informally interviewing him, I noticed that Alex had a circumspect way of answering some questions. When I asked him about the stress in his life, he discussed his different treatments for it but did not discuss his feelings. When I asked him about his work with Andrey, he discussed his work in broad terms but avoided details of how his work related to Andrey. He did openly acknowledge, however, that life in Leningrad was stressful.

Alex took the HVP test on 1 August 1991. Tables 1 and 2 have Alex's rankings of the phrases in the HVP. For Part 1, the instructions call for the respondent to rank the items in terms of their values, and, for Part 2, the instructions ask the respondent to rank items in terms of personal agreement or disagreement, the higher the rank, the more the respondent agrees with the phrase.

I questioned Alex about any possible misunderstandings with the test. Here is a summary of our discussion for Part 1 (world). I asked Alex why he ranked "A madman" in the top half of his answers. He replied that, often in the military, the boys would simulate being crazy (to get a rest). He also believed that artists and musicians are often crazy. I also asked him why he valued "Nonsense" positively (by putting it in the top half). He responded that Zen values "nonsense." I questioned Alex about his relative disvaluation of marriage since he placed "By this ring I thee wed" tenth. He told me that married life troubled him. Finally, I asked Alex if he understood what the phrase "A short circuit" meant since he also ranked it in the top half. (I had problems getting that phrase translated.) His reply showed that he did.

In Part 2, the response that jumped out at me was his ranking of the phrase "I enjoy being myself," which is first in the axiological norm, all the way down at fourteen. Here, the translation, which, back translated, meant "I am satisfied with myself," played a role. Alex explained that, in the Soviet Union, individuals are not expected to be satisfied with themselves. This idea is strong in the culture, has deep roots, and was an intellectual ideal before the Bolshevik Revolution. Since "self-satisfaction" is not the same as "self-enjoyment," this phrasing had to be updated in a later version of the test. See my dissertation for HVP test versions #2 and #3 and the overall test translation and back-translation process (Gallopin, 1999, pp. 625–634).

Obviously this flaw in this early translation of the HVP-PIV makes any results for Part 2 slightly suspect. Other respondents (N=16) using the same version had a more overall, positive evaluation of the phrase ranking it from second to sixteenth with an average ranking of 8.3 (standard deviation = 3.7). Given that the expected ranking of this phrase is "first," the sample suggests a problem.

Also note the extreme over disvaluation of the phrase "The world makes little sense to me," placed all the way at the bottom of his Part 2 rankings. This suggests that Alex was (excessively) confident in his ability to see his place in the world. (A quite low ranking of this item implies that the world makes a lot of sense to Alex.)

TABLE 1: Alex's HVP Response, Part 1

Test Date: 1 August 1991

HVP-PIV [PART 1–WORLD]

Alex's ranking		AXIOLOGICAL NORM
(1)	Love of nature	(2)
(2)	A baby	(1)
(3)	Good food	(6)
(4)	A technical improvement	(9)
(5)	A devoted scientist	(5)
(6)	A mathematical genius	(3)
(7)	Nonsense	(10)
(8)	A madman	(14)
(9)	A short-circuit	(12)
(10)	"By this ring, I thee wed."	(4)
(11)	A fine	(11)
(12)	An assembly line	(8)
(13)	A uniform	(7)
(14)	A rubbish heap	(13)
(15)	Blow up an airplane in flight	(17)
(16)	Burn a heretic at the stake	(16)
(17)	Torture a person in a concentration camp	(18)
(18)	Slavery	(15)

I continue with the evaluation of Alex to show that his Part 1 results (world) did show some stress pattern, but results combining Part 1 and Part 2 results (self) are not completely reliable.

The tests were scored using an algorithm developed by Robert S. Hartman in his *Manual of Interpretation* for the HVP (Hartman, 1973a). For more generalized information about the HVP and its scoring, see John Austin's "The Hartman Value Profile" in *Forms of Value and Valuation*, edited by Rem B. Edwards and John W. Davis (Austin, 1991, pp. 243–289).

Figures 1–4 show the results of Part 1 of Alex's test. The bar graphs are based on numerical results that are scaled qualitatively. (See Oleg's HVP for a different presentation style of results.) Note that the scales of possible qualitative results range from excellent to extremely poor. Here, the

TABLE 2: Alex's HVP Response, Part 2

Test Date: 1 August 1991

HVP-PIV [PART 2–SELF]

Alex's ranking	AXIOLOGICAL NORM
(1) I love the beauty of the world.	(3)
(2) The universe is a remarkably harmonious system.	(9)
(3) I love my work.	(2)
(4) I like my work—it does me good.	(6)
(5) The more I understand my place in the world, the better I get in my work.	(8)
(6) My work brings out the best in me.	(4)
(7) My life is messing up the world.	(16)
(8) My work adds to the beauty and harmony of the world.	(7)
(9) No matter how hard I work, I shall always feel frustrated.	(11)
(10) My working conditions are poor, and ruin my work.	(13)
(11) I feel at home in the world.	(5)
(12) The lack of meaning in the universe disturbs me.	(14)
(13) My work contributes nothing to the world.	(12)
(14) I enjoy being myself.	(1)
(15) I curse the day I was born.	(18)
(16) My work makes me unhappy.	(15)
(17) I hate my work.	(17)
(18) The world makes little sense to me.	(10)

axiological language is used primarily. Indexing different psychological dimensions as well as other personality features is also possible.

As you can see, the results of the HVP testing are potentially quite rich. Alex's scores ranged the gamut of possibilities from excellent scores in "balance" (BQr–quality and BQr–quantity) to extremely poor scores in his total capacity to value in terms of its "quality" (BQa–quality) and in his self valuation (Self Quotient–quality). (See Figure 4.)

Before turning to another example of the application and interpretation of the HVP, I want to summarize the results of Alex's test. Alex showed an overall better orientation to the world than to himself. A gross measurement of statistical correlation with the axiological norm, Rho, shows this (Figure 3). In Part 1 (world), he scored an Rho = 80%. In Part 2 (self), he scored a Rho = 55%. A poor Rho suggests some problem in test design, test administration, or test respondent. The Dim% scores (world and self acceptance) in Figure 1 are an indicator of "fantasy." Much like the L scale of the MMPI, you can use the

Dim% score to measure an individual's "honesty" in test taking. Alex's scores on self and world were both good, showing that he was giving authentic answers to it. Assuming that the test version Alex took was valid, which, as discussed above, we cannot, but assuming it is for the sake of demonstration, the Dim% scores show that we can consider Alex's responses to be reliable.

You may read an axiological profile in terms of its peaks and valleys. Alex's strengths lay in his world valuation with a good Differentiation world score and poor self score (Figure 1). He shows a stronger ability to value in terms of practical situations, very good Dim-E and Int-E scores in self and world (Figure 2). His ability to concentrate on the world (D.I.) is good (Figure 3). He also shows an excellent balance between world and self (BQr) in Figure 4, suggesting an absence of general or "surface" stress. Problems come in his "moral appreciation of the world" (Distortion–world in Figure 1) a score significantly worse than his self judgment in terms of "right and wrong" (Distortion–self).

While Alex firmly believes he understands his role in the system of the world (placing "the world makes little sense to me" last in Part 2), his moral understanding of that world (Distortion, Part 1) is poor. Moral misunderstanding of the world in a society dominated by the Soviet Union's brutal rule for seventy years is not surprising and maybe should be expected, but not all respondents to the Russian HVP indicated moral distortions. You need to consider other factors.

Here the question of cultural differences arises. Can we trust the test to measure moral distortion accurately? You can see the influence of Alex's interests in Zen and other experiences, where things like being crazy or making "no sense" have value. This is the influence of the East, which is strong in Russia.

You can see that Alex also has trouble with axiologically positive items such as "a uniform" and "an assembly line." In Soviet Russia, working and uniformity went hand in hand. The state, represented by uniforms, was the master. The worker worked for the master in the factory. In America, the uniform is worn as status, and the assembly line gives you a job, an income, and less expensive goods. Alex showed his disgust with working for a state by ranking "slavery" below heinous items such as "torture a person in a concentration camp," "blow up an airliner in flight," and "burn a heretic at the stake." Was being "dead" better than being "Red"?

I want to finish the discussion of Alex by pointing out the more psychologically oriented indicators in his test, Int% (Figure 1) and AI% (Figure 3). Int% is a measure of anxiety. AI% is a measure of depression. (Pomeroy *et al.*, 1985). Alex showed poor scores for both (ranging from average to very poor), indicating tension. This manifested itself in chain smoking, an inability to give direct answers to questions, bizarre dreams, and behavior that worried Andrey. (Andrey wanted Alex to take the test because

Figure 1: General Axiological Measures for Alex

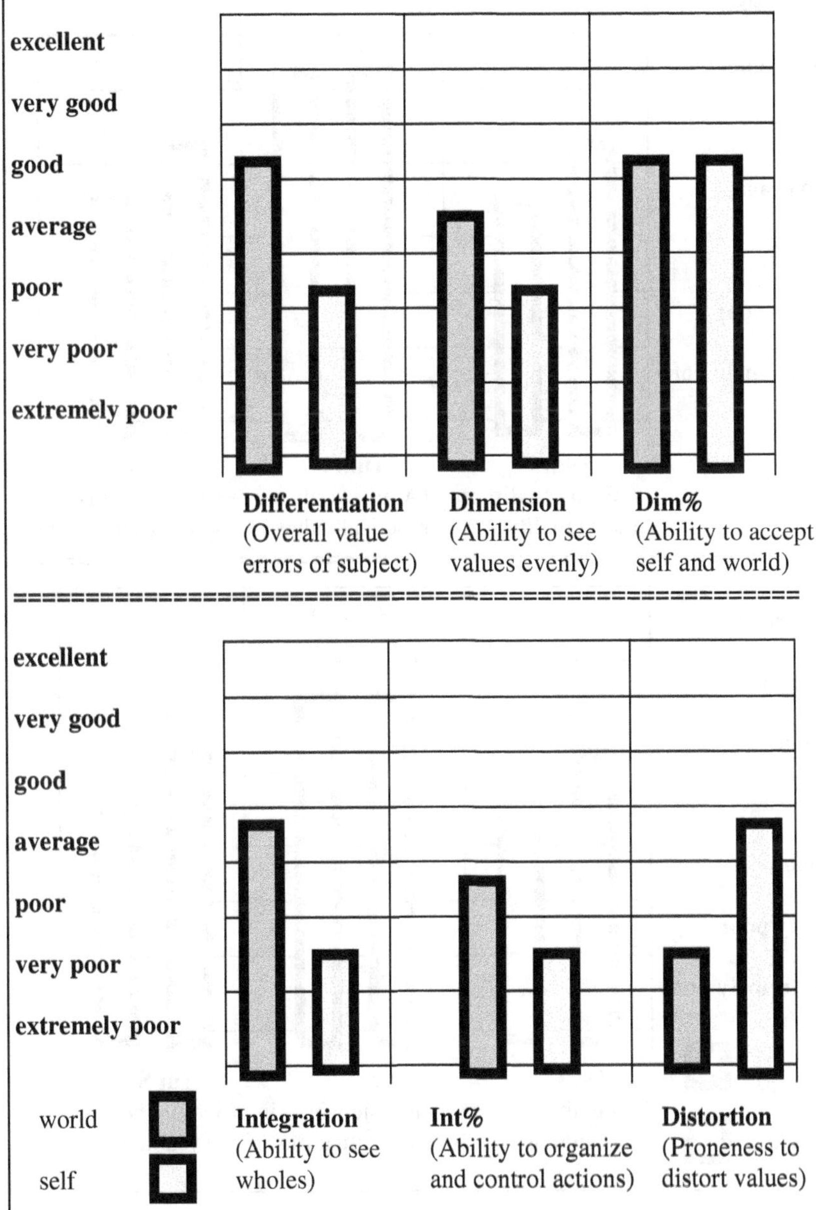

Figure 2: Axiological Measures (Dimensions I, E, S) for Alex

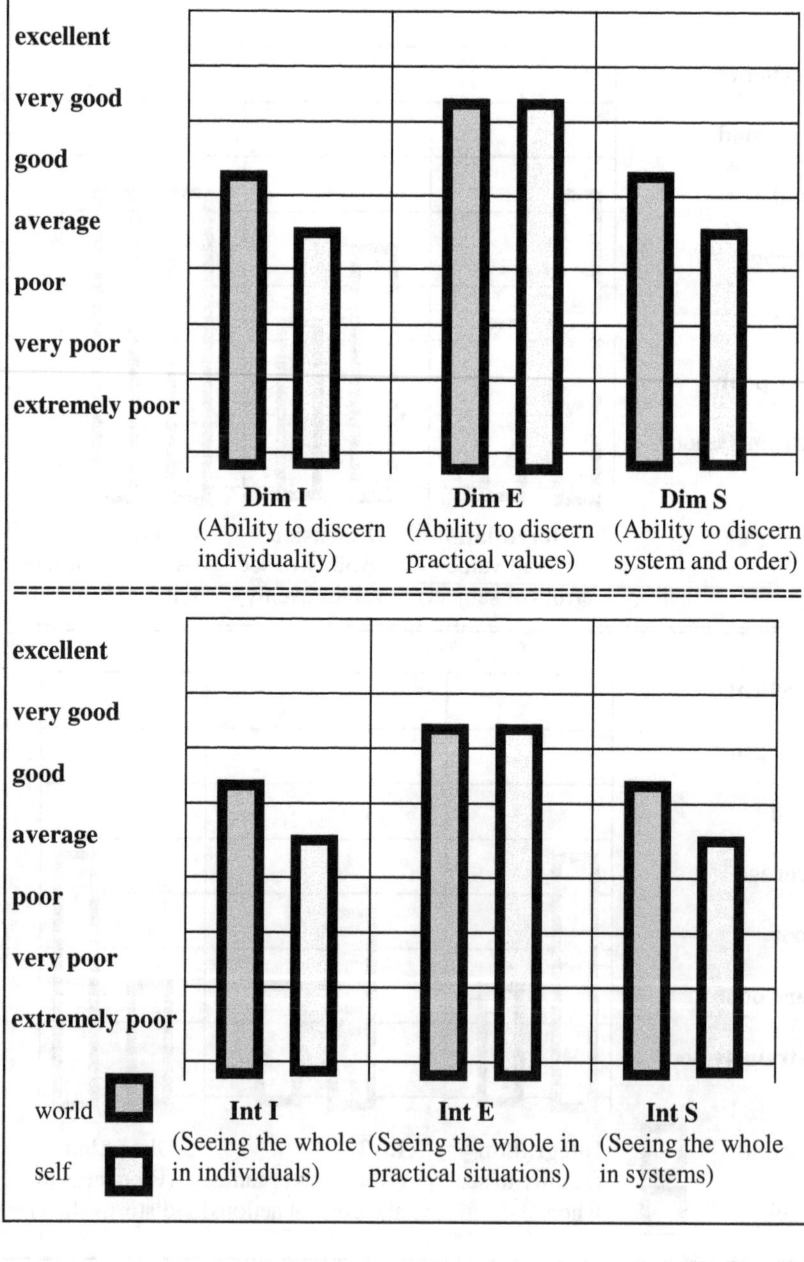

Figure 3: Additional Measures for Alex

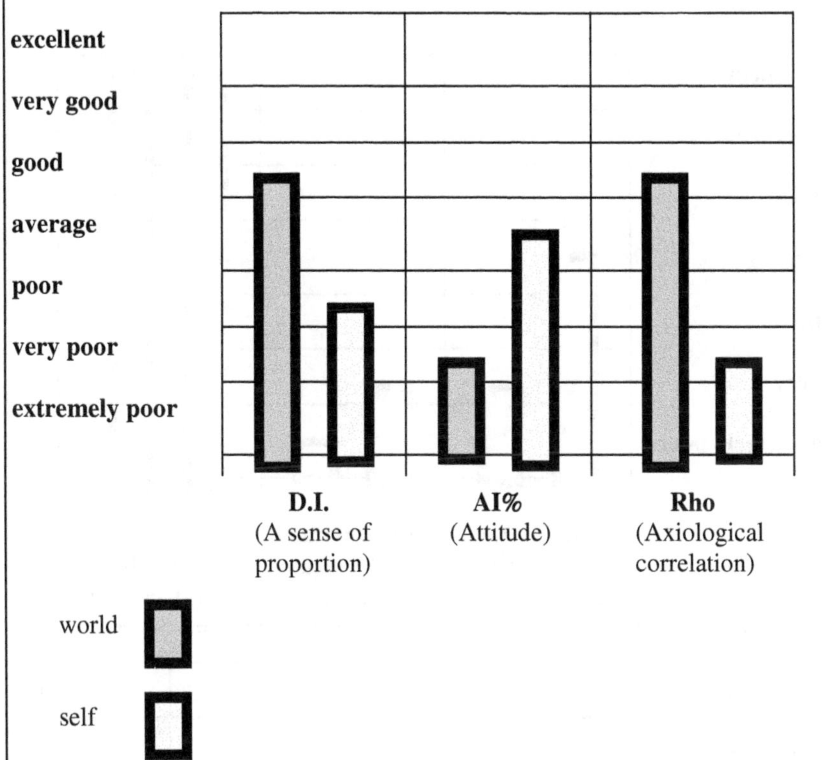

he believed the experience would be beneficial for him.) Alex also indicated "reaction depression" characterized by a very poor AI% for the world. This was an additional sign of anxiety and fear. His AI% for self score showed him to be tentative and timid with regard to his self-attitude. This showed up as a self-effacing nature when I spoke with him.

Alex's overall balance saved him—his general stress level was low (excellent BQr scores). This was probably a result of his different relaxation methods, but the surface calm masked some tensions measured by the test, suggested by Andrey's concern about Alex, and shown by Alex's self-report. A psychologist might say that Alex had psychological difficulties, which he handled with "brilliant defenses."

Alex was suffering but not to the extent that it was debilitating. Andrey's concern with him was not panic, merely a sign of paternalism for a younger colleague. I did not see much of Alex in the following years. Perhaps he dropped out of Andrey's group or finished his schooling at the University and

Figure 4: Combined Summary Indicators for Alex

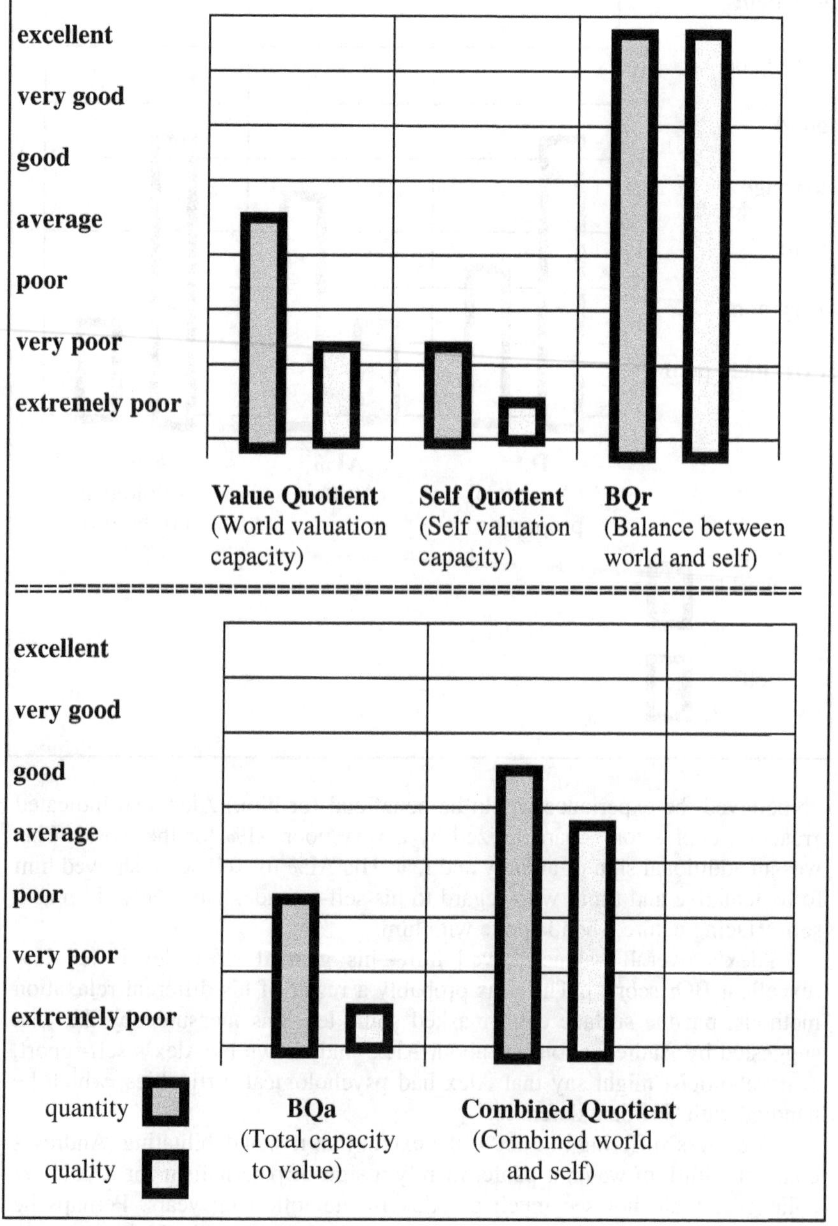

departed. Little was said about him in 1992, and he may have been around but played no role in my network. In 1993, he had left the scene entirely.

B. Second HVP Case Study

For my next case study, Andrey's oldest son, Oleg, is the subject. Oleg, having a working knowledge of English, opted to take the English version of the test. In this respect, he was the exception to those from Andrey's group who took the test in 1991. This turned out to be fortuitous. Even though he could not be considered as part of the Russian sample set for the purposes of Leon Pomeroy's validation, his test results are less questionable than my first demonstrated subject (Alex) because, by avoiding the imperfect Russian translation, Oleg took a test version that was reliable. The limitation here was Oleg's English language competence. I found Oleg's English understandable, so I believe that his test results are also reliable.

I did not interview Oleg during the test process. Andrey administered the test he took. This chain of custody may have introduced bias or misunderstandings of which I am not aware. Even so, I still have more confidence in his results than Alex's.

Tables 3 and 4 show Oleg's responses to the HVP-PIV, English version. Oleg, twenty years of age, was a male, single, student of economics, who had completed his fourth year of Russian college. (In Russia, college starts earlier than in America.) The test date was 2 August 1991.

Before discussing the evaluation of Oleg's results, note that in Part 1 he ranked the phrase "A uniform" at number fourteen. This heavy disvaluation of what is axiologically a (positive) value, along with Alex's disvaluation (he ranked it thirteenth) is suggestive of a cultural difference. Soviet Russia was by no means a popular system in 1991 among many Russians (Satter, 1996, pp. 73–77; Billington, 1992, pp. 28–29). Uniformity was identified with the state. Uniforms were not considered to be signs of status or allegiance to a system, but instead, a sign of control and power. Two test results cannot be conclusive, but they are noteworthy, especially since some of those helping me with the translation of the test brought up the problematic nature of this phrase. Chapter Seven included a discussion of the philosophical assumptions that the HVP-PIV makes and how cultural and national differences may impinge upon its translation to foreign languages. The phrase, "A uniform," is an excellent example of this.

In order to emphasize the HVP-PIV's use in the psychological dimension, I will use a different approach to the evaluation of Oleg's test. I evaluated Alex's test using the standard axiological language and with few psychological terms. Pomeroy evaluated Oleg's test (in September, 1991), and the psychological profile (Table 5) is based on a letter Pomeroy wrote to me.

TABLE 3: Oleg's HVP Response, Part 1

Test Date: 2 August 1991

HVP-PIV [PART 1–WORLD]

	Oleg's ranking	AXIOLOGICAL NORM
(1)	A baby	(1)
(2)	"By this ring, I thee wed."	(4)
(3)	Good food	(6)
(4)	Love of nature	(2)
(5)	A mathematical genius	(3)
(6)	A devoted scientist	(5)
(7)	A technical improvement	(9)
(8)	A short-circuit	(12)
(9)	An assembly line	(8)
(10)	A madman	(14)
(11)	A rubbish heap	(13)
(12)	A fine	(11)
(13)	Nonsense	(10)
(14)	A uniform	(7)
(15)	Slavery	(15)
(16)	Blow up an airplane in flight	(17)
(17)	Burn a heretic at the stake	(16)
(18)	Torture a person in a concentration camp	(18)

Oleg's test results are reliable despite a high fantasy score in Part 1 (world). This is because his fantasy score (DIM%) for Part 2 (self) is not high. A test is rejected if *both* fantasy scores are high, indicating the subject was not being authentic and "intellectualizing" the test according to some external system of valuation. We can say that Oleg accepts himself but not the world, in which he has little faith. For a young person growing up in the Soviet Union after the death of Leonid Brezhnev this is an appropriate response. By the time Brezhnev died, communism as an ideal pattern was bankrupt. All that the Soviets had left was a general sense of relatively good times under Brezhnev. *Perestroika* had not arrived yet, thus the worst secrets were yet to be revealed. In the course of growing into manhood, Oleg would have experienced the growing national realization that the Soviet Union was not the "greatest nation" on the planet, that it had severe problems, and that it had a checkered past. With *glasnost* came the final debate over the moral direction

TABLE 4: Oleg's HVP Response, Part 2

Test date: 2 August 1991

HVP-PIV [PART 2–SELF]

Oleg's ranking	AXIOLOGICAL NORM
(1) "I like my work—it does me good"	(6)
(2) "My work brings out the best in me"	(4)
(3) "I enjoy being myself"	(1)
(4) "The more I understand my place in the world, the better I get in my work"	(8)
(5) "I love my work"	(2)
(6) "I feel at home in the world"	(5)
(7) "My work adds to the beauty and harmony of the world"	(7)
(8) "I love the beauty of the world"	(3)
(9) "The universe is a remarkably harmonious system"	(9)
(10) "No matter how hard I work, I shall always feel frustrated"	(11)
(11) "My life is messing up the world"	(16)
(12) "The lack of meaning in the universe disturbs me"	(14)
(13) "My work contributes nothing to the world"	(12)
(14) "The world makes little sense to me"	(10)
(15) "My working conditions are poor, and ruin my work"	(13)
(16) "My work makes me unhappy"	(15)
(17) "I hate my work"	(17)
(18) "I curse the day I was born"	(18)

of the Soviet Union, a cacophony of voices pulling in different directions. Since he had no external moral compass, a father (Andrey) who had joined the party for the sake of expediency (personal communication from Russian contact Ann, 1991), and an uncertain future, I am not surprised that Oleg, who also had high abilities to value (very good RHO and DIF scores), would lose faith in the world.

Remarkably, the test picks up an "Achilles heel" of an otherwise well adjusted youth. Oleg was prone to "reactive depression" characterized by a certain wariness to the world (AI%-1). He took the HVP during the summer. Oleg had a strong reaction, according to his father, to light variations in the fall and winter, when long periods of darkness would follow shorter and more dully lit days. This physical sensitivity (a variant of seasonal affective disorder) would be compounded by Oleg's particular value structure. Thus his depression sensitivity would exaggerate the effects of darker days. I observed

Oleg react negatively to some gloomy days in October. His personality showed remarkable changes. He was much less outgoing and easygoing, acquiring an "underground man" personality (the type Fyodor Dostoyevsky described so well in his *Notes from the Underground*), difficult to be around, and bordering on the pathologically hostile. That October, some of his life circumstances had temporarily changed for the worse. Normally, he handled temporary set backs in stride. Without the irritation of those gloomy days, Oleg's very good sensitivity to values would have mitigated his tendency to become depressed. Once winter set in (or the threat of its arrival), his depression blossomed to its full potential. Where before he may have been only a bit hesitant toward the world, he instead became suspicious and angry. This may have happened because once winter arrived his "fantasy" about the world (DIM%-1) may have melted away. Measuring this by having Oleg take the HVP test during the time of his troubles would have been interesting. This was not possible because, during these periods, he was quite taciturn.

C. Third HVP Case Study

Glasha took the HVP twice, once in 1992, during the seminar Pomeroy and I gave about the HVP, and once in 1993, helping Yuri (Andrey's student assistant) and me test software that would be used in the upcoming CSAM 93 Congress. The difference between the two tests was startling. I present them here as a testament to how ongoing social changes could affect an individual in the former Soviet Union.

In 1992, when I first met Glasha, she was thirty-nine and had turned forty by the time I collaborated with her in 1993. She was married to her second husband, a colonel in the Red Army, and had a son (seven years old) by her previous marriage. Her second husband had married her under the condition that he not be responsible for her son. He already had several children by his previous marriages and was not interested in raising another one. Desperate for financial support, Glasha had agreed to this and left her son in her home town of Dnipropetrovsk, Ukraine, to be raised by her parents. Glasha spent her time shuttling between St. Petersburg and Dnipropetrovsk. Her career was in St Petersburg, but half her family was in Dnipropetrovsk.

If her life was not difficult enough, Glasha faced more problems in 1993. Due to a freeze in military wages caused by an economic downturn in 1993, Glasha's husband was unable to provide Glasha with the kind of financial assistance he had once provided her. Glasha meanwhile was making the difficult transition from graduate student to full time professional. She had a fledgling career in television journalism but was only making enough at the time to, in her words, "pay for dinner." She had not yet broken into the "inner circles" where people were paid well. Glasha also had to finish her graduate degree and was finding it difficult to do so. (This involved politics, which included struggling with Andrey, who sat on her thesis committee.)

Table 5: HVP-PIV SUBSCALE	OLEG	QUALITATIVE
RHO-1 WORLD VALUES	.87	VERY GOOD
RHO-2 SELF VALUES	.86	VERY GOOD
DIF-1 WORLD SENSITIVITY	36.0	VERY GOOD
DIF-2 SELF SENSITIVITY	38.0	VERY GOOD
DIM%-1 FAITH IN WORLD	58.0	VERY POOR *
DIM%-2 FAITH IN SELF	18.0	VERY GOOD
INT%-1 REACTIVE ANXIETY	31.0	LOW
INT%-2 EXISTENTIAL ANXIETY	37.0	SOME
AI%-1 REACTIVE DEPRESSION	67.0	HIGH **
AI%-2 EXISTENTIAL DEPRESSION	50.0	NONE
DI-1 CONCENTRATION: WORLD	13.0	AVERAGE
DI-2 CONCENTRATION: SELF	10.0	GOOD
BQR GENERAL STRESS LEVEL	0.86	LOW
DIMI-1 PEOPLE SKILLS	7 (-3)	CLEAR (LIKES)
DIME-1 PRACTICAL/SOCIAL SKILLS	10 (-2)	CLEAR (LIKES)
DIMS-1 DEALING WITH AUTHORITY SKILLS	19 (-7)	AVG. (NEUTRAL)
DIMI-2 SELF ESTEEM INDEX	8 (-2)	CLEAR (LIKES)
DIME-2 WORK WORLD ADAPTATIONS	15 (+7)	AVG.(OVERVALUES)
DIMS-2 STRENGTH OF INNER AUTHORITY	15 (-5)	AVG. (NEUTRAL)
DIS-1 MORAL DISTORTIONS: WORLD	2	SOME
DIS-2 MORAL DISTORTIONS: SELF	0	NONE
KNOW WORLD INTELLIGENCE		AV
KNOW SELF INTELLIGENCE		GOOD+

* Indicates fantasy; ** Hesitant; timid; reluctant

To top things off, Glasha and her husband were in the middle of moving from their rooms in a communal flat near the city center to an apartment in one of the suburbs on the outskirts of the city. Glasha was going to miss the kind of life afforded to those fortunate enough to live in proximity to the shopping and culture available in downtown St. Petersburg. The move had opened up some opportunities to Glasha, who had become involved in the new semi-legal (gray) housing market. When I started working with her in 1993, she already had several offers for her former room in the communal flat. She was considering selling it instead of returning it to the state-run housing pool.

Glasha possessed strong internal resources. She was bright, and spoke three languages—Russian, Ukrainian, and English. She was actively assisting Pomeroy and me with our research. She was energetic and had an entrepreneurial spirit. She also had many friends, some of them affluent like Nicholas (see Chapter Two).

I did not interview Glasha at the time she took either of the two tests, but I did get some general feedback from Glasha about the HVP and have incorporated that in my analysis. Also, for purposes of my analysis, I compare the two tests side by side. She took the first test on 3 September 1992 and the second test on 12 July 1993. Table 6 shows Glasha's rankings for Part 1 of the first test. Table 7 shows Glasha's rankings for Part 1 of the second test.

The first thing we notice when comparing these two results is the unusual ranking of "A madman" in the first position on the second test. A discussion of this will follow shortly. Notice also that "A technical improvement" has moved up from fifth position to second. The next three phrases, formerly ranked one to three, have been pushed down but retain their original order. This is crucial since it shows that Glasha's second test has retained some of the features of the first. A complete reordering of every phrase would not be typical of a retest of the same subject, but shifting around a few phrases while maintaining the order in the rest is a reasonable expectation. In this case, ten phrases retain their relative original positions, four are shifted up in the ranking ("A madman," "A technical improvement," "Nonsense," and "Burn a heretic at the stake") and four down ("A mathematical genius," "'By this ring I thee wed'," "A uniform," and "A rubbish heap").

What could have caused this dramatic shift? The first clue comes from a story Glasha told me concerning data collection she had been doing for Pomeroy in 1992. Part of Pomeroy's request was that Glasha collect some data from villages. At one of these villages, Glasha had had her data confiscated by a local official. The incident had shaken Glasha, and she apologized for not having data from the villages for us. I told her not to worry about it and that I was glad she was okay. I also urged her not to try to collect data in such a place again. Even though Glasha had been confident she could do so, we had been unwise to ask her. Her collection of data from university students had been much more successful.

Glasha brought back one anecdote from her rural experience that deeply impressed her. One villager (not from the same village where the confiscation had taken place) gave a strange answer to the test, the highlight of which was that he had ranked the phrase "Burn a heretic at the stake" at the top. Glasha questioned the man about this, and he replied that "heretics," which to him meant "witches," were dangerous to the village, and eliminating them was good. Glasha had gotten into an argument with the man over this. When I heard this, I told Glasha that, while most people would agree with her that this particular response was pretty bizarre, giving unusual answers to the test was

TABLE 6: Glasha's HVP Response, Part 1, test 1

Test Date: 3 September 1992

HVP-PIV [PART 1–WORLD]

Glasha's ranking		AXIOLOGICAL NORM
(1)	A baby	(1)
(2)	Love of nature	(2)
(3)	A devoted scientist	(5)
(4)	A mathematical genius	(3)
(5)	A technical improvement	(9)
(6)	"By this ring, I thee wed."	(4)
(7)	Good food	(6)
(8)	A uniform	(7)
(9)	An assembly line	(8)
(10)	A rubbish heap	(13)
(11)	A fine	(11)
(12)	Slavery	(15)
(13)	Nonsense	(10)
(14)	A short-circuit	(12)
(15)	A madman	(14)
(16)	Torture a person in a concentration camp	(18)
(17)	Blow up an airplane in flight	(17)
(18)	Burn a heretic at the stake	(16)

not forbidden. If that was how the man felt, then so be it. The test was designed to handle any ordering of the phrases.

From speaking with other Russians (Nicholas in particular), I had gathered that things like nonsense and madness were not automatically dismissed by Russians as being necessarily bad (as it might be by Americans). Many Russians not only associated madness with genius but considered it to be the source of genius.

At the time (summer, 1993), a tense political atmosphere existed in Russia. This was coupled with a sense that Russia needed a strong leader of great insight to lead it out of its morass; a political genius perhaps could do the job. Glasha could have made the association between madman and genius, and our discussion about bizarre answers to the test may have given her a "green light" to answer the test in this superficially bizarre manner. Note also that

TABLE 7: Glasha's HVP Response, Part 1, test 2

Test Date: 12 July 1993

HVP-PIV [PART 1–WORLD]

Glasha's ranking		AXIOLOGICAL NORM
(1)	A madman	(14)
(2)	A technical improvement	(9)
(3)	A baby	(1)
(4)	Love of nature	(2)
(5)	A devoted scientist	(5)
(6)	Good food	(6)
(7)	Nonsense	(10)
(8)	An assembly line	(8)
(9)	A mathematical genius	(3)
(10)	"By this ring, I thee wed."	(4)
(11)	A uniform	(7)
(12)	A fine	(11)
(13)	Slavery	(15)
(14)	A rubbish heap	(13)
(15)	A short-circuit	(12)
(16)	Burn a heretic at the stake	(16)
(17)	Torture a person in a concentration camp	(18)
(18)	Blow up an airplane in flight	(17)

"Nonsense," ranked thirteenth in the first test, has moved up to seventh in the second.

Other more mundane shifts took place as well. Glasha dropped her ranking of marriage ("By this ring I thee wed") by four places. Glasha at the time was having marriage difficulties. So this change makes sense. The shift of "A technical improvement" to second was consistent with the national emphasis on modernization and the growing national sense that Russia was behind the West technologically.

Taking a look at Part 2 of both tests (Tables 8 and 9), we see a fairly similar pattern. While ten phrases have kept their relative order, two have been shifted downward, and six have been moved up in the ranking. Though not as striking as the changes in Part 1, significant changes are here. Note that the phrases "My work brings out the best in me" and "The more I understand my place in the world, the better I get in my work" have been ranked significantly higher, meaning that Glasha agrees with them more. Note also

TABLE 8: Glasha's HVP Response, Part 2, test 1

Test Date: 3 September 1992

HVP-PIV [PART 2–SELF]

Glasha's ranking		AXIOLOGICAL NORM
(1)	"The universe is a remarkably harmonious system"	(9)
(2)	"I love the beauty of the world"	(3)
(3)	"I enjoy being myself"	(1)
(4)	"I feel at home in the world"	(5)
(5)	"I love my work"	(2)
(6)	"My work adds to the beauty and harmony of the world"	(7)
(7)	"My work brings out the best in me"	(4)
(8)	"I like my work—it does me good"	(6)
(9)	"The more I understand my place in the world, the better I get in my work"	(8)
(10)	"My working conditions are poor, and ruin my work"	(13)
(11)	"My work makes me unhappy"	(15)
(12)	"My life is messing up the world"	(16)
(13)	"My work contributes nothing to the world"	(12)
(14)	"The lack of meaning in the universe disturbs me"	(14)
(15)	"No matter how hard I work, I shall always feel frustrated"	(11)
(16)	"I hate my work"	(17)
(17)	"The world makes little sense to me"	(10)
(18)	"I curse the day I was born"	(18)

that she ranked the phrase "My work makes me unhappy" the lowest, meaning she strongly disagrees with it. "My work makes me unhappy" is axiologically similar to "Slavery" in Part 1. This suggests that Glasha strongly rejects some kind of interal slavery. The processed results show this more clearly.

Figures 5 and 6 contain general qualitative world and self scores for Glasha from both tests. Glasha's overall scores suffered in the 1993 test (Figure 6), but a couple of scores improved. The Dimension and Dim% scores for self both improved significantly. On the first test, we cannot trust Glasha's self-scores because her Dim%–self score (self-acceptance) is poor, which indicates that Glasha was intellectualizing when it came to judgments about herself. The improved Dimension–self score means that Glasha could see values associated with her internal world more evenly in 1993 than she could

TABLE 9: Glasha's HVP Response, Part 2, test 2

Test Date: 12 July 1993

HVP-PIV [PART 2–SELF]

Glasha's ranking	AXIOLOGICAL NORM
(1) "I love the beauty of the world"	(3)
(2) "My work brings out the best in me"	(4)
(3) "The more I understand my place in the world, the better I get in my work"	(8)
(4) "The universe is a remarkably harmonious system"	(9)
(5) "My work adds to the beauty and harmony of the world"	(7)
(6) "I enjoy being myself"	(1)
(7) "I feel at home in the world"	(5)
(8) "The lack of meaning in the universe disturbs me"	(14)
(9) "My life is messing up the world"	(16)
(10) "I love my work"	(2)
(11) "I like my work—it does me good"	(6)
(12) "My working conditions are poor, and ruin my work"	(13)
(13) "My work contributes nothing to the world"	(12)
(14) "No matter how hard I work, I shall always feel frustrated"	(11)
(15) "I hate my work"	(17)
(16) "I curse the day I was born"	(18)
(17) "The world makes little sense to me"	(10)
(18) "My work makes me unhappy"	(15)

in 1992, and the improved Dim%–self score means that Glasha saw herself more realistically.

Glasha's ability to judge the world without errors, ability to see external values evenly, ability to see the world as a whole, and ability to organize and control her actions in the world all diminished. Her proneness to distort values about the world increased. Only her *acceptance* of the world stayed the same. This pattern was overtly troubling and suggested Glasha was headed for trouble, but you cannot assess the tests looking at only some of the scores.

What these summary scores suggest is that in 1993 Glasha was experiencing some kind of transition. The transition involved a turn away from the world toward the self. Glasha was giving up external moral clarity (perhaps temporarily) in an effort to see herself, her internal values, more clearly. The first test shows that in 1992 Glasha was not realistic and idealized herself.

Figures 7 and 8 contain Glasha's scores across the three value dimensions, I (intrinsic), E (extrinsic), and S (systemic). Figure 7 is from the 1992 test and Figure 8 from the 1993 test. For the world, Glasha's Dimension (Dim) and Integration (Int) scores reveal an emerging pattern that is oriented toward the practical, given by the better extrinsic scores (Dim-E and Int-E) relative to Dim-I, Int-I, Dim-S, and Int-S, a pattern that becomes prominent in the 1993 test. This implies that in 1993 Glasha was looking at the world in terms of material, concrete, and functional value with a focus on class groupings and in a comparative way. She was doing so in her ability to discern practical values (Dim-E) and her ability to see the relevant in complex practical situations (Int-E). (In axiological parlance, "seeing the relevant in the complex" means seeing the situation as a whole.)

For herself, Glasha increased focus on her uniqueness as a person. In the 1992 test, Glasha's self scores were good but based on fantasy (the high Dim%). The 1993 scores show Glasha focused on her true strengths and limitations and on her self-esteem (Dim-I, Int-I). She was more aware of who she was, but she had trouble with inner authority (Dim-S) and knowing her role in the world (Dim-E). This could point to a discipline problem and a general dissatisfaction with her career, which, though hectic and exciting for her, was not rewarding her with adequate compensation. With her many duties as wife, mother, student, and professional, Glasha was being pulled in too many directions and could be distracted at times.

Additional scores (Figures 9 and 10) show more about Glasha's psychological states at the time of each test. The D.I. scores measure how well Glasha can focus on the appropriate value dimension for a given situation. In 1992, Glasha could focus on external situations with a very good sense of proportion; a better balance among her three value dimensions existed. In 1993, this had changed. Glasha fixated on extrinsic values at the expense of the other two dimensions and could only see the world for its practical value. This came out in several ways when I knew Glasha. In 1992, Glasha focused on the academic. In 1993, she appeared preoccupied with time and how much things cost. She loved to discuss for how much she might be able to sell her communal apartment room, often complained about her husband's diminished financial strength, and, at one point, wanted to know if my wife and I might want to buy a child (a young boy of four).

This was one of the last times I talked to Glasha, and her proposal stunned me. I quickly dismissed the idea with a flat refusal, but I wondered why she even thought of asking me. Part of the reason probably had to do with the fact that my wife and I did not have any children. Still, the proposal left me feeling that Glasha did not have a sense of what was decent. (Glasha probably thought that she was doing us a favor because a married couple not having any children was not decent, this attitude being more common in Russia than America.) Boris Yeltsin eventually addressed the disturbing and

Figure 5: General Axiological Measures for Glasha, test 1

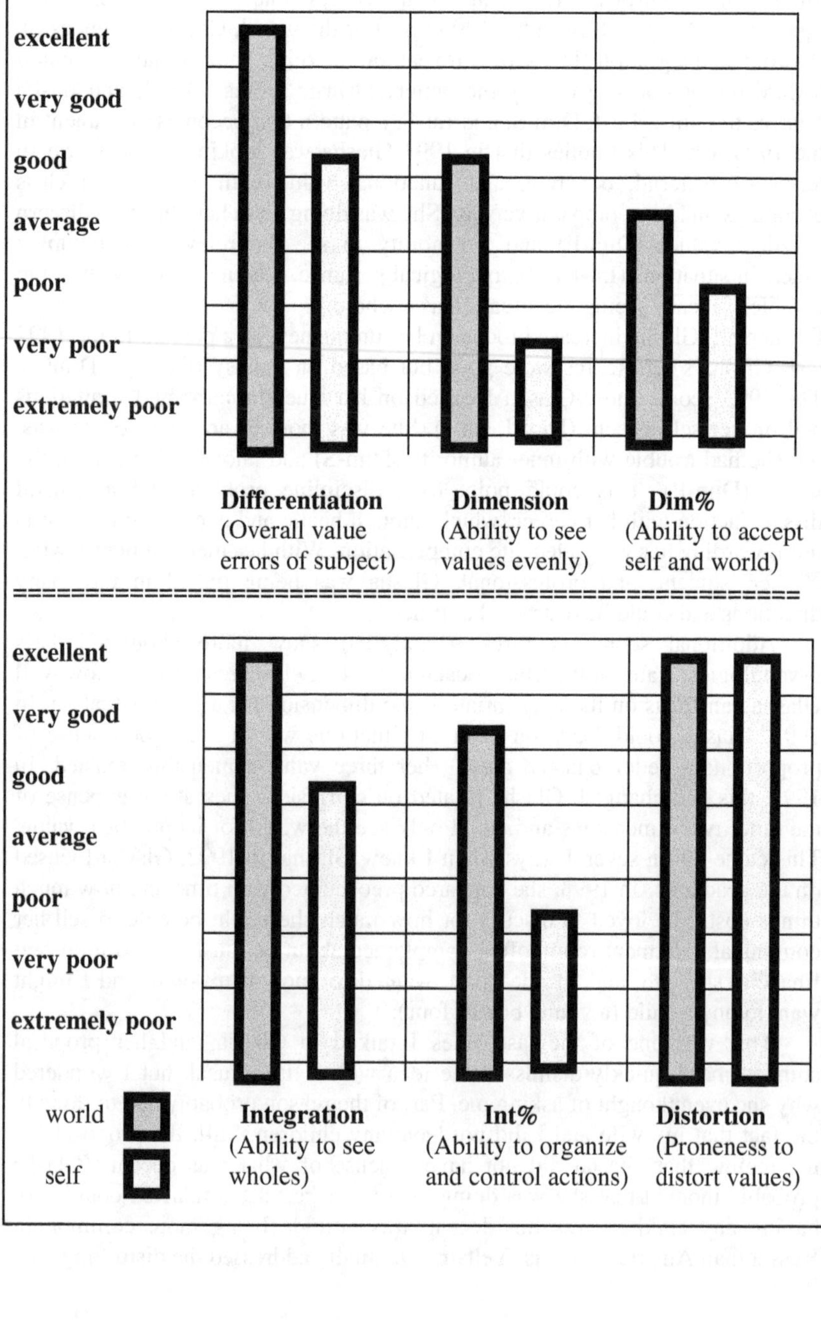

Figure 6: General Axiological Measures for Glasha, test 2

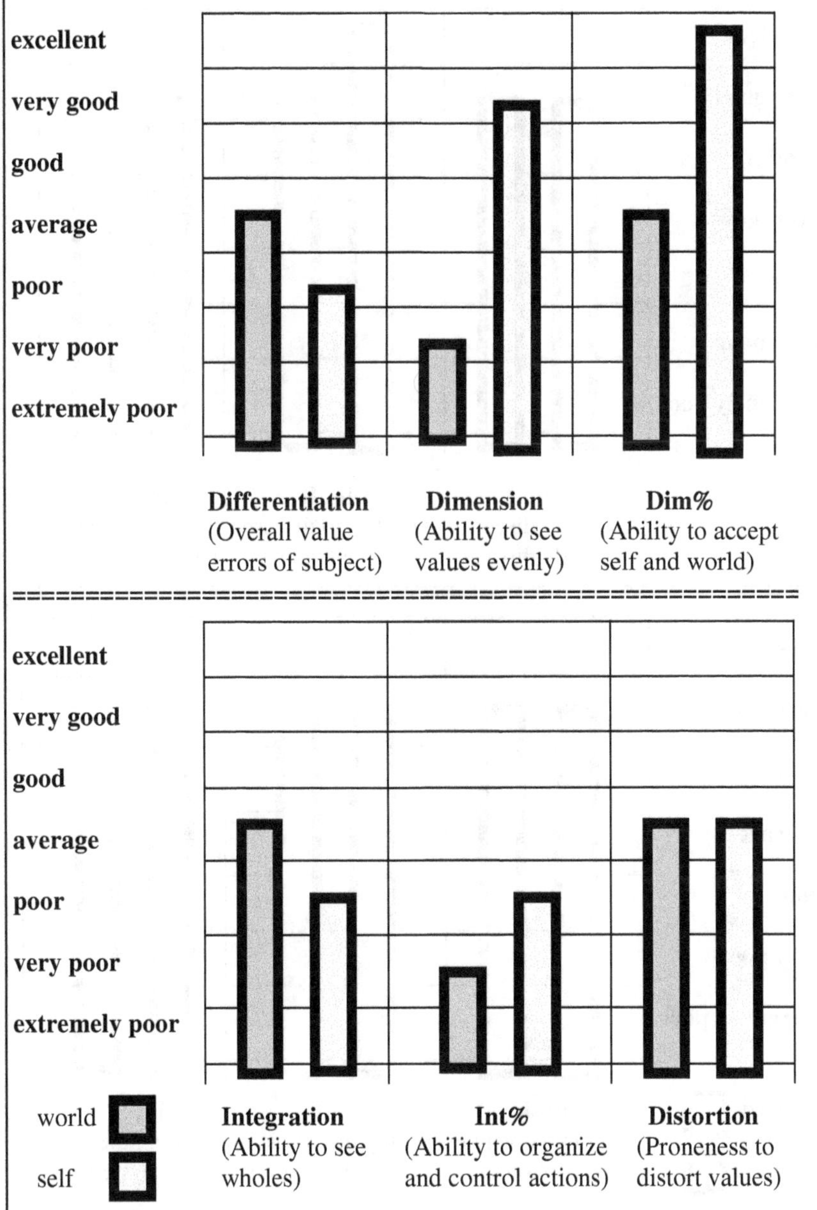

Figure 7: Axiological Measures (Dimensions I, E, S) for Glasha, test 1

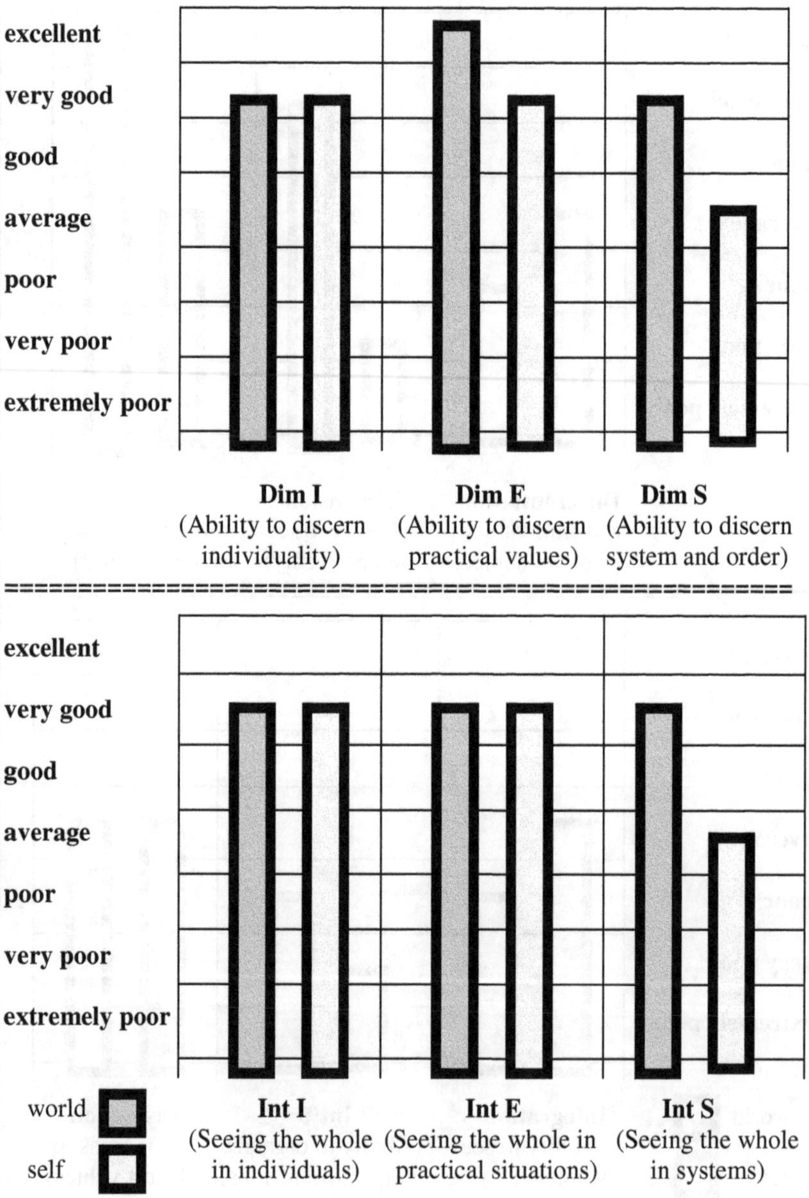

Figure 8: Axiological Measures (Dimensions I, E, S) for Glasha, test 2

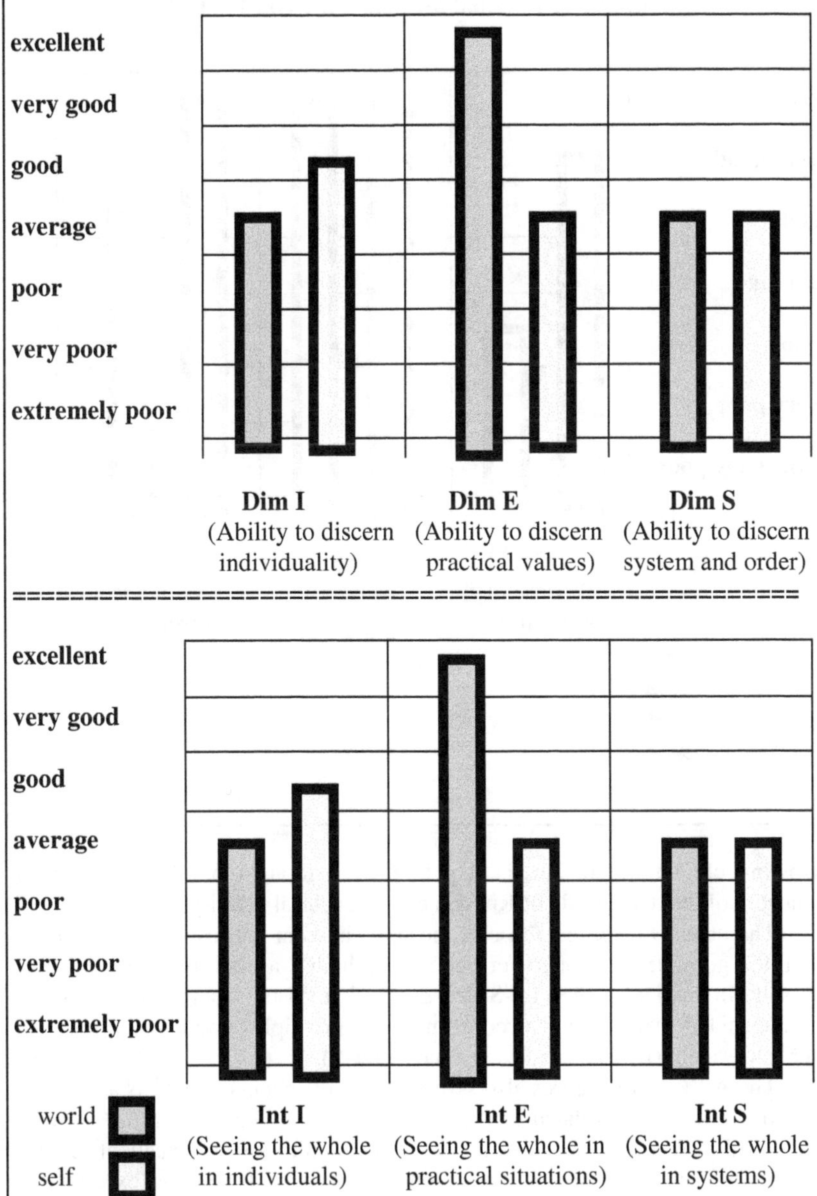

Figure 9: Additional Measures for Glasha, test 1

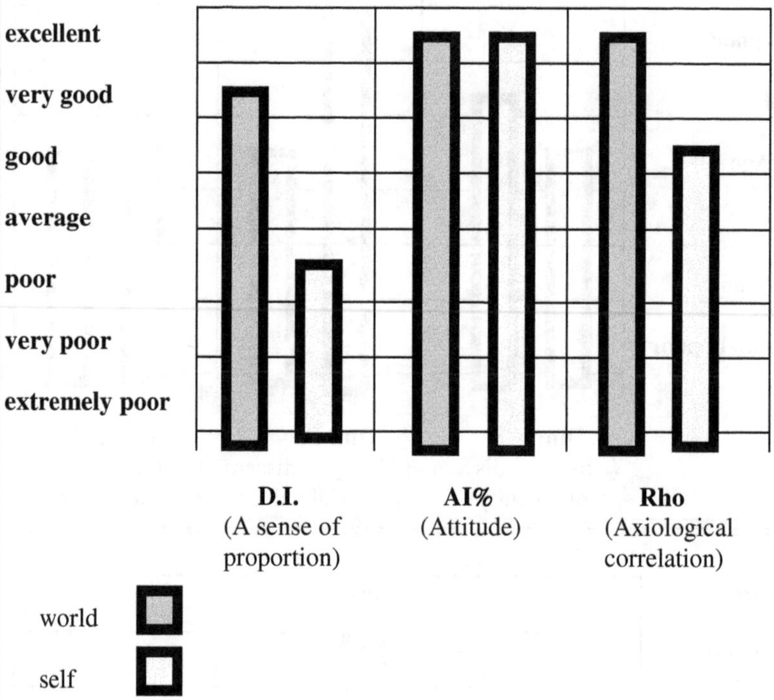

growing child trade in Russia. Up to then, I thought of Glasha as being innocent of the darker side of Russian entrepreneurial activity.

The other D.I. scores, those of the self, show an improvement from 1992 to 1993, going from poor to very good. Glasha has a more balanced sense of herself. In particular, her Int-S score, which measures her ability to solve problems and make decisions concerning her principles, improved *relative* to her self-esteem (Int-I) and role awareness (Int-E).

The A.I%–world scores also showed dramatic changes. AI% is a measure of attitude and is correlated to depression. In 1993, Glasha's attitude toward the world took a dramatic turn for the worse (sinking from excellent to very poor) while her attitude toward herself remained fairly steady (excellent to very good). AI%–world can measure "reactive" depression, which is depression about external conditions. Glasha was feeling quite low about her objective situation in 1993. Her lack of depression about herself was keeping her afloat.

Figure 10: Additional Measures for Glasha, test 2

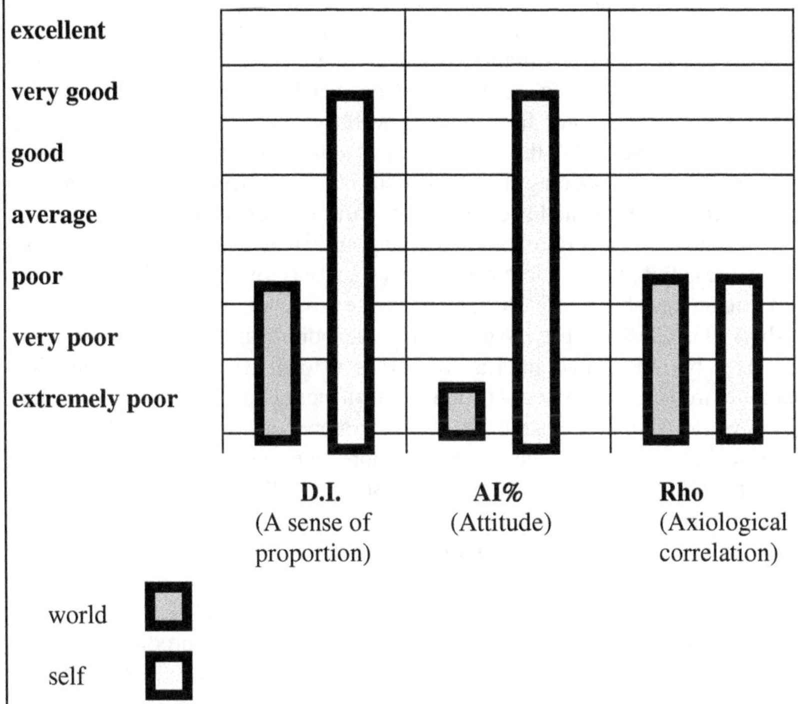

Turning to the final set of scores, the summary scores shown in Figures 11 and 12, we can get an overall measure of the changes in Glasha's capacity to value. Note that the self and world scores are treated separately and combined to yield a pair of indicators called quantity and quality (or harmony). The quantity score measures Glasha's depth of value vision, how much she can see, while the quality score measures the clarity of Glasha's value vision, how well she can see what she sees.

In 1992, Glasha could see much of the world in terms of its values, and she could see what she saw very well, but she could not see as much about herself and could not see that very well. Overall, Glasha could see a lot in terms of values (BQa–quantity was very good) but had more trouble seeing it well. Relative to 1993, Glasha lacked balance (or maturity) between her world view and self view (BQr). This tended to weaken her combined scores.

In 1993, Glasha suffered in her capacity to value the world and herself quantitatively and qualitatively, but the balance between her capacity to value the world and herself was excellent. This pulled up her combined scores to the point where Glasha had gained in her capacity to value harmoniously (good versus average). Glasha had matured in her ability to value from average in 1992 to good in 1993 (not shown on the figures).

Glasha had matured, but she had done so in an unusual way that had much to do with the circumstances of her life over the two years in question. Glasha had gone from a situation that was relatively comfortable—in 1992, the deteriorating economic situation had not yet hit many Russians, and the Russian military was noted for providing well for its officers—to one that was financially perilous. At the same time, new but morally questionable opportunities were opening up in Russia. Glasha faced an array of life decisions that accompanied such things as starting a new career, maintaining a difficult marriage, raising a son, and changing her place of residence. Going through these things in a stable prosperous society is tough enough, but having to do it in an unstable impoverished one is even tougher.

In 1993, Glasha must have felt that the bottom had dropped out from under her, but she found internal resources to deal with the situation. She became extremely pragmatic—to the point of being callous to people in the outside world—but at the same time became more sensitive to herself. Glasha improved her self-acceptance. This was more important since self-esteem is based on a foundation of self-acceptance (Branden, 1994, pp. 90–94).

3. Concluding Remarks

This chapter has examined three respondents using the HVP. Because the amount of analytical material this technique is capable of producing would make this book too cumbersome, my goal here has not been to produce an exhaustive survey of my Russian respondents. I collected far more material than is shown here. Instead, the goal has been to produce several in-depth studies of a few individuals and their struggles to cope with a changing environment. The point is to provide examples of what I did with the HVP in the field.

My subjects had differing levels of success. Alex appeared destined to play a game of catch up in life. Glasha and Oleg both showed great potential but faced major obstacles.

The HVP tests brought out highly detailed emotional and cognitive data but could not provide concrete data to accompany them. By combining my observations, the respondents' comments about themselves, and the tests (when results were available), I found it possible to flesh out the test results and seek corroboration and explication in the lives of the respondents. This worked best for the limited longitudinal testing I conducted with Glasha.

I believe a picture emerges from the results of these three respondents that complements the analytic results that Chapter Nine contains. The nature and pace of change in Russia, involving currents from the West, brought stress to my subjects, which they handled in a variety of ways. In Chapters Two

Figure 11: Combined Summary Indicators for Glasha, test 1

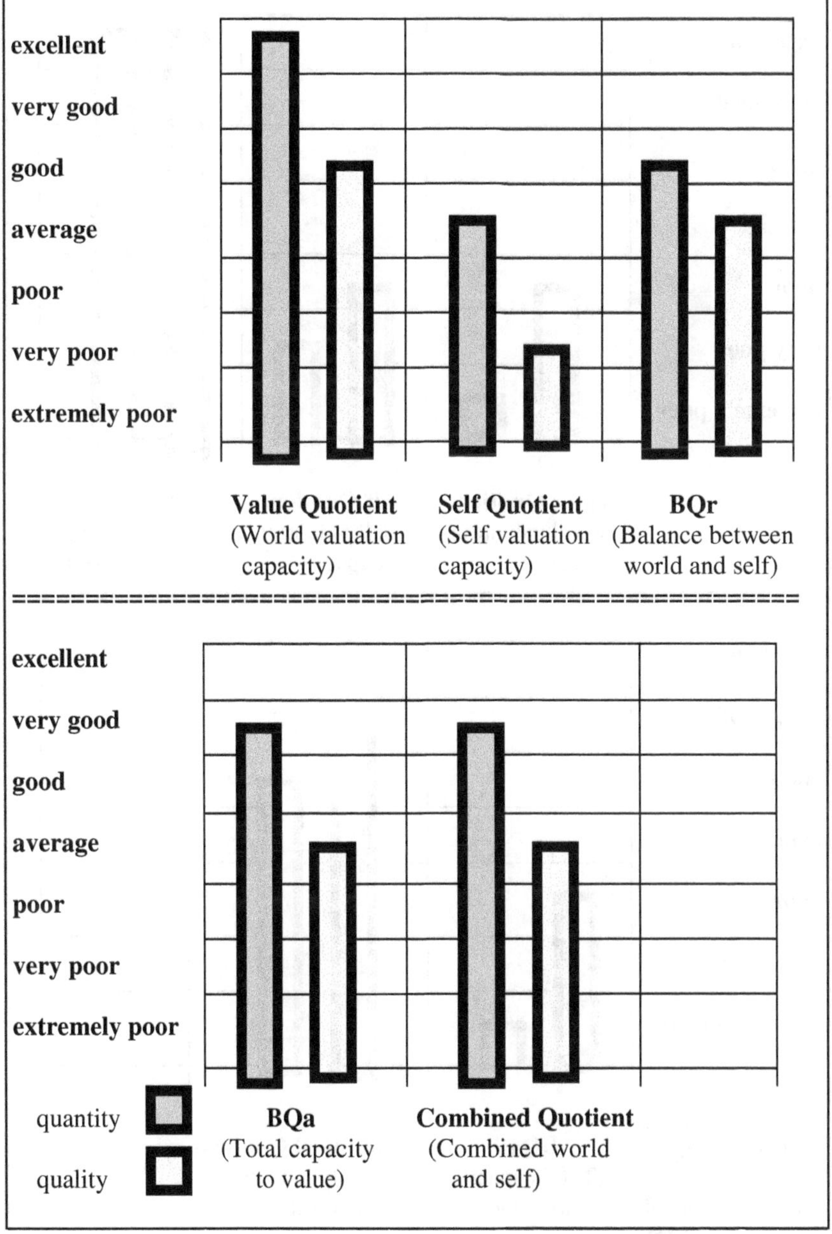

Figure 12: Combined Summary Indicators for Glasha, test 2

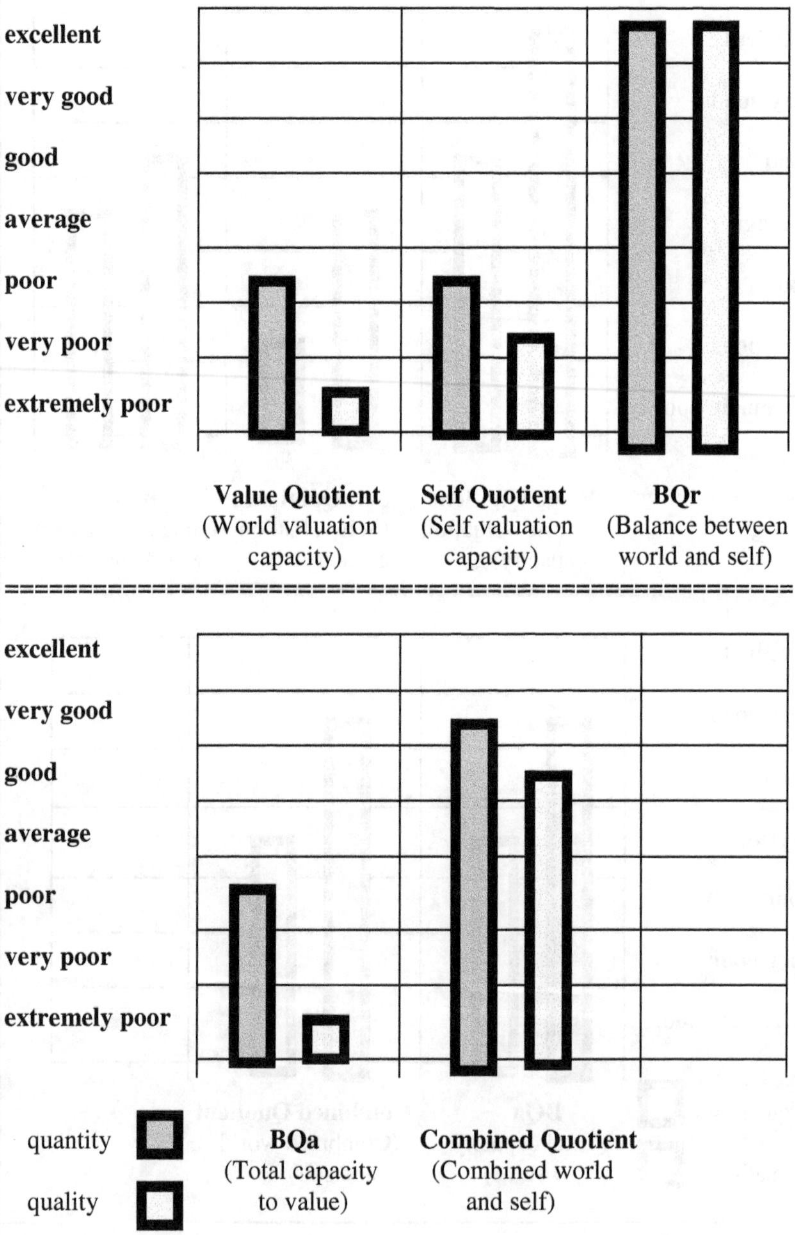

through Six, we see examples of this. We see Russians and other Soviets coping with a variety of difficult life conditions, which include poor health and sanitation, some kinds of shortages, and a cumbersome economic system that is prone to breakdowns and nagging inconveniences. Chapter Nine analyzes the values driving the coping mechanisms.

Chapters Two through Six contain selected results of ethnographic participant-observation that highlight the Russians' use of *blat* to organize their lives. Chapter Nine shows how extensive use of social contacts and the manipulation of the networks created by these contacts allowed Russians to cope with a difficult environment.

In this chapter, I focused on the individuals involved with such activity, their stories, and a glimpse of how their minds work, including a mother's struggle to make ends meet using her wits as well as state resources, a computer programmer's struggle with the pressures associated with life in a troubled society, and the son of a "workaholic" professor, who suffered from a lack of moral direction, manifested by an unusual psycho-biological disorder. Their personalities are self-controlled on the surface. Glasha went from being tense in 1992 to more calm in 1993 (shown by her BQr scores), and they are all depressed about the world. Glasha in 1992 was not depressed about the world but became so in 1993. Oleg's depression about external conditions has to be qualified since he had a high fantasy score about the world (see Table 11, Dim%-1). Also, Oleg's surface calm would be periodically interrupted by his struggle with seasonal affective disorder.

Stress plagued all the respondents. Each had different ways of coping with it. Glasha got busy with her career and took the time to make the long journey to visit her son and parents in Dnipropetrovsk, a rail journey of several hundred kilometers. Alex had his cigarettes and Zen meditation. Oleg probably had the most difficulties controlling his stress. I did observe one outlet—he enjoyed playing chess.

Several themes run through the results. These include the main concerns that my subjects expressed as well as things of which they were not aware but I observed. The book has touched on these themes. They include the difficulty of conducting a normal life in the former Soviet Union, a coming to grips with reality, and a struggle for personal identity in an environment that rewarded pragmatic behavior.

Two broad concerns occupied my respondents. First, they were concerned about their families. Alex and Glasha expressed difficulties with marriage. Glasha was separated from her son, who was left behind in the Ukraine. Oleg wanted to become independent.

Ironically, Oleg, though firmly ensconced in his family, wanted to leave it. His father disappointed him, he felt stifled by family life even though he had a room to himself, a rarity in Russia, and he felt the need to be on his own. One day, Oleg told my wife and me that he wanted to live separately as soon as possible. His parents could afford to send him to Germany for the summer but could not afford to get him a separate place. He was still dependent on them.

Besides family, careers preoccupied my respondents. Some found a career a necessity; others gave it priority over family life. Glasha, in 1992 a relatively comfortable student being supported by her well-to-do husband and only dreaming about a career, by 1993, with her financial support slipping away, plunged frantically into her career. Alex was working hard as a programmer for little pay. Oleg took a stab at finances with his interests in currency exchange and economics.

The three HVP respondents struggled between practicality and individuality. Alex's strengths for instance lay exclusively in the extrinsic value dimension. His emphasis was on practical situations in the world and his role in those situations. Oleg, by contrast, was a "people person." His strengths were in seeing the individuality of others as well as his own uniqueness. Oleg, at the time, was partially sheltered from the realities of post-Soviet life, where the former economic guarantees had been stripped away. Oleg accepted himself and had good self esteem. He could not accept the world and felt depressed by it (even though he intellectually endorsed the revolution going on in his country). Glasha, on the other hand, was undergoing a transformation. In 1992, she was practically inclined toward the world and undifferentiated toward herself (but had weaknesses with internal systems and self-discipline). In 1993, the murky picture cleared, and Glasha became oriented to practicality in the world and to individuality in herself.

Nine

VALUE ANALYSIS: THE IMPACT OF PERESTROIKA

1. Overview

During the 1980s, the Soviet Union was on the brink of an economic meltdown due to years of an increasingly corrupt government and a closed and isolated society. Coming aware of the approaching disaster for the country, Soviet leadership turned to an untested younger man, Mikhail Gorbachev. The new leader attempted to reform communism to revive the country's spirit. By introducing ideas, including the economic experiment of *perestroika*, more akin to an open Western-like society, Gorbachev released untapped social resources.

When I went to the Soviet Union in the summer of 1991, I witnessed the effects of Gorbachev's new ideas first hand, not at the national level, but more intimately among a handful of coteries. This chapter summarizes that summer's four week ethnographic adventure, much of it detailed in previous chapters, in terms of several major themes related to values and valuation. It presents an analysis of those themes using tools drawn from formal axiology, social network theory, and ethnology. Final conclusions are drawn about Russian concerns in the period following *perestroika*.

For the most part, the entrepreneurial activity growing out of *perestroika* is front and center. However, other themes intrude on occasion concerning such diverse topics as war-time ethics, secrecy, the connection between scientific research and making a living, the individual versus the state, public behavior and private behavior, and different issues concerning living conditions.

The entire justification for my trip, from the point of view of my hosts, was their attempt to make a profit from it. That this was occurring in a communist country was ironic, but Soviet life was still present in the way my hosts went about the project. They were secretive, manipulative, and, at times, ruthless. I could never be out of their sight. They took their obligation to "keep me out of trouble" to extremes. In many ways, I found the experience to be irritating and felt the need to be as independent of them as I could without upsetting the situation to an extent that would jeopardize the research.

A kind of buoyancy existed among Russians and other Soviets at that time that probably was not there before *perestroika*. The idea of making your own enterprise was novel and fresh, even though it had already been occurring in a subterraneous fashion for many years during Soviet times. In 1991, it was legal to some extent, so more and more Soviet citizens became involved, including just about all of my Russian contacts. Gorbachev introduced legal but limited free enterprise as part of his economic reforms in the 1980s

(Smith, 1992, p. 252). The reforms pertained to registered cooperatives with bureaucratic oversight (Hosking, 1990, p. 150). Most Russians did not participate formally, but the legalization of what had formerly been black market (illegal) activity had indirect consequences. Russians tended to view this development as giving tacit sanction to ongoing gray (semi-legal) market activities, thus energizing them. The semi-legal activities—such as Dmitri and Alisa providing room and board to a foreigner—thrived while fully legal business enterprises tended to remain in the discussion stages.

The tempo of burgeoning free enterprise increased in 1992 and 1993, but, as more and more Western influence came to St. Petersburg, the nature of the entrepreneurs changed so that Soviet characteristics, although still there, were less prominent. Because of this, 1991 was a better year to see the unusual combination of Soviet mores and an entrepreneurial spirit more akin to the West. In 1991, Russia was at the cusp of change.

Soviet mores included secrecy and surveillance (Smith, 1981, pp. 1–5, 464). Dmitri kept his overarching agenda hidden and acted as my minder. This confused and irritated me. Hiding what he had in mind kept me off-balance during negotiations, and keeping an eye on me prevented any mishaps that could have jeopardized his semi-legal activity. Beyond the immediate benefits of his tactics were deeper social considerations. Sociologist Georg Simmel noted that the use of secrecy in society represents a kind of maturity amongst those that do so (Simmel, 1964, p. 330). Delaying the exposure of your full knowledge and activity until the time is ripe expands the power of that knowledge and activity (Simmel, 1964, pp. 330, 331).

Observers of the Soviet Union noted the prevalence of social activity occurring outside of that which was legally permitted in the form of the black market and gray market (Smith, 1992, p. 248). This covert expansion of society is part of the power of hidden agendas. Secret activities increase the range of human agents in society. In the case of the Soviet Union, human agents using *blat* (*sviazi*) extended the economic scope of Soviet society.

In 1991, I witnessed this first hand. Keeping their secrets while uncovering mine (such as the amount of currency I carried into the country) reinforced my child-like stance in an unfamiliar environment and enhanced Dmitri and Alisa's mature social position relative to mine. They could play adults more comfortably while I was treated like "a baby" as they had promised Leon Pomeroy before I set foot in their country. I had not grasped the full implications of this remark at the time, thinking only that I would be well cared for without grasping the downside of such a position.

The rise of an entrepreneurial spirit in late twentieth-century Russia represented a revival of something long dormant in Russian society. Prior to the Bolshevik Revolution of 1917, which ushered in a sea change in the political climate that targeted and then snuffed out entrepreneurs, imperial Russia was known for having entrepreneurs as part of its economic system, the more successful of these coming from the peasant classes (Pipes, 1974, pp. 207–218). Capitalism came later to Russia than it did to America and most

European nations, but, when it did, Russia experienced a rapid rise in business activity (Kenez, 1999, p. 7). For a short period starting near the end of the nineteenth century, capitalism and entrepreneurs flourished side by side. Then war and revolution overthrew the old regime, replacing capitalism with communism.

A mode of negotiating life, long used during more repressive times, also permeated the atmosphere of the Russia I visited (Smith, 1981, p. 60). It entailed a heavy reliance on social connections (called *blat* or *sviazi*) and a group camaraderie that tended to produce economic units at the level of cliques as opposed to individuals or private corporate structures legally treated as individual entities. It was a different way of doing what the West refers to as "competition." Comparing Russia to America, units of economic production differ along social lines. In America, the ultimate unit is the individual. In Russia, the ultimate unit is a connected group with an associated "group ego" (Ledeneva, 1998, p. 150).

Intermixed with this fluid social environment was a moral conflict involving a changing legal and ethical environment. During the Soviet heyday, ideology ruled the life of Russians and corruption was criminal and dangerous. Then, as the Soviet elite classes became more and more engaged in subverting their idealized but impractical social system, the edges between legality and illegality became blurred as administrators and managers of different state and business functions turned to *blat* to get things done (Ledeneva, 1998, pp. 25–27). Authority turned a blind eye to unapproved but necessary economic activity, manipulating the enforcement of rules according to its needs (Ledeneva, 1998, pp. 77–79; Smith, 1981, pp. 300–306). Eventually, ethics changed. Speculative activity, long considered to be sinful, started to become acceptable in the latter years of Soviet rule.

The combination of enduring practices such as *blat* with a new legal and ethical environment constituted a cultural shift. Culture, the cultivation of values, was undergoing change that was measurable. After 1991, the military nature of Soviet society became de-emphasized. An emphasis grew on consumer goods; things that were in short supply but had become highly desired started to become available. New things that could be measured included material items imported from the West, such as new technology, new products, new films, and new television programs. Brand names associated with the West began to appear in different parts of St. Petersburg on store fronts and on billboards. These included Adidas sporting goods, Baskin-Robbins ice cream, different cigarette brands such as Camel and Lucky Strikes, and the Dutch-run Babylon supermarkets (Selby, 1996, p. 291). The major downtown bookstore *Dom Knigi* (House of Books) started carrying computer related products, including circuit boards, floppy disks, and packaged software products. On television, you could watch the soap opera "Santa Barbara" and the detective show "Crime Story." In theaters, Harrison Ford appeared in "The Fugitive." Kiosks, small enclosed stands that dotted the city, grew dramatically in number. They sold all varieties of small consumer items, including cosmetics, printed matter such as newspapers, books, magazines, fruits and vegetables, toys, liquor, candy, ice cream, other sweets, flowers, cigarettes, and so forth. The formerly almost empty state-run stores became stocked with foods. New cooperatives offered an even better variety of food items with many imported items, things not seen before except in the secret stores reserved for Soviet elite (Smith, 1981, pp. 30–34).

As shortages disappeared, prices rose, as did salaries. The changes were unevenly distributed. Some benefited; others did not. In concert with the burgeoning markets, a new vision of life arose that entailed a change in priorities. Less dependence on the state for your livelihood was one of these. More opportunities arose at all levels of society. No longer was your career path dictated by your position in a rigid structure that tended to reward a few at the expense of many.

However, influence continued to play a more important role than ability. Several of my Russian friends landed jobs with foreign corporations with well-known brand names. From what I could gather, good connections were required to get these positions. Once the connection was established, how you did was based on talent. Alena Ledeneva extensively documented *blat* during the Soviet and post-Soviet periods. According to her, *blat* did not suddenly disappear after the Soviet command economy was replaced by a more Western style economy (Ledeneva, 1998, p.206). For example, private job positions are assigned by group connection (Ledeneva, 1998, pp. 207–208), which leads to a more controllable labor pool. This is another example of the group-based nature of economic units in the former Soviet Union.

Ledeneva comments on the importance of studying *blat* because it has been largely overlooked by Sovietologists and analysts of the post-Soviet period (Ledeneva, 1998, p. 1). Here, I attempt to add to the extensive research she did by bringing in some fresh philosophical ideas and techniques drawn from axiology and cultural anthropology. Reciprocally, Ledeneva's research is invaluable to the value oriented areas I cover.

During 1990 and 1991, I became acquainted with a philosophical-scientific complex called formal axiology. In the summer of 1991, I carried a tool of measurement, the Hartman Value Profile, Pomeroy Interpretation Validation (HVP-PIV), derived from that complex into Russia as part of a preliminary field experience required by my doctorate. Though the HVP-PIV (hereafter referred to in its generic form as the HVP) was my main concern for the internship with Pomeroy, my primary concern for my anthropology work was to gather preliminary ethnographic data. The overall goal of my endeavor was to meld these two concerns into an overall project that would require more months of fieldwork and further collaboration with Russians on the HVP research. The project drew into itself more tools of analysis including those oriented to ethnographic and social analysis. My dissertation covered this expansive project (Gallopin, 1999).

My main concern here is to focus on value inquiry, so the main tool of analysis is drawn from formal axiology. The three dimensions of value, intrinsic, systemic, and extrinsic, are always present in any social situation, such as that which involved a graduate student of anthropology on a field trip designed to collect scientific data engaged with a pair of Soviet Russians pursuing novel private enterprise. The little society that temporarily formed itself around that novel situation constitutes the text for my analysis.

2. My Role as Observer-Participant

A social science like any other strives to be objective. In cultural anthropology this is possible only if the observer effect is considered. This is due to the intimate nature of the encounter between observer and focus group. A cultural anthropologist may spend weeks, months, and even years living amongst the subject peoples of his or her inquiry. During these extended time periods, the anthropologist's values are bound to affect those he (she) encounters in the focus culture. In Russia, I brought along my own set of psychological and ethical baggage, my prejudices, and my idiosyncrasies. I carried a set of knowledge, had physical and emotional characteristics, and possessed developed preferences.

One of the first and most obvious factors that affected me during the initial field study was my lack of preparation. Normally, at least a year is spent reading the literature and studying the language of the focus culture prior to setting foot inside its locale. Because I attained the Russia project at the last minute, this was not possible. A better understanding of the language would have been of immense help in communicating. It would also have made me less dependent of English-speaking Russians. Knowing Russian would have helped me with the process of getting the HVP translated into Russian.

A more detailed examination of the Soviet Union's contemporaneous politics would have helped me understand why entrepreneurial activity was on the rise. It would have also enabled me to be more sensitive to attitudes and other signs that rapid political change was imminent. Though I had an overall grasp that changes were occurring, I was in the dark about that particular summer's political events. Better political knowledge plus language knowledge would have enabled me to understand local news reports and newspapers and not leave it up to my hosts to relate crucial matters to me, which, for the most part, they did not. When the August 1991 coup attempt occurred two weeks after I left Russia, I was as surprised as most Americans were.

A thorough reading of a few tourist guides would have helped me understand the different forms of currency, including how traveler's checks were handled. It also would have provided information about the kinds of public facilities available, such as public transportation, phones, postal facilities, and it would have given me knowledge of restaurants and cafes. I would have had a better idea of the city's layout and the location of surrounding towns such as Petrodvorets and Pushkin. I would have been able to locate gift shops and to have some idea of the items they carried. This would have helped with the selection of gifts, which turned out to be more important than I expected. In different ways, having to learn about these things after I was already there hampered me.

Additional preparation could have included discussions with professors or students familiar with life in Russia, including knowledge of such things as average salaries of different professions and the cost of living. For example, Russians spent a larger percentage of their disposable income on food than any other budget item. On the other hand, their housing was subsidized and cost a fraction of what a typical American might pay in a large city. Such knowledge would have helped me negotiate a price for my stay with Dmitri and Alisa. Such discussions could have also given me a better idea of what a typical Russian family might like as a gift upon my arrival. These discussions occurred after my first trip.

To qualify for the doctorate, however, I could not delay this trip. The attainment of such knowledge had to wait until after the initial pilot trip. So I went into Russia as a "paratrooper dropped behind enemy lines." Since an invitation was required to travel to the Soviet Union, I had no guarantee that my first tenuous trip would not be my last. I depended on my Russian and Latvian contacts for even basic knowledge. I was fortunate to meet English-speaking Russians who would help me continue my research. I would eventually gain enough knowledge subsequent to my first trip so that, by 1993, I had a much better idea of what was going on in Russia, and I had more confidence in my ability to do the work.

Psychologically, my dependence on others for basics, combined with my own personality traits, left me feeling lost and helpless at times during my first trip. According to Ann, who observed me in Russia, I was "not with it." According to Pomeroy, from what I told him about my experience, I was "like a cork bobbing in the ocean." I was reticent by nature if under social stress. I also had to contend with culture shock, a debilitating phenomenon that is an occupational hazard for ethnographers (Bernard, 1988, pp. 164–167). I was not used to the harshness of Leningrad, nor the primitive conditions of Karelia. I tended to be more comfortable in tourist areas such as Petrodvorets. However, I eventually found my voice, so to speak, and asserted myself. This required that I risk social mistakes in an unfamiliar cultural setting, and I made plenty of them.

Illness also hampered by ability to make good judgments. I was not accustomed to the Russian diet and the amount of hard liquor some Russians consumed. I also did not know when to say "no." I only learned over time that to refuse food or drink and not be meticulously polite and compliant was okay. During the 1991 trip, I spent a good deal of energy and focus just trying to keep from getting seriously ill.

I also had to learn how to separate my feelings from my professional obligations. At first, I tended to behave more like a tourist than an anthropologist. My hosts felt that entertaining me was crucial for their business. I found it easy to go with the flow and become caught up in the notion that I was supposed to enjoy my experience and get a good deal for my money. This led to mistrust between my hosts and me. Halfway into the trip, I finally realized that buying my hosts presents was not a matter of whether I liked them but that it was necessary to maintain the kinds of ties I would need to progress in my research. I was not there to have a good time; I was there to work.

I had to learn to be more independent. The scene at the airport after my return flight from Latvia was telling. At first, I waited hoping that someone would show up miraculously to lead me "home" to Dmitri and Alisa's flat. When it finally sunk in that this was not going to happen, that I was going to have to make it happen, only then did I start making progress towards some form of autonomy and self-reliance.

Despite all the setbacks, my hosts were providing an opportunity otherwise not available to me for my professional and academic development. Toward the end of my 1991 stay, I began to appreciate this and did not hesitate to buy presents for my hosts. In 1992 and 1993, I made sure that negotiations took place up front and were not left to chance. I tried to distribute novel and useful gifts when appropriate. My relationships with my other hosts during that time were mostly better than those I had with Dmitri and Alisa. By the time I completed my doctorate in 1999, I put my 1991 experience in a wider context and appreciated its importance. In 2000, I traveled to St. Petersburg. While there, I contacted Dmitri and took him and one of his sons out to dinner as a way of showing my appreciation for his help in getting my doctoral research started.

3. Themes of Value and Valuation

The study of values here continues what was presented in the previous two chapters. The three value dimensions are represented in our language by a variety of terms that practitioners of formal axiology interpret into their appropriate value equivalence. For example, if something is practical or expedient, it can be said to have *extrinsic value*. If something is unique or priceless it can be said to have *intrinsic value*. If it is a mental construction, scientific, mathematical, or legal, it can be said to have *systemic value*. These interpretations of the character of objects or events may be ambiguous because of the imprecise nature of language, but they are all we have. An art exists in the proper translation of descriptive properties into the terms of formal axiology. In order to help the following discussion, I have prepared a table of terms (Table 1) commonly interpreted into their corresponding value dimension that I have drawn or inferred from sources that deal with formal axiology (Forrest, 1994; Hartman, 1969; Edwards, 1991; Davis, 1991; Edwards, 1991a). The table includes terms used in the value analysis.

I want to stress a theme used throughout my analysis, that of value convergence. This is an extension of the idea behind the HVP, that of matching up values. The idea of the test is to rank items according to their relative values. The closer you are to the axiologically derived correct ranking the better you do in the test. Perfection in this test means that your assessment of the items matches, item by item, the axiological value of the item. This is value convergence or harmony. Dissonance involves mismatches and is measured by the technological aspect of HVP scoring. Since no person matches all the items, the characteristics of a person's value vision are given by precise measures of the magnitude of value dissonance.

TABLE 1 — VALUE TERMS (I, E, S)

INTRINSIC	EXTRINSIC	SYSTEMIC
personal	social	legal
intimate	practical	formal
love	nature	law
private	public	rules
friendship	exchange	rank
sentimental	monetary	scientific
individual	collective	ideal
inventor	entrepreneur	official
creative	ambitious	righteous
ethical	economical	technical
priceless	expensive	$ 100.00
church	business	government
a human being	society	the state
nurture	entertain	teach
vocation	career	studies
son	making a living	HVP*
blat	networking	social network model**
empathize	negotiate for payment	discuss theory***

* An example of how Dmitri prioritized the value of things he was concerned with while I was there. The HVP was an interesting mental construction; getting food on the table was more important; raising his son(s) properly was paramount.

** Relative views of the same phenomenon, from Dmitri's view of informal connections as priceless in the life of a Soviet, to my conception of connections drawn from the American social practice of "who you know," to text-book theory about dynamic social structure.

*** What I did with Dmitri and/or his wife in order of their relative values. When I was able to empathize with their situation, money conflicts were resolved and theorizing became more relevant.

The measure I employ in my analysis is more general and more flexible. I am looking at situations that, to date, are not measurable by the HVP because, while the HVP is designed to measure an individual's cognitive value structure, the situations that interest me involve interactions between two or more individuals. However, the overall theory of formal axiology can be applied to these interactions by discerning the three value dimensions involved, singly or in combination. What I try to measure is the relative degree of harmony or dissonance in a situation. I do so by assessing and comparing the value assignment different individuals give to the same object, person, or experience.

As a researcher, I traveled into Russia with the idea of doing philosophical exploration, namely testing a complex theoretical construct and experimenting with an instrument derived from that theory. As such, I was bound up in *systemic valuation* (S). My hosts on the other hand received me with the idea of conducting business, extending their social connections, and raising their social status. As such, they were ostensibly bound up in *extrinsic valuation* (E). Somewhere in our meeting, personalities were bound to engage, tangle, dance, submit, conquer, adjust, and understand. Personality is a set of characteristics unique to an individual and involves aspects of *intrinsic valuation* (I).

Because positive combinations of value produce higher set cardinalities that are associated with infinite continuous sets, intrinsic value can also be reached through the combination of values. Therefore, even if the exchanges between Dmitri and I had remained in terms of scientific theory, a system of mental constructions (S), or negotiations and entertainment (E), some inevitability existed that, because these kinds of value would combine with the potential of enhancing value, our exchanges would reach *intrinsic valuation* (I).

An example of a way that I reached *intrinsic valuation* (I) can be found in the manner in which I went about my internship. In order to improve the HVP (S) by extending its applicability with a good Russian translation, I had to make social connections (E) in Russia to find language experts. Each successful connection (E) enhanced the HVP (S) at least potentially and provided a value *composition.*

A composition is a positive combination of values (Forrest, 1994, pp. 28–30). Using standard annotation, the composition created by combining the value of a social contact and the value of the HVP's improvement can be expressed as S^E (see this book, Chapter Seven, Table 1), where S stands for the systemic value of the HVP and E stands for the extrinsic value of a successful connection. The HVP's value is the base of the exponentiation and the connection's value is the exponent because the value of the connection is applied to the value of the HVP. In the mathematics of formal axiology, the cardinality of S^E is $\mathbf{X}_1$ (see this book, Chapter Seven, Table 1). $\mathbf{X}_1$ is short hand notation for an infinite continuous set.

Frank G. Forrest uses the term *value index* for "the cardinality of the meaning set associated with each type of concept," namely the concepts (mentioned in Chapter Seven) synthetic, analytic, and singular. Forrest refers to these concepts as types I, II, and III. A value index is assigned by Forrest to each of the value domains associated with the three kinds of concepts, respectively, systemic, extrinsic, and intrinsic (Forrest, 1994, p. 32). They are, as discussed in Chapter Seven, N, $\mathbf{X}_0$, and $\mathbf{X}_1$. Forrest uses different notation to stand for the same cardinalities. My point here is to introduce the notion of a value index associated with each of the value domains and extend the concept to include, as Forrest does, the results of value combinations. Therefore the cardinality $\mathbf{X}_1$ is the value index of the value composition S^E.

Note that Forrest uses a slightly different value calculus than Robert S. Hartman. He reasons that, even though intension sets of analytic concepts can be countable infinite sets, in practice these kinds of sets do not occur because the exposition of any analytic concept is always finite in experience. Forrest substitutes the value index **k** for $\mathbf{X}_0$, to which Hartman assigns extrinsic value. This number, **k**, is in general much larger than the value N given to a systemic value. However, **k** and N are finite and countable.

Since neither approach has conclusively been shown to be the correct one, I will stay with the original cardinality assignments of Hartman and use the term "value index" to mean the value dimension associated with a set cardinality rather than the set cardinality itself. This will help show the relationships between different value combinations and the base value dimensions, I, E, and S.

Forrest's aim and my aim are different. Forrest uses formal axiology to derive what he terms Hartmanian Algebra in an effort to resolve different moral dilemmas by calculating the value indices of the value combinations present in any complex moral situation (Forrest, 1994, pp. 41–67). My goal is explication of different social situations that involve value conflicts or value harmonies. These social situations are derived from the ethnographic reports I produced about Russia. But they could be derived from any ethnography.

Note also that my use of set cardinalities leaves out the axiological differences employed by the HVP where several value combinations (compositions and transpositions) share the same cardinalities but different axiological rankings. Hartman uses the base of the combinations to "break ties." At this stage, I am only after gross measurements to get a rough sense of comparative evaluations of the same things by different social players.

Getting back to the example above, $\mathbf{X}_1$ is also the mathematical cardinality of intrinsic value. Therefore, the value combination symbolized by S^E, standing for the practical enhancement of the HVP through connections, equals something *similar to* intrinsic value; $\hat{I} = S^E$. I use the symbol, $\hat{I}$, instead of I to distinguish between an axiological *value index* derived from a calculated cardinality ($\mathbf{X}_1$) and an axiological *value assignment* (I). This must be done to avoid the problem some Hartman followers have with the asserted equivalence, I = S^E. In the model I am developing, Î stands for a value index that is *potentially* intrinsic. Potentially intrinsic values are those that share intrinsic value's cardinality but are ranked axiologically lower than intrinsic value. Value combinations S^E and E^E fall into that category.

Note here that the value combination in the example represents the work in which I was engaged (which added to the systemic value of the HVP) and not the HVP itself, which was only technically improved, S^S. (See Chapter Seven, Table 3: S^E—my work added to the "beauty and harmony" of the HVP). The best example of this situation occurred when I made contact with Andrey and Ann, socialized with them, and fashioned a working agreement with them. The richness of the value of doing this is confirmed by the fruitful research collaboration that ensued and revolved around the HVP. An entire constellation of work was linked to it, including Pomeroy's cross-national research project, Sergey's international science congress (CSAM 93), my doctoral dissertation, and the work of other students and scientists in Russia and America that assisted us with or participated in these projects.

My research also led to *intrinsic value* because it involved *blat*. Some Russians (those that think like Dmitri) believe social connections are "priceless." Ledeneva uncovers the "priceless" nature of *blat* indirectly by noting its absolute necessity in Soviet Life: "…The use of informal channels in Soviet type society was not a matter of choice; it was an enforced practice necessitated by perpetual conditions of shortage" (Ledeneva, 1998, p. 36). The use of *blat* was not just convenient; it was vital. Ledeneva further notes that *blat* has two dimensions. It has personal and occupational characteristics. Therefore, a *blat* network may consist of personal and occupational connections (Ledeneva, 1998, pp. 104–105). Not all Russians valued *blat* in the same way that Dmitri did. For example, Lena acknowledged the existence of *blat* describing it as "*a way of life* due to shortages," but saw it more as a practical matter, something necessary for those things in short supply, which involved contacts but not necessarily friendships.

Anthropologist Dorothy Lee views "a way of life" as involving more than just practical matters. She gives examples of how some cultures eschewed the conveniences introduced by Western contact in order to preserve those ways of organizing life that they held sacred because their identity as a people was intimately wrapped up in them (Lee, 1959, pp. 73–76). So, Lena was unconsciously endorsing the idea that *blat* was more than practical, even though overtly she thought it was merely practical. The best way to view *blat* is as something that covered a range of values for Russians from extrinsic to intrinsic.

Something that is priceless has a value beyond a quantifiable or discrete measure, which can only be continuous and infinite. This is *intrinsic* by definition. Therefore my methodology employed what many Russians valued intrinsically, namely, the informal social connection. What I valued as part of my scientific research in combination with a practical necessity overlapped with what many an ordinary Russian considered to have intrinsic value for its life-sustaining and identity-sustaining quality. For Russians like Dmitri, the informal social connection, in and by itself, had infinite and continuous value because of its infinite possibility and malleability and because it made you "Russian." I saw connections as being practical, and only in positive combination with mental constructs did they become something approaching intrinsic value. Dmitri assumed that I placed the same kind of value on connections that he did. I assumed that he understood that connections enhanced my research. The reason that, in spite of communication difficulties, no irreconcilable breakdown occurred was because we both valued the same general phenomenon at the same cardinality. Here, *intrinsic valuation* (I) and value index Î (potential intrinsic) converged at $\mathbf{X}_1$ to serve as "common ground." This common ground can be described as being at the cusp between extrinsic valuation and intrinsic valuation.

This notion may appear curious at first sight, but the following example illustrates why I believe this to be the case. Because of its implicit value richness, *intrinsic valuation* (I) may be assigned to a situation, event, or object in a variety of ways. People may agree for instance that a particular object has intrinsic value but differ in how they reach this assessment. One way of thinking about this is to use the example of a fictional hero in Western culture. James Bond, as an iconic figure, appeals to a wide range of people who want to identify with him. (Bond does not appeal to all, but many culture heroes exist to choose from for such an example.) Bond's suave manner and extensive knowledge of and access to the finer things in life has appeal for sophisticates. His unusual competence, courage, and athleticism appeal to men (and women) of action and those who wish to be so. His luck and prowess with beautiful women appeal to many women and to men who seek to be successful with women. Bond, as the representation of an individual human being (Hartman, 1969, pp. 116–119) and as a metaphor (Hartman, 1969, pp. 266–267), has intrinsic value. Those who value Bond intrinsically may not give the same classifiable reasons (E) for admiring him, but they are united by the same culture hero. All (who value Bond) agree that he represents something beyond the specific qualities they find in him, yet they only have these qualities with which to describe him.

Here we see a convergence of the extrinsic (classifiable qualities) with the intrinsic (the culture hero). The potential intrinsic, I believe, acts as a kind of bridge between the extrinsic and the intrinsic. The mathematics of this remains to be worked out and would require another book. So here it remains as a supposition.

The flexibility of the intrinsic level of value (whether achieved potentially through a value index derived from a value combination or directly through a straight value assignment) allowed Dmitri and I wiggle room in an otherwise too tight a space. Because I was after the systemic and he was after the extrinsic, a potential for clashes existed. However, since we each operated with our independent but axiologically similar valuations, we could swim side by side. His metaphor was that of the life sustaining nature of every social connection he wanted me to make. He was doing me (and himself) a favor with each one. I felt he was doing me a favor, because I needed to find those connections that would help me with the HVP.

Dmitri was also doing a favor for those to which he introduced me. They may have been pressuring Dmitri for an audience with an American. For example, I met a man from far away Tuva, a remote province in Siberia, that asked me to send a fax to him when I got back home. The simple novelty of meeting an American impressed him, and he wanted to show his friends that he had met one.

Throughout the first part of my stay, a constant theme was in play. I was introduced to one Russian (or Soviet citizen) after another. Even though most of them were not helpful to me, they kept coming, so I always felt that I would find the person who would help. The game ended when I met Andrey and Ann, not directly through Dmitri, but by chance in a context that Dmitri's connection with Anatol provided. They were the people for which I was looking. The best Dmitri had done was his introduction to Anatol. Though Anatol wanted to help with the HVP, he wanted to do a Latvian version. This was outside the scope of my immediate concern. When I established a social connection with Andrey, Dmitri's stream of introductions ceased.

Our meeting at the intrinsic level of value did not last, and, for Dmitri and me, meeting at another level of value, the extrinsic or systemic, was more problematical. There, cultural misunderstandings abounded. These conflicts are worth exploring since they shed light on Russian culture as well as mine, and they further extend an understanding of how the value dimensions interact with each other.

A. The HVP and Systemic Versus Extrinsic Value Conflict

Dmitri and I clashed often at the extrinsic level, but the most damaging of our clashes occurred at the systemic level. The basic problem revolved around our mismatched understandings of the HVP and of its purpose. The breakdown in Latvia concerning Dmitri's administration of the test was representative of this. Ostensibly this was a practical problem, but it stemmed from Dmitri's failure to understand the nature of how the HVP was constructed.

He occasionally would demonstrate his technical misunderstanding of the HVP in his conversations with me. Signs of this (covered in the narrative) included his trouble understanding the concept "atychal," his reference to the HVP as a heuristic device that could be employed in his role as an educator, the disproportionate length of time he spent on the translation, and his feeling that, once the translation was complete, his scientific obligation to me was over. The value of the HVP lies in its accurate use, which includes understanding the theory behind it. This includes not switching the subject to your pet theories about value, which Dmitri often did. The power of the HVP's diagnostic capabilities should not be short circuited by merely using the phrases for "classroom stimulation" (heuristic device), nor is the HVP merely a good starting point for research with the idea that then other theories will be substituted (also heuristic). It is a durable tool that can be translated into different languages and used extensively because of its scientific nature. Sample collection is paramount to test the accuracy of an HVP translation. Whatever the reason was, Dmitri failed at this. Even though Dmitri did put much effort into translating the HVP phrases into Russian, and I appreciated this, he failed to follow through on other aspects of the work.

The following example (not covered in the narrative) of Dmitri's misunderstanding of the HVP research is revealing. Sometime after I returned from Riga in one of our many conversations, Dmitri referred to how Pomeroy was using the HVP in his cross-cultural research as "stone soup." Dmitri was fond of using folksy analogies to get his points across, and he appeared to have formed his impression based on his initial contact with Pomeroy in Japan, interactions with me in Russia, and communications with Pomeroy via letters and telephone. It was a mature impression and not an off the cuff remark.

As the story goes, a peasant invited neighbors as his guests to a meal. The peasant said he would serve them "stone soup." Curious, the neighbors gathered around a large pot of simmering water with a large clean stone at the bottom. The peasant tasted the soup and commented that it needed more salt so he asked one neighbor to fetch a little salt. Once the salt was added, the peasant tasted the soup again and commented that the soup was too bland. He asked another neighbor to bring him a turnip to put some zip in the soup. Once the turnip was added, the peasant commented that the soup was too sharp. Perhaps some carrots could be added to make it more mellow. The process was repeated again and again. The soup was too thin, so starchy potatoes were added; it was too weak, so some animal fat was added. This went on until the peasant was satisfied. At this point, he removed the large stone from the pot and served his guests.

Dmitri viewed the HVP-PIV as the "stone" in "stone soup," and he believed that the "soup" represented Pomeroy's research. He meant that Pomeroy was collecting data indirectly by employing his HVP test as a kind of ruse. The crucial facts that Pomeroy pursued were those that he requested *in addition* to test samples. Dmitri saw me collecting data apart from the HVP. He believed that Pomeroy had other students doing the same in other countries. This was true to some extent, but Dmitri did not understand that I had my own goals independent of Pomeroy. This was true of others Pomeroy employed in different countries. The most important thing was that Dmitri did not understand that Pomeroy and I represented a whole group of people seriously interested in the HVP for its own sake and that it already had a rich background of results that stood in their own right apart from whatever additional information might come our way.

Perhaps Dmitri was projecting onto us how he might use such a test. To Dmitri, the HVP was a "black box" that he did not care to unravel, because, for his immediate needs, he saw no reason to do so. He also saw it as ultimately disposable. As such, he failed to appreciate the systemic value of the HVP. Most of the ex-Soviet scientists I encountered did not understand the true nature of the HVP. Andrey began to grasp its true power only after months of collaboration.

My enthusiasm for the HVP, unlike Dmitri, was based on its scientific potential. My shortcomings revolved around my relative inexperience with the HVP. Though I knew enough to know that Dmitri exhibited little understanding of the HVP, I knew that I was more or less in the same boat. I lacked the expertise that was required to properly educate Dmitri, which involved overcoming his resistance to its technical side. He was much more concerned with the language of the HVP test and showed no interest in the sophisticated technical and interpretive process that translated a filled out test into philosophical and psychological results. In 1991, the HVP was still relatively new to me. I needed to gain more experience.

Andrey and Ann immediately valued the HVP as a systemic value and quickly gained my confidence and, later, Pomeroy's. Andrey, as a professor, recruited some bright students to help him understand the technical aspects of the HVP. In 1992 and 1993, Andrey, Ann, Lara (Andrey's wife), Yuri (a student assistant), and other Russians collaborated with Pomeroy and me on some fruitful research employing the HVP in Russia. Our work included extensive collection of HVP samples, a joint Russian-American seminar (Pomeroy and Gallopin, 1992), and a joint paper at an international scientific congress, CSAM 93. More details can be found in my dissertation (Gallopin, 1999, pp. 316, 395, 396, 398, 542, 543, 570, 609, 611, 612, 631–634, 652).

Some common ground did exist for Dmitri and me in terms of systemic value (S). We had frequent theoretical discourses intended to clarify concepts in history, psychology, anthropology, education, and sociology. (See Chapter Five, Section 3, Subsections C, E, and I, and Chapter Six, Section 2, Subsections D and E for those conversations covered in the narrative.) However, with the notable exception of the discussion of social networks, these discourses contributed little to my research goals. Believing that our conversations (S) were futile, Alisa implicitly evaluated the situation with her occasional interruptions of our discussions to get some pressing task (E) accomplished. Examples of this included interrupting us to get me to address the issue of paying them (E) for my stay or to get Dmitri to help her in the kitchen (E). Dmitri once abruptly ended a theoretical discussion to tell me that, at that time in the Soviet Union, doing theoretical science (S) was viewed as a "luxury" because of the more immediate problem of struggling to get food on the table (E). All these were examples of placing extrinsic value over systemic value E > S.

This is proper valuation according to formal axiology, at least in the immediate sense. Implicit in this observation is that, to axiologically equal or surpass the value of coping with tough economic conditions (E), theoretical science, having only systemic value, must be positively combined with something that has extrinsic or intrinsic value. Note that, while he faced similar economic difficulties, unlike Dmitri, Andrey took a longer view and did not consider science to be a "luxury" but an absolute necessity if the nation was to overcome its problems.

While Dmitri may have undervalued the systemic by failing to see its long run potential, I made the mistake of overvaluing it. I tended to indulge Dmitri and myself in theoretical discussions, believing that they were worth pursuing in order to further my technical understanding. For example, when our theoretical discourses (S) sharpened my understanding (S), the resulting value of the composition (S^S) lay below *extrinsic valuation*. This can be seen by evaluating the cardinality of the axiological formula S^S as $N^N = N$. Meanwhile E has cardinality $\mathbf{X}_0$. The following functional notation can be used to show these relationships: $C\{S^S\} = N$; $C\{E\} = \mathbf{X}_0$. Since $\mathbf{X}_0 > N$, axiologically, $S^S < E$. (The base of the exponential formula, S^S, represents my understanding; the exponent represents the theoretical discussion.)

Fruitful results of *systemic valuation* (S) occurred when it was combined with a higher value. One example of this was the connection I made with Andrey, a social connection (E) made possible and enduring by our mutual *systemic valuation* of the HVP (S). The scholarly results mentioned above (S) followed our collaboration. You can say that a value composition resulted from the scientific enhancement (S) of our collaboration (E). This value composition is represented by the axiological formula E^S. Evaluated mathematically, $C\{E^S\} = \mathbf{X}_0$. Since $C\{E\} = \mathbf{X}_0$, Andrey did not dismiss my scientific interest as having no direct practical value, while Dmitri (and Alisa) did. Notice for example that, during the business seminar in Latvia, Dmitri gave the HVP test as an aside, during a break, and he did so carelessly. The idea of making it a part of his work occurred to him, but only much later, and only as a remote possibility. Andrey and Anatol grasped that idea almost immediately, and both urgently asked me to bring Pomeroy to their country to help them incorporate the HVP into their projects.

Andrey sought a higher axiological goal than scholarly work. He wanted to create a commercial application (E) of our collaboration. Pomeroy, Andrey, and Yuri contributed ideas, which included applying the HVP to career counseling, writing a popular book about formal axiology, and creating a computer program designed to transform the pencil and paper HVP into a more flexible version that could be taken on a computer screen and instantly evaluated. If these applications had been developed, the following value composition would have resulted: S^E, commercial applications valuing a theoretical construct. Since $C\{S^E\} = \mathbf{X}_1$, the value index here would have been î.

Although some progress was made, we never accomplished the long range goals. I could not stay in Russia indefinitely, and Pomeroy had more pressing business. Once I returned from the field to write my dissertation and Pomeroy turned his attention to other countries, our Russian friends lost interest because they wanted a long range time commitment from us before they would further commit their resources.

However, as evaluated above, my research activity during 1991 did achieve value index Î because I made a successful connection that allowed the Russian version of the HVP to be tested for validity. Once this had been accomplished, a gate was opened leading to two years of further collaboration with our Russian contacts. This enabled Pomeroy and me to pursue separate and joint research goals.

B. Dmitri and Alisa's Scheme

Dmitri and Alisa had a plan before I set foot in Russia. They were Russian entrepreneurs. Coming from the West, with its superficial popular view of the Soviet Union, the last thing I expected to encounter was "go-getters." As mentioned before, a little study would have prepared me for something like what I encountered. I was prepared to meet scholarly people like me. Friction might revolve around ideology, and academic topics like philosophy, religion, socialism, and international politics. I was not prepared to meet a Russian version of American used car salesmen.

Dmitri treated the HVP like a "conversation piece" in that it could stimulate theoretical discussions. He considered it to be no more than an interesting "card trick," something that could attract attention and raise curiosity. Unlike Andrey, he saw little scientific value in it. To Dmitri, the HVP's value lay in the practical fact that it had gotten me to Russia and hopefully would get Pomeroy there as well. Dmitri and Alisa wanted to use Dmitri's scientific connections to run a homespun guest service for scientists who were interested in visiting Russia. Dmitri later confirmed that they were using me as a prototype for this kind of service, a fact of which I was unaware. I can imagine Dmitri gaining the confidence of other scientists by expressing interest in their research.

To Dmitri and Alisa, in so far as their entrepreneurial activity (E) was concerned, Pomeroy's interest in doing scientific research (S) in Russia and my attempts, as his proxy, to make that occur were a fortuitous coincidence. They used Dmitri's position in science to attract scientists who could then pay them money to be entertained. The "bait" was the apparent scientific interest. The "hook" was the promise to collaborate. Once in Russia, the "fish" would be drawn into the "net" and charged a fee.

This does not mean that Dmitri was not interested in science *per se*. He was, having an overtly natural curiosity about many things in that realm. It only means that *as a team* Dmitri and his wife were not very interested in science and definitely interested in business.

Ethically, Dmitri and Alisa were no better or worse than a retailer employing "bait and switch" tactics. Axiologically, their activity created a complex situation bound to lead to breakdowns and value confusion. In 1993, a similar situation faced me. Svetlana, my friend from Pushkin, used the pretext of helping me with my research to try to lure me into paying her to be my "tour guide," a time-wasting situation. By then, I was savvy enough to steer clear.

In 1993, I had developed my social network to such an extent that ending my association with Svetlana, though awkward, was not impractical. By contrast, in 1991, I was pretty much stuck with Dmitri, since severing that relationship prematurely would have left me without a research site. The setback may have been grievous enough to foreclose my doctorate. Only after I was confident that I could continue my Russian research with Andrey did I suspend collaboration with Dmitri, a move that Pomeroy endorsed. Meanwhile, I endured the situation and strove to find value in it.

Superficially, the problems I encountered with Dmitri and Alisa appear to be no more than the kind of situation any traveler might encounter when not using established tourist facilities. However, I was not an ordinary traveler, and I have an obligation to look beyond the surface issues of "getting fleeced." The tell-tale sign that more was involved than a commercial dispute was the depth of the emotions invested by both sides in working out a suitable arrangement. When I telephoned Dmitri in 2000, after the initial surprise had worn off, he wanted to know if had any "business." I assured him that I wanted nothing more than to take him to dinner, something I was never able to do in 1991. When we met at the restaurant, he told me that he had entertained several scientists after 1991, trying to give them a smoother time than I had had. Of all the people he and his wife had entertained, only I had gotten in touch with him afterwards. We had connected deep under a choppy surface of squabbling and created a bond that brought me back to him across cultures, time, and distance.

Initially, I had been disappointed with Dmitri, but as I came closer to finishing my doctoral work, I became nostalgic for that time in my life when I was so unsure of myself and the situation, completing my doctorate appeared like a pipe dream, and I was sure I would never go back to Russia after such a rough time. When I had been in Russia with Dmitri, all that had not mattered much, the experience itself being all-consuming and challenging. My major advisor told me not to lose hope, and assured me that I had accomplished more than I realized on my first trip. I should go back to Russia and try again.

My experiences with Dmitri, Alisa, and their circle had given me more than the lead of social network research, crucial as that became for my dissertation. They had also provided a set of value problems to ponder. Paramount was the nature of how I had been treated. Central to this were partially hidden agendas driven by the circumstances in which we found ourselves.

Before evaluating the overall ethical nature of Dmitri and Alisa's scheme, I will explore different value subtexts that arose from my presence in their apartment and my attempts at collaboration with Dmitri. First, Alisa's interruptions of my theoretical discussions with Dmitri stemmed from her evaluation of them as being impractical. Therefore *systemic valuation* (S) was being disvalued as being impractical, or unworthy of *extrinsic valuation* (E). This is an axiological transposition or *dis-valuation* (Forrest, 1994, pp. 28–30) represented by the formula S_E. Evaluating, $C\{S_E\} = 1/\mathbf{X}_1$. In my judgment, Alisa's interruptions constituted an event (E) that interrupted a stream of thought (S). This is also represented by S_E.

Alisa and I shared an overall disvaluation ($1/\mathbf{X}_1$) of the situation at value index $1/\hat{\imath}$. This is a potentially intrinsic disvaluation. We had different things in mind when making the evaluation. Our level of disgust was mutual but our reasons for the disgust were different. Unfortunately, we swam in antipathy. We could have become enemies as much as Dmitri and I could have become friends. For the first half of my stay, the only enduring "harmony" I had with Alisa was an antipathy *shared* (harmoniously?) at the same axiological value index. This antipathy was submerged when we got along by necessity and overt when it would surface now and again in dramatic flare ups over money.

Meanwhile, Dmitri was enjoying our discourses as entertainment and believed that I was also. This value composition is represented by S^E with value index $\hat{\imath}$. To the extent that I enjoyed our discourses, and I did, Dmitri and I swam in the potential intrinsic. I believed that we were forming a friendship ($I^I = \mathbf{X}_2$).

This situation, with Dmitri and I potentially becoming friends and Alisa and I potentially becoming enemies, put pressure on all of us. It threatened to cause disharmony in their marriage. A social balancing reaction took place. Dmitri began to seek flaws in me to resist friendship. He began to analyze me and my motives, especially when it came to my behavior in Riga. He wanted to know more about my academic background. He chided me for being naïve about what it took to get by in the Soviet Union. Alisa strove to find my good side. She congratulated me on fixing my jacket in Karelia. She asked me to dance with her at the management conference party in Riga. She urged Dmitri to let me go downtown alone back in Leningrad. When I did act in a way that pleased her, such as delivering a payment or proper gifts, she showed it. She went out of her way to find milk for me when I was ill in Pushkin, and she helped arrange a going away party for me when I was about to leave.

Dmitri and Alisa adjusted their behavior toward me to remain loyal to each other in terms of their *social* roles as husband (E) and wife (E). This value composition, E^E, of husband and wife maintaining their roles as a married couple, had value index $\hat{\imath}$; $C\{E^E\} = \mathbf{X}_1$. Its intrinsic value (potential) overcame the disharmony that I, as a foreigner (an American) with "unusual" ideas and behavior, introduced to the order of their world.

A value transposition can model this disharmony, where 1/S stands for the disorder introduced to the functioning of their marriage (E). The transposition is E_S with value index 1/E; $C\{E_S\} = 1/\mathbf{X}_0$. This is extrinsic dis-valuation. The negative impact of the extrinsic disorder was not as great as the positive quality of their potentially intrinsic relationship. However, it was still detrimental, and Dmitri asked me to "repair my relationship with Alisa" when I came back from Latvia.

The struggle between harmony and disharmony affected my relationship with Dmitri. Differing evaluations of our conversations were a source of disharmony. I sensed that something was not quite right because Dmitri could also devalue our discourses in the same way that Alisa did. He had done so in two ways. First, when our discussions were interrupted, Dmitri did not appear to mind. Our discussions might as well been chit-chat. Also, he made a point in one of our discussions to talk about the uselessness of theoretical science (S) under the "present circumstances" (E) in the Soviet Union and to emphasize that he had to wait a long time to buy a lot of sugar because of its scarcity. Because our mutual enjoyment (E) of the systemic (S), yielding the potentially intrinsic (Î), could be phony (1/S), I often felt empty and unsatisfied. A value transposition represented by the formula $(S^E)_S$ was occurring.

Hartman shows how a complex axiological formula with multiple combinations of values can be evaluated using a chain of calculations each reducing a combination or transposition to its axiological equivalent (Hartman, 1969, pp. 276, 289). Evaluating, $C\{(S^E)_S\} = (\mathbf{X}_1)^{-N} = 1/\mathbf{X}_1$. The value index is 1/Î. This is a second way in which I was induced into disvaluing the situations that arose from the interruption of our theoretical discussions in a potentially intrinsic way.

These degradations of value, Alisa's being overt and Dmitri's more subtle and less conscious, made me feel as if I was being attacked on two fronts. This was, to say the least, demoralizing. As time went on, I began to sink into the morass of seeing our theoretical discussions as sometimes pointlessly entertaining (E) Dmitri with a theory he did not appreciate and Alisa saw as a waste of time (1/S). At other times, I felt that they were just an empty way of sharpening my knowledge of theories (S^S) that did not help me with my research. I sensed that something similar was going on with Dmitri. We appeared to be connecting less and less with these kinds of conversations. Our minds had been split off from the intrinsic and, because of this, undervalued. The situation that I had believed to be valuable (S^E) was just killing time through pointless entertainment (E_S).

After our conflict over negotiations (E_E) was resolved, a new kind of conversation took the place of the original kind, and some value was restored to our discussions. These conversations had more to do with me in that, even if they turned out to be theoretical, they started with a situation that concerned me. Two examples of this were the conversation about comfort zones (Chapter Five, Section 3, Subsection I) and the conversation about social networks (Chapter Six, Section 2, Subsection E). The first concerned Dmitri's praise of my gift giving after the confrontation with Alisa. The second was based on comments Dmitri made after my comment that I felt alone. Both were valuable experiences. The first taught me to be more forthcoming and to participate in the culture. It made me a better ethnographer, as I was no longer hanging back all the time, merely observing. The experience (E) enhanced my professional (S) goals: (S^E). The second experience helped systematize (S) my research (E) providing the value composition (E^S).

In both cases, my personality was involved, and my dedication to science. This value composition can be described by I^S. The value index here is intrinsic (I); $C\{I^S\} = \mathbf{X}_1$. By concentrating on *me* and not just abstractions, Dmitri was able to enhance the value of our conversations. Also, note that the conversation about social networks began with a comment that Dmitri made on the day we went to Petrodvorets, where we shared a richly valuable cultural experience and were able to relax. The day had lingered and reached a quality that is associated with intrinsic value. As Hartman put it, you want a positive intrinsic experience to last, while a negative intrinsic experience is one you want to end as quickly as possible (Carter, 1991, pp. 118–119). An intrinsic experience had put us in the mood to open up, me by sharing my feelings with Dmitri, and him by giving me a valuable insight into his culture.

After my struggle in 1991, I decided that the fieldwork I did for my life's vocation or calling (I), namely anthropology, would have to take a different form. I needed to collect a wider array of information gathering techniques (S) applicable to a wider range of situations (E). I concentrated on social network formation (E), Russian language competency (S) and (E), and interviewing techniques (S) designed to record conversations and produce classifiable data (E). I sought value compositions designed to enhance anthropological knowledge—viewed as a set of empirical classifications based on experiences in the field, (E)—and further my vocation in the sense of a career (E) and enrich it as a calling (I).

For example, an interview with Natalie and Rastislavna (Liza's aunt and grandmother) yielded analyzable data about a respondents life experiences in Russia (Gallopin, 1999, pp. 447–526). I met Liza, a Russian who was a student and teacher of English in 1993, and she became a student in my English seminar because of her interest in learning the American version of English. I cultivated the relationship, and she introduced me to Natalie and Rastislavna who agreed to be interviewed. The interview became part of my dissertation, which was published as a contribution to anthropology.

This was a successful endeavor containing multiple value compositions. The successful employment of a classroom technique (S) in the field (E) yielded the value composition E^S. I was applying a technique to systematically gather data from a stream of Russian life. It had practical value; $C\{E^S\} = \mathbf{X}_0$, value index **E**. Since the technique (S) produced analyzable data (E), it yielded the value composition S^E, where the data valued the technique used to produce them. This yielded potential intrinsic value ($\hat{I}$); $C\{S^E\} = \mathbf{X}_1$. My successful development of a social connection (E) to attain interviews (E), yielded the value composition E^E, also with value index $\hat{I}$; $C\{E^E\} = \mathbf{X}_1$. I was swimming in the potential intrinsic ($\hat{I}$) connected to my vocation (E, I). To put it in the vernacular, I was "with it."

In 1993, I had come a long way from my state in 1991, when, according to Ann, I was "not with it." I had transcended the intrinsic because my activity (E) was valued by the intrinsic results of valuing my calling (I), yielding the value composition E^I. $C\{E^I\} = \mathbf{X}_2$, a value index higher than intrinsic (**J**). This is the axiological equivalent of "love of nature" (see Chapter Seven, Table 2) or "creative engineer" (Hartman, 1969, p. 272). In my case, I was a "fully engaged and productive ethnographer totally immersed in the culture of interest." The fulfillment of my vocation valued the work I put into it.

This value progression from the systemic and extrinsic to the intrinsic and beyond as a result of productive activity is noteworthy. It can be applied as is shown below to some situations in Russian culture.

By contrast, during 1991, my research stumbled along in axiological valleys, ruts, and ditches. I was struggling to make the connections I would need without yet realizing the range of value in those connections. I was mostly having connections made for me by Alisa and Dmitri, as part of their extrinsic valuation of my presence. How they valued me clashed with how I wanted to value my work. In order to understand the roots of this clash, we will examine the nature of Russia's economy at the local level.

C. Economy and Social Networks

Russia, during the late 1980s and early 1990s, underwent a fundamental transformation. Overtly, this was seen in the political upheaval that transformed Russia from the one-party Communist dictatorship called the Soviet Union to the Russian Federation, which, by 1994, had become a constitutional, multi-party democracy with a democratically elected President and Duma (Congress). While *glasnost* opened up the country for open political debate and introduced a free press, *perestroika* decentralized the Russian economy and introduced legal free enterprise. As the state withered away so did the state-run social safety net, which included guaranteed housing, medical care, and jobs. The new conditions provided extra incentive for ordinary Russians to become private businessmen and businesswomen. While the initial impetus of Gorbachev's reforms focused on *glasnost*, which created a cultural atmosphere akin to America's hippie movement of the 1960s, the second impetus focused on *perestroika* with its economic theme. Freedom of expression was replaced by commercial adventures.

According to Lena, Russians were tired of being poor. They were jealous of "minorities," those people living at the edges of the USSR, who appeared to have a higher standard of living. If Latvia was representative of this, Lena was right because, from what I observed, Latvians did enjoy a wide variety of consumer goods not available in the Russian republic. While Latvians and other fringe republics valued political independence more than economic autonomy and broke away, Russians embraced reforms and defended them during the 1990s. Dmitri and Alisa, Andrey and Ann, Vasili and Sonia, and even Pavel (the kayak instructor at the Karelian camp) all demonstrated enthusiasm for entrepreneurial activity.

Still, *perestroika*, in and by itself, remained too murky a concept to carry the day. By the time of the August 1991 coup attempt by reactionaries, *perestroika* had lost some of its momentum. Vasili saw it as "scattering toys around to start a new game." The general mood of Russia reflected this. In July of 1991, outside observers were having a hard time sensing which way the country was headed. Some Russians I knew did not grasp what *perestroika* was all about, or they felt that it had passed them by (Gallopin, 1999, pp. 359–363).

A more organized approach was needed because Gorbachev's economic reforms were limited and tentative in nature. Boris Yeltsin would finally bring about the sharp political break needed to implement the beginnings of a fully endorsed capitalism in Russia. Nevertheless, Gorbachev had introduced some of the ideas of capitalism into Russia's mainstream. Since Russia's past was culturally more oriented to local communes, individual entrepreneurs were rare in 1991. A kind of half-baked capitalism emerged with small groups taking the economic role more commonly filled by the individual (or individually treated tax entities called "corporations") in Western countries. Dmitri and Alisa together with some of their social contacts constituted such a group.

In order to better understand how this group operated, a network diagram is useful. Figure 1 shows such a diagram. It includes those individuals who were connected to Dmitri in some fashion during my stay in 1991. This network, like many such networks in the Soviet Union, was fluid. If I were to have visited Dmitri in 1992 or 1993, his social network would have changed. I knew this indirectly by observing Andrey's network and others change during 1992 and 1993. I also knew from my meeting with Dmitri in 2000 that, when the Soviet Union dissolved at the end of 1991, links to the break away republic of Latvia were broken. Dmitri could no longer easily travel to Riga. New visa regulations and travel restrictions made assembling a large group of former Soviets for a business conference in Riga difficult. As a result, Anatol shut down his Managers Club, and so Dmitri lost his consulting work and his Latvian contacts. Some of Dmitri's contacts were more permanent than others, such as links to his wife and other members of his family. I can also presume that his links with Vasili and Sonia were enduring. In 2000, he still had them as friends. The links to Latvia proved to be more tenuous and those in Karelia, with the possible exception of Pavel, were hardly permanent.

Some of Dmitri's contacts were more permanent than others, such as links to his wife and other members of his family. I can also presume that his links with Vasili and Sonia were enduring. In 2000, he still had them as friends. The links to Latvia proved to be more tenuous and those in Karelia, with the possible exception of Pavel, were hardly permanent.

FIGURE 1 — DMITRI'S NETWORK IN 1991

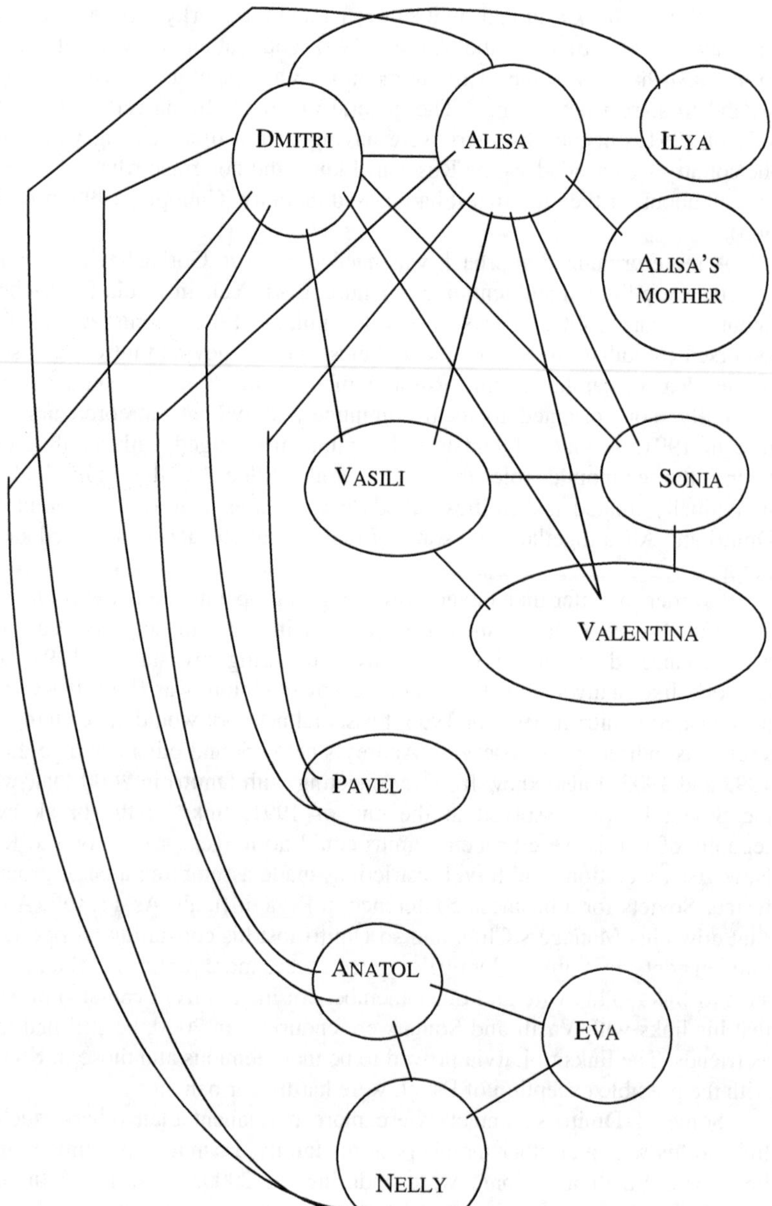

FIGURE 2 — NETWORK DISTRIBUTING SUGAR

(1) VASILI AND DMITRI ARE FRIENDS.
(2) SONIA IS MARRIED TO VASILI.
(3) SONIA GIVES TIP TO DMITRI ABOUT WHERE AND WHEN SUGAR WILL BE SOLD.
(4) DMITRI BUYS SEVERAL KILOGRAMS OF SUGAR AND GIVES THEM TO ALISA.
(5) ALISA CARRIES PART OF THE SUGAR IN SEVERAL JARS TO HER MOTHER.
(6) ALISA'S MOTHER FURTHER DIVIDES THE SUGAR BETWEEN HERSLEF, ILYA, AND OTHER RELATIVES.

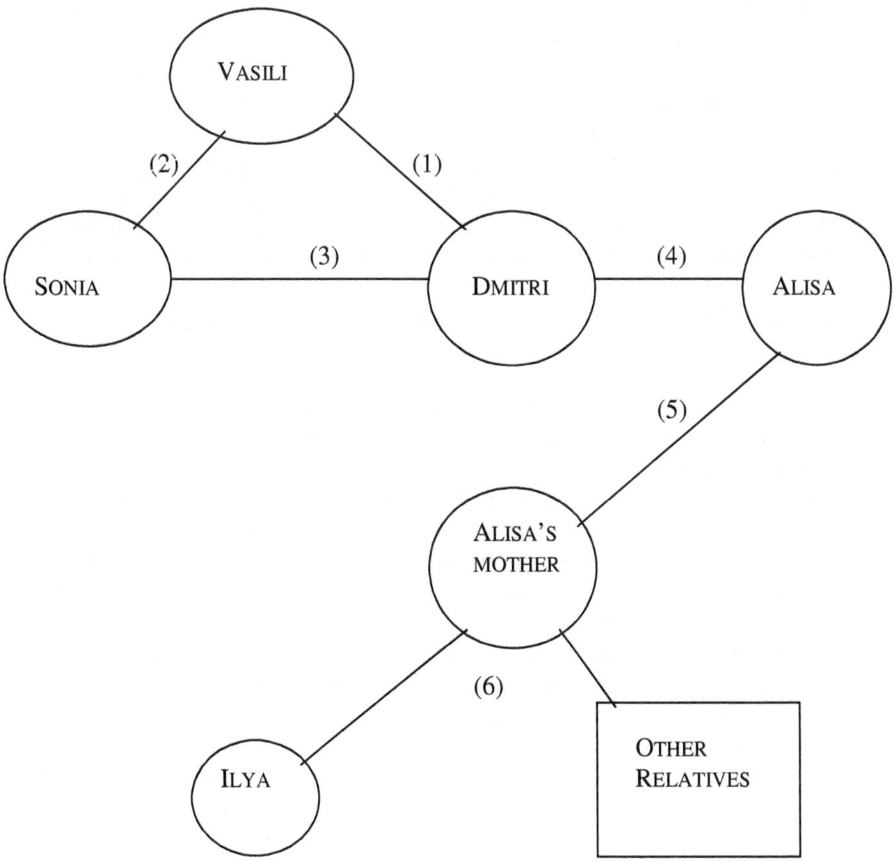

Each kind of link can be classified using the value triad. Systemic links are conceptual. Extrinsic links involve material exchange. They are concrete and not ephemeral like systemic links. Intrinsic links involve personal relationships of substance. They are more enduring than extrinsic links.

A link in name only, being a link because some kind of fleeting contact exists, can be classified as systemic, so can knowledge of a person who is linked to a person with which you have a face-to-face relationship. For example, my link with Alisa's mother was systemic because, while I stayed at Alisa's home, I knew about her mother but never met her in person. An example of a fleeting contact might be saying "hello" to a neighbor you otherwise do not know. An either-or relationship exists for this kind of link. A contact has been made or it has not; knowledge of the person may exist or it may not. To distinguish a systemic link in a network from an extrinsic link, we need to examine whether any kind of practical exchange has taken place.

When Dmitri approached Mikhail (the first man who offered help with our boat) at the Karelian camp ground in order to gain assistance, he was setting up an extrinsic link. In exchange for meeting an American, Dmitri secured Mikhail's assistance with the leaky kayak. An extrinsic link could involve a series of practical exchanges. In America, such links are common. For example, repeated visits to the same grocery store involve extrinsic links with its employees as long as they only involve a *functional* relationship. These kinds of links existed in Russia as well. The different stores I visited with Dmitri contained extrinsic links in his network. (Since they are too numerous, I do not include them in a network diagram.)

Intrinsic links are quite different. Such links can be connected to *blat*. The basis of *blat* is a friendship. Recall how Dmitri referred to the simple example of acquiring a train ticket for his son, Ilya. Due to the scarcity of train tickets, he needed to be friends with a ticket seller to get one. The unused train ticket generated when I decided to return from Latvia to Leningrad by plane instead of by train was gone by the time Clara and I got to the train station to say goodbye to Dmitri and Alisa. Scarcity created high demand, and relationships were exploited to divert the ticket from the province of scalpers (a profit driven, extrinsic phenomena, not considered to be *blat*) to that of a non-monetary gift exchange.

Dmitri's relationship with Vasili provides some examples of *blat*. Dmitri had no car but could get rides from Vasili. Dmitri used these rides to entertain his American guest. Vasili's wife, Sonia, gave Dmitri a tip about where he could find a shop selling sugar, a rationed item. Judging from the quantity Dmitri purchased he probably exceeded the official allotment size. What could he do, or any person in that situation? If he did not take advantage of information, his family would have to do without sugar for an unknown period of time.

The sugar was distributed by Dmitri's wife to her relatives. The network of sugar distribution is given in Figure 2. All of the connections making up this distribution network could be characterized as intrinsic. This includes family relationships, which may be presumed to be tight since no evidence to the contrary existed. I have included those relationships that I observed first hand or could be reasonably deduced by what I was told.

Intrinsic relationships can be characterized by their enduring nature and, in the case of friendships, their informality. Family ties have to be evaluated. A dysfunctional family may reduce the nature of contact to extrinsic or merely nominal, existing in name only, and, as they are reduced to an idea only, systemic. Because of their intimacy and enduring nature, intrinsic ties provide an excellent medium through which exchanges can flow. So, intrinsic links can also be valued extrinsically if they are only seen as being practical. Friendships can also provide security, emotional sustenance, and intimacy. *Blat* can be seen as reducing a friendship to only its practical aspects, but, because *blat* is based on friendship, it cannot be equated with the impersonal and temporal practical exchange of a strictly extrinsic relationship.

A good example of an attempt to build an intrinsic relationship, thus setting up the possibility of *blat*, was our encounter with Pavel in Karelia. Dmitri and Alisa made a good effort to get to know him. Socializing included a camp dinner arranged by Pavel, a boat ride, and a late night talk with me. In exchange, Dmitri attempted to help Pavel make an arrangement with the idea of inviting Americans to his kayak school through me. Dmitri also was willing to lend his psychological expertise to some moral dilemmas about which Pavel had long thought. Even though the arrangement with me did not bear fruit, a more general goal may have proved useful. Dmitri was attempting to establish an enduring relationship with a man who frequented the same campgrounds they did. Future exchanges were possible. Meanwhile, Dmitri got his kayak fixed by an expert.

Reciprocity was involved in this relationship, but it was not the kind of reciprocity where exact figures are kept and exchanges are intended to balance. The reciprocal gestures were a kind of coded communication, an overture to further interaction. Also, notice the level of effort involved *compared* to that of the exchange with Michael. In extrinsic valuation, terms such as good, fair, average, and poor apply. Degrees of goodness exist. In this case, the relationship with Pavel was better than the one with Michael. Dmitri and Alisa were building a relationship that had more properties of a good exchange relationship. Several meals and activities were shared. An exchange of visits occurred. Stories were shared. Underlying this process was a secondary process that was even more valuable. By getting to know each other, the two parties were building trust, the foundation of friendship.

We have uncovered a process whose steps are observable, beginning with the knowledge (systemic) that two men interested in kayaks may be of mutual benefit to each other, moving to a series of exchanges (extrinsic), and finally to mutual trust heading toward friendship (intrinsic). This process must have been repeated countless times in Russia in different situations. The knowledge that someone whom you trusted existed in an area of your interest and could help you if the need arose was valuable in itself. Making use of such a contact was even more valuable.

When Nelly called Dmitri and Alisa from Latvia as if she was ringing up a friend in her city, I was pretty certain that they had more than a one-time working relationship. The relationship that Alisa and Dmitri had with her was the end product of a process similar to the one they were just beginning to engage in with Pavel. Obviously, Dmitri and Alisa had tapped into a rich network of relationships in Latvia, some of which I glimpsed while I was there. Included in this network was the possibility of meeting people from all over the Soviet Union that attended the kinds of business and research related conferences sponsored by Anatol's group.

When I attempted to make my own way amidst this social network, I was met with resistance from Dmitri and Alisa. They appeared to be jealous of my activity and fearful of any success I may have had. To me, I was having an experience more full of promise than any I had had in Leningrad or in Karelia. I eventually made my way into a network as rich in Leningrad through Andrey and Ann. Our fortuitous meeting in Riga provided the crucial link that allowed me to jump from one social group into another. The leap enabled me to successfully complete my doctoral research.

I did not know it at the time, but I had temporarily acted as a broker between rival networks, manipulating the situation as a *blatmeister* might. A *blatmeister* was an influential person who was skilled at moving between social networks to accomplish tasks of which ordinary citizens were not capable (Ledeneva, 1998, pp. 115–121). This was due to my unusual situation as an American who was being sought out simultaneously by two competing Russian social groups. I manipulated the situation so that the research activity was shifted from Dmitri's group to Andrey's. While in Latvia, I kept Anatol's group (which overlapped with Dmitri's) involved in a different translation of the HVP so that they did not become rivals of Andrey's group.

The more Western-oriented cultural atmosphere in Soviet Latvia most likely played a role in facilitating the role that I played. This cultural atmosphere provided familiar guide posts that enabled me to maneuver with more confidence than I could in Soviet Russia. These included access to English speaking people, the feasibility of using commercial devices such as traveler's checks and credit cards, and more services made available to the individual traveler. These systemic (commercial system), extrinsic (services), and intrinsic (individual attention) values created a medium in which I could, so to speak, swim. In Russia (RSFSR), at the time, I felt like a fish out of water.

In the Soviet Union, individual attention amounted to constant monitoring and the implicit mistrust that that kind of behavior engenders. The (unmonitored) individual had no worth in the eyes of the state nor in the particular customs prevalent at the time. By contrast, a group of tourists could be understood as a mobile social network and handled as such. My experiences with Dmitri's constant monitoring were by no means unique. My supposition that this kind of monitoring was endemic was corroborated by Eileen's recounting of her experiences. She felt smothered by her host. Add my experience boarding the plane in Latvia, where I was first isolated from the rest of the passengers in the terminal and then checked by security once on board the plane, and you have three examples of uncomfortable situations generated by the Soviet mistrust of the loner.

Services were non-existent or, if they did exist, often rude. I recall commenting to Dmitri after one such experience in a post office. He explained that the clerks were "tired of foreigners." This was odd. A service should welcome tourism as added business. However, the idea of making a profit in a state enterprise was antithetical to the principals of the Soviet Union and the ideals of socialism. The system required obedience and not profit. Doing your duty was necessary, but smiling was not.

Russia had a double-tiered payment system for train travel and tourist sights such as museums. "Poor Russians" were subsidized while "exploitative and greedy foreigners" paid "world prices," which were relatively much higher (Gallopin, 1999, pp. 287–290). The state wanted to reinforce the idea that it was taking care of its own people. Dmitri took advantage of this when he had me travel with him as "a Russian" on the train to Latvia so that he could save money.

My experience on the way home from Pushkin with Dmitri and Alisa via a rail system that was showing signs of age showed that some Russians regarded government subsidies as their prerogative and were jealous of foreigners taking advantage of the low prices. I am referring to the agitated man on the overcrowded train who spotted me as being an American foreigner. The fact that I was "taking advantage of" inexpensive rail travel (as if the time lost and aggravation were worth it), in effect not paying a higher price to travel back to Leningrad some other way, demonstrably troubled him.

The commercial system was antiquated, and modern conveniences basically had to be found in expensive hotels or shops catering to tourists. Both required "hard currency," U.S. dollars or other acceptable foreign currency. (*Nomenklatura*, Soviet elite, could shop in special shops set aside for them.) The Soviet economy had generally been organized around military concerns and all that implied. It emphasized systemic concerns, and, while providing extrinsic value to an extent, it discriminated against individuals. Therefore, in this sense, it undervalued intrinsic aspects of life.

As a sort of counterbalance to these public phenomena, Russian domestic life was warmer than might be found in the typical American home. This warmth did not abate when a guest appeared. Besides some perfunctory considerations such as putting on *tapochki* when inside a Russian apartment, you were made to feel at home. The informality and joy of the "Russian kitchen" were stark contrasts to the coldness and harshness of a Russian's public life.

By the end of my 1991 trip, I had successfully moved from one Russian kitchen to another when Andrey introduced me to his wife, Lara, and let me stay in his flat for a couple of days. Andrey and Ann introduced me to their colleagues at the State University of Leningrad. I tapped into Andrey's expansive network, which was based partly at his university and partly in his family. This provided the medium that enabled me to conduct more research. Although Dmitri was no stranger to *blat*, Andrey was closer to being a *blatmeister*.

When I returned to Russia in 1992, I knew that I should not pursue my contact with Dmitri any more though he was only a phone call away. We had both been rattled by our 1991 experience. My report to colleagues at home had for the most part turned them away from the idea of pursuing that relationship. Pomeroy was strongly against my returning to Dmitri's group once he was convinced by me (and Andrey) that the new lead was worth pursuing. Andrey began to deliver data (Russian HVP results) via the (at the time, novel) internet well before I returned to Russia. Pomeroy immediately grasped that sharing information with more than one clique in Russia could lead to conflict and disrupt potential research. The idea was to milk one network instead of scattering myself among several.

The conflict I had been embroiled in between Andrey's circle and Dmitri's circle in Latvia was based on group rivalry. This is a central aspect of Russian life. In the United States, the middle class tends to view circles as a matter of temporary convenience, moving out of old circles into new ones as life pathways unfold. Permanent networks tend to occur at the extremes of American society, among the rich and powerful, "the loose association of billionaires and millionaires," and among the poor, such as urban Afro-Americans (Liebow, 1967). In Russia, a sense of loyalty to one circle appears to endure. For example, I watched Andrey move from job to job or hold several jobs down at the same time in the course of three years. Meanwhile, his circle of friends and colleagues remained fairly intact. Some players may have drifted in and out of it, but the core group remained the same. Perhaps this can be compared to a schooltime coterie or a close and extended family. Groups like this may also be found in American business establishments but (except at the highest levels) rarely spread over several enterprises.

As stated before, a social network may be founded on intrinsic or extrinsic value. A network founded on intrinsic value will tend to be more enduring and reflect deeper bonds. In her study of Soviet Russians, Ledeneva shows the characteristics of a *blatmeister's* network:

> As a rule *blat* networks [of *blatmeisters*] originated in long-term relationships and consisted of regular access to each other's resources rather than just favour-for-favour exchanges…. There was no clear-cut quantification of reciprocity within such networks, there was a more intuitive sense of mutual obligations supported by eagerness to belong to the system and fear of being excluded from it (Ledeneva, 1998, p. 115).

This idealized kind of social network can be found in other societies. In America, for instance, it may be found in disadvantaged groups living in the margins of the overall society. Anthropologist Elliot Liebow, who studied social networks among poor Afro-American males living in Washington, D.C. (Liebow, 1967), described the ideal personal network aspired to by any one of them:

> The pursuit of security and self-esteem push [the Afro-American male] to romanticize his perception of his friends and friendships.... He prefers to see the movement of money, goods, services and emotional support between friends as flowing freely out of loyalty and generosity and according to need rather than as mutual exchange resting securely on a quid pro quo basis (Liebow, 1967, p. 176).

These were the kind of social networks Dmitri had in mind. A network founded on extrinsic value will tend to be more temporal and reflect relationships of convenience. In American society, you may find that middle-class individuals shifting from group to group as they pursue a career hold strong nostalgia for their school days and wish to reunite with their old chums in periodic formal events. These reunions may be their only chance to feel that they are part of a group connected by intrinsic value. While, in America, being part of such groups later in life is not entirely out of the question, in Russia, they are much more a fixed part of the social landscape.

Starting with the social gatherings at Vasili's residence, continuing with the informal social gatherings at the Managers Club in Latvia, and ending with my introduction to Andrey's group at Leningrad University, I was impressed by the ease with which the people took me into their circles. I was to find this situation repeated several times in 1992 and 1993.

While the ideally functioning social network in Russia requires deep bonds at the level of intrinsic value, the goal of these groups is to provide practical benefits. The trust engendered by the ambience of durability facilitates the exchanges. Compare this to American life where formal enforceable laws prop up a series of exchanges in temporal relationships. Why does each form predominate in its respective country?

We can employ some simple axiological formulas to understand this phenomenon. The underlying idea is the similarity of value. A well-formed Russian social network has intrinsic value (I). The primary form of exchanges in America involves temporal relationships. Such exchanges entail social networks with extrinsic value. A typical social network may include a series of links from the farmer who grows the food to the wholesaler who purchases it and sells it to a processing plant, where the food is transformed into a transportable product that is distributed by a transportation network and eventually winds up in a grocery store, supermarket, or restaurant. The consumer of food products constitutes the final link in such a network. These networks do not rely on friendships. What gives this arrangement its strength is the systemic value of the laws that support the entire network. The rule of law, something that was in scarce supply in Soviet Russia, guides every temporal relationship in the American commercial networks. A system of legal relationships (S) is employed by temporal exchangers of goods, services, or other practical things (E). This value combination can be expressed as S^E. The Russian model can also be expressed as a value combination, namely as a system (S) based on friendships (I). This value combination can be expressed as I^S. In this case, the system is "natural," a kind of *spontaneous order* arising from informal relationships based on self-interested individuals who seek to circumvent systemic restraints on the economy.

Evaluating each of these combinations we come up with the same set cardinality, $\mathbf{X}_1$. They are axiologically similar, but they are not equal since S^E has value index $\hat{\imath}$ (potential intrinsic) and I^S has value index I (intrinsic).

At first blush, the Russian compensation for the state-induced shortages appears to be more robust: intrinsic value versus potential intrinsic. However, many other value combinations are associated with the "natural" system employed by Russians. These arise from the value environment created by the state's undermining of economic conditions via imposed restrictions on free enterprise and include two value transpositions, E_S and S_E. The first transposition represents shortages, defined as goods that are unavailable, where goods are taken to be extrinsic and unavailability is systemic (a good is present or it is not). The second transposition represents a bad economy devaluing the state that is responsible. The first transposition involves the practical challenges facing *perestroika*-era Russians, and the second involves the psychological conditions created by the despair of tough living conditions and hidden resentment toward the Soviet state.

In the decade prior to *perestroika*, these conditions were alleviated by favorable world oil prices for the Soviet Union's vast oil industry, which created an artificial wealth, which in turn masked the underlying economic problems (Malia, 1994, p. 337). *Perestroika* was a response to the emergence of these underlying problems with the gradual decline of world oil prices during the 1980s. Gorbachev was brought into the top of the Soviet leadership precisely because he promised a fresh political approach with programs designed to address the looming problems.

Gorbachev's programs did not go far enough toward unfettering the Russian entrepreneurs. This promising social class, while becoming aware of the problems as more information was exchanged via *glasnost*, became increasingly disillusioned with the dim prospects of ever being able to do something about it. Consequently, they provided grassroots support for a liberal political movement instead of the backbone of an economic renaissance. This movement pushed the Soviet regime toward its downfall.

Beyond these economic considerations are the problems that arise when friendships are continuously exploited for their practical advantages. A friendship that cumulatively acquires a pragmatic character cannot remain intimate. Friends devolve into "buddies" or acquaintances, falling back into extrinsic value. Liebow, in his study of under-employed Afro-Americans in an urban setting, noted how the friendships formed by them had a fragile or volatile nature (Liebow, 1967, pp. 181–182, 204). Friendships could easily devolve into something less, including enmities. They did this so often that they could be characterized as being unreliable, especially when put under stress (Liebow, 1967, p.182).

Russians found themselves in a similar position, living in relative poverty compared to the Soviet elite. Crowded into bleak urban settings and with few prospects of economic advancement, they concentrated on the formation of friendship networks, as did their urban Afro-American counterparts in America. Russians faced the same kinds of problems maintaining friendships that Afro-Americans did. Ledeneva notes that, whereas Russians valued friendships, *blat* itself could carry a stigma since it involved activities that could be illegal and went against the equality implied by socialism (Ledeneva, 1998, p. 68). Russians preferred to think of it as "helping out" instead of being in it for yourself (Ledeneva, 1998, pp. 61–62). The best situation involved being part of a circle wherein you could expect a free flow of mutual aid without calculation (Ledeneva, 1998, p. 115).

The trouble of maintaining the intrinsic value of social networks together with the value transpositions created by a state system antithetical to the pursuit of an economically advantageous life made the Russian approach to having a good life problematic. The basic American articulation of value S^E proved to be more reliable than the valiant but doomed Russian gamble on the intrinsic.

Here we have two juxtaposed nations locked in a bitter ideological struggle over the course of about seventy years. Each of them arrived at value-similar systems to feed, house, and clothe their people. America's economic system, starting with an almost pure capitalism, slowly devolved into a mixed economy with many government controls. America over this course of time became increasingly militaristic. As opportunities contracted, the use of "networking" (a predominantly extrinsic form of employing social networks to advance careers) became more prevalent among those seeking an advantage in the competitive labor markets.

Russia's economic system, after the violent Bolshevik Revolution, followed a communist model as much as it could, but it continually relied on an illegal, mostly underground, and quasi-capitalist economy to prop up the militaristic Soviet government. The Soviet economic policy attempted to create the same kind of systemic-extrinsic series of economic links that America had. Because of the centralized nature of the Soviet economy, conditions existed that made it impossible for these kinds of commercial networks to operate efficiently. A centralized-command economy is incapable of making the thousands upon thousands of continuous local decisions that must be made to deliver goods in a cost effective way. The rule of law is non-existent because the laws make little economic sense and, because of this, are constantly undermined. The rule of corruption replaces the rule of law. Soviet leaders realized this almost from the beginning, turned a blind eye to the corruption, and participated in it themselves.

Ignoring state laws was not something that arose only after the Russian Empire was replaced by the Soviet Union. For much of the time, the Russian Empire was not highly urbanized. It was a largely rural society populated mainly by peasants accustomed to a communal way of life. Peasants often resisted different attempts imposed by the ruling classes to modernize. The peasant's main aim was to acquire land that they felt was rightfully theirs. They preferred to follow their customary law and often ignored (at their peril) laws imposed on them by the autocratic state. Russians were notorious for their circumvention of the law long before the Soviet Union existed (Figes, 1998, pp. 98–102).

I witnessed a scene in Karelia that, though not directly involved in the Soviet economy, was highly symbolic of the economic situation in Russia. This was the scene of the policemen fishing with their uniforms on (Chapter Three, Section 3, Subsection H). In America, this kind of behavior would be immediately condemned. A policeman's uniform represents law and order, the legal system necessary for capitalism to function. To see the uniform worn as vacation wear would be quite disturbing. Such a situation was not only tolerated in the Soviet Union but most likely welcomed, for the kinds of laws that were metaphorically "on vacation" were the very laws that forced Russians into the *blat* relationships that made any kind of economy possible.

Blat was the substitute for the rule of law, and it undermined Soviet laws. In order for *blat* to work, some amount of "looking the other way" on the part of authority must have existed. Ledeneva describes how this worked:

> On the social level, for ideological reasons, *blat* could not have been recognized by the state as an attribute of the Soviet system. Rather *blat* was either left unnoticed (unmentioned in official discourse) or subject to a limited, usually satirical, critique. It was criticised as an anti-Soviet phenomenon deriving from the moral perversion of some individuals.... Power institutions could not eliminate what in effect supported them and what they were coupled with.... The inability to recognize that *blat* was rooted in the institutions of power led to a situation where the success of a campaign was judged by the detection and punishment of scapegoats while the phenomenon as such remained untouched (Ledeneva, 1998, p. 68).

The state did maintain a psychological hold on its citizens despite its apparent permissiveness. This was done by creating an atmosphere in which punishment for transgressions could always be potentially leveled upon any one it chose (Ledeneva, 1998, pp. 77–78). Justice, if you can call it that, was not distributed evenly. It depended on your social position. This was a further incentive to engage in the use of *blat* to protect oneself from the arbitrary enforcement of Soviet laws. However, the engagement in *blat* carried its own risk. So Russians learned to play a "misrecognition" game in which they rarely referred to what they were involved in as *blat* (Ledeneva, 1998, pp. 66–72).

D. Living with *Blat*

Social networking was as endemic to Soviet life as retailing was and is to American life. As post-Soviet Russia builds commercial structures, the emphasis on *blat*-oriented social networks will dissipate. By 2000, new retail outlets were firmly established in St. Petersburg. The American fast food restaurant, McDonald's, was one of the most evident features of the new climate of retailing. Private construction was evident in and around the city. This was occurring to some extent in 1993, but the number of American enterprises was still low then. Most of the new supermarkets and clothing outlets were of European origins. The European-style stores were still novelty items. Lines would form outside these stores as if they were theaters or museums.

In 1992, a store selling Rifle jeans was vandalized. The newcomers had to contend with resentment against a variety of perceived injustices. At the time, inflation was high, and many had lost savings. The prices for high fashion jeans were out of reach for the ordinary Russian. Many wanted the restoration of communism, and nascent capitalism was still perceived negatively, as it had been officially during Soviet times. In 2000, a store selling Lee and Levi-Strauss jeans at "world prices" (rather steep) was doing great business. By then, enough *nouveau riche* existed to justify these stores. General perception had changed as becoming rich appeared to be within reach of more and more. Also, Russian economic and political structures, although strained, had not disintegrated as had been predicted at the beginning of Russia's experiment with freer markets. Russians had accepted the new conditions while the reformation of the economy and government had been accomplished without a disastrous civil war.

In 1991, all of the coming changes were only pregnant possibilities. Enough was known to make the new ideas worth pursuing, but only barely, because the prevalent attitude was still tainted by the gloominess that characterized the era of Stalin in the Soviet Union. By 1991, the hard lessons of communism had been learned. Ann reflected this when she and Andrey took me to a nice park south of Leningrad only a day or two before I was to leave Russia that year. We were buying some ice cream, and, as we approached the vendor, Ann told me not to expect too much variety. "There's only one choice here." She was right; only one flavor was available. Still, it was good ice cream. This was another characteristic of Russia at the time—making the best of a bad situation.

The use of *blat* was one way in which Russians made the best of a bad situation. Thousands upon thousands of continuous *blat* based exchanges and the associated permanent and temporary networks associated with them formed the basis for the economic distribution of goods and services throughout the former Soviet Union. This in turn kept the economy viable and the country from political chaos. Held together from below, the Soviet Union never faced a severe political crisis until its leaders induced one.

The signal for the demise of the Soviet order came in August of 1991, a few weeks after I left. The occurrence of the coup did not signal the end, since a coup had been used to replace Khruschev with Brezhnev in 1964. The end was marked by the failure of the coup to replace Gorbachev with a candidate suitable to the hard liners who launched the coup. Instead, the President of the Soviet Russian Republic (RSFSR), Boris Yeltsin, emerged as Russia's new *de facto* leader. By the end of 1991, this became official.

The popular support that Yeltsin received was made up of liberal minded politicians cultivated by *glasnost* and the ambitious businessmen and business women who emerged from the fledgling class of Russian entrepreneurs cultivated by *perestroika*. Gorbachev's twin programs, by stirring things up and weakening the authority of the state, had unleashed the forces that had been frozen inside complex webs of social relationships. *Blatmeisters*, such as Andrey and Dmitri, who had been seeking business relationships through the semi-clandestine medium of *blat* now had a chance to pursue such relationships openly following Western models. This switch released the pent up extrinsic value stored in the multitude of practical relationships held in social networks.

The way *blat* had been practiced prior to this constituted a form of investment. *Blatmeisters* (and anybody who used *blat* to a smaller extent) invested time and energy into the cultivation of numerous contacts. Payoffs were not only hard to calculate; they were uncertain. Therefore some amount of risk was involved in this enterprise. However, *blat* continued to be practiced because it was the only way to "get ahead" in a system designed to "make everyone equal." This fact of human nature was eventually recognized by Soviet authority. Therefore, they turned to the strong, the ambitious, and the enterprising in a desperate attempt to preserve a system that was not succeeding. The extrinsic value of tolerated activity undermined the egalitarian ideals (systemic) of the Soviet Union: S_E.

Another kind of activity undermined the bureaucracy that supported the state. This was the personalization of the Soviet bureaucratic system (Ledeneva, 1998, p. 83). In order to make the system work, Soviet bureaucrats had to turn to informal personal relationships (intrinsic) to assure continuity in their procurement and distribution of materials, goods, and services; otherwise the economy would not have run, and the unpredictability of political developments would have been overwhelming (Ledeneva, 1998, pp. 83–87; Smith, 1981, pp. 300-306).

As an economic activity, the personalization of the Soviet bureaucratic system undermined the ideals of the state (S_E) while at the same time making the system viable (S^E). In this manner, a kind of value equilibrium was maintained. However, in terms of friendship relationships, this activity was an example of an intrinsic value, the personalization of the bureaucracy, undermining a systemic value, the idealism used to justify the state: S_I. It was also an example of intrinsic value supporting a state that had a bad system: $(S_S)^I$. Overall, the personalization of the otherwise formal relationships in the Soviet bureaucratic structure had a strong negative effect on the morale of the nation as a whole.

Dmitri alluded to the personalization of the bureaucracy when he discussed *blat* with me (Chapter Six, Section 2, Subsection E):

> Dmitri continued: "Because, coupon...because buy sugar with coupons, it is very little. This is only example. But the same. I must connect with my friend from Baltic (Anatol) [to handle] different problems, for example, your problem."
>
> "Your problem" was Dmitri's reference to his arranging an official invitation that made it possible for me to get a visa to travel to the Soviet Union. He had solicited Anatol's help with this. He was comparing this case to the one involving sugar, saying that they were two instances of the same sort of thing. Both involved informal relationships and connections.
>
> I was getting interested. Dmitri went on: "It's not [possible], official way."
>
> "I understand," I concurred, expressing curiosity.
>
> "It's not official way. So, if I feel that..."
>
> Dmitri was cut off by Alisa who needed his help in the kitchen. He returned shortly and tried to pick up where he left off: "...so in order to develop, we must [join] and [rejoin] many relationships...ah, friendly relationships, because...not friendly relationships very cost, very expensive. Unofficial..."
>
> "Unofficial way?"
>
> "Unofficial way, unofficial way..."
>
> "Less expensive?"
>
> "Not only less expensive...Unofficial way [is] the main...friendly way."
>
> "Main, friendly. I see."
>
> "Simply unofficial way, very expensive too...destroy law, unofficial way... Do you understand?"

The "official way" was following the rules of the bureaucracy ("red tape"). The "simply unofficial way" entailed breaking the law or ignoring regulations. The "main friendly way" was using *blat*, in this case, personalizing the bureaucracy, and the official involved was Anatol, or someone that Anatol knew. I did not grasp it at the time, but Dmitri was introducing me to a phenomenon that would be considered to be important enough to be thoroughly documented by a Russian scholar several years later (Ledeneva, 1998).

This phenomenon was a way of life for Dmitri, for Andrey, and for every Russian I met, whether or not they participated in it. To be a Russian meant to be involved, in one way or another, with the cultivation of personal contacts to deal with the ubiquitous Soviet bureaucracy. Nobody could get away from it. Mastering the process meant you did better in Soviet society.

Mastering the process also meant never acknowledging the process directly. When I asked others about *blat*, I usually got no response or some indication that another person was involved with it. For example, Yuri referred to it as something "from the past." Andrey, who had access to special stores and who had ancestors considered to be *nomenklatura*, never mentioned *blat*. However, when asked what he considered most damaging about the effects of the Stalin era on post-Stalin times in the Soviet Union, he regretted having to pass on techniques of dissembling and deception to his children. The most ubiquitous form of deception involved *blat* and its misrecognition by those engaged in it.

Blat was more than a game played by those coping with shortages and those seeking favors to advance their private interests. It was a way of life. One example should illustrate this nicely. Seryozha, Lena's brother, was one of my Russian hosts in 1993. I spent some time hanging out with him and one of his friends. I knew that Seryozha engaged in *blat* because he had apparently unlimited access to concert and theater tickets through some of his friends (Gallopin, 1999, pp. 401–406).

One day, I asked him to take me shopping so I could see more of what was involved with dinner preparation. Before he and his friend could purchase groceries they needed to have some hard currency (U.S. dollars) exchanged into rubles. I thought they would head for the nearest official currency exchange place, at banks and other designated outlets available all over St. Petersburg. Instead they headed for a kiosk near the corner of his apartment building. At first I thought the reason he was going to the "street" to do this "*na lyeva*" (on the side) was for convenience, to save time spent on a metro ride or a longer walk. But by the time the process was completed, we had spent about the same amount of time it would have taken us to go to an official place. The delay was due to the fact that after his friend went into the kiosk to chat with the proprietor—a person he apparently knew because I doubt the proprietor would have let a stranger go in—we went back to the street and walked around killing time. Then we headed back to the kiosk to make the exchange (Gallopin, 1999, 600–602).

I mulled over this little scenario for sometime, wondering what motivated Seryozha and his friend to take a chance on a potentially illegal way of exchanging dollars when a legal and perhaps even more convenient way of exchanging currency was available to them such as using the banks. Perhaps they were after a better rate, but, from what I had heard, getting a better rate on the street, though possible, was rare. What finally dawned on me was that they were used to doing things this way. It was habitual and part of their routine. They were cementing a *blat* relationship. Further than that, it helped identify them as Russians "sticking it to the system."

E. Dmitri and Alisa's Scheme Reconsidered

In Section B of this chapter, I discussed Dmitri and Alisa's "bait and switch" tactics used to lure Pomeroy and me into a cooperative scientific effort with me travelling to the Soviet Union as Pomeroy's student representative. I also discussed Dmitri's nonchalant attitude toward the scientific aspect of the effort, while he concentrated on "entertaining me." Meanwhile his wife concentrated on extracting what they felt was an appropriate payment for their "tourist" services. These developments left me in a state of moral confusion.

My friends and colleagues in the United States believed Pomeroy and I had been duped. I heard about and read about similar Soviet practices. I was fully convinced that Pomeroy and I had made the correct decision to cut our ties with Dmitri. From our point of view, we were right, but that was not the only context to consider.

From Dmitri's point of view, he had to find a way to make a living in a changing economy. Before, the state had supported scientists. In 1991, state support was no longer adequate. In 1992 and 1993, I watched while Andrey and his wife organized scientific events with the intent of making a profit. Their methods may have been more sophisticated and the amount of work greater, but they were doing the same sort of thing, trying to make a business out of their scientific interests. They also provided accommodations for my wife and me. Negotiations over a price for this were smoother, and by then I knew better than to be surprised that a price was necessary. By 1992, Russia was no longer the Soviet Union, and free enterprise was no longer a subterranean activity. I knew how to operate under those conditions.

The picture in 1991 was much murkier, and I was at a loss as to what to expect. Therefore, I should have let Dmitri take the lead and not made assumptions about what was correct behavior under his circumstances. Information was hidden from me until I arrived, because the withholding of information was common, not because Dmitri and Alisa were applying unusual methods. Journalist Hedrick Smith (Smith, 1981, p. 464) observed the prevalence of secrecy in the Soviet Union, at least, among officials, including members of the Communist Party, which Alisa was. If Dmitri spent much of his time introducing me to other people he knew, this was because he wanted to cultivate contacts, not because he did not understand my research goals. Dmitri was not an idle man and had a busy schedule even in the summer holiday period. For him, a professor, to make time to host an American student meant less time devoted to other activities. He would seek to gain something from it, and, since times were tough economically in the Soviet Union, he would want to make money. Nominally, the state still supported scientists and professors but, in reality, the economic structure was breaking down, and the future of the state was uncertain. In the light of Dmitri's context, his and his wife's actions were not unreasonable.

I was upset by the aggressive nature of his wife when she was demanding and collecting money from me, including holding my luggage hostage in Latvia. Still, I was an unknown quantity to them, and any landlord faced with a renter who has not paid them on time may resort to draconian measures to secure a payment. In America, this is usually done legally. In the Soviet Union, clear laws for our situation were not available. Our mutual language difficulties, my lack of knowledge about the importance of gifts to Russians, their lack of sensitivity to the effects of culture shock on an American suddenly immersed in Soviet culture (I had a lot of trouble cashing my traveler's checks), and their secretive operations were aggravating factors in our rent dispute.

My interpretation can only go so far in evaluating Dmitri and Alisa's activity. By using formal axiology, we can evaluate the situation more precisely. Since the situation abounded in value combinations, some of which have already been discussed, here I concentrate on more encompassing value combinations.

The overall situation can be captured by two axiological formulas. The first, from my context, is being tricked into being a tourist as opposed to a scientist so they could make some money: $(E^E)^{1/E}$, where E^E is the making of money and 1/E is the trickery (E_S = 1/E). (Note here that the trick they employed was not meant to be a personal attack. It was impersonal. Otherwise the combination I_S would have to be used with quite different results.) Arriving at a value index for this is more complicated than for the value combinations we have seen so far. The first step is to determine an intermediate cardinality: $C\{(E^E)^{1/E}\} = \mathbf{X_1}^{1/\mathbf{X}}\mathbf{_0}$. Forrest evaluates a formula like this by using an equation such as $\mathbf{X_1}^{1/\mathbf{X}}\mathbf{_0} = z$ (Forrest, 1994, pp. 89–96). Solving for z: $\mathbf{X_1} = z^{\mathbf{X}}\mathbf{_0}$, with two solutions, z = N or $z = \mathbf{X_0}$.

Evaluated under the first context, we can see that a positive result is reached. We can conclude that a systemic value index is achieved by the scheme of my hosts. The idea of making money has been preserved. The second solution to the axiological equation shows a positive extrinsic value and can be interpreted as practicality. Their scheme, though underhanded, achieved a kind of practical value. Both outcomes fall short of what they would have achieved if they had made money without employing trickery, E^E. $C\{E^E\} = \mathbf{X_1}$; a potentially intrinsic value index. The manifestation of the price they paid for employing trickery was the simple fact that, in the process of making money, they destroyed the relationship they had with Pomeroy and me.

Dmitri and Alisa's scheme achieves a different result under the second context, theirs. At a basic level, they saw themselves as making ends meet by providing a service using culturally accepted methods. Their circumvention of the state apparatus added some intrigue to what they were doing. For example, on the journey to Riga, they had me travel "as a Russian." A complex value combination captures their activity (operate within the culture by using *blat* to circumvent the state (S_E) so they can make ends meet by providing a service (E^E): $(E^E)^S{}_E$. Note here that operating within the culture means that Dmitri and Alisa felt no ethical obligation to let me in on their secrets. As a temporary member of their culture I had to accept "customary activity." Note also that undermining the state was impersonal and *blat* was being used as a practical tool.

We may evaluate the second combination in the same manner. First, the cardinality is determined: $C\{(E^E)^S{}_E\} = \mathbf{X_1}^{1/X}\mathbf{1}$. Then, we try to solve the equation, $\mathbf{X_1}^{1/X}\mathbf{1} = z$: $\mathbf{X_1} = z^X\mathbf{1}$. No solution exists for z in this equation. Forrest calls these equations *indeterminate*; z = **d** (Forrest, 1994, pp. 91, 92, 95).

We can see that Dmitri and Alisa operated in a moral "gray area." Forrest's valuemetrics show that an indeterminate result of the value combination produced by an activity means the action cannot be justified (Forrest, 1994, p. 92). Why is this? Why should not they have sought to make money in spite of the state's attempt to curtail such activity? After all, the state was stifling normal human aspirations and could be considered to be evil. Why not subvert it?

I believe that the key to the answer lay in the overall nature of the relationship between the individual and the state at the time in the Soviet Union. By coincidence, Dmitri's new friend in Karelia, Pavel, provided a vital clue when he brought up a moral question that had troubled him since he was a child. In the next section, I will attempt an answer to this complex question by placing it in a wider context through an exploration of Pavel's moral dilemma.

Before proceeding, a partial answer to the question lies in the preceding discussion about the personalization of the Soviet bureaucracy. As adultery does to a marriage, *blat* helped to prolong the Soviet state while subverting it. As adultery taints a marriage so did *blat* taint the Soviet Union. Dmitri's "successful" scheming and all others like it at the hands of untold numbers of Soviet citizens only prolonged the agony of the Soviet decline.

4. More Values and Valuation

The discussion so far has established some themes. These include Russians' preoccupation with the business of surviving a rough economy and an oppressive state, an inconsistent attitude toward systemic aspects of life such as governmental regulations and scientific research, and a preoccupation with personal and informal relationships in order to deal with bureaucratic structures. Another theme implied in these is the individual versus the state and the moral dilemmas this entails. This section rounds out my value analysis by focusing on this theme.

In Karelia, Dmitri and I had a significant discussion with Pavel concerning an incident that occurred during the Great Patriotic War (Chapter Three, Section 3, Subsection G):

> As we sat around the fire, Pavel began to tell more stories. He told us about an incident that occurred when he was a young boy during the Great Patriotic War (World War II). A German [soldier] had gotten caught behind enemy lines in Russian territory. He sought refuge in the home of his parents. They had kept him for only a short time when a Russian officer came looking for the man. The Russian was a cruel man and, upon arresting the German, began to beat him. Pavel's parents intervened, driving the officer away. Pavel remembered biting the officer on the leg. Pavel did not relate what consequences his parents suffered after this incident. He was still preoccupied with the ethics of the situation. Were they right to protect the German from the Russian officer? After all, the Germans were the enemy responsible for the devastation of Russia.
>
> I expressed the opinion that he and his parents did not act immorally. It was a natural reaction. They were protecting a man's life, regardless of the larger picture. He shook his head and said that it was not so simple. The conversation turned to the general conditions of the Soviet Union at the time. He seemed bitter that many Russians left the Soviet Union. I said that, given the horrendous conditions, they had every right to leave if they could. He countered by saying that they abandoned their country in its time of greatest need.
>
> This is a crucial question when it comes to Russians and the Soviet Union. How did most Russians react to their leaders' calls for sacrifice? What is a country's value? Is it more valuable than an individual human being? Is it an abstraction that is not worth the cost in human toll?

The most obvious "solution" to this dilemma is to note that the individual has intrinsic value, note the state has systemic value, and conclude that the individual's value trumps that of the state. An equally superficial way of looking at this is to invoke patriotism. After all, this was the Great *Patriotic* War, and, like they do in America, Russian leaders naturally called for "sacrifice" on behalf of the nation.

The value issues here are more subtle and complex than this polarized pair of bromides. The problem with the first answer is its academic naivete. Once you have framed the question in a convenient formula, just do the math. However, how do we know that the matter is merely that of the state versus the individual? Do not we have to first understand the nature of the state? What is an "individual" in the abstract? Should we lump individuals together, mixing hardened criminals with innocent babies? On the other side, does not patriotism mean love of country instead of love of the state? Can you love a country ruled by a repressive regime?

One of the interesting things about this dilemma is its stark contrast to the mundane nature of fighting a state bureaucracy over day-to-day matters in clandestine ways. The war was a matter of life or death in an immediate and dramatic nature. More than a state was at stake. A country, a nation, and perhaps even an ethnic group was in danger. Yet the same basic value categories were involved, intrinsic and systemic. (Extrinsic value was involved as well, but it was not at the heart of the conflict.) So Pavel's dilemma was, in an unusual way, related to the same basic dilemma facing Russians in their day to day choices.

We need to isolate the values implied in Pavel's dilemma. Before doing that we need to examine Pavel's reference to "country," which is more than a state or a nation. A state is "an organized political community under one government" (Thompson, 1995, p. 1360). A nation is "a community of people of mainly common descent, history, language, etc,, forming a state or inhabiting a territory" (Thompson, 1995, p. 905). A country is "a territory containing its own language, people, culture, etc." It is also "the territory of a region containing its own government" (Thompson, 1995, p. 307). A territory is "the extent of the land under the jurisdiction of a ruler, state, city, etc." (Thompson, 1995, p. 1440). The question is, does a country have intrinsic value? A country includes the systemic value of the structure governing its people, of its regulations and laws, and it includes the systemic value of its technology. A nation is closer to extrinsic value: Ethnic groups are social; they are collections of individuals. For an individual, being Russian, for example, is a category.

The defining characteristic of a country is the land. An appropriate question for Pavel would have been whether he considered the land of the Soviet Union (of Russia) to be sacred? For, if he did, then he was assigning it intrinsic value. Another question to consider is whether the things contained by the land, the people, the culture, its natural features, and so on, contribute to its value. Before deciding how to evaluate "a country," I want to go back to other side of the value equation.

When Pavel's parents defended the German soldier (I am assuming he was in the German armed forces) against the Russian officer, they were not thinking in terms of categories. Obviously, if they had given the man shelter, they were considering him in his full sense as a human being. No evidence existed that Pavel's parents were politically on the side of Germany, only that they had acted in a humanitarian fashion by considering the intrinsic value of the human being in front of them, one they knew, not an abstraction.

This is the difference between the academic "solution" mentioned before and the concrete valuation performed by Pavel's parents. To apply formal axiology properly you must judge situations on a case by case basis. If we say that any individual under any circumstances has more value than the state, we miss the point. Otherwise, no justification would exist for punishing a person who commits treason.

As a boy, Pavel's emotional reaction was to act in concert with his parents. No dilemma existed at that time. Only after Pavel grew into a man with a full knowledge of the context of the situation that existed at the time of the incident did he question the actions of his parents and himself. Whatever retribution Pavel's parents suffered as a result of their actions (they must have) is not known. Pavel chose not to reveal this, but obviously it would have affected him deeply.

The discussion about those who chose to leave the Soviet Union or as Pavel put it, "abandoned their country in its time of greatest need," extended the dilemma facing Pavel but did not provide a solution. For one thing, knowing why they left is crucial. More than one reason probably was in play and varied from individual to individual. Dmitri had mentioned this in one of our discussions (Chapter Six, Section 2, Subsection D):

> After our break, the subject of immigration arose. I was discussing the work of Ruth Benedict with Japanese immigrants (*Sword and the Chrysanthemum*), which I used as a reference in my first proposal, when Dmitri asked me why Japanese people immigrated to the United States. I said that they did because they wanted a better life. Dmitri asked if this was for economic reasons. I concurred. Dmitri concluded that the Japanese had different motivations to go to the United States than Russians, who went there primarily for political reasons (to escape persecution). Only recently had Russians gone for perhaps economic reasons. According to Dmitri, only "advanced" Russians, not simple Russians, emigrated from the Soviet Union. Simple Russians could not get cooperation from the Soviet government.

Two reasons existed, an economic one and a political one. The political one was the one more likely to have been the reason Russians were fleeing during the Soviet Union's time of "greatest need." Therefore the dilemma was one more of personal safety than one of better practical circumstances. This is an intrinsic value related reason.

A value dilemma implies some kind of value balance. Pavel was having difficulty deciding the proper courses of action in two related value situations: protecting a human being versus turning in an enemy of the state and perhaps the country as a whole, and avoiding persecution versus remaining loyal to your country under difficult circumstances. To a Western eye, your country may be valuable, but you and your loved ones are more valuable, especially when survival or freedom is involved. The land that the country represents is more a matter of practical value—a piece of nature to be conquered and divided. However, we know that other cultures, Native Americans for example, consider the land to be something that feeds them, clothes them, provides them with shelter, and has mystical meaning. They believe the land is sacred and "living."

One of the most difficult dilemmas facing post-Soviet Russia was the question of private land ownership. Making land an economic priority, by privatizing it, was not an easy thing to do even after many other parts of the Russian economy were privatized (Aron, 2000, pp. 665, 674, 682). The reason for this was an ages long conviction by Russian peasants stretching back to the early days of the Russian empire that land was to be shared in a communal and egalitarian fashion (Figes, 1998, p. 521; Lawrence, 1969, p. 98). The ancient *mir* or land commune ruled the way in which peasants organized agriculture and inheritance patterns (Lawrence, 1969, pp.98–100). This cultural practice had deep roots and constantly was a source of resistance to attempts by Russia's imperial regimes to modernize agriculture (Figes, 1998, pp. 232–241).

The struggle over land continued right up to the end of the empire. The advent of the Soviet Union was marked by the reversal of many of the land reforms attempted by Nicholas II's ministers and the fledgling Russian Duma (Figes, 1998, pp. 361–367). After the 1917 revolutions, the peasants not only reverted back to communal patterns of land distribution; they also undermined the imperial landed gentry, destroying their manors and confiscating the land (Figes, 1998, pp. 361-367, 462–464, 530–533). Until Soviet collectivization of the late 1920s and early 1930s (Lawrence, 1969, pp. 278–281), which forcibly restored the state's ascendancy in the perennial struggle over land, the peasants enjoyed a temporary ideal situation: They owned the land, dividing it among themselves by traditional means, becoming small holders in the process (Figes, 1998, pp. 361–367, 530–532, 752; Lawrence, 1969, pp. 238–239).

Forced collectivization was the Soviet state's method of reasserting control of the land. It turned Russians back into *de facto* serfs binding them to state-owned or collectively owned agricultural combines—the imperial system with a new class replacing the lords of the manors. Concessions were made to the Soviet farmers in terms of tiny household plots, which were owned privately. This continued a tradition that existed for centuries, since the medieval landowners also allowed the peasant serfs private plots (Smith, 1981, p. 267). During Soviet times, these plots produced much of a Russian household's available supply of fruits, vegetables, meats, wool, and dairy products and in a much more efficient manner than the large state-run combines (Smith, 1981, pp. 266–268). This showed how much the latter day "peasants" still valued the little land they could call theirs.

After the Soviet Union fell, the question of how to manage the land arose. All agreed that the state owned combines were inefficient, but they could not agree on how land reform was to occur or if it was worth it. Privatizing the collective farms was a point of contention. Since this meant opening land up for sale and creating a market for land, in other words, turning it into a commodity that could be bought and sold, a political clash occurred between those who wanted an egalitarian form of land distribution and collective ownership, the *status quo*, and those who favored the commercialization of land based on private property (Aron, 2000, pp. 265, 318, 331, 433,495–496, 644, 665, 674, 682).

I believe that this conflict over what land means to a typical Russian influenced Pavel's dilemma. When I asked Dmitri to tell me, out of the people I had met, whom he felt was the most "Russian," he named Pavel. By staying in the Soviet Union during hard times instead of fleeing, Pavel had demonstrated, not only his loyalty to the state, but also his loyalty to the country as a whole, to "Mother Russia."

In the 1970s, journalist Hedrick Smith asked some Russians he met to name the best time in Russia's history. One of them named the War (Great Patriotic War). This surprising answer was explained this way (Smith, 1981, p. 403):

> "Because at that time we all felt closer to our government than at any other time in our lives. It was not *their* country then, but *our* country. It was not *they* who wanted this or that to be done, but *we* who wanted to do it. It was not *their* war, but *our* war. It was *our* country we were defending, *our* war effort."

Part of Pavel's tourist related proposal to me included a tour of Leningrad, so he could show visitors to his kayak school, not only the sport of kayaking, but also the Russian cultural heritage. He also was willing to make concessions to modern times by opening his country to outsiders in order to encourage its economic development. However, he was careful to note that "you can exploit the situation" but that he was not interested in any profit, thus keeping his anti-capitalist ideals. The richness of valuation of a person devoted to all aspects of a country despite its hardships, including its peoples, its traditions, its culture, its economy, its government, and its land, shows a deep and abiding love for it. This is intrinsic valuation of an extrinsic value. Pavel's love for his country provides the intrinsic valuation. A country is a collection of classifiable items (people here are considered as a group), and so it is an extrinsic value.

In order to agree with me that his parents did the right thing in their protection of the German soldier, Pavel would have had to give up a substantial amount of his values. The conflict remained in his mind. This conflict can be summarized by the following value combination: prevent cruel treatment of a captured enemy soldier whom you have sheltered. Note that Pavel's parents were not objecting to the capture of the soldier. They were objecting to the beating of a man for which they had sympathy. However, since they interfered with the capture of an enemy soldier, they had to bear that responsibility. So in order to prevent the unnecessary cruel treatment they had to act against the Russian officer who was there on behalf of the Soviet state. The force they used did not permanently harm the Russian officer. No evidence exists that they were acting cruelly against him. So their action constitutes acting against the state. The harm of the state is represented by S_E. The physically cruel treatment of the German prisoner is I_I. Prevention means that their action disvalues the Russian officer's cruel treatment of the German. Combined the axiological formula is $(I_I)_Y$, where $Y = S_E$. Note the base here represents the cruel treatment of the soldier. Evaluating the cardinality, $C\{(I_I)_Y\} = (\mathbf{1/X_2})^{-1/\mathbf{X}_1} = \mathbf{X_2}^{1/\mathbf{X}_1}$. Using the same procedure as above, we solve for z: $\mathbf{X_2}^{1/\mathbf{X}_1} = z$; $\mathbf{X_2} = z^{\mathbf{X}_1}$: $z = N$, $\mathbf{X_0}$, or $\mathbf{X_1}$. This result represents three possible positive values—systemic, extrinsic, or intrinsic. A systemic valuation of Pavel's parents action means they acted in a manner consistent with their idea that this man's life was valuable. An extrinsic valuation of their actions means they preserved their own and their son's psychological integrity. To watch the man being beaten to death in front of them would have caused irreversible psychological damage. Also, the German's life was preserved for a time. This constitutes intrinsic valuation. To sum up, Pavel's parents had intervened in a potential war crime.

On the other side of the value equation, we have the consequences that Pavel's parents must have borne, the Soviet Union's retaliation. Pavel's dilemma is concerned with how much value he placed on the Soviet Union at the time of the incident. During the Great Patriotic War, as mentioned above, the Russian population rallied around the war effort and the regime, despite the regime's previous crimes against its own people. One of the reasons for this was the evil nature of the Nazi regime conducting the war against the Soviet Union. Since the war was a battle between two bad regimes, the Russians chose to fight for theirs as long as it was acting to defend Russia at the time. A general mood of Russian solidarity dominated Russia at the time, and nostalgia for that period lingered long after the war ended.

The actions of Pavel's parents, humane though they may have been, broke with that solidarity. So, besides the direct "crime" against the Soviet state, Pavel's parents were behaving in an anti-social manner. Their actions could also have been construed as unpatriotic, perhaps even un-Russian. Pavel's comment that those who fled Russia to avoid persecution and to seek a better life did so in "its time of greatest need" shows that he felt they were betraying Russia, and it shows his deep faith in his country despite its flaws. All these factors contributed to Pavel's feelings of moral ambivalence. On the one hand, he loved his parents and as a boy had helped them drive away the Russian officer. On the other hand, he had grown up in a country dominated by an all-pervading state, its communist ideology, and the rise of Russian nationalism during and after the Second World War.

We have seen an axiological evaluation of the situation from the point of view of Pavel's parents. Next, we will evaluate it from Pavel's point of view many years later. As discussed above, Pavel saw his parent's transgressions at three levels. Their action violated the Soviet state. This can be captured by the transposition S_E. Their action violated Russian social solidarity during the war. This can be captured by the transposition E_E. Their action violated the sacred trust Pavel held for his country. This can be captured by the complex value combination $(E^I)_E$.

In order to complete the complex value combinations that capture Pavel's dilemma, I will assume that Pavel shared his parent's sentiments about the German soldier; he saw his humanity as they did. Therefore we can set up the following three combinations

(1) $(I_I)_Y$, where $Y = S_E$
(2) $(I_I)_Y$, where $Y = E_E$
(3) $(I_I)_Y$, where $Y = (E^I)_E$

The first combination yields the result as shown above $z = N$, $\mathbf{X_0}$, or $\mathbf{X_1}$. The second combination, since $C\{S_E\} = C\{E_E\} = \mathbf{1/X_1}$, also yields $z = N$, $\mathbf{X_0}$, or $\mathbf{X_1}$. So far, our evaluations show no value conflict between Pavel and his parents. The third combination yields a different result: $C\{I_I\} = \mathbf{1/X_2}$. $C\{Y\} = C\{(E^I)_E\} = \mathbf{1/X_2}$. $C\{(I_I)_Y\} = (\mathbf{1/X_2})^{\mathbf{-1/X}}\mathbf{2} = \mathbf{X_2}^{\mathbf{1/X}}\mathbf{2}$. Using the same procedure as above, we solve for z: $\mathbf{X_2}^{\mathbf{1/X}}\mathbf{2} = z$; $\mathbf{X_2} = z^{\mathbf{X}}\mathbf{2}$: $z = \mathbf{d}$. The result is indeterminate. The action is not justified.

Therefore, in light of Pavel's development as a native of Russia under the Soviet regime, he moved further and further away from what he had emotionally grasped as a boy, but now considered a youthful indiscretion. He no longer shared the values of his parents. He saw less and less what they did as a humane act and the prevention of a war crime. He saw it more as the betrayal of a trust, the trust they should have had in Russia, whom the Russian officer represented. All those who fled Russia also betrayed the same trust. As long as Pavel continues to frame this moral question in the same way, he will continue to be confounded by its indeterminate nature and will be lost in the moral void it represents.

Dmitri and Alisa found themselves in a similar moral void when it came to dealing with me. They appeared to share Pavel's deep faith in Russia. After all, they endorsed Russia with Dmitri's boast of its accomplishments and Alisa's endorsement of its Communist elite, and they endorsed Pavel as being truly Russian. I contrast them with other Russian contacts such as Andrey, Ann, Lara, and Lena, who all admitted that Russia had made terrible mistakes and was paying the price. This second group looked to the West for answers. That does not mean that this group rejected Russia outright. It only means that they wanted to see Russia change for the better and felt this was only possible if the nation as a whole was willing to accept that it had failed to achieve a moral state and, as a result, the entire country had suffered.

We have an insight into two Russia's, that of the Slavophiles (Russophiles), represented by Dmitri's circle, and that of the Westernizers, represented by Andrey's circle. Scholars have documented these two kinds of Russians and the competing influence these two intellectual cultures have had on the development of the nation (Smith, 1981, pp. 569–572, 574–574, 595; Lawrence, 1969, pp. 99, 187, 201). Here we have gained an axiological insight into what divides them.

5. Concluding Remarks

We started this chapter with me as a student struggling to find his way in an unfamiliar culture and to overcome cultural differences in order to push a research agenda forward. We end this chapter noticing a cultural divide among the Russians I was studying. The combined tools of formal axiology and social network analysis have helped to make sense of an ethnographic narrative. They help to bring into focus the murkiness of the machinations described by the narrative. Traditional anthropological tools providing interpretive analysis are based on morally neutral "scientific" accounts that stress facts and discount value-oriented insights. Or they are based on value-oriented accounts using the anthropologists' own culture or the studied culture as the "norm." Social network analysis has given shape to the mini-society I was studying. Formal axiology has helped to structure the value dynamics I encountered without the attendant problems of cultural bias.

I was not aware of it at the time, but the two groups competing for my attention in 1991 represented the Slavophiles and Westerners. Slavophiles like Dmitri believed in Russian superiority. They did not find much value in Western ideas or technology, except perhaps for their esthetic appeal. Dmitri appeared to collect Western scientific treatises and Western scientists like a dilettante collects art and artists. Westerners like Andrey believed that the West held the keys to Russia's future. They sought out Western technology and ideas and were quick studies in understanding how to use them. *Perestroika* represented different things to each group. The Slavophiles (such as Gorbachev) hoped *perestroika* would save Russia's latest incarnation as the Soviet Union, which preserved some of the old Russian institutions such as the empire and collective agriculture. Westerners (such as Yeltsin) hoped *perestroika* would transform Russia into a modern nation on a par with the Western nations.

This does not mean that each Russian fell neatly into either category. It just means that these two cultural constellations existed. Russians such as Seryozha embraced Russian customs such as *blat* but equally felt themselves to be out of the system. Those who appeared to be in one camp or the other were not completely consistent. Dmitri, after all, invited Western scientists to visit him or else I would not have been there in the first place. He also included Western-oriented Latvians such as Anatol in his circle. He and his friend Vasili dabbled in ideas imported from the West. (See Chapter Three, Section 3, Subsection B; Chapter Four, Section 2; Chapter Five, Section 3, Subsections A and E; and Chapter Six, Section 2, Subsection G.) Lena, while rejecting the Soviet Union's repressive past, blamed many of its problems on the West. Andrey, who avidly sought out Western scientists and business representatives, still continued to enjoy perks reserved for Soviet elite (Gallopin, 1999, pp. 610–611) and dutifully tended his garden near a *kholhoz* (Soviet collective farm) like a good Russian peasant (Gallopin, 1999, pp. 573–578).

The two groups were not completely distinct. Both groups employed *blat*, and both groups valued its practicality, but Dmitri also valued it for its Russian cultural qualities. These groups shared a common cultural feature underneath their differences. Every Russian I met also shared a common concern for the fate of their country. Dmitri was concerned about a possible civil war. Andrey was concerned about the economy. Lena was concerned about the role of minorities in the break up of the Soviet Union.

Their struggle was also my struggle—to grow professionally, and be challenged ethically—for to engage in Russia at that time meant sharing Russians' moral dilemmas. Pavel's "Russian-ness" meant, among other things, his willingness to share moral concerns with others, strangers, and even foreigners. Lacking adequate political and religious outlets, the kind that allow Americans to channel their ethical convictions into churches, mosques, temples, and other worship centers of choice, and their political convictions into *meaningful* elections and *accountable* representatives, Russians had only each other. Before 1991, these kinds of outlets were in a nascent but largely unrealized state in the Soviet Union. Since 1991, that situation has changed in the former Soviet Union, perhaps its biggest change.

My first foray into Russia put me there at a critical time in Russia's history. The Russian people were already disillusioned with *perestroika*. Post-*perestroika*—the period that began when Gorbachev's attempts to reform Russia sputtered and stalled and the Soviet regime began its downward death spiral—was in its infancy. One of the challenges facing post-*perestroika* Russia was the moral legacy left behind by Stalinism, namely, the lack of any kind of core values that could unite the Russian people (Aron, 2000, pp.690–691). This value indeterminacy, noted above for situations that faced Pavel and Dmitri when they tried to operate in or think seriously about a changing Russia, faced every Russian.

WORKS CITED

Agar, Michael H. (1996) *The Professional Stranger: An Informal Introduction to Ethnography.* San Diego.: Academic Press.

Aron, Leon (2000) *Yeltsin: A Revolutionary Life.* New York: St. Martin's Press.

Aslund, Anders (1995) *How Russia Became a Market Economy.* Washington, D.C.: The Brookings Institute.

Austin, John (1991) "The Hartman Value Profile (HVP & HVP II)." In *Forms of Value and Valuation: Theory and Applications.* Rem B. Edwards and John W. Davis, eds. Lanham, Maryland: University Press of America, pp. 243-289.

Barner-Barry, Carol and Cynthia A. Hody (1995) *The Politics of Change: The Transformation of the Former Soviet Union.* New York: St. Martin's Press.

Barraclough, Geoffrey (1982) *The Times Concise Atlas of World History.* Maplewood, New Jersey: Hammond.

Bernard, H. Russell (1988) *Research Methods in Cultural Anthropology.* Newbury Park, California: Sage Publications.

Billington, James H. (1992) *Russia Transformed: Breakthrough to Hope.* New York: The Free Press.

Boissevain, Jeremy (1973) "Preface." In *Network Analysis: Studies in Human Interaction.* Jeremy Boissevain and J. Clyde Mitchell, eds. The Hague: Mouton & Co., pp. vii-xiii.

Boissevain, Jeremy and J. Clyde Mitchell, eds. (1973) *Network Analysis: Studies in Human Interaction.* The Hague: Mouton & Co.

Borovkova, A. (1989) *Zapad Tsentralnoy Aziyi.* Moscow: Nauka.

Branden, Nathaniel (1994) *The Six Pillars of Self-esteem.* New York: Bantam.

Carter, Robert E. (1991) "The Norm of Intrinsic Valuation." In *Forms of Value and Valuation: Theory and Applications.* Rem B. Edwards and John W. Davis, eds. Lanham, Maryland: University Press of America. pp. 105-124.

Clifford, James and George E. Marcus, eds. (1986) *Writing Culture: The Poetics and Politics of Ethnography.* Berkeley: University of California Press.

CSAM'93 (1993) *Abstracts of the St. Petersburg State University International Congress on Computer Systems and Applied Mathematics (CSAM'93), July 19–23.* St. Petersburg, Russia: Center of Modern Communications, POLYLOG.

Davis, John W. (1991) "Extrinsic Value and Valuation." In *Forms of Value and Valuation: Theory and Applications.* Rem B. Edwards and John W. Davis, eds. Lanham, Maryland: University Press of America, pp. 59–80.

Dunlop, John B. (1993) *The Rise of Russia and the Fall of the Soviet Empire.* Princeton, New Jersey: Princeton University Press.

Eckenrode, John, ed. (1991) *The Social Context of Coping.* New York: Plenum Press.

Edwards, Rem B. (1991) "Systemic Value and Valuation." In *Forms of Value and Valuation: Theory and Applications.* Rem B. Edwards and John W. Davis, eds. Lanham, Maryland, University Press of America, pp. 37–58.

———. (1991a) "Universals, Individuals, and Intrinsic Goods." In *Forms of Value and Valuation: Theory and Applications.* Rem B. Edwards and John W. Davis, eds. Lanham, Maryland: University Press of America. pp. 81–104.

Edwards, Rem B. and John W. Davis, eds. (1991) *Forms of Value and Valuation: Theory and Applications.* Lanham, Maryland: University Press of America.

Ellis, Albert (1962) *Reason and Emotion in Psychotherapy.* Secaucus, New Jersey: The Citadel Press.

Figes, Orlando (1998) *A People's Tragedy: The Russian Revolution, 1891 – 1924.* New York, New York: Penguin Books.

Folkman, Susan, Margaret Chesney, Leon McKusick, Gail Ironson, D. S. Johnson, and T. J. Coates (1991) "Translating Coping Theory into an Intervention." In *The Social Context of Coping.* John Eckenrode, ed. New York: Plenum Press, pp. 239-260.

Forrest, Frank G. (1991) "Value Combinations." In *Forms of Value and Valuation: Theory and Applications* Rem B. Edwards and John W. Davis, eds. Lanham, Maryland: University Press of America, pp.125-170.

———. (1994) *Valuemetrics: The Science of Personal and Professional Ethics.* Amsterdam: Rodopi.

Freilich, Morris, ed. (1970) *Marginal Natives: Anthropologists at Work.* New York: Harper and Row.

Gallopin, Gary (1999) *A Witness to Culture Shift: Anthropology amidst the New Russian Entrepreneurs of the Former Soviet Union.* Ann Arbor, Michigan: UMI Dissertation Services.

Granville, Brigitte (1995) *The Success of Russian Economic Reforms.* London: Royal Institute of International Affairs.

Hartman, Robert S. (1969) *The Structure of Value: Foundations of Scientific Axiology.* Carbondale, Illinois: Southern Illinois University Press.

———. (1973a) *The Hartman Value Profile (HVP): Manual of Interpretation.* Muskegon, Michigan: Research Concepts.

———. (1973b) "Axiology as a Science." *Journal of Human Relations*, 21 (1), pp. 31–53.

Hartman, Robert S. and Maria Cardenas Trigos (1970) *The Hartman Value Profile (HVP).* Muskegon, Michigan: Research Concepts.

Hosking, Geoffrey (1990) *The Awakening of the Soviet Union.* Cambridge: Harvard University Press.

Humphreys, Rob and Dan Richardson (1994) *St. Petersburg: The Rough Guide.* London: The Rough Guides.

Kann, Pavel (1990) *Leningrad: A Guide.* Moscow: Planeta Publishers.

Kapuscinski, Ryszard (1994) *Imperium.* Klara Glowczeska, trans. New York: Random House.

Kenez, Peter (1999) *A History of the Soviet Union from the Beginning to the End.* Cambridge, UK: Cambridge University Press.

Kudryavtsev, E. (1986) *I Hereby Apply for an Apartment (Proshoo Predostavit Kvartiroo).* Aini Lekhto, trans. Moscow: Progress Publishers.

Laqueur, Walter (1994) *The Dream That Failed: Reflections on the Soviet Union.* New York: Oxford University Press.

Lawrence, John (1969) *A History of Russia.* New York: The New American Library.

Ledeneva, Alena V. (1998) *Russia's Economy of Favors:* Blat, *Networking and Informal Exchange.* Cambridge, U. K.: Cambridge University Press.

Lee, Andrea (1984) *Russian Journal.* New York: Random House.

Lempert, David H. (1996*) Daily Life in a Crumbling Empire: The Absorption of Russia into the World Economy.* Boulder, Colorado: East European Monograph.

Liebow, Elliot (1967) *Tally's Corner: A Study of Negro Streetcorner Men.* Boston: Little, Brown and Company.

Lieven, Anatol (1994) *The Baltic Revolution*: *Estonia, Latvia, Lithuania and the Path to Independence.* New Haven: Yale University Press.

Malia, Martin (1994) *The Soviet Tragedy: A History of Socialism in Russia, 1917-1991.* New York: The Free Press.

Maybury-Lewis, David (1965) *The Savage and the Innocent.* Cleveland: World Publishing Company.

———. (1967) *Akwe-Shavante Society*. Oxford: Clarendon.

McDonnell, Lawrence (1994) *October Revolution*. Staplehurst, Kent, United Kingdom: Spellmount Limited.

McElroy, Ann and Patricia K. Townsend (1989) *Medical Anthropology in Ecological Perspective* (Second Edition). Boulder: Westview Press.

Milroy, Lesley (1987) *Language and Social Networks*. Oxford: Blackwell.

Morrison, John (1991) *Boris Yeltsin: From Bolshevik to Democrat*. New York: Dutton.

Nagayama, Yahusiha, ed. (1990) *Abstracts of the 22nd International Congress of Applied Psychology (July 22-27, 1990) Kyoto, Japan*. Osaka, Japan: Faculty of Human Sciences, Osaka University.

Noble, Mary (1973) "Social Network: Its Use as a Conceptual Framework in Family Analysis." In *Network Analysis: Studies in Human Interaction*. Jeremy Boissevain and J. Clyde Mitchell, eds. The Hague: Mouton & Co., pp. 3-14.

Paulsen, Mats (1991) "Night Life." *Leningrad News: Aeroflot Leningrad Inflight Magazine* (Summer) 4: pp. 8, 26-27, 35.

Phillips, Catherine, Christopher Rice, and Melanie Rice (1998) *St. Petersburg* (Eyewitness Travel Guides). New York, New York: DK Publishing.

Pipes, Richard (1974) *Russia under the Old Regime*. New York: Charles Scribner's Sons.

———. (1990) *The Russian Revolution*. New York: Alfred A. Knopf.

Platonov, Sergei F. (1972) "Peter the Great not a Revolutionary Innovator." In *Peter the Great Changes Russia*. Marc Raeff, ed. Lexington, Massachusetts: D. C. Heath and Company, pp. 179-182.

Pomeroy, Leon (1985) "Beyond Terrorism and War: An Introduction to Behavioral Axiology." *Journal of the Organization for the Study of Group Tensions*, pp. 58-67.

Pomeroy, Leon and Arthur R. Ellis (1991) "Psychology and Value Theory." In *Forms of Value and Valuation: Theory and Applications*. Rem B. Edwards and John W. Davis, eds. Lanham, Maryland: University Press of America, pp. 291-314.

Pomeroy, Leon and Gary Gallopin (1991) "Preliminary Russian Data and the Study of Values and Valuation Update." Paper presented at the Annual Conference of the Hartman Institute, University of Tennessee, Knoxville, Tennessee. October 10-12.

———. (1992) "Behavioral Axiology Part III: Introduction to a New Cognitive Science for Psychology, Social Scientists and Business Applications." Two Day Seminar Given Before the Faculty and Students of St. Petersburg State University (September 3-4), St. Petersburg, Russia.

Pomeroy, Leon and Richard Bishop (1989) "Cross-Cultural Studies Employing the Hartman Value Profile (HVP)." Paper presented at the Annual Conference of the Hartman Institute, University of Tennessee, Knoxville. September.

———. (1990a) Introduction to Behavioral Axiology, Part II: A Cross-Cultural Validation of Hartman's Valuemetrics and Value Science assumptions as a New Orientation in Cognitive Psychology. In *Abstracts of the 22nd International Congress of Applied Psychology (July 22-27, 1990) Kyoto, Japan.* Yahusiha Nagayama, ed., Osaka, Japan: Faculty of Human Sciences, Osaka University, pp.300-301.

———. (1990b) "Cross-Cultural, Cross-National Study of Values and Valuation Update." Paper presented at the Annual Conference of the Hartman Institute, University of Tennessee, Knoxville. October.

———. (1991) "Behavioral Axiology: Cross-Cultural Study of Values." In *Forms of Value and Valuation: Theory and Applications.* Rem B. Edwards and John W. Davis, eds. Lanham, Maryland: University Press of America, pp. 315-328.

Pomeroy, Leon, Elaine Fox, Richard Bishop, and John Davis (1985) "A New Tool for Health Psychology and Behavioral Medicine." *VA Practicioner*, July, pp. 50-52.

Pomeroy, Leon, Gary Gallopin, and Richard Bishop (1997) "Planting the Tree of Formal Axiology on Russian Soil: A Comparison of Russian and Ukrainian Value Dynamics Employing the HVP." Paper presented at the Annual Conference of the Hartman Institute, University of Tennessee, September.

Pomeroy, Leon, R. Bishop, G. Gallopin, A. Voitenko, D. Kirsanov, and S. Voitenko (1993) "Telecommunications in Psychology." In *Abstracts of the St. Petersburg State University International Congress on Computer Systems and Applied Mathematics (CSAM'93), July 19–23.* St. Petersburg, Russia: Center of Modern Communications, POLYLOG, pp. 262–263.

Pomeroy, Leon, Richard Bishop, and Gary Gallopin (1992) "Cross-Cultural Behavioral Axiology: USA vs. Japan vs. Russia." Paper presented at the Annual Conference of the Hartman Institute, University of Tennessee, Knoxville, Tennessee. October 1-3.

Pratt, Mary Louis (1986) "Fieldwork in Common Places." In *Writing Culture: The Poetics and Politics of Ethnography.* James Clifford and George E. Marcus, eds. Berkeley: University of California Press, pp. 27-50.

Pryce-Jones, David (1995) *The Strange Death of the Soviet Empire*, New York: Henry Holt and Company.

Raeff, Marc, ed. (1972) *Peter the Great Changes Russia.* Lexington, Massachusetts: D. C. Heath and Company.

Riasanovsky, Nicholas V. (1969) *A History of Russia.* London: Oxford University Press.

Rogers, Alisdair and Steven Vertovec, eds. (1995) *The Urban Context: Ethnicity, Social Networks and Situational Analysis*. Oxford: Berg Publishers.

Rosaldo, Renato (1989) *Culture and Truth: The Remaking of Social Analysis*. Boston: Beacon Press.

Satter, David (1996) *Age of Delirium: The Decline and Fall of the Soviet Union*. New York: Alfred A. Knopf.

Selby, Nick (1996) *St. Petersburg: A Lonely Planet City Guide*. Hawthorn, Australia: Lonely Planet Publications.

Selye, Hans (1978) *The Stress of Life*. New York: McGraw-Hill.

Shipler, David K. (1983) *Russia: Broken Idols, Solemn Dreams*. New York: Penguin.

Simmel, Georg (1964) *The Sociology of Georg Simmel*. Kurt H. Wolff. trans. and ed. New York: The Free Press.

Smith, Gordon B. (1992) *Soviet Politics: Struggling with Change*. New York: St. Martin's Press.

Smith, Hedrick (1981) *The Russians*. New York: Ballantine Books.

Speer, Albert (1970) *Inside the Third Reich*. Richard and Clara Winston, trans. New York: MacMillan.

Sumner, B. H. (1972) "Peter's Accomplishments and Their Historical Significance." In *Peter the Great Changes Russia*. Marc Raeff, ed. Lexington, Massachusetts: D. C. Heath and Company, pp. 188–194.

Thompson, Della, ed. (1995) *The Concise Oxford Dictionary of Current English* (Ninth Edition). Oxford: Clarendon Press.

Tucker, Robert C. (1987) *Political Culture and Leadership in Soviet Russia*. New York: W. W. Norton and Company.

Ulam, Adam B. (1992) *The Communists: The Story of Power and Lost Illusions: 1948–1991*. New York: Charles Scribner's Sons.

Vaksberg, Arkady (1991) *The Soviet Mafia*. John and Elizabeth Roberts, trans. New York: St. Martin's Press.

Veveris, Ervins and Martin Kuplais (1989) *In the Latvian Ethnographic Open-Air Museum*. Riga: Avots.

Waitzkin, Fred (1993) *Mortal Games: The Turbulent Genius of Garry Kasparov*. New York: G. P. Putman's Sons.

Whitten, Jr., Norman E. (1970) "Network Analysis and Procedures of Adaptation Among Ecuadorian and Nova Scotian Negroes." In *Marginal Natives: Anthropologists at Work.* Morris Freilich, ed. New York: Harper and Row, pp. 339–402.

Yanov, Alexander (1981) *The Origins of Autocracy: Ivan the Terrible in Russian History.* Stephen Dunn, trans. Berkeley: University of California Press.

Yeltsin, Boris (1990) *Against the Grain: An Autobiography.* Michael Glenny, trans. New York: Summit Books.

———. (1994) *The Struggle for Russia.* Catherine A. Fitzpatrick, trans. New York: Random House.

Zemtsov, Ilya (1985) *The Private Life of the Soviet Elite.* New York: Crane Russak.

ABOUT THE AUTHOR

GARY G. GALLOPIN, PH D. (SUNY- Buffalo, 1999, *A Witness to Culture Shift: Anthropology Amidst the New Russian Entrepreneurs of the Former Soviet Union*) is Adjunct Professor of Anthropology at College of Dupage in Chicago, Illinois. He also lectures at Moraine Valley Community College. He specializes in the Maya and in Russian area studies, Russian culture, and peoples of North Asia. He is interested in the new bio-cultural paradigm in anthropology. Accordingly, he teaches courses in both biological and cultural anthropology and is currently teaching and developing a course in North Asian studies. In 1991, with Vernon Scarborough, Dr. Gallopin coauthored a seminal article ("A Water Storage Adaptation in the Maya Lowlands") published in the leading scientific journal *Science* about ancient Mayan water storage management at Tikal, Guatemala, based on his Master's thesis research at the University of Cincinnati (*Water Storage Technology at Tikal, Guatemala*). In 1991, at New Orleans, Dr. Gallopin lectured about his and Dr. Scarborough's findings at the Annual Meeting of the American Archaeological Society. Together with Leon Pomeroy, he collected data in the former Soviet Union from 1991 to 1993 for the HVP-PIV, a revolutionary value-metric instrument designed by Robert S. Hartman, and interpreted and validated by Leon Pomeroy. In 1992, at St. Petersburg, Russia, he provided technical, computational, and logistical support for Dr. Pomeroy's introduction of formal axiology to Russian scientists and business leaders. In 1993, Dr. Gallopin lectured in the same city at the international meeting of CSAM (Computer Science, Applied Mathematics). Dr. Gallopin is friend to the Robert S. Hartman Institute for Formal and Applied Axiology in Knoxville, Tennessee, where he has given a series of lectures about his axiological and ethnographic research in Russia. Dr. Gallopin worked with the newly emerging class of Russian entrepreneurs. In addition, he has a former background in engineering including a Bachelor of Science degree in Operations Research from Cornell University, and computer-programming experience garnered while working and consulting for top US corporations including IBM, Morgan Stanley, Metropolitan Life Insurance, and Allstate. With this and with his academic credentials, Dr. Gallopin represents a new breed of intellectual, grounded in the rigorous reasoning of the established theoretical and applied sciences and attuned to the moral sensitivities of nations around the world.

INDEX

VIBS

The **Value Inquiry Book Series** is co-sponsored by:

Adler School of Professional Psychology
American Indian Philosophy Association
American Maritain Association
American Society for Value Inquiry
Association for Process Philosophy of Education
Canadian Society for Philosophical Practice
Center for Bioethics, University of Turku
Center for Professional and Applied Ethics, University of North Carolina at Charlotte
Central European Pragmatist Forum
Centre for Applied Ethics, Hong Kong Baptist University
Centre for Cultural Research, Aarhus University
Centre for Professional Ethics, University of Central Lancashire
Centre for the Study of Philosophy and Religion, University College of Cape Breton
Centro de Estudos em Filosofia Americana, Brazil
College of Education and Allied Professions, Bowling Green State University
College of Liberal Arts, Rochester Institute of Technology
Concerned Philosophers for Peace
Conference of Philosophical Societies
Department of Moral and Social Philosophy, University of Helsinki
Gannon University
Gilson Society
Haitian Studies Association
Ikeda University
Institute of Philosophy of the High Council of Scientific Research, Spain
International Academy of Philosophy of the Principality of Liechtenstein
International Association of Bioethics
International Center for the Arts, Humanities, and Value Inquiry
International Society for Universal Dialogue
Natural Law Society
Philosophical Society of Finland
Philosophy Born of Struggle Association
Philosophy Seminar, University of Mainz
Pragmatism Archive at The Oklahoma State University
R.S. Hartman Institute for Formal and Applied Axiology
Research Institute, Lakeridge Health Corporation
Russian Philosophical Society
Society for Existential Analysis
Society for Iberian and Latin-American Thought
Society for the Philosophic Study of Genocide and the Holocaust
Unit for Research in Cognitive Neuroscience, Autonomous University of Barcelona
Whitehead Research Project
Yves R. Simon Institute

Titles Published

Volumes 1 - 173 see www.rodopi.nl

174. Dixie Lee Harris, *Encounters in My Travels: Thoughts Along the Way*. A volume in **Lived Values:Valued Lives**

175. Lynda Burns, Editor, *Feminist Alliances*. A volume in **Philosophy and Women**

176. George Allan and Malcolm D. Evans, *A Different Three Rs for Education*. A volume in **Philosophy of Education**

177. Robert A. Delfino, Editor, *What are We to Understand Gracia to Mean?: Realist Challenges to Metaphysical Neutralism*. A volume in **Gilson Studies**

178. Constantin V. Ponomareff and Kenneth A. Bryson, *The Curve of the Sacred: An Exploration of Human Spirituality*. A volume in **Philosophy and Religion**

179. John Ryder, Gert Rüdiger Wegmarshaus, Editors, *Education for a Democratic Society: Central European Pragmatist Forum, Volume Three*. A volume in **Studies in Pragmatism and Values**

180. Florencia Luna, *Bioethics and Vulnerability: A Latin American View*. A volume in **Values in Bioethics**

181. John Kultgen and Mary Lenzi, Editors, *Problems for Democracy*. A volume in **Philosophy of Peace**

182. David Boersema and Katy Gray Brown, Editors, *Spiritual and Political Dimensions of Nonviolence and Peace*. A volume in **Philosophy of Peace**

183. Daniel P. Thero, *Understanding Moral Weakness*. A volume in **Studies in the History of Western Philosophy**

184. Scott Gelfand and John R. Shook, Editors, *Ectogenesis: Artificial Womb Technology and the Future of Human Reproduction*. A volume in **Values in Bioethics**

185. Piotr Jaroszyński, *Science in Culture*. A volume in **Gilson Studies**

186. Matti Häyry, Tuija Takala, Peter Herissone-Kelly, Editors, *Ethics in Biomedical Research: International Perspectives*. A volume in **Values in Bioethics**

187. Michael Krausz, *Interpretation and Transformation: Explorations in Art and the Self*. A volume in **Interpretation and Translation**

188. Gail M. Presbey, Editor, *Philosophical Perspectives on the "War on Terrorism."* A volume in **Philosophy of Peace**

189. María Luisa Femenías, Amy A. Oliver, Editors, *Feminist Philosophy in Latin America and Spain*. A volume in **Philosophy in Latin America**

190. Oscar Vilarroya and Francesc Forn I Argimon, Editors, *Social Brain Matters: Stances on the Neurobiology of Social Cognition*. A volume in **Cognitive Science**

191. Eugenio Garin, *History of Italian Philosophy*. Translated from Italian and Edited by Giorgio Pinton. A volume in **Values in Italian Philosophy**

192. Michael Taylor, Helmut Schreier, and Paulo Ghiraldelli, Jr., Editors, *Pragmatism, Education, and Children: International Philosophical Perspectives*. A volume in **Pragmatism and Values**

193. Brendan Sweetman, *The Vision of Gabriel Marcel: Epistemology, Human Person, the Transcendent*. A volume in **Philosophy and Religion**

194. Danielle Poe and Eddy Souffrant, Editors, *Parceling the Globe: Philosophical Explorations in Globalization, Global Behavior, and Peace*. A volume in **Philosophy of Peace**

195. Josef Šmajs, *Evolutionary Ontology: Reclaiming the Value of Nature by Transforming Culture*. A volume in **Central-European Value Studies**

196. Giuseppe Vicari, *Beyond Conceptual Dualism: Ontology of Consciousness, Mental Causation, and Holism in John R. Searle's Philosophy of Mind*. A volume in **Cognitive Science**

197. Avi Sagi, *Tradition vs. Traditionalism: Contemporary Perspectives in Jewish Thought*. Translated from Hebrew by Batya Stein. A volume in **Philosophy and Religion**

198. Randall E. Osborne and Paul Kriese, Editors, *Global Community: Global Security.* A volume in **Studies in Jurisprudence**

199. Craig Clifford, *Learned Ignorance in the Medicine Bow Mountains: A Reflection on Intellectual Prejudice.* A volume in **Lived Values: Valued Lives**

200. Mark Letteri, *Heidegger and the Question of Psychology: Zollikon and Beyond.* A volume in **Philosophy and Psychology**

201. Carmen R. Lugo-Lugo and Mary K. Bloodsworth-Lugo, Editors, *A New Kind of Containment: "The War on Terror," Race, and Sexuality.* A volume in **Philosophy of Peace**

202. Amihud Gilead, *Necessity and Truthful Fictions: Panenmentalist Observations.* A volume in **Philosophy and Psychology**

203. Fernand Vial, *The Unconscious in Philosophy, and French and European Literature: Nineteenth and Early Twentieth Century.* A volume in **Philosophy and Psychology**

204. Adam C. Scarfe, Editor, *The Adventure of Education: Process Philosophers on Learning, Teaching, and Research.* A volume in **Philosophy of Education**

205. King-Tak Ip, Editor, *Environmental Ethics: Intercultural Perspectives.* A volume in **Studies in Applied Ethics**

206. Evgenia Cherkasova, *Dostoevsky and Kant: Dialogues on Ethics.* A volume in **Social Philosophy**

207. Alexander Kremer and John Ryder, Editors, *Self and Society: Central European Pragmatist Forum*, Volume Four. A volume in **Central European Value Studies**

208. Terence O'Connell, *Dialogue on Grief and Consolation.* A volume in **Lived Values, Valued Lives**

209. Craig Hanson, *Thinking about Addiction: Hyperbolic Discounting and Responsible Agency.* A volume in **Social Philosophy**

210. Gary G. Gallopin, *Beyond Perestroika: Axiology and the New Russian Entrepreneurs.* A volume in **Hartman Institute Axiology Studies**

www.ingramcontent.com/pod-product-compliance
Lightning Source LLC
LaVergne TN
LVHW020650300926
849161LV00004B/886